D0207834

The Great Powers and the End of the Ottoman Empire

Edited by

MARIAN KENT
School of Social Sciences, Deakin University

London
GEORGE ALLEN & UNWIN
Boston   Sydney

© George Allen & Unwin (Publishers) Ltd, 1984.
This book is copyright under the Berne Convention. No reproduction
without permission. All rights reserved.

George Allen & Unwin (Publishers) Ltd,
40 Museum Street, London WC1A 1LU, UK

George Allen & Unwin (Publishers) Ltd,
Park Lane, Hemel Hempstead, Herts HP2 4TE, UK

Allen & Unwin, Inc.,
9 Winchester Terrace, Winchester, Mass. 01890, USA

George Allen & Unwin Australia Pty Ltd,
8 Napier Street, North Sydney, NSW 2060, Australia

First published in 1984.

British Library Cataloguing in Publication Data

The Great powers and the end of the Ottoman Empire.
1. Ottoman Empire—Foreign relations—Europe
2. Europe—Foreign relations—Ottoman Empire
I. Kent, Marian
326.5604   DR578
ISBN 0–04–956013–1

Library of Congress Cataloging in Publication Data

Main entry under title:
    The Great powers and the end of the Ottoman Empire.
Bibliography: p.
Includes index.
1. Eastern question (Balkan)   2. Europe—Foreign
relations—Turkey.   3. Turkey—Foreign relations—
Europe.   4. Europe—Foreign relations—1871–1918.
5. Europe—Foreign relations—1918–1945.   6. Great
powers.   I. Kent, Marian.
D465.G753   1984   327.5604   83–15896
ISBN 0–04–956013–1

Set in 10 on 12 pt Plantin by Inforum Ltd, Portsmouth
and printed in Great Britain by Mackays of Chatham

Contents

Preface

This volume originated some years ago in informal discussions among the three Australian contributors on European activities in the Ottoman Empire. Each of these contributors was engaged in university teaching and research in his or her particular Power's interests in the Ottoman Empire. It seemed a useful idea to consider an even wider co-operative venture in a formal publication bringing together specialists on the interests and activities of all the European Great Powers in the Ottoman Empire. This book is the end product of that idea.

Such activities by the European Great Powers have often been considered to be the cause of the Ottoman Empire's collapse after the First World War. It seemed desirable, therefore, to examine this belief in the context of a comparative, factual study, the product of precise research based on the widest range of archival and other sources. In such a way an informed and balanced answer could be attempted. The book aims primarily at the specialist reader, whether researcher or undergraduate. It is, none the less, hoped that it might be interesting and valuable to a wider readership.

In order to produce a work of original research that would provide authoritative and up-to-date interpretations of the subject fairly tight limits of time-scale were needed to give the work a manageable size and integrated form. The book follows a clear overall theme. At the same time the individuality of the separate chapters has been preserved, through each contributor pursuing an individual theme based on the particular national concerns of his or her Great Power. Cross-referencing helps the reader make comparisons among the chapters as he proceeds, and each chapter attempts to draw a conclusion on the relative responsibility of that Power for the fall of the Ottoman Empire.

In putting together the individual conclusions a consensus does emerge. The spreading of the exact proportions of responsibility will, however, inevitably involve some weighing up by the reader. It would appear clear, nevertheless, that responsibility must be shared, both among the Great Powers and between them and the Ottoman Empire itself. The vicious circle postulated in the first chapter seems a valid concept.

One matter that should be mentioned here is that of spelling. As anyone familiar with this field knows, there are wide variations in the spelling of places and personal names of this part of the world. The contributors have decided not to standardise these spellings. Each is writing from the standpoint of his or her particular Great Power and therefore it seemed appropriate to retain the forms of spelling (or of their anglicisation) normally occurring in the contemporary documentation of the individual Powers. The first chapter, on the Ottoman Empire itself, uses spelling acceptable to present-day Turkish scholarship.

It is not possible in a composite work for each contributor to make detailed thanks by name to the archive personnel, scholars and others who are always so helpful in any research undertaking. We are always indebted to such help. But as most of the editing of the draft chapters occurred while this editor was visiting the Department of Middle East and Islamic Studies of the University of Toronto special thanks are due to that department for its hospitality and to the University for use of its excellent resources at that time. This editor is also grateful to Professor W. N. Medlicott, formerly of the London School of Economics, for his advice on the project. Finally, I should like to thank my colleague, Ray Duplain, who drew the maps.

Marian Kent
Geelong, 1982

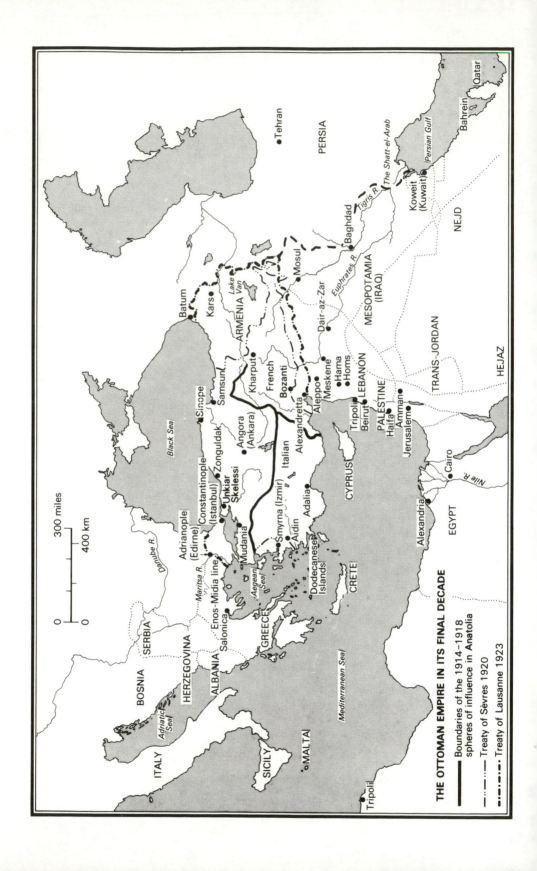

THE OTTOMAN EMPIRE IN ITS FINAL DECADE

—— Boundaries of the 1914–1918
spheres of influence in **Anatolia**

·–·–·– Treaty of Sèvres 1920

·■·■·■· Treaty of Lausanne 1923

300 miles

400 km

Danube R.

ITALY

BOSNIA

SERBIA

HERZEGOVINA

ALBANIA

Adriatic Sea

SICILY

°MALTA

Salonica

GREECE

Maritsa R.

Enos-Midia line

Adrianople (Edirne)

Mudania

Aegean Sea

CRETE

Mediterranean Sea

Tripoli

Constantinople (Istanbul)

Unkiar Skelessi

Zonguldak

Black Sea

Sinope

Samsun

Angora (Ankara)

Italian

Smyrna (Izmir)

Aidin

Adalia

Dodecanese Islands

CYPRUS

Alexandretta

Aleppo

Meskene

French

Bozanti

Kharput

Batum

Kars

ARMENIA

Lake Van

Mosul

Dair-az-Zar

Euphrates. R.

Tigris R.

Baghdad

MESOPOTAMIA (IRAQ)

The Shatt-el-Arab

Persian Gulf

Koweit (Kuwait)

Bahrein

Qatar

NEJD

PERSIA

Tehran

Hama

Homs

LEBANON

Tripoli

Beirut

Haifa

PALESTINE

Amman

Jerusalem

TRANS-JORDAN

HEJAZ

Cairo

Alexandria

EGYPT

Nile R.

Tripoli

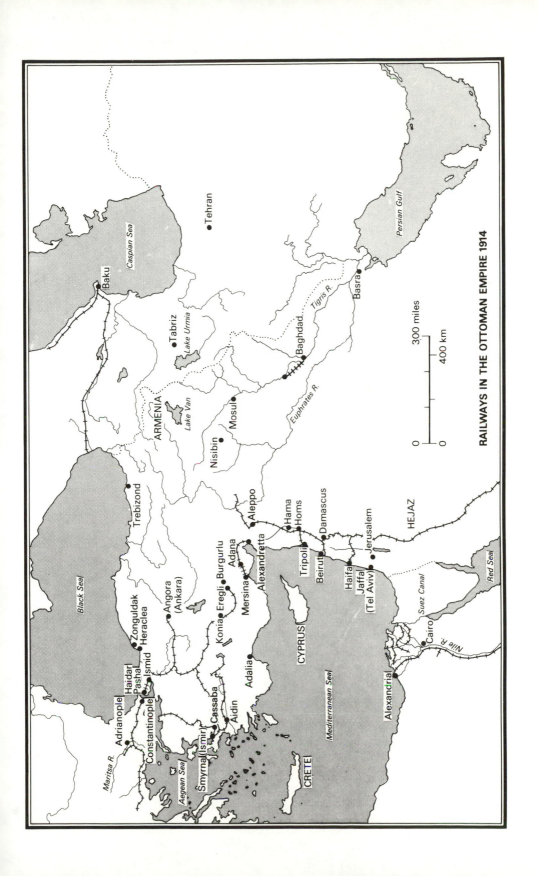

RAILWAYS IN THE OTTOMAN EMPIRE 1914

Introduction

By the beginning of the twentieth century the Great Powers had considerable interests in the Ottoman Empire. Political, economic, strategic and cultural, these interests had been largely acquired in the course of the eighteenth and, especially, the nineteenth century. Throughout the nineteenth century the periodic crises of the Eastern Question – that threatened fragmentation of the Ottoman Empire with its implied threat to European peace – had produced rivalry and tension in the political relations among the Powers. Each Power had its particular concerns in the Ottoman Empire as well as its particular areas of concern, but so long as the Powers did not encroach seriously on each other's interests or special areas of interest significant disturbance was avoided from such a quarter. The crises of the Eastern Question arose when such infringements occurred, whether through direct Great Power action, or indirectly, resulting from the actions of client Balkan national groupings or of the Ottoman government or its vassal rulers.

The Ottoman Empire was, after all, vulnerable to many pressures. Spread over a vast area stretching from the borders of the Austro-Hungarian Empire in the west to the Russian Empire, Persia and the Arabian peninsula in the north and east and, to the south, Egypt and north Africa, it contained many subject peoples and many diverse regions. Fighting a rear-guard battle against nationalist independence movements within its borders and European imperial ambition from without them, the Empire had, by the turn of the century, one trump card. This was the general desire of the European Powers for it to survive as a political entity, for its total disintegration was a worse alternative.

Its survival, none the less, was not without considerable cost and required much flexibility from Turks and non-Turks alike. Europeans within the Ottoman Empire were protected by the Capitulations – treaties ensuring them privileges and extra-territorial rights and protection by their own government agencies. Their governments, too, had acquired political and economic strength through their rights under the Capitulations and the activities of their nationals. The Ottoman government, right up to the First World War (when it thankfully unilaterally abrogated the Capitulations) was, accordingly, in a difficult situation. This situation was made worse by the government's own political and economic administration, outdated, mismanaged and venal. Worse, its authority and power were declining at the very time that burgeoning technological innovation could contribute materially to modernising and reforming the Empire, and was to put additional pressures on it. The Empire's progress was thus effectively in the hands of the European Great Powers, and the financial advantage largely returned to them.

Such 'progress' included the Empire's initiation into the realm of international loan finance in 1854. Turkey's resultant increasing indebtedness from then on – until by 1875 over half its borrowing was for principal and interest payments on former loans (owed largely to foreign creditors) – led to its virtual bankruptcy that year, made final in 1879. Following this bankruptcy Turkey's creditors succeeded in reorganising the country's finances and some of its main revenue-producing areas of the economy through the medium of the Ottoman Public Debt, set up in 1881 under the Decree of Mouharrem. These creditors, or bondholders, had as their delegates on the Council of the Ottoman Public Debt Administration financial figures representing all the Great Powers; and these figures, in effect, worked in close harmony with their governments. If considerable reform and improvement in Turkish economic management did indeed result from establishing the Debt Administration, it represented, none the less, a serious and deeply resented infringement of Turkey's sovereignty.

Symptomatic of the power of the Debt Administration was the position of the Imperial Ottoman Bank. By the later nineteenth century this was the single most powerful bank in the whole Empire, with its own seat on the Debt Council, for it was the agency through which the Ottoman government was able to contract almost all of its loans, being able to guarantee – or withhold – quotation on the Paris Bourse. Founded first in 1856, and reorganised in 1863, the bank was originally a British and then an Anglo-French institution; but soon it became in effect French. It was the only bank able to issue currency (apart from the Ottoman government itself), and it quickly became involved in economic investment in the Ottoman Empire, as did other, European-controlled banks there.

Participation in development concessions was the other main source of European economic power in the Ottoman Empire. The Empire had neither the resources nor the ability to develop its own economic potential. But the European Powers did. The nineteenth century saw European involvement in developing virtually every aspect of the economy – communications, transport, services, factories and mines, and trade – while by the early twentieth century the Empire's three main creditor European Powers, France, Germany and Britain, supplied advisers to the Ottoman government over a very wide range of its activities. This was quite apart, of course, from the very great involvement in the Turkish economy after 1881 by the Debt Administration. Concessions were sought by groups of financiers, banks or business entrepreneurs, and the more important concessions were usually obtained through intervention by their sponsor governments with the sultan. He was unable to refuse if he wished to attain any of his own goals, although he did become expert at playing one Great Power off against another to his best advantage. But Sultan Abdul Hamid II himself, who was in power from 1876 to 1909, through much of the period of Great Power financial domination of the Empire, sought not only to modernise his realm but also to do so in such a way as to strengthen his own position. The most ambitious of all these concessions, and that most fraught with political friction among the Powers, was the

German Baghdad Railway scheme. Begun in 1899, it was seen by the sultan as a vital strategic link across the mountainous backbone of his territories.

This scheme, the great scheme of German imperial economic endeavour in the Ottoman Empire, symbolised also the aggressive emergence of German interests into Europe's established areas of influence. These now represented a unified and dynamic Power, determined to carve its own modern position in the Empire. The other Great Powers, for all their rivalries and friction, felt threatened by this sudden German expansion, and their efforts in the two decades before 1914 were concerned to contain or neutralise this unstable interferer in their established spheres of influence.

Even in enterprises where no economic profit was made the European Powers had a strong position. Apart from their own consular courts, prisons and post offices they ran schools and hospitals and had longstanding religious interests and foundations in the Empire. Religious divisions within the Empire's populations both weakened the authority of the Ottoman government and enhanced that of the Powers, making some of them into religious protectors to significant portions of the Empire's population. There was also a considerable expatriate community in the Empire engaged in trade and other commercial or professional activities. These, too, under the Capitulations, were also an important source of both external interference and local leverage by the Powers in the affairs of Turkey.

All in all, therefore, without pre-empting the more detailed discussions in this book of individual Great Power involvement in the Ottoman Empire and of the Empire's internal situation, there were clearly large, vested Great Power interests combined with serious internal structural weaknesses of the Empire which, in combination, were to produce, in the strain of war and nationalist revolution, its ultimate disintegration.

What this book seeks to investigate, therefore, is the nature and motivation of each Great Power's particular interests in the Ottoman Empire and the extent to which these interests and involvement might have contributed to the end of that Empire. The interests of each Power in the Empire are seen against the background of that Power's broader foreign-policy concerns, and also against the machinery and personnel through which its Turkish policy was framed and operated.

Clearly the chief preoccupations of any one Power were likely to differ to some degree from those of its fellows. Such differences mean that the thematic approach of the different chapters as well as the specific issues discussed or the way in which the same material might be handled varies considerably from chapter to chapter. As a result, each chapter contributes to a composite picture of Great Power involvement in the Ottoman Empire while at the same time it presents a very individual contribution to the book. Each chapter has its own themes, focal points and relevant parameters. For instance, some Powers had had interests in the Ottoman Empire for much longer than other Powers, or interests which were of far more basic concern to them than to their fellows.

Some Powers, too, lost this interest earlier than the other Powers, whether through ceasing to exist, like the Austro-Hungarian Empire by the end of the First World War, or by changing the ruling ideology and regime, like Russia in 1917. Some, like Germany, had a comparatively late revival of interest in the Ottoman Empire, though a lateness more than compensated for by the fervour with which it was pursued. Other Powers – Britain, France and (to a much lesser extent) Italy – were instrumental in the practical dismantling of the Ottoman Empire after the First World War. Different Powers, too, as has been suggested earlier, had geographical areas that were of particular interest to them. France, for instance, was especially concerned with Syria; Britain with Mesopotamia and the Persian Gulf; Russia with the Straits and northern Anatolia; while Austria, after the turn of the century, replaced her interest in Crete and Albania with Macedonia and with the turbulent Balkan areas near her south-eastern frontier generally. Considerations of strategy, economic gain, political prestige, too, all played their part. The Turkish government itself was a far from passive observer of Great Power intrusion into its affairs, and its major concerns and problems are discussed in the first chapter of all, setting the scene for the succeeding chapters.

In the course of this book, therefore, and within the parameters discussed above, a great deal of ground is covered and information, interpretations and up-to-date references are provided. Certain limitations have been accepted by the contributors, arising from their individual thematic approaches and from the inevitable restrictions of space. Where a contributor has written in depth on an aspect of his or her Power's involvement in the Empire in another publication that material tends not to be reproduced here in any detail. Instead, the reader is given the appropriate references to the fuller account and the contributor is able to devote more attention to other aspects of his theme and to putting it into a broader perspective. In any case, it would be impossible to cover every aspect of interest to any chapter. Selectivity, therefore, has been essential in preparing the chapters, but it is hoped that the individual themes they present, their complementary character, and the broad picture that they paint will together add considerably to the understanding of the role of the Great Powers in the end of the Ottoman Empire.

1 The Late Ottoman Empire

Feroz Ahmad, University of Massachusetts – Boston

The meeting at Reval between King Edward VII and Tsar Nicholas II in June 1908 suggested to Turkish minds that the two great antagonists of the Eastern Question might be burying their differences and reaching agreement to dismember the Ottoman Empire.[1] The fear of dismemberment was never far from Turkish thoughts, especially after the Congress of Berlin in 1878. There the Great Powers abandoned the principles of maintaining the integrity of the Ottoman Empire and non-interference in its internal affairs – principles they had adopted at the Paris Congress in 1856.[2] At Berlin, the Ottoman Empire not only lost territory, it was also forced to reconcile itself to foreign intervention, ostensibly to supervise reform on behalf of the Porte's non-Muslim subjects though more usually to further the interests of one Power or the other. That encouraged nationalism and separatism among subject peoples and created an explosive situation for the Porte. It may therefore be argued that the Powers were responsible for hastening the collapse of the Empire if only because they exploited a situation not of their making.

The Ottoman Empire, like the other multi-national, multi-religious empires, had become an anachronism in a Europe dominated by nation states. Its rulers tried to meet the challenges of industrial capitalism and a rapidly emerging world market by reforming their own state and society. If they failed, they were not alone. A far more homogeneous Chinese empire succumbed to the same challenges, as did the empires of Austria-Hungary and Tsarist Russia. It seems as though reform alone could not stave off the fatal day of final destruction, and none of the ruling classes, least of all the Ottoman, could go beyond reform to the restructuring of society; only the Bolsheviks did that after they seized power and therefore still had an 'empire', albeit in a new form. Nevertheless, the Ottoman Turks tried till the very end to reform and struggle for survival. Ultimately they were forced to accept the inevitable; to abandon the idea of empire and settle for a national republic.

The end of the Ottoman Empire ought not to be any cause for surprise; the puzzle is that it survived as long as it did. One authority on the Eastern Question has noted that 'The Ottoman Empire in 1774 was still stagnant and archaic. Its chances of survival now seemed to many observers very small.'[3] If the Empire survived for almost another century and a half, that was due more to the rivalries of the Great Powers and their failure to reach agreement on how to divide 'the sick man's' legacy than to the patient's will and determination to survive. Yet Ottoman state and society as they approached the end of empire were very different from the description of 1774. In the century and a half that had elapsed, major changes were introduced into the entire structure of the Empire. These changes did not save it but they did lay new foundations without which there could have been no nation state.

The Empire at the beginning of the nineteenth century may best be described as a 'tributary state'.[4] The military–bureaucratic ruling class rested on no specific socio-economic foundations (as did the ruling class in pre-industrial Europe whose power was based on land ownership). Instead, it appropriated surplus in the form of revenue from all sectors of the economy: the land, internal and foreign trade, and manufacturing. Out of their own self-interest, Ottoman rulers protected all these sectors without allowing any one of them to influence state policy and to emerge dominant over the others. Thus, while landholders and merchants acquired great wealth and were vital to the economy, they were never permitted to exercise political power. These economic groups failed therefore to develop as a political class.

The great Ottoman transformation coincided with the Napoleonic episode in the Levant. The state was threatened internally by reactionary rebellions against reform and externally by Napoleon's invasion of Egypt. In the ensuing turmoil, new political forces – namely, the landed provincial élite supported by the reformist bureaucracy – intervened on behalf of the sultan. After defeating the reactionaries – at least, temporarily – they forced the sultan to confirm their own rights and privileges.[5]

The signing of the 'deed of agreement' (*sened-i ittifak*), Turkey's Magna Carta, in 1808 marked the emergence of landed interests as a political force at the centre. Despite setbacks, by 1826 the alliance of sultan, landed élite, and bureaucracy had succeeded in defeating the reactionaries. Soon after, the bureaucracy at the Sublime Porte virtually seized control of the affairs of state. It launched a series of reforms whose aim was to create a modern state apparatus and limit the autocratic powers of the sultan.[6] In the years 1840–70 three statesmen – the Grand Vezirs/Foreign Ministers Mustafa Reşid Pasha (1800–58), Âli Pasha (1815–71), and Fuad Pasha (1815–69) – ran the Empire and conducted its foreign relations. They were convinced 'Westerners', who, having seen Europe at close quarters, concluded that it was futile to resist her advance and wiser to emulate her by adopting her ideas and institutions. Better still, they believed, make the Empire a part of the European system by letting it be integrated into the rapidly expanding world economy, the impact of whose exports was painfully apparent in the Ottoman economy as early as the 1820s.[7] The policies of these 'Westerners' soon created modern-sounding state institutions, but they also had a disastrous effect on the economy and society, leading to bankruptcy and foreign control.

There was a popular reaction against these men and their policies because they were held responsible for making the Empire subservient to the West. Âli Pasha was described as 'the ambassador of that European power which was most influential in Istanbul rather than the foreign minister of the Ottoman Empire'.[8] As a result, the sultan became a popular figure, the symbol of opposition to the West, and regained the initiative from the bureaucrats. For the next generation, Sultan Abdul Hamid II (1876–1909) ruled the Empire from Yıldız Palace, aided by a clique of favourites and sycophants who created their own closed 'palace system'. There was a marked degeneration in the power of the Grand Vezirate and the Foreign Ministry, both being closely associated with the discredited 'Westerners'.[9] Such ministers became creatures of the sultan, dependent for their official survival upon patronage and intrigue within the Palace clique. Thus, in the years 1871–85 there were more than twenty changes at the Foreign Ministry; only thereafter was there a semblance of stability with Kürd Said Pasha and Ahmed Tevfik Pasha acting as foreign ministers during the years 1885–95 and 1895–1909 respectively.[10] The Foreign Ministry had become a technical appendage to the Palace where policy was actually made. In such circumstances, the Under-Secretary at the Ministry, especially if he were as talented as Artin Dadian Pasha, became more important than the Minister, for he supplied the information on which policy was based. By and large, career diplomats played a secondary role, while Abdul Hamid used his confidants as negotiators and ambassadors. This state of affairs lasted until the constitutional revolution of 1908.[11]

The Young Turk revolution marked the end of the Hamidian system and the temporary resurgence of the Sublime Porte to its former glory. With the establishment of political parties and parliamentary politics, the element of ideology was injected into the bureaucracy, including the Foreign Ministry. It is thus possible to chart the course of the revolution by the changes at the Grand Vezirate and the Ministry of Foreign Affairs alone.

Even though the Constitution was restored in July 1908, Abdul Hamid's Grand Vezirs, Said and Kâmil Pashas, and his Foreign Minister, Tevfik Pasha, continued in office. It is true that they were now independent of the sultan and were taking measures to strengthen the Porte against the encroachments of both the Palace and the Committee of Union and Progress (CUP) – the most radical organisation in the Young Turk movement – but Said and Kâmil were nevertheless men of the old regime. Only after the CUP had engineered the fall of Kâmil Pasha in February 1909 were the Unionists able to replace Tevfik, who, 'perhaps because of his long habituation of the Hamidian system, did not seem to know anything about the regulations supposed to govern his ministry'.[12]

Tevfik's successor, Mehmed Rifat Pasha (1860–1925), was a career diplomat. He joined the translation bureau of the Foreign Ministry in 1882, became minister to Athens in 1897 and Ambassador to London in 1905, whence he was recalled to be Foreign Minister. Rifat's sympathy for Unionist aspirations was as important as his professionalism in leading to his appointment. Socially he belonged to the declining class of Turkish Muslim merchants whose fortunes the CUP hoped to revive by instituting protectionism and abolishing the privileges of foreigners. Rifat's father and brother were merchants of the Balkapı district in Istanbul, and his brother Şefik joined the CUP and was elected to Parliament. Rifat himself was considered sufficiently loyal to the Committee to be given a safe parliamentary seat for Istanbul.[13]

Rifat Pasha was succeeded in September 1911 by Mustafa Asim, another career diplomat with Unionist sympathies, who was immediately replaced by the anti-Unionist government of Ahmed Muhtar Pasha (1839–1918) in July 1912. This Liberal government brought to the Foreign Ministry Gabriel Noradunghian, an Armenian nationalist, in the fond hope of swaying the Great Powers towards Turkey during the Italo-Turkish and the First Balkan wars.[14] After the Unionist *coup d'état* of January 1913, except for the interim appointment of Muhtar Bey, the Foreign Ministry was always occupied by someone from the inner circle of the CUP. Said Halim Pasha (1863–1921), the Egyptian prince from the house of Muhammad Ali, who was already Foreign Minister, became Grand Vezir in June 1913 and remained in office until October 1915. He was succeeded in the Ministry by Halil (who adopted in 1934 the family surname Menteşe), a key member of the Committee, who was replaced by Ahmed Nesimi, a confidant of Talât Pasha, when the latter became Grand Vezir in February 1917.

The Unionists considered diplomacy to be too important to be left to diplomats. Thus, even when they were not in power they engaged in diplomatic manoeuvres independently of and unknown to the government. Until they came to power in 1913, the Unionists were the self-appointed guardians of the new regime, exercising power without responsibility. They were often impatient with official procedures and suspicious of the Foreign Ministry, which they regarded as being both cautious and timid in its dealings with foreign states. Moreover, they believed that many of their professional diplomats had leanings towards Liberal political groups which made them willing to reach compromise with the Powers over the Empire's sovereignty – the very thing the CUP was determined to regain.[15] The Committee, therefore, sent its emissaries and deputations to convey its views to foreign embassies and governments. Even after the Unionists had gained control of the Foreign Ministry, their delegations, supported in technical matters by career men, continued to deal with matters of war and peace, as well as with the search for alliances. The same methods were used throughout the war, until the resignation of Talât Pasha's Cabinet in October 1918. It was replaced by a government untainted by association with the war party in the hope that the Allies would give better armistice terms to such a ministry.

The fall of the CUP allowed the Palace to regain the initiative once again, though only for less than a year. In those months, Sultan Mehmed VI Vahdettin (1918–22) reverted to the diplomacy of the Liberal Young Turks and that meant total reliance on and subservience to Great Britain. Old and discredited members of the Ottoman *ancien régime* were resurrected in order to form ephemeral governments and conduct personal diplomacy. Thus, Tevfik Pasha formed two ministries between November 1918 and March 1919, to be followed by Abdul Hamid's brother-in-law Damad Ferid Pasha (1853–1923), who led three cabinets in seven months. Damad Ferid, having served in diplomatic missions throughout Europe during the Hamidian era, and having been acquainted with European statesmen during his tenure as a Liberal politician, was considered an asset in the negotiations for the very survival of the Ottoman state and dynasty. Such hopes proved illusory. The British-backed Greek invasion of Anatolia on 15 May 1919 and the paralysis of the Istanbul government ended any hope that the sultan's regime had of gaining popular acceptance.[16]

Meanwhile, local notables had begun organising resistance to the foreign occupation of Anatolia. By the summer of 1919, a national movement was taking shape under the leadership of Mustafa Kemal Pasha (1881–1938), named Atatürk, or 'Father Turk', in 1934. The nationalist movement's Representative Committee soon became an alternative focus of power and a direct challenge to the Istanbul government. After the capital was occupied by Allied troops on 16 March 1920, the nationalists announced the formation of a government in Ankara on 23 April. They claimed, with much justification, that the sultan was a 'prisoner' of the Allies and was therefore no longer capable of acting on behalf of the Turkish people. So far, nationalist diplomacy had been confined to unofficial contacts with representatives of foreign powers in Anatolia. But, having declared themselves a government, the nationalists had to organise a Foreign Office. In May 1920 the National Assembly elected Bekir Sami as its first Foreign Minister.[17]

Bekir Sami (1864–1932), a former Unionist provincial governor, had joined the nationalist movement during its organisational phase and worked closely with Kemal Pasha, winning his trust and confidence. The same was true of Yusuf Kemal (Tengirşenk) (1878–1969) and İsmet (İnönü) (1885–1973), who succeeded Bekir Sami and served as Foreign Ministers until the proclamation of the Turkish Republic in October 1923. Both men enjoyed Mustafa Kemal's trust, and that was perhaps the most important qualification required for the post of Foreign Minister. Policy, formulated collectively by Kemal Pasha's inner circle on the advice of seasoned diplomats like Ahmed Rüstem Bey de Bilinski,[18] had to be implemented to the letter if the struggle for a sovereign and independent Turkey were not to be compromised at the negotiating-table. Thus, Bekir Sami was asked to resign in May 1921 'for having made economic concessions' to European powers during talks in London, thereby violating 'the principles of the National Government'. He was denounced by Mustafa Kemal as 'an adherent of peace at any price',[19] suggesting that the Kemalists would continue fighting for their programme of self-determination. After this event, the Foreign Minister had even less authority, for he was invariably accompanied by a small group of advisers who made sure that he did not go beyond his brief.[20] Even İsmet Pasha at Lausanne had constantly to seek instructions from Ankara, and that resulted in prolonged negotiations.

If the method of making and implementing policy differed from regime to regime during the last years of the Empire, the aim of policy remained virtually unchanged until the end of the First World War. The fundamental aim was to maintain the integrity of the Empire threatened by the aggressive designs of the Great Powers and the nationalist aspirations of the subject peoples; the latter invariably sought Great Power patronage in order to achieve their ends. Only in 1919 was there a dramatic clash between the aspirations of the old ruling class and those of the national movement. The sultan of the defeated Empire was willing to accept a truncated state in a partitioned Anatolia, even under a foreign mandate, so long as he was allowed to retain some vestiges of his traditional authority.[21] The nationalists, on the other hand, refused to settle for anything less than self-determination for a sovereign Turkish nation. This, they argued, was in keeping with the principles proclaimed by President Wilson. The approach of these two antagonists to foreign relations differed sharply; but so did the approach of those regimes united in the aim of saving the Empire.

The Turkish 'Westerners', led by Reşid, Âli and Fuad Pashas, believed that the Ottoman Empire could be saved by being integrated into the Western political and economic system. They had a vested interest in promoting Westernisation at home, for it strengthened their position *vis-à-vis* an autocratic sultan who, under the traditional order, enjoyed the power of life and death over his bureaucrats. The Charters of 1839 and 1856 and the 1876 Constitution altered that by establishing equality for all before the law, as well as placing other restraints on the sultan's autocracy.[22]

The motives of this Westernising bureaucracy were not entirely self-serving. The reformers sincerely believed that it would be wiser for Istanbul to join rather than resist Europe, as Ottoman conservatives proposed. The Empire would benefit from joining the world economic system (it was happening anyway) and finding a place in the new division of labour. That was the logic behind Reşid Pasha signing the Treaty of Baltı Liman in 1838 – the agreement to establish free trade throughout the Empire.[23] While its implementation undermined existing manufactures by making them even less competitive against virtually duty-free imports, it enhanced the export of raw materials to Europe. The treaty also liberated landholders from the buying monopoly of the state and permitted them to sell directly to foreign buyers or their agents at the higher market prices. The landed class emerged strengthened both politically and economically. Within a generation it provided the socio-economic foundation for the Ottoman state which no longer controlled commerce and industry, now largely the preserve of Europeans and their Christian clients.[24]

The policies of the 'Westerners' were successful in so far as they gave the Empire the semblance of modernity, with Western institutions, palaces and furniture in the French style, and frock coats. There was even a hint of acceptance by the Powers when the Empire was included in the Concert of Europe in 1856 and its integrity guaranteed. But the burden of free trade and superstructural Westernisation proved too heavy for the traditional sectors of the economy and society. Psychologically, the provision of legal equality for non-Muslim subjects, already more advanced materially, affected adversely the Ottoman Muslim psyche accustomed to enjoying a totally false sense of superiority *vis-à-vis* the 'infidels'. All these complex factors produced a reaction against the 'Westerners' and Westernisation. The sultan, posing as the champion of the traditional order, but also alarmed by Western penetration, seized the initiative from his bureaucrats. Even though the movement against Westernisation had an Islamic character, it was by no means reactionary. It was essentially anti-imperialist and a response to increasing Western dominance in the Islamic world and Asia. It provided Abdul Hamid with the opportunity to exploit his position as caliph to mobilise sentiment throughout the Islamic world (including India) against the West – something the CUP regime continued to do, especially during the First World War.[25]

The new balance of power in Europe marked by the defeat of France and the emergence of Germany and Italy as Great Powers facilitated the sultan's task of trying new options in foreign relations. By turning to Germany, Abdul Hamid hoped to counter the Russian threat by means other than support from Paris and London. At the same time, he hoped to challenge what he saw as the Anglo-French monopoly over Ottoman affairs.

The German card was in fact an old one; Ottoman sultans had used it against Russia in the eighteenth century.[26] Abdul Hamid came to rely on it despite Bismarck's initial snub. He had great admiration for Prussia even before he became sultan and is said to have wagered a hundred liras (then worth about £100 sterling) on a Prussian victory in the war against France. Abdul Hamid, noted his personal physician, hated Russia, had contempt for France, feared Britain, and saw Germany as a faithful ally.[27] By the 1890s the German card was even more potent because of Germany's increasing strength and ambition as a world power. That suited Abdul Hamid's pan-Islamism since Germany, unlike England, France and Russia, did not colonise Muslim lands and therefore was not suspect in Muslim eyes as an imperialist power. On the contrary, Kaiser Wilhelm was able to present himself to the Muslim world as the champion of Islam against its enemies, rather as Napoleon had tried to do in an earlier age.[28]

Apart from the ideological and personal factors which brought Berlin and Constantinople together, there were also other factors which united these empires, the most important being the economic and the geopolitical. Abdul Hamid believed that by giving economic concessions to Germany, especially concessions like the Berlin–Baghdad railway, he would give her an economic stake in the Ottoman Empire, obliging her to intervene on the Porte's behalf in both political crises and wars. The German railway concession would facilitate the movement of troops to assist him from Europe as well as from within the Empire, and could not be threatened by English sea power.[29] The link was strengthened even more when the sultan asked the Kaiser to train the Ottoman army.

Abdul Hamid's strategy of attacking the positions of England, France and

Russia in the Ottoman Empire by involving Germany undoubtedly worked. Germany soon became a serious rival to the other imperialist powers, and tensions between them sharpened. Whether that helped to prolong the life of the Empire, as Abdul Hamid hoped it would, or hastened its demise, is debatable. It certainly made the Great Power rivalry more complex and therefore more difficult to resolve. Had Germany been kept out of Ottoman affairs – extremely unlikely given German power – it is possible that the Entente Powers might have established a condominium over the Empire. They could then have partitioned it at their convenience. Such a scenario, however, assumes the Ottoman Empire in the role of a passive victim awaiting its destiny in a fatalistic frame of mind. That was never the case.

If Abdul Hamid was successful in making the Eastern Question more complex through German participation, he was never able to commit Berlin to the defence and integrity of the Empire. He also never tried to go beyond the policy of playing off the Powers against each other by offering to become Germany's formal ally. That would have required, if nothing else, a strong army, since Germany was not likely to form an alliance with a liability; and Abdul Hamid, despite his high military spending and his commitments to army reform, saw a strong army as a threat to his own position.[30] His internal policies, though reformist in character, were designed to strengthen the *status quo* rather than to introduce structural social change. Be that as it may, the erosion of Ottoman society went on apace with Western penetration, and the sultan could do little to arrest this process. Finally, in 1908 he succumbed to revolution, which, as in everything else, began the active phase in Ottoman foreign relations, with the search for a European ally.

The Young Turk revolution commenced with the limited goal of restoring the 1876 Constitution. Its long-term aims, however, were far more ambitious. They were nothing less than to rejuvenate and transform Ottoman society so as to make the Empire accepted as an equal by the Great Powers. Nothing describes the ambitions of the Young Turks better than their claim to be the 'Japan of the Near East'.[31] Internally, that meant converting the Empire from the status of a semi-colony, controlled and exploited by the European Powers, to a sovereign capitalist state, exploiting its own imperial resources for its own benefit. It is important to emphasise that to the Unionists 'modernisation' or 'Westernisation' had come to mean adopting capitalism, and not just reforming institutions. They understood that a capitalist society had its own class structure, including a bourgeoisie, to sustain it, and they began to take steps to create such a society.[32]

The first task of the Young Turks was to win acceptance from the Great Powers and have them abandon all the privileges they enjoyed through the Capitulations. They believed that Europe, especially England and France, would be sympathetic to a revolution which was struggling to set up a constitutional system modelled on those of Europe. After all, the principal reason why Europe insisted on retaining the Capitulations was its claims that its citizens residing in the Ottoman Empire could not be expected to live under an alien and archaic system of law and government. If this obstacle were removed, and a system of government acceptable to Europe instituted, then there would be no reason for the Capitulations.

Initially the Young Turks – Unionists and Liberals – turned to Britain for support. Germany had supported the Hamidian regime and acquired a strong foothold in the Empire through the concessions granted by the old regime. By encouraging Britain to compete against Germany and France for new concessions, the Young Turks hoped to break France and Germany's hold and acquire greater autonomy for the Porte. Hostility to Germany increased when her ally Austria-Hungary annexed Bosnia and Herzegovina in October 1908. The pro-Unionist *Tanin* went so far as to suggest that Vienna's motive in carrying out this act was to strike a blow against the constitutional regime and assist reaction in order to bring about its fall.[33]

The Young Turks found themselves isolated and let down by the attitude of the Powers in view of the violation of the Treaty of Berlin they themselves had signed. There was little the Turks could do except vent their frustration by organising a boycott of Austro-Hungarian goods.[34] The Unionists, however, decided to approach Britain with an offer of alliance. Two prominent Unionists, Ahmed Rıza and Dr Nâzım, were sent to London to discuss the matter with Sir Edward Grey and Sir Charles Hardinge. The proposal was politely rejected. Grey told them

that our habit was to keep our hands free, though we made ententes and friendships. It was true that we had an alliance with Japan, but it was limited to certain distant questions in the Far East.

They replied that Turkey was the Japan of the Near East, and that we already had the Cyprus Convention with Turkey which was still in force.

I said that they had our entire sympathy in the good work they were doing in Turkey; we wished them well, and we would help them in their internal affairs by lending them men to organise customs, police, and so forth, if they wished them.[35]

Despite this rebuff, the Unionists did not abandon their pro-British attitude. They considered Britain the lynchpin of the Triple Entente and, if she could be won over, France and Russia would be, too. They were optimistic that their programme of reform would impress Britain and they were willing to bide their time. The CUP continued to support the anti-Unionist but pro-British Kâmil Pasha, and when the Committee forced his resignation in February 1909 they promised to withhold their support from any ministry which might succeed him unless it pursued his policy of friendship for England.[36] Hüseyin Hilmi Pasha, who succeeded Kâmil as Grand Vezir, personally went to assure the British Ambassador that 'his policy towards England would be the same as that of his predecessors, and that he would continue to count on the support and advice of HMG'.[37]

Not even the British embassy's anti-Unionist attitude during the counter-revolution of April 1909 could undermine the CUP's anglophilism. This was not based on sentiment but on political realism and expediency. The counter-revolution had been crushed by the Third Army, and that brought Mahmud Şevket Pasha and the senior officers on to the political stage. The senior officers, many of them German-trained, were thought to be pro-German, and Şevket Pasha, who became the Empire's strongman, was considered positively Germany's man at the Porte. He had spent ten years in the German army and was said to be close to Field-Marshal von der Goltz, who was again in Turkey to train the army. However, there was no question of Şevket Pasha seizing power in order to set up a regime devoted to German interests, as the CUP press claimed.[38]

Nevertheless, the Unionists, who were predominantly civilian, resented the intrusion of the army into government. One way to challenge and undermine the army's position was by attacking Germany in the press and supporting friendship with Germany's rival, Great Britain. But neither Britain nor France responded to Unionist professions of friendship. In fact France resented the Porte's desire to acquire financial autonomy. When in 1910 the Finance Ministry tried to negotiate a loan without political and economic strings, the French supported by Britain offered humiliating terms which amounted to establishing French control over Turkish finances. The Unionists refused to accept such terms, and after protracted negotiations in Paris, London, and Berlin finally floated the loan in Germany.[39]

The first three years of relations between the new regime and the Powers were demoralising and frustrating for the Turks. The Powers refused to make any concessions over the Capitulations and loosen their grip over the Empire's internal affairs. The Turks were powerless because the Great Powers, despite their rivalries, were united on the issue of defending their privileges against Turkish assaults. In September 1911, when the Turco-Italian War broke out, the Porte was still isolated and totally without Great Power support.[40] Germany was sympathetic but unable to help Turkey against her own ally, Italy. The Porte therefore turned once again to Britain and appealed for her support in the war. A month later, in October 1911, there followed a formal proposal of alliance with either Britain alone or with the Triple Entente.[41] This time Grey's rejection was not outright. Once peace had been restored between Turkey and Italy, he would be ready, he wrote, 'to discuss and examine . . . the measures which might be adopted for establishing on firm and durable basis a thoroughly good understanding between the Ottoman Empire and this country'.[42] But that was in the future. Meanwhile the war struck a critical blow at the fortunes of the CUP, bringing about its fall in July 1912.

The Liberals were in power when the First Balkan War broke out in October. Peace was made with Italy, and the octogenarian anglophile Kâmil Pasha was appointed Grand Vezir in the hope that he would be able to win Britain's support. Kâmil launched his diplomatic offensive with an appeal to

Grey to intervene immediately in the current crisis. He reminisced about Anglo-Turkish friendship since the Crimean War, perhaps hoping to strike a sentimental note in Sir Edward's heart. But Grey remained unmoved. He informed Kâmil in no uncertain terms that the Powers would not intervene to save Edirne (Adrianople) for the Turks, and that the idea of territorial integrity was a dead letter. He advised Kâmil to cede Edirne to the Bulgars before they lost other things that were not already lost[43] – a chilling reminder that the capital, threatened at that moment by the Bulgars, might also fall and be lost to the Empire.

It is not possible to understand Unionist policy and behaviour after 1913 without realising what a traumatic effect the disaster of the Balkan Wars had on the Turkish psyche. The Turks had lost the very lands that had provided the life-blood of the Empire for centuries. Moreover, the capital had come within an ace of falling to the enemy, spelling the end of their Empire. Throughout this entire catastrophe the Great Powers had stood by, even though at the outbreak of hostilities they had declared that they would not permit a change in the *status quo*. That declaration was based on the assumption of Turkish victories; after Turkish defeats these words, it seemed, were conveniently forgotten.[44]

The Unionists, who seized power in January 1913, were more convinced than ever that only an alliance with Britain and the Entente could guarantee the survival of what remained of the Empire. In June, therefore, the subject of an Anglo-Turkish alliance was reopened by Tevfik Pasha, who restated his proposal of October 1911. Once again the Turkish offer was turned down.[45] Sir Louis Mallet, who became Britain's Ambassador to the Porte in 1914, noted that 'Turkey's way of assuring her independence is by an alliance with us or by an undertaking with the Triple Entente. A less risky method [he thought] would be by a treaty or Declaration binding all the Powers to respect the independence and integrity of the present Turkish dominion, which might go as far as neutralisation, and participation by all the Great Powers in financial control and the application of reform.'[46]

The Unionists could not possibly accept such proposals. They felt betrayed by what they considered was Europe's anti-Turkish bias during the Balkan Wars, and therefore they had no faith in Great Power declarations regarding the Empire's independence and integrity; the termination of European financial control and administrative supervision was one of the principal aims of their movement. Sir Louis Mallet seemed totally oblivious to that.

The following year, in May 1914, Talât Bey, *primus inter pares* in the Unionist movement, offered an alliance to Russia, but that, too, was not accepted.[47] The Committee's final attempt to reach an understanding with an Entente Power was the approach to France. Cemal Pasha, another leading member of the CUP with francophile proclivities, was sent to Paris in July 1914 for this purpose. He returned to Istanbul with French military decorations but no alliance.[48] Meanwhile, negotiations with Berlin had been opened, and

Cemal's failure in Paris gave an impetus to them. Even the pro-Entente Cemal Pasha recognised that Turkey had no choice but to conclude an agreement with Germany to avoid being left isolated in another moment of crisis. That alliance was duly signed on 2 August 1914 as the First World War gathered momentum.[49]

There was a general consensus among Turks in favour of the German alliance, for it ended Turkey's isolation – a factor of great psychological significance in 1914. But Unionists differed as to whether or when Turkey should become a belligerent. After all the disasters the Empire had suffered in the recent past, most Unionists would have preferred to stay out of the war, maintaining a benevolent neutrality in favour of Germany. The war party, composed mainly of junior army officers led by Enver Pasha, might have wished to enter the war lest Turkey be left out of peace negotiations and be partitioned herself following a quick and inconclusive end, anticipated by almost everyone; but Enver was not strong enough to drag a reluctant government into war, had the country's financial situation not been desperate and the psychological pressures overwhelming.

The financial and economic crisis was itself triggered by the outbreak of the Austro-Serbian War in late July. There was a panic in Istanbul which paralysed economic life as European-controlled enterprises suspended their operations. Navigation companies stopped using Turkish ports, while insurance companies refused to insure goods which might be confiscated as contraband of war. The imperial treasury was exhausted with only 92,000 liras in ready cash on 3 August and no European government willing to provide a loan.[50] Germany alone was willing to meet the Porte's financial need, but only if the Porte joined the war.[51]

The Turks were convinced that the Entente Powers, especially England, took Turkey's neutrality for granted. In London there was no awareness of the impact the Allied blockade of the Straits would have on Turkish public opinion, or that the embargo on the two warships, just completed in Britain and destined for the Turkish fleet, would anger ordinary Turks who had subscribed to the 'Fleet Fund' for their purchase. The CUP, with its control of the press, exploited these incidents against the Entente Powers. Once the war became general, there was a sense of relief among the Unionists because the Great Powers could no longer practise gunboat diplomacy against Turkey. The government declared armed neutrality and general mobilisation at the beginning of August. It also began to make preparations to abrogate the Capitulations unilaterally so as to be able to act as a sovereign state again.

With their newly found freedom, the Unionists came to see the war as an opportunity to renovate their entire society and regain their pride and self-respect. The Turkish press noted with obvious approval how Japan had seized the opportunity provided by the war to consolidate its position in East Asia, forcing Germany to abandon its possessions in China. 'Who can say when Japan will do the same to France and England . . .?' asked *Tercüman-i Haki-*

kat.[52] Turkey watched Japanese activity with great admiration and envy; one senses a strong desire to emulate Japan's example amongst the Turks, humiliated for so long by the West.

The Porte took the first step to regain 'for the Ottoman people its sovereignty and the nation its independence' by unilaterally abolishing the Capitulations on 9 September 1914.[53] The announcement that foreigners would no longer enjoy a position of privilege in the Empire boosted the morale of the Turkish people, though it had the opposite effect among the Christian population. There were spontaneous expressions of popular support for the government of the type witnessed when a people acquire their independence after generations of foreign subjugation. The CUP manipulated this sentiment by organising mammoth demonstrations, and declaring that the suppression of the hated Capitulations had concluded the first stage of the revolution and the nation was now ready for the second.

If sovereignty and independence were won by a courageous stroke of the pen, pride and self-respect were regained at great cost on the battlefield. The defence of the Straits at Gallipoli against the Allied onslaught did much to restore Turkish self-esteem. Failure in this long and bitterly waged campaign would have meant the destruction not only of the Ottoman Empire, but perhaps also of the Turkish people just as they were beginning to organise themselves as a nation. The Gallipoli campaign was therefore seen as a struggle for survival. Having emerged from it victorious, the Turks came to believe that they had won the right to be treated with respect by their enemies and as equals by their German and Austro-Hungarian allies.[54] In the overall war effort, the Unionists were convinced that Turkey's contribution was second to none. Turkish armies had tied down large numbers of Allied troops on various fronts, keeping them away from theatres in Europe where they would have been used against German and Austrian forces. Moreover, the Turks claimed that their success at Gallipoli had been an important factor in bringing about the collapse of Russia, resulting in the revolution of April 1917. They had turned the war in favour of Germany and her allies.

The newly found sense of dignity and self-respect explains Turkish attitudes towards Germany and Austria which both allies, accustomed to subservience, found arrogant and chauvinistic. The Turks refused to make concessions even to their allies, whose businesses, for example, were told to work through the medium of Turkish and to employ intermediaries who knew the language. This was part of the Unionist scheme to further Turkish economic interests and to create an indigenous bourgeoisie.[55] In 1917 the Cabinet went so far as to consider maintaining relations with Washington after the United States had declared war on Germany on 6 April. But the views of the war party prevailed and they insisted on maintaining a common front with their allies. Thus, relations with America were broken on 20 April 1917.[56] In return for such a show of solidarity, the Unionists expected reciprocity from Germany when it was time to negotiate a peace treaty with the enemy. They expected Germany to continue fighting until Ottoman territories in the Arab provinces lost to England had been regained. They expected Germany to allow a Turkish sphere of influence to be established in the Caucasus after Russia was dismembered at the peace-table. Unionist illusions were soon shattered when at Brest-Litovsk they found that Berlin expected them to subordinate their interests to those of Germany. For example, the Turkish delegation could not ask for a Russian withdrawal from eastern Anatolia because the Bolsheviks would ask for the evacuation of their territories occupied by the Germans. The Germans refused to do that, and the Turks had to pay the price.[57] In the final analysis, the Unionists simply lacked the power to back up their dreams and aspirations for a new Turkish empire in the Caucasus, and their allies knew it.

The Unionists signed the German alliance and entered the war convinced that neutrality would be disastrous for Turkey since it would leave her isolated and at the mercy of all the belligerents. The alliance was a gamble which the CUP believed gave Turkey a fighting chance to survive. The Turks could now prove themselves as the allies of a Great Power and again win the respect of Europe. With their experience of the Powers, there was no question of using Germany for their ends. Rather, seeing that the alliance was signed *after* the outbreak of war, the Unionists realised that they were the ones who could be used. But even that was preferable to isolation and a sense of impotence they knew so well. Was Turkish participation in the war the final nail in the coffin? Possibly. It is unlikely, however, that a neutral Turkey would have been allowed to remain neutral by the Triple Entente; it was strategically vital and it was likely to have been subverted and occupied, as were Greece and Persia. Moreover, because of its multi-national character, it is improbable that the Empire would have survived intact the declaration of the Wilsonian principle of self-determination. But without participating in the war it would not have been possible for the Unionists to carry out the transformation so necessary for laying the foundations of the new state and society that were to result in the Turkish Republic.

The victory of the Entente signalled the end of the Ottoman Empire; the question was what would succeed it. The sultan and the Liberals in the capital returned to the old policy of total dependence on Britain in the hope of salvaging whatever they could of their former territories. As we saw above, they tried to placate the Allies by forming a Cabinet willing to subordinate itself to Allied wishes.[58] While the sultan placed all his hopes in British support, even a British mandate, a group of intellectuals in the capital formed the Wilsonian Principles Society in the belief that an American mandate would be preferable for Turkey.[59] Both groups had lost the will to struggle for independent survival and had come to accept the inevitability of foreign tutelage.

Outside the capital, however, a national movement was taking shape despite the defeatism of the old ruling class. The new social forces – principally the landholders and the bourgeoisie – which had developed during the Young

Turk period and which had much to lose from the Allied scheme to dismember the Empire, including Anatolia, rallied to the nationalist cause.[60] The nationalists, under Mustafa Kemal's leadership, abandoned all imperial and pan-Turkist irredentism and fought for a sovereign, national Turkey in keeping with Wilsonian principles. They were fortunate in having to face a war-weary Europe, too exhausted after 1920 to impose its will on Turkey. Moreover, the Allies were divided because of their imperialist rivalries over the partition of Anatolia. Mustafa Kemal was able to exploit these rivalries with the same skill as the Ottomans. A working relationship with the Soviet regime in the north proved to be most important for the nationalists. Whatever the ideological differences between these two movements, their common imperialist enemies kept them together in an alliance of convenience.

Soon after the nationalists formed their Foreign Office and elected Bekir Sami as Foreign Minister in May 1920, they sent a diplomatic mission to Moscow, thus effectively ending their international isolation. A draft treaty was initialled in Moscow on 24 August, two weeks after the sultan had signed the humiliating Treaty of Sèvres, accepting the partition of Turkey. In Anatolia, the nationalists began to take measures to abort the Armenian state to which the Treaty of Sèvres was to give birth. By November they had advanced beyond Kars, and the Bolsheviks who had just captured the government of the Armenian state from the Mensheviks prevailed upon it to make peace with the nationalists. Thus, Ankara's first international treaty was signed on 2 December 1920, establishing Turkey's new boundaries in the east.[61]

Nationalist policy continued to be a fine mix of military force and diplomacy. Successes on the battlefield against Greek forces yielded diplomatic gains, such as the Treaty of Ankara with France (October 1921), which followed the victory at Sakarya in August.[62] This pattern continued until the Greek army was driven out of Anatolia, and Britain, which had supported the Greeks, decided to negotiate with the nationalists. After protracted negotiations, the nationalists achieved their aim of establishing a sovereign and independent republic.

The all-pervasive character of European intervention in Ottoman affairs needs to be explained. What were the special circumstances in the Ottoman Empire that enabled Europe to interfere so effectively? The simple answer is that the nineteenth century was the European century *par excellence*, and hardly any part of the globe escaped Europe's attention. Even distant China and Japan were 'opened up' to Europe's – and America's – expanding economy. Given its strategic location and its proximity to Europe, the Ottoman Empire could hardly have escaped European encroachments. Besides, each of the Great Powers had a lively interest in the Empire, and the pursuit of this interest is the theme of the other chapters. Here we need only look at some of the special characteristics of the Ottoman situation which facilitated European penetration.

The vastness of the Empire which stretched from the borders of Austria-Hungary in the west to the Red Sea in the east made it difficult to control in an age of poor communications. Despite the railways and the telegraph, central authority was shadowy even in Anatolia, let alone in the borderlands of the Empire. Like other pre-modern empires – Spain, for example – the Ottoman Empire never integrated its conquests economically and therefore never established a binding link with its colonies. As the Empire was integrated into the world economy, certain of its regions (the Balkans, Egypt, Iraq, and Hijaz) established closer economic links with Paris and London, even with British India, than with Istanbul. Abdul Hamid recognised the weakness of his Empire and attempted to compensate for it by integrating local ruling groups (Albanian, Arab and Kurdish) into his system by according to each certain privileges and a measure of autonomy. When the Unionists attempted to restore central authority, they were confronted with rebellions and general discontent, supported in part by some of the Powers. The Austrians interfered in Albania, the Russians in the Balkans and eastern Anatolia, and the French in Syria. The Unionists were forced to accept reality and adopt limited decentralisation as a policy most likely to keep their Empire intact.[63]

The Ottoman Empire differed, however, from other pre-modern empires in that its ruling class made no attempt to integrate conquered peoples culturally. The sultans had no policy of converting the non-Muslims of the Balkans or Anatolia to Islam or turkifying the non-Turks; the idea of nationality simply did not exist, and the Turks – at least, the rulers – called themselves Ottomans. All the Ottomans did was to settle small islands of Muslim Turks in a sea of Christians.[64] Over a period of time there were conversions and some cultural integration, but the process never amounted to much. Besides, the *millet* system, which was not as watertight as it was once thought to be, could always be resurrected by the leaders of the religious communities to emphasise and exaggerate the differences between the communities and erode whatever integration had taken place over the centuries. That is what happened in the nineteenth century under the influence of nationalism.

The history of the *millet* system dates back to the reign of Mehmed II, known as the Conqueror (1451–81), who, having conquered Constantinople in 1453, guaranteed the Greek church religious freedom, and to its appointed head, the patriarch, granted full religious and civil authority over the Greek Orthodox community of the Empire. That bound the patriarch to the sultan since the former's authority over his *millet* was entirely dependent on the support of the latter.[65] Later, these privileges were extended to the Armenian and Jewish communities.

Until the nineteenth century, the *millets* had a purely religious character. Greeks and Slavs, if Orthodox, were members of the Greek community, while Armenians formed separate *millets* depending on whether they were Gregorian or Catholic. By the middle of the century, however, the national ideal had begun to penetrate the *millet* framework, and the Porte, seeing that as a way to divide the opposition, recognised a separate Bulgarian Exarchate in 1864.[66]

It does not require much imagination to see how the Powers could manipulate this system to further their own ends. The *millets* themselves benefited from foreign protection, especially those individuals who were able to acquire foreign citizenship. But the long-term effects of patronage were disastrous for the Empire and tragic for the communities. The process of patronage began with the Treaty of Küçük Kaynarca in 1774, which recognised Russia as the protector of the Orthodox *millet*. Later, other Powers claimed similar rights to protect communities with whom they shared a religious affinity. France became the protector of the Catholics, Britain and America of Protestants, so that all non-Muslim *millets*, save the Jews, found a Great Power protector.[67] Evangelical missionary activity played its role in the process, for that, too, came under the protection of one Power or the other. Mission schools and colleges were instrumental in introducing modern ideas, especially the idea of nationalism among non-Muslims and non-Turks, thereby alienating them from the existing culture and society.

Another institution that undermined Ottoman sovereignty was the Capitulations, or extra-territorial privileges enjoyed by foreigners residing in the Empire. Originally these privileges were granted unilaterally by the sultan to foreign merchants, and later they were extended to states whose citizens traded in the Ottoman Empire. The Capitulations arose out of the same concept as the *millets*, and European merchant communities were treated in much the same way as a religious community. 'Thus, the English were recognised in the sixteenth century as the "Lutheran Nation", and non-English Protestants were regarded as being under their protection.'[68] The English community in the Empire enjoyed virtual freedom from Ottoman law, being subject to its own laws which were enforced by English consular officials in the capital and the provinces.

In time this practice designed to facilitate intercourse between Ottomans and Europeans became a burden on the Ottoman state. The Powers could obstruct virtually any measure being considered by the Porte if they felt that it violated their privileges, now considered rights. Thus, the foreign embassies protested against the Law Concerning Vagabonds and Suspected Persons in May 1909; it stipulated flogging as a punishment, and they refused to envisage any of their subjects being flogged by the Turkish authorities.[69] Moreover, the Powers no longer considered the Capitulations as a unilateral grant to be revoked unilaterally by the donor. That was the Ottoman view. The American Ambassador expressed the Great Power view when he responded to the Porte's note informing him that the Capitulations had been abolished. He stated that

. . . the capitulary regime, as it exists in Turkey, is not an autonomous institution of the Empire, but the result of international treaties, of diplomatic agreements and of contractual acts of various sorts. The regime, consequently, cannot be modified in any of its parts and still less suppressed in its entirety by the Ottoman Government except in consequence of an understanding with the contracting Powers.[70]

Because of the war, the protests of the Great Powers did not intimidate the Porte; the Powers were in no position to back their threats with force. Thus, once abrogated, the Capitulations would never be restored in their old form.

These two institutions – the *millet* system and the Capitulations – were most consequential in undermining the authority of the Ottoman state and hastening its end. The rapid rise of nationalism among the non-Turkish population would not have been possible without European patronage. Without the collusion of the Powers members of the non-Muslim bourgeoisie would have been unable to acquire foreign citizenships, thereby being able to evade Ottoman laws and taxes. Without this privilege such groups might have tried to further their interests via the Ottoman state, by supporting its development rather than stunting its growth. The active participation of the non-Muslims would have strengthened both state and economy and perhaps provided the basis of a multi-national society, and therefore a different end to our story. It is worth noting that the commercial elements among the non-Muslims were not, by and large, nationalists; their interests were better served in a large multi-national empire than in a small nation state. Thus, the Greek of Istanbul preferred to live on in the Turkish republic rather than move to Athens. But, given the choice of foreign or Ottoman citizenship, non-Muslims of this class – the Muslims of this class had no choice – gave up Ottoman citizenship and lived in the Empire as foreign subjects.[71] They had every interest in keeping the Ottoman state weak, though not so weak as to bring about its demise. Such a fine balance could not be maintained indefinitely.

In the long run it was not possible to hold together an empire which lacked most of the characteristics necessary for cohesion: a common race, religion, language, culture, geography and economy. The Great Powers accelerated the process of disintegration by encouraging the centrifugal forces in the Empire. One could argue that the Powers propped up the Empire by their failure to agree to a partition scheme. But that was in the nature of imperialist rivalries. When it became necessary to agree on partition, as in 1915, the Entente Powers did so. By the end of the nineteenth century, however, there was a *de facto* partition of the Empire into spheres of influence, tacitly accepted by the Porte. The Turks never challenged British supremacy in Egypt until they entered the war in November 1914. They asked that Cyprus be returned to them only after Brest-Litovsk when the provinces lost to Russia in 1878, and in return for which Britain took Cyprus, were regained. Syria, including Lebanon, was recognised as France's sphere, while Russia was grudgingly acknowledged as the dominant power in the Balkans and north-eastern Anatolia. The wartime Allied partition plan followed these well-established lines closely, taking into account changed circumstances, such as the inclusion of Italy.

The Unionists intended to restore Ottoman authority wherever possible, but their dreams were rudely shattered by the Balkan Wars. The expulsion of the Muslim–Turkish population from the lost provinces in Rumelia weakened the impulse for irredentism and forced the Turks to concentrate on Anatolia. That soon led to the awareness of a narrower nationalism of the Turks living in Anatolia, the very basis of the republic-to-be.

Even though the Turks fought hard during the war for the Arab provinces, there was a general acceptance of their loss, except for regions where there was a strong Turkish presence as in northern Syria and northern Iraq. This was partly the result of Anatolian Turkish nationalism taking root, and partly the recognition that Turkey would have to live in a world of nations. Following the Bolshevik revolution, and what seemed like the break-up of the Tsarist empire, pan-Turanist Unionists toyed with the idea of setting up a union of Turkic peoples, mainly in Russia, led by Istanbul. That scheme also ended with defeat and was totally rejected by the nationalists.

The Ottoman Empire also suffered from basic structural defects (as was the case with other pre-modern tributary states) which made it unsuited to survive the challenge from the industrial West. The Western challenge was twofold: military and economic. To meet the military threat, the entire state structure of the Empire had to be reformed so as to be efficient. But reform required large sums of money which the traditional revenue system, geared to simpler needs, could not generate. By way of example, the old bureaucracy, the scribal service in 1800, had between 1,000 and 1,500 officials on its rolls. A century later, the number of officials in the reformed bureaucracy has been estimated at between 50,000 and 100,000.[72] The treasury of a declining economy could hardly provide regular salaries for such large numbers, to which ought to be added the ever-growing military establishment. Rampant corruption was inevitable as irregularly paid officials supplemented their salaries with bribes.[73] The Ottoman dynasty also appropriated a substantial portion of state revenues, which it used to maintain its imperial pretensions.[74]

Had the economy been dynamic, the revenues necessary to finance reform might have been generated from within Ottoman society. Western economic domination ended that possibility. Revenues formerly obtained from commerce and manufacturing were substantially reduced after the introduction of free trade practices in 1838. Initially the landholders benefited because they exported more of their produce at higher prices. But for the last twenty years of the nineteenth century there was a slump in farm prices when Turkish produce failed to compete with American grain. Because of the Capitulations the state could not raise a tariff barrier and the farmers had to wait for the upturn in prices which came around 1900. Meanwhile revenues declined, though the squeeze on the peasantry was not relaxed. The peasant's contribution continued to rise throughout this period. In the fiscal year 1872–3 it was estimated at 77 per cent of total revenue, though 'the farmers also contributed to the remaining 23 per cent'. By 1903 the direct taxes on land had risen to 84.7 per cent of all revenues, and to 87.2 per cent in 1910.[75] The outbreak of war in 1914 increased the demand for revenues tremendously, and once again the state turned to the peasant.[76]

One method of closing the yawning gap between revenues and expenditure was by contracting foreign loans. The *Tanzimat* statesmen seemed to believe that the Ottoman disease could be cured with a stiff dose of money, which the Porte's allies in 1854 were willing to provide. The first loan was floated during the Crimean War; the expenses of the war and the willingness of her allies were instrumental in pushing the Porte to borrow 2½ million gold liras.[77] Thereafter foreign loans became the established method of meeting state expenditures, most of which were devoted to unproductive ends.[78]

When the state declared itself bankrupt in 1875, its yearly charges on these debts were as high as 14 million gold liras out of revenues of about 17 or 18 million gold liras.[79] The Porte, unable to meet its obligations to its foreign creditors, was obliged to accept foreign financial control in 1881 under the Ottoman Public Debt Administration. With the example of Egypt before their eyes, the Ottomans feared that the alternative to the Debt Administration was direct Great Power control. In Egypt, the khedive had actually appointed an Englishman as Finance Minister and a Frenchman as Minister of Public Works. Such foreign trusteeship would undermine the independence of the state even more and had to be avoided at all costs. The Public Debt represented only the bondholders and, as such, was the lesser evil; it could not interfere directly in the affairs of state – or so the sultan and his advisers believed.[80]

In fact, the Public Debt could and did interfere in state affairs because it controlled one-quarter of state revenues. With a bureaucracy larger than the Finance Ministry it was a state within a state, administering choice revenues so as to pay back both domestic and foreign creditors. Its efficiency was responsible for restoring the Porte's financial standing in foreign money-markets, enabling the Porte to continue borrowing abroad. Between 1881 and 1908 the Ottoman government borrowed 51.5 million liras, receiving 45 million, or 87.4 per cent of the total, at an average interest rate of 4.1 per cent. Borrowing increased, and at higher interest rates, during the troubled times of the constitutional period. Between July 1908 and July 1914, the Young Turks borrowed 46 million liras, of which they received 39 million, or 84.8 per cent, at an average interest rate of 4.6 per cent.[81] Once war broke out the Porte had to turn to her German ally to meet her financial needs and ended up with a huge debt which might have had disastrous consequences for Turkish sovereignty had Germany won the war.

One result of the Empire's indebtedness and the Public Debt's hold on its finances was that there was never sufficient capital to invest in order to increase the productive capacity of the economy. To do so, the Porte had to turn to the Public Debt and obtain capital at high rates which the Ottoman state could hardly afford.[82] Unable to find money to put into public works, so vital for a desperately needed economic infrastructure, the Porte was forced to grant concessions to foreign entrepreneurs for, among other things, roads and railways. Such concessions, especially those for railways, which had great economic as well as strategic value to the Powers, became another source of Great Power rivalry and conflict, further eroding the prestige of the Ottoman state.[83]

Despite this crippling indebtedness, the Porte continued to devote about 50 per cent of state revenues to military expenditures – a massive drain on an overburdened treasury. The burden becomes greater if the 'extra-ordinary expenditures', which were almost entirely devoted to military needs, are taken into consideration.[84] Military spending was justified by the growing internal and external threat to the Empire. The growth of nationalism in the Balkans created potential enemies within Ottoman borders and irredentist states outside. The Porte's military establishment was intended as a safeguard against such opponents rather than against the Great Powers, whose military strength it could hardly hope to match.

The threat was real enough. Between 1878 and 1882 the Ottoman Empire lost 232,000 square kilometres of territory and over 6 million in population. The losses of the Young Turk period, especially in the Balkan Wars, were much more dramatic. Within a generation the Empire had lost 32.7 per cent of its territory and 20 per cent of its population.[85] Again the Ottomans were trapped inside a vicious circle: they spent huge sums to prevent the collapse of their Empire yet that process increased their indebtedness and dependence on the European Powers, and accelerated the pace of collapse.

The relationship between expenditure and imperial prestige must not be neglected. The Hamidian regime naturally attached great importance to it and devoted a considerable sum of money to maintaining it. The Young Turks continued to stress the imperial tradition and the CUP even married some of its members into the royal family – the most famous being Enver Pasha. The Young Turks also supported imperial pretensions financially, and Grand Vezir Hakkı Pasha promised that, while he would cut expenditures, that would never be at the expense of the dignity and prestige of the Empire. He added, in his address to Parliament, that the Ottoman Empire was a Great Power with a vast coastline and extensive borders, and that he would give his utmost attention to the needs of the army and the navy.[86] Later, when the military budget was debated, some Unionists, like Finance Minister Cavid Bey, criticised the high military spending, claiming that much-needed reform was being sacrificed to the exigencies of the armed forces. When he asked that military spending be curtailed and more money devoted to productive ends, War Minister Şevket Pasha replied that security was the first need of the Empire and without security public works and the reorganisation of finances would be a futile exercise. He asked that the military budget be voted unanimously, so that everyone might see that the Ottoman nation had resolved to maintain its power.[87]

Only after the Unionists had seized power in January 1913 was the military budget cut. Ironically, Cavid presented the 1914–15 budget showing an approximate decrease of 30 per cent in military spending only two months before the outbreak of war. It came before Parliament on 4 July and passed without much discussion.[88]

The declaration of mobilisation in August made the matter entirely academic. The Porte now had to borrow huge sums to wage a long and costly war. By 1918, Turkey was so heavily indebted to Germany that the German ambassador proposed using his nation's financial position to make Turkey into Germany's Egypt.[89] Germany's own defeat, however, saved Turkey from that unhappy fate.

The relationship between the Ottoman Empire and the European Powers was dialectical in nature. On the one hand, this relationship was destructive and corrosive in its impact on traditional Ottoman society; on the other hand, it provided the very basis for its renewal so as to enable it to cope with a world in rapid change. The destructive elements – the Capitulations, manipulations and the alienation of the Christian minorities, the loans – have already been considered at some length. Other influences were equally important; without them, the Empire could not have been formed into a viable nation state.

It is important to emphasise here Western influences on the rising national class of the 1880s rather than the influence of Western ideas on the ruling class, which resulted in modernising only the state structure to the neglect of society as a whole. While the rulers accepted the liberal economy of Adam Smith, the nationalists drew attention to the economic ideas of the German political economist, Friedrich List (1789–1846), who favoured, among other things, state intervention in the economy. Once this idea was adopted by the Young Turks after 1908, they began to create a new social basis for the state. Their success in doing so partly explains the failure of Britain, France and Italy to carve Anatolia into spheres of influence. The sultan's regime in Istanbul might have gone along with this scheme under protest. But it no longer had the broad social basis so necessary for its very survival, since it now served only the narrowest interests. In contrast, the nationalists propounded a new ideology – populism, or *halkçılık* – adopted from the narodniks via Turkish émigrés from Russia, and mobilised a national liberation movement whose supporters identified with the emerging nation state. Overall, however, the Ottoman–Turkish experience with Europe was a bitter one and it has left deep scars on the Turkish psyche. Its memory continues to haunt the Turkish people to this day.

Notes: Chapter 1

1   Ernest Ramsaur, Jnr, *The Young Turks: Prelude to the Revolution of 1908* (Princeton, NJ, 1957), pp. 133–4.
2   Enver Ziya Karal, *Osmanlı Tarihi*, Vol. VIII (Ankara, 1962), p. 78; see also M. S. Anderson, *The Eastern Question 1774–1923* (London, 1966), p. 143.
3   ibid., p. xxi.
4   The term is adopted from Samir Amin, *The Arab Nation* (London, 1978).

5 Bernard Lewis, *The Emergence of Modern Turkey*, 2nd edn (London, 1968), pp. 75–7; see also Niyazi Berkes, *The Development of Secularism in Turkey* (Montreal, 1964). For a contrary opinion, see Şerif Mardin, *The Genesis of Young Ottoman Thought* (Princeton, NJ, 1962), pp. 147–8.

6 Carter V. Findley, *Bureaucratic Reform in the Ottoman Empire: The Sublime Porte 1789–1922* (Princeton, NJ, 1980), passim.

7 Lewis, *Emergence*, p. 457. Musa Çadırcı writes that the Muslim merchants were unable to get the sultan to protect them from European competition and consequently their position declined rapidly. See his '11 Mahmud Döneminde (1808–1839) Avrupa ve Hayriye Tüccarları', in Osman Okyar and Halil İnalcık (eds), *Social and Economic History of Turkey (1271–1922)* (Ankara, 1980), pp. 237–41.

8 M. K. İnal, *Osmanlı Devrinde Son Sadrıazamlar*, Vol. I (Istanbul, 1955), p. 34.

9 See Findley, 'Civil–bureaucratic hegemony of the Tanzimat', *Bureaucratic Reform*, pp. 151–5.

10 ibid., p. 255. In 1909, Tevfik Pasha was briefly Grand Vezir during the counter-revolution and then was sent to London as ambassador. He was again appointed Grand Vezir during the armistice period. See below, p. 7.

11 ibid., p. 263.

12 See Feroz Ahmad, *The Young Turks: The Committee of Union and Progress in Turkish Politics, 1908–1914* (London, 1969), pp. 14–36; the quotation is from Findley, *Bureaucratic Reform*, p. 299.

13 Rifat was retained by the government of the counter-revolution because he was considered to be close to London, having been ambassador there. He was ambassador in Paris 1911–14 and in Berlin in 1918. He refused to serve in the anti-national armistice governments, preferring early retirement. See Ahmad, *Young Turks*, p. 177.

14 Noradunghian Efendi joined the Foreign Ministry in 1870 under the patronage of Âli Pasha. He was sent to study law in Paris and later joined the Porte's legal department. In 1908 he was appointed senator and also served in Kâmil Pasha's Cabinet. In 1911 he joined the Liberal Union and was also a member of the Armenian National Assembly, whose president he became in 1914. See Celâl Bayar, *Ben de Yazdım*, Vol. III (Istanbul, 1966), pp. 757–9 and 906–11.

15 In the context of this chapter, Liberal with a capital 'L' refers to supporters of anti-Unionist political groups like Ahrar Fırkası and Hürriyet ve İtilâf Fırkası. Members of these parties described themselves as Liberals when addressing foreigners.

16 Sina Akşin, *İstanbul Hükümetleri ve Milli Mücadele* (Istanbul, 1976), has provided the most detailed and comprehensive account of the activities of the Palace during the armistice period. See also Lewis, *Emergence*, pp. 239–42, 250–2 and passim.

17 Roderic Davison, 'Turkish diplomacy from Mudros to Lausanne', in Gordon Craig and Felix Gilbert (eds), *The Diplomats 1919–1939* (New York, 1963), p. 183.

18 On Ahmed Rüstem see Mine Erol, *A. Rüstem Bey* (Ankara, n.d.). Son of a Polish convert to Islam and an English mother, a member of a well-known British family resident in Istanbul, Ahmed Rüstem (1862–1935) was a career diplomat. As a result of exposing corruption in the Hamidian diplomatic service he was forced to live in exile between 1900 and 1908, being recalled after the revolution. Ahmed Bey was appointed ambassador in Washington in 1914 but was declared *persona non grata* in September because he retaliated to American criticism of his government's policies by denouncing the lynching of Blacks in the South and the use of water torture in the Philippines. In 1919 he joined the nationalists and served as adviser on foreign affairs.

19 *A Speech Delivered by Mustafa Kemal Atatürk 1927*, new edn (Istanbul, 1963), pp. 496–500; Davison, 'Turkish Diplomacy', p. 189. Kemal's speech was originally entitled *A Speech Delivered by Ghazi Mustafa Kemal, President of the Turkish Republic, October 1927* and was published in Leipzig in 1929.

20 There is a strong hint here of the Soviet system of political commissars to make sure that the diplomats toed the nationalist line.

21 This is evident from the sultan's acceptance of the Treaty of Sèvres in 1920. See Paul Helmreich, *From Paris to Sèvres: The Partition of the Ottoman Empire at the Peace Conference of 1919–20* (Columbus, Ohio, 1974); and Lewis, *Emergence*, p. 247.

22 ibid., pp. 106 ff.

23 See Charles Issawi (ed.), *The Economic History of the Middle East, 1800–1914* (Chicago, Ill./London, 1966), pp. 38–40; and Oya Köymen, 'The advent and consequences of free trade

in the Ottoman Empire', in *Etudes Balkaniques*, Vol. II (Sofia, 1971), pp. 47–56. The most detailed study of Anglo-Ottoman economic relations during this period is to be found in Muhabat Kütükoğlu, *Osmanlı-İngiliz İktisadi Münasebetleri 1839–1850*, Vol. II (Istanbul, 1976).

24   The emergence of a Turkish landed class as a political force still awaits study. The passage of the 1858 Land Code is, however, symptomatic of its rise. See Issawi, *Economic History*, pp. 65–90, and Lewis, *Emergence*, pp. 448–51. In Iraq such a class did emerge. See Hanna Batatu, *The Old Social Classes and the Revolutionary Movements of Iraq* (Princeton, NJ, 1978).

25   On pan-Islam see Berkes, *Secularism*, pp. 253 ff.; Lewis, *Emergence*, pp. 340–43; and Karal, *Osmanlı Tarihi*, Vol. VIII, pp. 539–50.

26   ibid., pp. 161–6.

27   ibid., p. 173, quoting the diaries of Abdul Hamid's physician, now located in the archives of the Turkish Historical Society.

28   ibid., p. 180. Karal seems correct in interpreting the Kaiser's 'promise' to defend the Muslim world for the sultan-caliph as being limited to the defence of Anatolia and the Arab provinces; the predominantly Christian Balkans were regarded in Berlin as Austria's sphere. The Kaiser also flattered Abdul Hamid by being the first European ruler to visit the sultan, which he did in 1889.

29   ibid., pp. 175–7. While Anglo-French lines, e.g. the İzmir–Kasaba line, were designed largely to carry raw materials from the interior to the coast for shipment to Europe, German railway projects were expected to open up Anatolia and bring prosperity to the land by providing cheap transportation for local produce. That was the only hope for local produce being able to compete against the grain imports from America.

30   According to German instructors training the sultan's army, Abdul Hamid had an 'instinctive rather than conscious fear of the power a good army would wield'; Alfred Vagts, *Defense and Diplomacy: The Soldier and the Conduct of Foreign Relations* (New York, 1956), p. 191, where he cites Gen. W. Giesl von Gieslingen, *Zwei Jahrzehnte im Nahen Orient* (Berlin, 1927), p. 47. Karal, *Osmanlı Tarihi*, Vol. VIII, pp. 179–80, quotes von der Goltz's argument, stated after the Balkan War, that while the Ottoman Empire had such vast borders and so many enemies no power would wish to form an alliance with it. On the decline of the army under Abdul Hamid, see ibid., pp. 369–75.

31   Ahmed Rıza and Dr Nâzım's interview with Sir Edward Grey in letter from Grey to Lowther, private, 13 Nov. 1908, FO 800/184A, quoted in Feroz Ahmad, 'Great Britain's relations with the Young Turks 1908–1914', *Middle Eastern Studies*, Vol. II, no. 4 (1966), p. 306.

32   For details see Feroz Ahmad, 'Vanguard of a nascent bourgeoisie: the social and economic policies of the Young Turks 1908–1918', in Okyar and İnalcik (eds), *Economic History*, pp. 329–50.

33   *Tanin*, 8 Oct. 1908, p. 1.

34   There is a useful article on the boycott and its implications for the Turkish economy. See Erdal Yavuz, '1908 Boykotu', in Orta Doğu Teknik Üniversitesi, *Gelişme Dergisi: 1908 Özel Sayisi (türkiye iktisat tarihi üzerine araştımaları)* (Ankara, 1978), pp. 163–81. See also Bridge, below, pp. 35, 38.

35   As in no. 31, p. 309. The Unionist mission had no governmental authority, and Grand Vezir Kâmil Pasha complained to Lowther that 'they spoke as if they represented the Ottoman Government'. See dispatch no. 855 from Lowther to Grey, 13 Dec. 1908, FO 371/546/43987.

36   Hüseyin Cahit, 'Kabinenin Sükutu ve İngiltere', *Tanin*, 15 Feb. 1909; dispatch no. 51 from Lowther to Grey, 14 Feb. 1909, FO 371/760/5984.

37   Dispatch no. 53 from Lowther to Grey, 15 Feb. 1909, FO 371/760/6275.

38   Hüseyin Cahit, 'Almanlar ve Osmanlılar', *Tanin*, 17 Dec. 1909, p. 1; on Mahmut Şevket Pasha see article by Feroz Ahmad in *Encyclopaedia of Islam*, 2nd edn (Leiden, 1953–).

39   Ahmad, *Young Turks*, pp. 72 and 75 ff. See also Marian Kent, 'Agent of empire? The National Bank of Turkey and British foreign policy', *Historical Journal*, Vol. XVIII, no. 2 (1975), pp. 374–81; and below, Kent, p. 179, Fulton, p. 151, 157, and Bridge, p. 40.

40   See Bosworth below, pp. 60–3.

41   Memorandum from Turkish Minister of Foreign Affairs to Foreign Office, 31 Oct. 1911, FO 371/1263/48554. This time it was an official proposal.

42   Quoted in Ahmad, *Young Turks*, p. 319, n. 31.

43   ibid., pp. 319–20. See also Marian Kent, 'Constantinople and Asiatic Turkey, 1905–1914', in F. H. Hinsley (ed.), *British Foreign Policy under Sir Edward Grey* (Cambridge, 1977), pp. 154–6, and below pp. 183, 185.

44 During the 1914–18 war, Talât Pasha reminded the American Ambassador of this: 'They promised that we should not be dismembered after the Balkan war and see what happened to European Turkey then.' Henry Morgenthau, *Ambassador Morgenthau's Story* (New York, 1918), p. 99.
45 See Ahmad, *Young Turks*, p. 321, n. 31. Meanwhile in Cairo, in March 1914, Kâmil Pasha saw Viscount Kitchener. He told him of 'the probability of another revolution in the very near future [an abortive coup against the CUP took place in May] and asked Grey to consider "the question whether some adequate foreign control might not be established in regard to the administration in Turkey" . . .' Quoted in Ahmad, *The Young Turks*, pp. 127–8. In a crisis, the Liberals invariably turned to Britain.
46 Minute by Sir Louis Mallet, undated, FO 371/1826/28098.
47 See also Bodger, below, p. 96.
48 See also Fulton, below, p. 161.
49 Djemal Pasha, *Memories of a Turkish Statesman, 1913–1919* (London, 1920), pp. 103–5. See also Trumpener, below, pp. 124–6, 127–8.
50 Mehmet Cavit, 'Meşrutiyet devrine ait Cavis Bey'in Hatıraları', *Tanin*, 21 Oct. 1944; and his testimony at the trial of Unionists conducted by the Istanbul government in 1919 as a way to evade the war-guilt question. See *Harp Kabinelerinin isticvabı*, ed. Hakki Tarik Us (Istanbul, 1933), pp. 82–3 and 93.
51 Cavid's diary entry of 27 Sept. 1914 reads: 'I am certain that Germany will not give us any money unless we enter the war.' See *Tanin*, 12 Nov. 1944. Negotiations opened in Berlin, and Cavid noted on 12 October: 'They will give us 250,000 liras ten days after the agreement is signed, 750,000 ten days after we enter the war against either Russia or England, and the rest (4 million liras) would be paid in 400,000 lira instalments each month, thirty days after the declaration of war. If the war came to an end, so would the payments.' See *Tanin*, 15 and 16 Nov. 1944, and Ulrich Trumpener, *Germany and the Ottoman Empire 1914–1918* (Princeton, NJ, 1968), pp. 271–84, for a discussion of financial matters based on German documents, and below, p. 125.
52 'Orient for the Orientals', *Tercüman-i Hakikat*, 20 Aug. 1914.
53 *Tanin*, 10 Sept. 1914, p. 1.
54 Later, the capture of the British army at Kut-ul Amara, along with Gen. Townshend, boosted Turkish morale even more. See A. J. Barker, *The Bastard War: The Mesopotamian Campaign of 1914–1918* (New York, 1967).
55 See n. 32.
56 Cavid, *Tanin*, 1, 2, and 5 May 1945.
57 A. K. Kurat, *Türkiye ve Rusya (1798–1919)* (Ankara, 1970), pp. 352 ff., where Ottoman Foreign Office documents are extensively quoted; see also Stefanos Yerasimos, *Türk-Sovyet İlişkileri* (Istanbul, 1979), pp. 11–15; and Trumpener, *Germany*, p. 170.
58 Akşin, *Istanbul Hükümetleri*, pp. 64 ff.
59 ibid., p. 117; Lewis, *Emergence*, p. 241.
60 This fact emerges quite clearly from the proceedings of the Economic Congress of Turkey held in Feb. 1923. The ideology of the new state that was established thereafter consistently favoured the interests of these groups. The proceedings of the Congress are now conveniently in *Türkiye İktisat Kongresi: 1923 İzmir* (Ankara, 1968), compiled and edited by A. Gündüz Ökçün.
61 Davison, 'Turkish diplomacy', pp. 186–7; for a detailed account based on Turkish documents, see Kurat, *Türkiye ve Rusya*, pp. 396–494.
62 Davison, 'Turkish diplomacy', pp. 193–4.
63 Ahmad, *Young Turks*, pp. 133 ff.
64 See von der Goltz's observations and his advice to withdraw to Anatolia, cited in Karal, *Osmanlı Tarihi*, Vol. VIII, p. 179.
65 See the chapter 'The Dimmis' in H. A. R. Gibb and Harold Bowen, *Islamic Society and the West*, Vol. I, pt 2 (Oxford, 1957), pp. 207–61; Stanford Shaw, *History of the Ottoman Empire and Modern Turkey*, Vol. I (Cambridge, 1976), pp. 58–9; and Lewis, *Emergence*, p. 335.
66 Stanford Shaw and E. K. Shaw, *History of the Ottoman Empire and Modern Turkey*, Vol. II (Cambridge, 1977), p. 161. In 1900, the Serbian petition to be made a *millet* was granted by the Porte in order to divide Serbs and Bulgarians in Macedonia. See Sir Charles Eliot, *Turkey in Europe* (London, 1965), p. 331.
67 Feroz Ahmad, 'Unionist relations with the Greek, Armenian, and Jewish communities in the

Ottoman Empire 1908–1914', in Benjamin Braude and Bernard Lewis (eds), *Christians and Jews in the Ottoman Empire* (New York, 1981), Vol. I, pp. 401–34.

68 Lewis, *Emergence*, p. 335. Abdul Hamid tried to play off Germany against France by recognising Germany as the guardian of German Catholics in Palestine – a right traditionally enjoyed by France. See Karal, *Osmanlı Tarihi*, Vol. VIII, p. 177.

69 Letter no. 588 from Lowther to Grey, 26 July 1909, FO 371/779/28919.

70 Ambassador Morgenthau to the Minister of Foreign Affairs, Therapia, 10 Sept. 1914, in US Department of State, *Papers Relating to the Foreign Relations of the United States, 1914* (Washington, DC, 1917), p. 1093. Ironically, the power that protested most strongly was Turkey's ally Germany. Ambassador Wangenheim is said to have threatened the Porte in the following terms: 'If you persist in suppressing the Capitulations and do not revoke your action, we will abandon the war, unite with the Entente powers and turn against you.' Quoted by H. C. Yalçin, *Siyasal Anılar* (Istanbul, 1976), p. 216; and Cavid's diary, *Tanin*, 1–5 Nov. 1944.

71 As Leland Gordon points out, many emigrants from the Ottoman Empire to America lived there just long enough to become naturalised citizens. They then returned to Turkey, where as American citizens they enjoyed the privileges of the Capitulations which exempted them from local taxation and military service. See Leland Gordon 'Emigration from Turkey to the US', *Levant Trade Review*, Vol. XVII, no. 2 (1928), p. 418.

72 Findley, *Bureaucratic Reform*, pp. 167–8. This massive increase was in part a way for the state to provide employment for Muslim Turks unable to survive in the world of commerce and manufacturing. In the same way, the state took care to maintain a stable price structure to protect the salaried, bureaucratic class, even though it was 'bad economics'.

73 Officials were paid six months a year by the Hamidian regime, and that with difficulty, writes Abdürrahman Şeref, himself an official, minister and historian of the period. See the new edition of his *Tarih Muhsahabeleri* (Istanbul, 1924), reissued as *Tarih Konusmaları* (Istanbul, 1978).

74 In the fiscal year 1872–3, the royal family consumed 6.1 per cent of total expenditure, the fourth highest after public debt (42.2 per cent), army and navy (22.1 per cent), and civil administration (13.6 per cent). See Issawi, *Economic History*, pp. 111–12. This pattern continued up to the 1908 revolution whereafter the royal family was given less: 1.4 per cent according to the expenditures for the fiscal year 1911–12. See W. W. Cumberland, 'Public Treasury' in E. G. Mears (ed.), *Modern Turkey* (New York, 1924), p. 399.

75 Reşat Aktan in Issawi, *Economic History*, pp. 110–11. Ahmad, *Young Turks*, p. 70, gives figures for 1909 and 1910 which show an increase in taxes which must in part be explained by the upturn in commodity prices since the turn of the century.

76 The most vivid account of the exploitation of the peasantry during the war is in chapter 1, 'Agriculture and the position of various classes in the village', of A. D. Novichev, *Ekonomika Turtsii v period minovoi voini* (Leningrad, 1935).

77 According to Fuad Pasha, 'the Ottoman Empire may be the sick man of Europe but the cure for his sickness is money'. Quoted in E. Z. Karal, *Osmanlı Tarihi*, Vol. VII (Ankara, 1956), p. 129. The first loan is discussed in Issawi, *Economic History*, p. 99.

78 See, for example, the budgets cited in nn. 71 and 72.

79 Issawi, *Economic History*, pp. 101–2. A more detailed account may be found in D. C. Blaisdell, *European Financial Control in the Ottoman Empire* (New York, 1929).

80 Engin Akarlı, 'Economic problems of Abdulhamid's reign (1876–1909)', fo. 41, unpublished paper based on the sultan's archives. I am obliged to the author for letting me read his excellent paper.

81 ibid., fos 41–2; Issawi, *Economic History*, pp. 100–6.

82 Akarlı, 'Economic problems', p. 42.

83 See E. G. Mears, 'Levantine concession-hunting', in his *Modern Turkey*, pp. 354–83.

84 Akarlı, 'Economic problems', p. 42.

85 ibid., pp. 48–9. The population loss was not so great because of the expulsion of Muslim and Turks from territories lost in the Balkans and their migration to Anatolia.

86 *Yeni Tanin*, 26 Jan. 1910, p. 1, cited in Ahmad, *Young Turks*, p. 70.

87 *Tanin*, 17 June 1910, p. 1, in ibid., p. 71.

88 *Stamboul*, 1 June and 6 July 1914.

89 See J. Bernstorff, *Memoirs of Count Bernstorff* (New York, 1936), pp. 188, 193–6.

2 The Habsburg Monarchy and the Ottoman Empire, 1900–18

F. R. Bridge, University of Leeds

At first sight it might indeed seem that the interests of the Habsburg Monarchy and the Ottoman Empire in their declining years were identical; and that there was an element of historical necessity in their common struggle in the war that ended with their almost simultaneous disappearance.[1] After all, even in the late eighteenth century the Austrians had begun to doubt the wisdom of co-operating with Russia in wars against an Ottoman Empire that had ceased to be an expansionist power. In the nineteenth century they came to believe that, in the south-east at any rate, the chief threat to the Habsburg Monarchy came from that same Balkan nationalism that was undermining the Ottoman Empire; and that the Ottoman Empire, for all its faults, was the best possible neighbour for the Monarchy. Certainly, any power combination that replaced it would be worse, whether it be a collection of irredentist states looking to Russia for support, and with designs on territories of the Monarchy, or direct Russian control over the area. 'A Slav conformation of the Balkan peninsula under . . . Russian protection would cut our vital arteries' – thus an Austro-Hungarian Foreign Office memorandum of 1884;[2] and in 1903 the Austro-Hungarian Foreign Minister warned Wilhelm II that the moment Russia were to establish herself in Constantinople 'Austria becomes ungovernable'.[3] The destinies of the Habsburg and Ottoman empires seemed inextricably bound together.

But this picture is too simple. Whatever broad theoretical considerations might suggest, Austria-Hungary could never do much to uphold the Ottoman Empire in practical political terms. To use force to resist Greek, Slav or Romanian national movements, whether these enjoyed Russian support or not, was never an attractive proposition. In the first place, the Monarchy's military weakness, and its large Slav and Romanian populations, made such an attempt extremely hazardous; in the second, the whole Christian Balkans would simply have been driven into Russia's arms, producing that very constellation the Austrians were most anxious to prevent. This had been axiomatic for the Austrians ever since the Russo-Turkish War of 1877–8, when they had resigned themselves to trying to limit the danger arising to their interests from the weakening of the Ottoman Empire. They tried to establish understandings with Russia to control the Balkans jointly; hence the Three

Emperors' Alliance of 1881–7 and the Austro-Russian *entente* of 1897 which was still in operation when this period opens. But when these efforts failed – in the later 1880s and after 1908 – they fell back on trying to establish Austro-Hungarian influence in the successor states themselves. It cannot be emphasised too strongly, in fact, that throughout the period under review the Habsburg Monarchy, as a neighbour of the successor states, could never make its Turkish policy simply in terms of relations with Constantinople, as Germany did. There were always the Balkan states to be considered; and, although there was no desire in Vienna to do anything that might hasten the demise of the Ottoman Empire, an out-and-out turcophile policy was unthinkable.

This same ambivalence characterised Austro-Turkish commercial relations in these years. For example,[4] the percentage of Austro-Hungarian exports going to Turkey rose from 3.26 to 5.4 between 1899 and 1913 – small in proportion to the 38.3 per cent going to Germany in 1913, but still not a negligible amount for a relatively backward power in a period of intensifying competition for markets and, after 1907, of recession. On the other hand, exports to the Balkan states accounted for 6.38 per cent of Austro-Hungarian exports in 1899 and 8.9 per cent in 1913 – of which 3.5 per cent and 4.3 per cent went to Romania alone. Here, too, therefore, there could be no question of any concentration on markets in the Ottoman Empire as opposed to those in the Balkan states – especially after the expulsion of Turkey from Europe after the Balkan Wars.

The likelihood of Austria-Hungary's developing extensive and overriding commercial links with the Ottoman Empire was further diminished by the competition she faced from other Powers. The geographical advantages of proximity and the Danube and Orient Railway links that had earlier helped to sustain her against remoter competitors were by the twentieth century proving ineffective as British and, especially, German competition developed. The Austrians struggled as best they could, devising a whole series of railway projects in the early years of the century. The most famous of these was the so-called Sanjak Railway project, a scheme to link the Austro-Hungarian network in Bosnia directly to the Turkish network by building a line through the Sanjak of Novibazar (the strip of territory separating Serbia from Montenegro, in which, at the Congress of Berlin, Austria-Hungary had secured the right to have railways and commercial routes). But even here it should be noted that the Sanjak Railway was only one of a series of schemes designed to promote trade not only with the Ottoman Empire, but also with Serbia, Montenegro and Greece.[5] It was the whole Balkan peninsula that the Ambassador in Constantinople had in mind when he wrote of the opportunities the Sanjak Railway would open up to Austro-Hungarian commercial influence, 'which is obviously bound to go hand-in-hand with the development of our political influence in these territories'.[6] And equally, when the schemes came to nothing, partly owing to the refusal of the Austrian and Hungarian governments to put up the money for the Serbian link, it was the loss of commercial opportunities 'in the Balkan peninsula' that Aehrenthal lamented – 'which we must safeguard as our natural market and our influence and predominance in the face of powerful competitors'.[7] The Foreign Minister was thinking just as much of opportunities in the Balkan states as in the Ottoman Empire. And, if even as a commercial power the Monarchy found itself hamstrung by domestic weakness and foreign competition, its role as a financier of the Ottoman Empire was never of any significance at all. In 1912 the Ottoman Empire drew 88 per cent of its foreign capital from Germany, France and Britain. Austria-Hungary herself was chronically short of capital; and although, unlike Russia, she occupied a seat on the Council of the Ottoman Public Debt Administration, her financial interest in it was 'about nil'.[8] In short, commerce and finance could never form the basis of an indissoluble link between the Habsburg and Ottoman empires.

In some respects, Austro-Hungarian commercial interests even served not only to worsen Austro-Turkish relations but also to undermine the Ottoman Empire. Austria-Hungary was always as tenacious as any of the Great Powers in upholding the Capitulations – including the treaty of 1862 which obliged the Turks to seek the permission of the Powers before raising their customs duties – and thereby helped to hold the Ottoman Empire in fee to the economic imperialism of the Great Powers and to hinder its economic development. True, Austria-Hungary's stubborn insistence on her rights under the Capitulations was motivated less by considerations of economic advantage than by that obsessive concern with prestige that characterises a Great Power in decline. This was equally true in the case of Turkish customs increases (over which the Austrians were generally quite amenable in practice); of the rights of the foreign post offices in Turkey, where the Austrians took the lead in resisting the sultan's encroachments; and of the rights of the Austrian emperor to 'protect' groups of Catholics, mainly in Albania and Macedonia (the so-called *Kultusprotektorat*, which dated back to 1606).[9] In all these cases the Austrians refused to make any concessions that might reflect adversely on their prestige. But the end effect, when it did not actually weaken the Ottoman Empire, was to create an insuperable obstacle to the establishment of really close relations between Vienna and Constantinople.

The final responsibility for Austro-Hungarian foreign policy lay with the emperor. Although, after the annexation of Bosnia in 1908, Franz Joseph had no territorial ambitions at the expense of the Ottoman Empire, he felt little sympathy for the Turks. *En route* for the opening of the Suez Canal in 1869 he had been entertained by Abdul Aziz; but, in glaring contrast to Wilhelm II, he never met any subsequent sultan. The first Austro-Hungarian state visit to Constantinople was that of Karl I in May 1918 – a deathbed reconciliation indeed. Franz Joseph loyally supported the efforts of the Powers to compel a recalcitrant Abdul Hamid to reform the administration of Macedonia, and he had no particular liking for the regime that replaced him: the Young Turkish

Committee 'seemed to him to terrorise and render ineffective the official government of Turkey'.[10] As for his Foreign Ministers, Goluchowski (1895–1906) cultivated the Russian *entente* and was generally equally haughty towards both Turkey and the Balkan states; whereas Aehrenthal (1906–12), faced with the collapse of the Russian *entente*, began to pay more attention to the Balkan states, partly with an eye to safeguarding Austro-Hungarian interests against the day of the Ottoman Empire's inevitable collapse. Neither minister was prepared to fight to maintain the Ottoman Empire. And even in the period of the wartime alliance a whole succession of Austro-Hungarian Foreign Ministers shrank from committing themselves to underwrite the Ottoman Empire.

These last were undoubtedly influenced by the advice – which they themselves sought – of the embassy in Constantinople. But this was partly a reflection of the fact that after 1915 a succession of relatively inexperienced men found themselves in charge of the Austro-Hungarian Foreign Office. For the most part, the Foreign Ministers of the period were no more inclined to be led by ambassadors than by Foreign Office officials – the latter being generally treated, particularly by Aehrenthal, as mere clerks. Goluchowski certainly doubted the capacity of both Calice (Austro-Hungarian Ambassador in Constantinople since 1881) and his aged Russian colleague – 'the old buffers at Constantinople, who had become so oriental as to be perfectly tolerant of Turkish methods'[11] – and Archduke Franz Ferdinand was scathing enough about Calice's successor, Pallavicini: 'so far the Turks have led this great diplomat by the nose'.[12] Yet in fact Calice, as doyen, was consistently energetic in pressing the Turks to treat their Macedonian subjects more equitably; and Pallavicini was respected by those who knew him as 'an excellent man of business, a very fast worker, very clear-headed and practical'.[13] Although, having to deal with the Turks face to face, he was sometimes less keen than his chiefs in Vienna to take a strong line, he was remarkably perceptive in reporting Ottoman affairs, had no illusions about the deficiencies of the Young Turkish regime, and by the closing years of the war was listened to with great respect by the policy-makers in Vienna.

The rest of the embassy personnel was of little account in the making of Austria-Hungary's Turkish policy. The military attaché usually confined himself to sending reports to the War Office, the political content of which was largely lifted from Pallavicini's dispatches. There was no naval attaché at all. The Austrians involved in supervising the administrative reforms in Macedonia before 1908 were generally well thought of by their colleagues and often had considerable experience in south-east Europe (Civil Agent Oppenheimer, for example, had served on the international financial commission in Piraeus).[14] But, although the Germans complained that the Austro-Hungarian *gendarmerie* commandant in Macedonia, Baron Giesl, was a turcophobe and a very bad influence on Calice, these people had no influence on policy-making – any more than did the twenty or so Austro-Hungarian consuls. When, in 1915, the Austro-Hungarian consul in Adrianople signed a declaration denouncing the persecution of Armenians, Pallavicini specifically adjured him to confine himself to what he defined as a consul's 'usual activities' – the simple writing of reports.[15]

The influence of public opinion on Austro-Hungarian policy-making in the Ottoman Empire was minimal. The Austrian Parliament had no constitutional right to discuss foreign affairs at all; and the Hungarians, although having this right, were in these years almost completely absorbed with internal matters. The British consul reported that the Hungarian press 'scarcely alluded' to Macedonia, and generally confined itself to deploring expenditure on the army and navy or on an active foreign policy – all held to be exclusively to the advantage of Austria or the dynasty.[16] Even on the outbreak of the Balkan Wars, Hungarian opinion, although generally sympathetic to the Turks, as it had been since the days of Kossuth, was firmly against action. Complaints from commercial interests suffering from the Ottoman boycott of Austro-Hungarian trade may have helped to push Aehrenthal into making concessions to the Turks during the Bosnian crisis; and Aehrenthal could never quite ignore the strident defence of the *Kultusprotektorat* by the clerical press, if only because of its links with Franz Ferdinand and the court. But such instances were sporadic. Most of the Austro-Hungarian press was in Jewish hands, but even the *Neue Freie Presse*, described in a British report as 'the leading representative of Jewish interests on the continent', was of negligible weight as far as the official policy of the Foreign Office in the Ballhausplatz was concerned.

By the turn of the century the attention of Austro-Hungarian policy-makers was shifting away from those areas of the Ottoman Empire that had pre-occupied them in the 1890s: Crete, Albania and the Straits. Crete the Austrians were content to leave to the supervision of the four Protecting Powers. This was always provided that the Protecting Powers consulted Vienna about any fundamental change in the international status of the island; that they refrained from encouraging Balkan irredentism by making concessions to the movement for union with Greece; and that they sought permission before increasing the Cretan customs duties – after all, Austria-Hungary had more trade with the island than any other Power had. In Albania, the Austrians simply trusted to their agreements of 1897 and 1900 with Rome to prevent an Italian military occupation of the coast. Such an occupation would be 'equivalent to closing the Adriatic, the keeping open of which is for us a question of most vital interest'.[17] There was little they could do to check the propaganda activities in Albania of churches and schools sponsored by France, Italy and the Vatican working together in what the Austrians regarded as an unholy alliance to undermine the *Kultusprotektorat*.[18] Defence of the Straits against Russia the Austrians complacently decided to leave to Britain alone, and early in 1903 Goluchowski refused to associate himself with Lansdowne's protests against the passage of unarmed Russian torpedo-boats into the Black Sea. To him this seemed a matter 'of very minor importance'[19] compared with the opportunity of tackling in close co-operation with St Petersburg that aspect of the Eastern Question that was now beginning to preoccupy his thoughts: the growing chaos and violence in Macedonia.

The Austrians were as well aware as anybody that the disorders in Macedonia[20] stemmed from a combination of Turkish misrule and the rivalries of the Christian inhabitants of the area, who found allies and arms in the neighbouring Balkan states in their struggle to secure the promised land for themselves, crushing or slaughtering rival elements, Christian or Turkish. Wherever the chief blame ultimately lay – with the Turks, the Christians, or with the statesmen who at Berlin in 1878 had handed the area back to the Turks – the pressing danger to European peace lay in the fact that the Ottoman Empire could hardly survive a blow so severe as the loss of Macedonia; and that its fall at that juncture would precipitate war between the Balkan states, and possibly a European war. It was, above all, to guard against this danger that the Austrians and Russians joined together to seek for the Ottoman Empire a new lease of life; and it was to this end that they initiated a series of proposals, culminating in the Mürzsteg Punctation of October 1903. This was designed to compel the sultan to reform the administration of Macedonia so as to make life tolerable for his Christian subjects there. Reforms were to be introduced under the 'dual control' of Austro-Hungarian and Russian civil agents, assisting an Ottoman inspector-general, and assisted in turn, in the second rank, by personnel from the other Great Powers.

For the Austrians, the Mürzsteg reform scheme proved a disheartening experience, and not merely because the reform programme was seen as irrelevant by the warring Christian bands. In the first place, the sultan, who regarded the scheme primarily as an onslaught on his sovereign rights, did everything in his power to obstruct the reforms; and he was encouraged in this by the Germans, who, the Austrians complained, 'think only of doing business deals and humouring the sultan and leave us in the lurch at every turn'.[21] The Austrians, by contrast, found their position in Constantinople severely shaken; and, if they were successful in helping to establish European control of the *gendarmerie* and financial administration of Macedonia by the end of 1905, they found the Turks 'becoming very arrogant and tenaciously making difficulties for us, not only in the reform question but in every other conceivable respect'.[22] If this were not enough, their Russian partners, weakened by war and revolution and seeking a *rapprochement* with Britain, began to yield to humanitarian pressure from London in favour of drastic reform proposals that Aehrenthal feared the Concert, let alone the sultan, would never accept. By the end of 1907, Aehrenthal had little faith in the long continuance of a conservative Austro-Russian dual control and determined to press ahead with such Austro-Hungarian interests as the Sanjak Railway project while some Russian goodwill still remained. The sultan obligingly granted an *iradé* for the railway project on 4 February 1908 – an apple of discord which immediately disrupted the Concert and freed him from the imminent threat of judicial reforms in Macedonia which the Mürzsteg Powers had been organising. The upshot was that Britain and Russia took the lead in the planning of future reforms, while Austria-Hungary abandoned completely the leading position she had hitherto occupied.

The view that Austro-Turkish relations had become particularly close in these months does not bear examination.[23] It is true that on the day following the issue of the *iradé* for the Sanjak Railway concession the ambassadors in Constantinople all accepted a German proposal to defer the projected judicial reform for further consideration; and that this was widely interpreted in *entente* circles as proof that the Austrians had 'played the mean game'[24] of sacrificing the reform scheme in order to secure the railway. But Austrian archival evidence shows pretty conclusively that Aehrenthal was making serious efforts to secure both the reforms and the railway. He had himself already rejected several German proposals – including an appeal from Wilhelm II to Archduke Franz Ferdinand – to postpone further reforms; and he now rebuked Pallavicini for his feebleness. Certainly, there is no evidence of an Austro-Turkish deal. The Turks tried to give that impression in order to disrupt the Concert, and even circulated spurious telegrams – allegedly emanating from the Ottoman embassy in Vienna – to that end.[25] And the Austrians, for their part, once Britain and Russia took the lead in Macedonia, made no attempt to come forward as the spokesmen of Turkey. Aehrenthal was at some pains to dissociate himself from the efforts of the German press to depict the two Central Powers 'as Siamese twins defending the rights of the sultan and the *status quo*'.[26] On the contrary, he observed, 'a complete identity of German and Austro-Hungarian interests in the Balkans does not exist'; a Big Bulgaria would be quite compatible with Austro-Hungarian interests, and he was certainly not prepared to commit himself to defending the integrity of the Ottoman Empire at any cost.[27]

The same complacency characterised Austro-Hungarian – in contrast to German – reactions to the Young Turkish revolution in July 1908. True, Aehrenthal was initially nervous and advised Britain and Russia to go cautiously with any new reform proposals.[28] He had always warned of the danger of upheavals if the Powers proposed drastic schemes that favoured the Christians at the expense of the sultan's rights; and he now wondered if the sickness were not spreading from Macedonia to the whole Empire.[29] Pallavicini, however, was more cheerful, calculating that with the fall of the Hamidian camarilla Austro-Hungarian commerce might recover some of the ground lately lost to its German competitors.[30] By mid-August, when terrorist activity had entirely ceased in Macedonia, Aehrenthal, too, had recovered his nerve and decided that the revolution had after all only achieved what five years of reforms had failed to achieve. As a token of his goodwill he sent the Austro-Hungarian officers serving with the Macedonian *gendarmerie* on unlimited leave, and told Mensdorff, ambassador in London and a cousin of

Edward VII, that he intended to adopt 'a sympathetically expectant attitude' towards the new regime.[31] Franz Joseph told Edward VII himself how much he welcomed the revival of British influence in the area.[32]

Undoubtedly, certain lingering misgivings about future developments in the Ottoman Empire were an important factor in the Austro-Hungarian decision to proceed with the annexation of Bosnia and the Herzegovina at this time.[33] Not only were Young Turkish newspapers talking about summoning the sultan's Bosnian subjects to send representatives to a parliament in Constantinople, damaging though this would have been to the prestige of an occupying power of thirty years' standing. The Austrians were perhaps even more concerned lest the ambiguous international position of the provinces should drag the Monarchy into the mêlée in the event of further upheavals occurring in Turkey, perhaps even in the Sanjak of Novibazar. In such an event, Austria-Hungary's rights in the Sanjak would be simply a dangerous entanglement. It must be emphasised that the Austrians in no sense saw the decision to annex the provinces and to withdraw from the Sanjak as an anti-Turkish move. It was intended, rather, to put an end to all ambiguity by drawing a clear line between what was Austro-Hungarian and what was Turkish, after which the Monarchy would be able to assume an attitude of benevolent detachment towards the neighbouring Empire. There is no reason to doubt the sincerity of Aehrenthal's assurance to the British Ambassador that he 'earnestly desired the success of the constitutional movement in Turkey, if only because Austria-Hungary needed a strong government in Constantinople if her traders were to extract all the legal profit from her advantageous geographical position'.[34] Indeed, he advised the Bulgarians after their declaration of independence to become 'an element of peace and order' – above all, by restoring good relations with Turkey.[35] Three days after the annexation, Pallavicini was still writing home in high hopes that the move would cause no great stir.[36]

Events showed that the Austrians had miscalculated. The Turks quite failed to appreciate the deeper, fundamentally conservative motives behind Austro-Hungarian policy, and not for the first or last time: the same misapprehensions had bedevilled Austro-Turkish relations after Mürzsteg and were to do so again over Albania. At any rate, the Turks simply took the annexation at its face value, as the seizure of an Ottoman province. They refused to recognise it without financial – let alone territorial – compensation, and backed up their demands by a boycott of Austro-Hungarian wares throughout the Empire. This last certainly alarmed Austro-Hungarian traders, who bombarded Aehrenthal with complaints. But the Ballhausplatz saw the dispute primarily in terms of the Monarchy's prestige. For three months Aehrenthal stubbornly refused to consider paying financial compensation, which the impecunious Austrian and Hungarian governments were refusing to provide anyway, and he refused to negotiate with Constantinople unless the boycott ended. By December the deadlock was complete, and Austro-Turkish relations so strained that to some observers war seemed a not unlikely outcome.

In the end, Aehrenthal accepted a diplomatic defeat at the hands of Turkey. He was still at odds with Russia, Britain and the Balkan states, and decided that, after all, 'the centre of the political depression lies in Constantinople and the political difficulties in Europe would easily be overcome if we can appear before the forum of Europe armed with an agreement with Turkey'.[37] Moreover, the alternative, a costly and dangerous military action against the Ottoman Empire, appealed to him as little as it did to the Austrian and Hungarian governments. But if the Austrians thought that their agreement to pay financial compensation to Turkey, made on 12 January 1909, marked the end of their humiliations they were mistaken. It was not until 26 February that the Turks ceased to haggle over the details. As Pallavicini observed, 'experience shows that in negotiations with Turkish statesmen the greatest difficulties arise when one thinks one is at the end'.[38] The sudden replacement of the anglophile Grand Vezir, Kiamil Pasha, by Hilmi Pasha – former inspector-general of Macedonia and an old friend of the Austrians – met with only a grudging reception in Vienna, where it was regarded as proof of the continuing influence of the occult Committee of Union and Progress.[39] The Austro-Turkish settlement was by no means synonymous with an Austro-Turkish *rapprochement*. Ottoman behaviour since October left a heritage of resentment in Vienna, and when in April the Turks began to ask the Powers finally to wind up the Macedonian financial commission Aehrenthal saw no reason to hurry. Austria-Hungary, he said, had 'already been too conciliatory to Turkey'.[40]

The Turks continued to give the Austrians new grounds for irritation and scepticism until well into the summer of 1909. They deliberately discriminated against the Monarchy, offering alternative employment to British, French, German and Italian personnel from the Macedonian financial commission, giving a British admiral and German and Italian generals high positions in the army and navy, while showing no interest at all in Austrian or Hungarian personnel. To Aehrenthal this seemed an unwarranted blow at the prestige of the Monarchy, particularly since 'we gave the constitutional regime proofs of our friendship from the start and great concessions in the protocol' of 26 February.[41] In retaliation, therefore, he continued to drag his feet in the matter of the abolition of the financial commission. The abortive counter-revolution of April 1909 had already caused 'considerable alarm' in Vienna, as a portent of perpetual instability in the Ottoman Empire;[42] and, although Aehrenthal welcomed the restoration of order, and, indeed, hoped briefly that the military might at last get a grip on the government and push the Committee into the background, it soon became clear that the Committee of Union and Progress remained firmly in the saddle. Altogether Aehrenthal, who had 'no faith in the lasting predominance of the Young Turks',[43] saw no reason to align the Monarchy more closely with their regime.

If Austro-Turkish relations started to improve – on the Turkish side at least – in the late summer of 1909, this was simply because the Turks discovered that they had even more pressing grievances against other Great Powers. The four Protecting Powers of Crete, for example, insisted in July on withdrawing from the island the contingents of troops that were stationed there to protect the sultan's sovereign rights; and Grey even went so far as to tell the Turks to address their complaints about Greek irredentist activity not to Athens but to the six Powers who had previously been responsible for Macedonia. That the Turks turned to Aehrenthal for sympathy was not altogether surprising. Far from approving of the actions of the Protecting Powers, he had made clear his attitude of complete abstention in the Cretan question – after all, it was hardly to Austria-Hungary's disadvantage if this question made trouble between Turkey and the Protecting Powers;[44] and he refused to countenance anything that savoured of a return to international intervention in the internal affairs of the Empire. He refused to co-operate when in 1910 Grey suggested joint pressure in Constantinople to put an end to an Ottoman boycott of Greek goods; and he even refused, despite pressure from clerical circles in Vienna, to take any serious steps to press the Turks to relax their brutal Ottomanisation of the Albanians. The new Turkey, he said, was no longer that of 1878: Europe could no longer take charge of the Macedonian question; any reform must come from Constantinople.[45] However, pleased as he was to observe that the Young Turks seemed to have established a modicum of stability in the Empire, from Austro-Hungarian abstention to a serious Austro-Turkish *rapprochement* was a long way.

It was initially the Turks who seemed most eager to improve Austro-Turkish relations, putting out feelers to the Ballhausplatz and to Austrian diplomats abroad describing Austria-Hungary as Turkey's 'alliée naturelle'.[46] The visit of the Grand Vezir, Hakki Pasha, to Aehrenthal in Marienbad in August 1910 went off well enough; and when it was followed by the participation of impecunious Austria-Hungary, for the first time, in a German loan to Turkey it even gave rise to some bad-tempered speculation in the Western press about Turkey's imminent adhesion to the Triple Alliance.[47] But in fact all this could not move Aehrenthal from his reserve. He had disapproved of the fall of Hilmi Pasha at the end of 1909 as a sign of the continuing influence of the Committee of Union and Progress.[48] He blamed the Turks' misgovernment, especially their bad choices of provincial officials, for the disturbances that were breaking out in the Yemen, Kurdistan and Albania.[49] Certainly, for him, there could be no question of an alliance with such an unpredictable and unstable power. He had no desire to do anything to weaken the regime: it was, after all, 'the lid on the pot that keeps the stuff inside from boiling over'.[50] But he came to adopt a somewhat cavalier indifference as Pallavicini continued to report on the strife prevailing early in 1911 between government, Parliament and Committee in Constantinople: 'these things reflect the peculiar conditions of the Orient'.[51] At any rate, his faith in the Committee sank to a new low point when the boycott of Greek goods was resumed and a serious rising broke out in Albania in the spring of 1911.

The bloody attempts by the Turks to suppress the rising posed an awkward problem for Aehrenthal.[52] On the one hand, he did not feel he could simply ignore the slaughter. He was under strong pressure from clerical circles at home, and complete abstention could all too easily allow Italy to assume the role of saviour of the Albanians. On the other hand, he had no liking for Grey's suggestions for Great Power intervention backed by international guarantees to the Albanians: the experience of Macedonian reform showed that this might only involve the Powers in endless disputes with Turkey. His solution was to warn the Turks privately of the dangers of destroying a race which they might some day need to counter the Slav threat, and, through an article in the semi-official *Fremdenblatt* of 8 June, to summon Constantinople to behave with moderation and humanity. But this 'middle way' failed. The Turks settled with the Albanians direct, fobbing them off with promises that were worthless – 'a disgrace', Franz Ferdinand's *Reichspost* raged, 'which touches Austria-Hungary in particular, who for three hundred years has called herself the protector of the Catholics of Albania'.[53] As for the Turks, they failed, as usual, to discern the deeper motivation of Aehrenthal's policy – in this case, the desire to preserve Ottoman rule in Albania by means of timely concessions – and simply saw in the *Fremdenblatt* article a gratuitous and unfriendly interference in their affairs.[54] The Russians were not unperceptive when they noted with satisfaction that Austria, by the prominent role she had assumed in the Albanian question, had been digging her own grave in Constantinople.[55]

Austro-Turkish relations were already decidedly cool, therefore, as the Italo-Ottoman quarrel over Tripoli reached its climax in September. It was hardly surprising that when the Turks appealed to Aehrenthal for support he coldly informed them that his reports showed that Turkey's behaviour towards Italians in Tripoli left much to be desired, and he could only advise Turkey to mend her ways.[56] Although he at first toyed with the idea of Austro-German mediation to end the war and improve the position of the Central Powers in Constantinople, the formal annexation of Tripoli by Italy in November convinced him that a compromise was for the time being unattainable.[57] He was certainly alarmed by unofficial Russian proposals for a Russo-Turkish alliance and a Balkan league (October–December), and advised the Turks to reject them – which they eventually did for reasons of their own. But for Aehrenthal, as for Berchtold who succeeded him in February 1912, the Italian ally and the neighbouring Balkan states always counted for more than distant non-aligned Turkey. In January 1912, Aehrenthal declined the most serious offers of alliance he ever received from the Turks. He was unwilling to commit himself to opposing Bulgaria's aspirations indefinitely; and so long as the war with Italy lasted and the situation in Constantinople remained confused he believed a Turkish alliance was out of the question.[58] Berchtold, it is true, jibbed at Italian operations in the Straits and in the Aegean Islands, but this was less from a love of Turkey than from a fear that Italy might establish herself permanently in the Aegean. In fact, the Tripoli War was not entirely unwelcome to Berchtold, in so far as it weakened and distracted Italy.[59] But this calculation was to prove shortsighted by the summer as the war, combining with a new Albanian revolt, brought about the fall of the Young Turkish government in July and again raised the whole question of the future of the Ottoman Empire.

At first the auspices did not seem unfavourable, as the Cabinet of All the Talents strove to conciliate both the Albanians and the Italians. And, for a time, the revolution in Constantinople, like the Young Turkish revolution four years earlier, seemed to offer a new and promising start for Austro-Turkish relations. The Austro-Hungarian Foreign Office, government and press were unanimous in welcoming the efforts of the new regime.[60] But Berchtold's proposal of 13 August that the Powers encourage Constantinople to extend to the whole of Macedonia the administrative concessions recently offered to the Albanians proved to be a disastrous mistake. It was unfortunate that Pallavicini's perceptive analysis of the situation did not reach Vienna till the end of August. 'Turkey was not, and is not now', he warned, 'a state in the European sense of the word.' The system of government under the old regime had been very centralised in theory but decentralised in practice. The Young Turks had tried to make centralisation a reality but had shown too little consideration for local conditions: hence their fall. The new government had brought a change of methods, but even they would not give up the principle of centralisation. In sum, 'no Turkish government can be decentralist'.[61] At any rate, the Turks, still victims of their simple friend–foe mentality, again interpreted well-meant if critical advice as evidence of hostile intentions. Their suspicions of Austro-Hungarian designs in Albania at once revived, and their instructions to the Ottoman embassy in Vienna now began to assume an 'unusually harsh tone'.[62] The Balkan states, for their part, recognised Berchtold's aims for what they were; but an attempt by a Great Power to prolong the life of the Ottoman Empire was for them yet another argument for speedy action to destroy it. Berchtold had not only estranged the Turks, but had also helped to precipitate the very conflict he had hoped to avert.

There was in fact no more chance of Austria-Hungary's coming to Turkey's assistance in the Balkan Wars than in the Tripoli War. Yet, here again, Vienna's attitude was determined not by the state of Austro-Turkish relations, indifferent as those were, but by considerations of Allied solidarity and Austria-Hungary's Balkan, as opposed to Turkish, interests. Quite apart from the fact that Turkey was still at war with Austria-Hungary's ally, intervention to help Turkey would have been the very thing to unite the whole of the Christian Balkans against the Monarchy. Berchtold himself had in any case become as disillusioned with the Turks as his predecessors and, first of all the statesmen of the Great Powers, recognised at the end of October that the Ottoman Empire's territorial base in Europe was shattered beyond repair. The Austrians then concentrated their efforts on securing their interests in areas in which they now accepted that Turkey would cease to rule. Turkish interests were very much a secondary consideration.

Hence Berchtold had no hesitation in joining the other Powers in their efforts to force the Turks to evacuate Adrianople – efforts that destroyed the Liberal government in Constantinople and brought the Young Turks back to power in January 1913. Indeed, in the Second Balkan War he held out almost alone for the retention of Adrianople by the Monarchy's Bulgarian protégés, although without German support his efforts proved futile. The effect of all this was, of course, a further cooling of Austro-Turkish relations. The Turks were soon discriminating against Austrians and Hungarians in their appointments to the new advisory posts they were creating in what remained of their Empire.[63] And this did not augur well for Austria-Hungary's chances of participating in the military reforms the Turks were planning with German assistance. Despite considerable diplomatic efforts by Berchtold and Pallavicini between June and December 1913 the Austrians had to accept German reluctance for their company and, when the Entente Powers began to agitate against the Liman von Sanders mission, abandoned their pretensions altogether.[64]

The incident over the German military mission was only one of a series that illustrated the fundamental differences between German and Austro-Hungarian policies towards the Ottoman Empire in the last years of peace. Germany's aim was simply to preserve the Ottoman Empire long enough for Germany to establish firm footholds in Asia Minor against the day of partition; and this carried the corollary that Turkey should avoid European entanglements that might draw it into a war and precipitate the collapse before the Germans were ready to secure their share.[65] In Asia Minor, at least, Austro-Hungarian aims were broadly similar. The Austrians certainly had no interest in an early partition; they had as yet no footholds at all there and could only trust that so long as Ottoman rule continued the area would remain 'a vast field of activity' for all the Powers.[66] But the Austrians saw the future of Turkey as only one, relatively minor aspect of a complex and wider picture. In contrast to the Germans, the Austrians cared less about the fragility of Ottoman rule in Asia Minor than about Turkey's potential usefulness in helping to deal with the irredentist threat on the very frontiers of the Monarchy; hence their stubborn efforts to draw Turkey into concluding a military convention with Bulgaria, directed in effect against Serbia and Greece. All this diplomacy went on behind the backs of the German allies and ultimately proved futile. Altogether, Vienna and Berlin were quite unable to agree on any common and effective policy in the Ottoman Empire.

The Germans were infuriated, for example, when the Austrians, angling for a loan in Paris, planned to admit France to a share in the Turkish section of the Orient Railway. With the return of the Turks to Adrianople this railway had assumed a new importance for Germany as a vital link to the Baghdad Railway.[67] The Turks, for their part, took umbrage at the Austrians' reluctance to support German demands that Bulgaria first agree to take over a proportion of the Ottoman debt before she could be granted a loan.[68] They were also offended by Austria-Hungary's support for Russia's attempts to secure a seat on the Council of the Ottoman Public Debt Administration as the price of agreeing to the latest Turkish request for a 3 per cent customs increase – especially as the Austrians were hoping thereby to get Russian support for their own efforts to control, together with Italy, the economic development of the new Albanian state.[69] The Turks were in fact by no means prepared simply to accept Austro-Italian domination of what was, after all, a predominantly Muslim area, so recently part of their own dominions. They had been involved since January 1914 in sporadic attempts to set up a Muslim regime and to topple the throne of the Prince of Wied, a nominee of the Powers but a protégé of Austria-Hungary. In these affairs the Austrians received no support whatever from the Germans, although they doggedly persisted in their efforts to establish their protégé's position in the face of the express disapproval of both Berlin and Constantinople.

The same overriding concern with Austro-Hungarian prestige, coupled with a somewhat cavalier disregard for the interests of other Powers and leading in the end to failure and embarrassment characterised Austro-Hungarian diplomacy in the Asiatic parts of the Ottoman Empire. When discussions started in the summer of 1913[70] about a possible reform scheme for Armenia under European control, Pallavicini was full of foreboding: 'I see the same process being prepared in Asiatic Turkey as that which put an end to Turkey in Europe.' As the wars of 1911 and 1912–13 had shown, the threat to the Ottoman Empire came not from within, but from without. In the end, he was sure Russia would get the lion's share, fobbing off the other Powers with, at best, colonies that would for most be 'in the air' and would have to be defended in Europe. As for Austria-Hungary, who had not yet even established a foothold in the area, she would probably get nothing at all.[71] By March 1914 the Turks, by threatening to refer the whole matter to the forum of the six Powers, had in fact forced Russia and Germany to modify their scheme to eliminate any traces of effective foreign control, and to employ Europeans, not from the Great Powers, but only from the middle states. This the Austrians regarded as satisfactory. They had got nothing, but neither had any other Great Power. As for the condition of Armenia, Pallavicini blandly observed that 'the reform programme is consigned to the same fate that has awaited all attempts at reform in Turkey'.[72]

Even more futile were Austria-Hungary's attempts in 1913–14 to lay the foundations for a colony incorporating much of the south coast of Anatolia.[73] True, there was some anxiety in Vienna lest a partition of the area between the other powers might mean the end of the Open Door, with deleterious consequences for Austro-Hungarian trade. But, for the Ballhausplatz, the issue yet again was primarily one of prestige. As Berchtold emphasised to Pallavicini in November 1913, the essential point was that 'we do not want to be the only power to come away empty-handed'.[74] But when Germany and Italy, who had already with Turkey's blessing staked out claims in the area, refused to make room for their ally the Austrian plan was doomed to failure. By July 1914, Berchtold was reduced to talking of putting pressure on the unco-operative Turks by supporting Italy in her long-drawn-out wrangle with the Turks over the interpretation of the 1912 Treaty of Lausanne. Even so, that Berchtold should consider intervening in this remote and tedious legal dispute, humouring Italy at the cost of further estranging Turkey, perhaps only reflected the change in Austrian priorities after the Sarajevo assassinations of 28 June. There now appeared the prospect of an Austro-Serbian, or even a European war.

Certainly, Austro-Turkish relations as such had hardly improved at all during the six months preceding the outbreak of war. In February 1914 the Ballhausplatz coupled 'the incalculability of the present military dictatorship in Turkey' with Serbian irredentism as the two chief sources of the prevailing uncertainty.[75] Pallavicini lectured the Turks repeatedly[76] on the 'great dangers' involved in fostering a national–Islamic movement which, if it as yet concentrated its wrath on Greeks and Armenians, might soon develop into a general xenophobia that could seriously injure European trade; on their foolish persecution of the Greeks in Thrace – one of the most productive elements in the Empire – and on their mishandling of the Arabs. On an international level, too, Vienna was dismayed by the flirtations of prominent Young Turk politicians with the Entente Powers.

It was hardly surprising, therefore, that as the July crisis moved towards its climax Pallavicini agreed with his German colleague that there ought to be no question of running after a Turkish alliance for the present.[77] Turkey was as yet in no condition to resist Russia in Armenia, let alone to render active assistance in the Balkans. The best that could be hoped for was to prevent Turkey's actually joining the Entente camp or coming to blows with Bulgaria.[78] When the Turks themselves proposed an alliance to Germany on 27 July, Berchtold had great reservations, especially about an alliance involving Austria-Hungary. It was only under German pressure that he agreed to participate, and then only as an acceding party to the German–Turkish treaty of 2 August.[79] Even at this stage, Austro-Turkish relations were characterised by that same wariness and lack of enthusiasm that had distinguished them in the last years of peace.

This pattern continued during the war as the Germans, intent above all on victory and taking very little thought for the morrow, steadily extended their obligations to Turkey simply in order to keep her in the war. In January 1915, for example, negotiating over a redefinition of the *casus foederis*, they agreed to drop the restrictive adjective 'non provoquée' as applied to attacks on Turkey by the Entente Powers or by a coalition of Balkan states. The Austrians, by contrast, were mindful not merely of present concerns, but also of the prospect of living cheek by jowl with Turkey and the Balkan states after the war was over.[80] Pallavicini stiffened Berchtold's resistance to the alteration, emphasising that 'one just has to reckon with the Turkish mentality':

> if the Turks feel that they will always . . . be supported by us and Germany, they will exploit the situation to play tricks on [*chicanieren*] the three [Entente] powers in every conceivable way and take measures affecting foreign schools and the rights of foreigners etc. which would be against our interests too.[81]

It was becoming 'increasingly clear' to him, the more the Turks insisted, 'how important it is to avoid giving the Turks *carte blanche*'.[82] When in March 1915 the Austrians, fearing that the Dardanelles expedition might otherwise knock Turkey out of the war, finally acceded to the Turco-German alliance of 11 January, they confined themselves to the less solemnly binding diplomatic form of an exchange of notes. They also insisted that, if the alliance were to continue after the war, the limitations and conditions of Austria-Hungary's obligations would have to be closely defined in a separate military convention.[83]

Later, too, the Austrians objected when the Germans promised the Turks, in September 1916, that they would not make peace without Turkey's consent if Ottoman territory were in enemy occupation. The Austrians certainly had no wish to continue the war simply to expel Russia from Armenia. Pallavicini admitted that 'if we refuse to accede . . . our position in Turkey and our relations here will be unpleasantly affected';[84] but when the Foreign Minister, Burián, asked him for his advice Pallavicini still insisted that, whatever assurances Austria-Hungary might give the Turks, 'in no circumstances' could she negotiate a formal treaty like the German one.[85] Similarly, when in May 1917 the Germans slightly extended their obligations to assist Turkey against Britain, Pallavicini again warned of the danger that Turkey might 'intentionally provoke a conflict, for example, for the reconquest of Baghdad . . . and a world conflagration would start over a purely Turkish interest'.[86] At any rate, 1917 closed with Pallavicini and his new chief, Czernin, firmly determined to delay the whole question of Austria-Hungary's formal adherence to the modified treaties until the war was over.

Meanwhile, the domestic activities of the Constantinople government continued, as before the war, to work against any really close co-operation between the Habsburg and Ottoman empires. True, Pallavicini, instructed by Burián in November 1915 to raise the question of the deportation of Armenians, tried to avoid an open quarrel with the Turks. He tactfully reminded the Grand Vezir that the Armenians were among the most industrious elements in the Empire; but he had to point out that, if Turkey's allies were accused of encouraging the persecution, they would have no choice but to lay the blame squarely on Constantinople.[87] When the Austro-Hungarian consul in Adrianople, who found it 'depressing as the representative of a *Kulturstaat* to have to observe these medieval goings-on [*Treiberei*]',[88] joined his Bulgarian colleague in signing a declaration condemning them, Pallavicini immediately called him to order and pointed to the bad impression his behaviour would make in Constantinople.[89] In March 1916, however, even Pallavicini was impressed by further horrific reports from the consul, and went to see Talat about them. But he was fobbed off with assurances that almost immediately turned out to be arrant lies. In such circumstances, 'eloquent of conditions prevailing here',[90] Pallavicini, while having no illusions left about the nature of the regime, concluded that there was little he could do to help the Armenians.

By the end of 1917 the issue was having awkward political repercussions. As the Austro-Hungarian chargé d'affaires in Constantinople reported:

> The nearer the end of the war comes, the clearer it becomes how greatly the government suffers from . . . the consequences of the cruelties against the Armenians . . . The Turkish government itself finds its freedom of ma-noeuvre restricted by the Armenian question in all plans and schemes for peace. It is not so much the fear of losing the Armenian provinces – perhaps they would even get over such a loss relatively easily – but rather the feeling that the Armenian question will be taken up by all the Powers (friend and foe) in order to meddle as before in the internal affairs of Turkey, and that thereby at the peace conference Turkey may forfeit her achievement of the present war – to have shaken off the capitulatory system.[91]

Nor was it long before Turkish demands for Austria-Hungary's unconditional adherence to the German–Turkish treaty of 18 February 1918 abolishing the Capitulations provoked a further round of arguments between Vienna and Constantinople. (The Austrians wished to make their adherence conditional on a successful end to the war, and to reserve the right to most-favoured-nation treatment should any of the Entente Powers manage to restore the Capitulations.) As Pallavicini explained to Czernin on 23 March,[92] the Turks had swollen heads: 'Turkey has always lived in fear of Russia, and it was this fear that moved her to join our side at the time. Now, however, Russia has ceased to be the bogeyman for Turkey; now she has a heightened self-confidence, dreams of conquests, and thinks in all seriousness that before Turkey, who has assumed the leadership of about 60 million Muslims, England will tremble.' He urged the utmost caution in dealing with the new, presumptuous Turkey.

True, under renewed pressure from the Germans, who explained that their promises to Turkey meant little, the Austrians acceded to the treaty abolishing the Capitulations in May 1918; and by June to most of Germany's supplementary commitments to Turkey.[93] But they still refused to negotiate separate Austro-Turkish treaties like the German ones. They refused even to accede to the German pledges regarding enemy-occupied territories and determined to handle the ratification of such accession agreements as they had made as dilatorily as possible.[94] Distrust of Constantinople remained as lively as ever in the Ballhausplatz until the very end of the war.

This was well illustrated by two incidents in 1918.[95] When in February the Navy Ministry proposed[96] that the Monarchy should negotiate a convention with Turkey to provide for naval co-operation after the war, and suggested that a start might be made by accrediting a naval attaché to the embassy in Constantinople, the Ballhausplatz completely failed to respond. In the summer, Burián became extremely agitated when he learned that the army authorities had been negotiating, with the emperor's approval but behind the backs of both the Foreign Ministry and the German allies, for a military convention which would establish Austro-Hungarian officers in the Ottoman army after the war, as a countervailing force to the Germans.[97] In addition to pointing to the futility of embarking on such negotiations without German approval, he went on to observe that, 'so long as the present war continues, such an agreement is superfluous, whereas after the war its value seems to me problematical as the policy which Turkey will pursue in future cannot be predicted with certainty today, and it is not out of the question that after the conclusion of peace Turkey will turn away from us and towards our enemies'[98] – a devastating comment on the state of the alliance in the closing months of the war. But his observations were not acted upon, merely filed away in the archives of the Ballhausplatz. They had been overtaken by events. The Habsburg and Ottoman empires were already in their death-throes.

The simultaneous collapse of the two empires at the end of 1918 might suggest that their destinies had been inextricably linked. Certainly, the expulsion of the Turks from Europe in 1913 had sharpened international tensions, in so far as it had greatly intensified the threat posed by Balkan nationalism to the continuance of both the Habsburg Empire and the international states system in its existing form. The First World War created a new system in which neither empire found a place. Moreover, the reluctance of policy-makers in Vienna throughout the period under review to take any action that might weaken the Ottoman state might also suggest an awareness of a broad community of interests between the two conservative empires.

In reality, a wide gulf existed between an appreciation of a broad community of interests in principle and its application in terms of practical politics. In the first place, Austria-Hungary was a member of an international states system composed of five or six Powers: the 'Concert of Europe'. Although Turkey had officially been declared a member of the Concert in 1856, she had never really been treated as an equal by any of the Powers. As the Austrians were wont to point out, Turkey was 'not a state in the European sense of the word'. Certainly the behaviour of a succession of regimes in Constantinople helped to perpetuate the isolation of the Ottoman Empire from all the Great Powers in these years. So also did those Powers' interference in and criticism of Turkey's domestic affairs. And Austria-Hungary in particular, as both a member of a Concert of Christian Powers and as a neighbour of the Balkan states, could never formulate its Turkish policy simply in terms of relations with Constantinople. These were never of overriding importance to the Ballhausplatz.

As an old and declining Power inordinately sensitive about its prestige, Austria-Hungary was perhaps more determined than the others to assert her rights as a Christian Great Power in the Ottoman Empire, ruthlessly enforcing both her own *Kultusprotektorat* and the whole capitulatory system. The former was largely symbolic but still immensely damaging to Ottoman pride, the latter certainly restrictive of the economic development of the Empire. Herein no doubt lies a measure of Austro-Hungarian responsibility for the failure of the Ottoman Empire to develop into a viable member of the European states system. Moreover, a cultural and political gulf continued to divide the Habsburg and Ottoman empires even in the days of the wartime alliance. It is not an inexorable community of fate, but simply the coincidence in time of the blows sustained by the two empires in the First World War, that accounts for the fact that in their deaths they were not divided.

Notes: Chapter 2

Abbreviations

AR Haus,- Hof,- und Staatsarchiv, Vienna, Administrative Regisratur
BD *British Documents on the Origins of the War, 1898–1914*, ed. G. P. Gooch and H. W. V.
   Temperley, 11 vols (London, 1926–38)
FO Foreign Office records, Public Record Office, London
GP *Die Grosse Politik der Europaïschen Kabinette, 1871–1914*, ed. Johannes Lepsius, A.
   Mendelssohn-Bartholdy and Friedrich Thimme (Berlin, 1922–7)
OUA Oesterreich-Ungarns Aussenpolitik
PA Haus,- Hof,- und Staatsarchiv Vienna, Politisches Archiv

1 For a more detailed examination of this subject, see F. R. Bridge, 'Austria-Hungary and the Ottoman Empire in the twentieth century', *Mitteilungen des österreichischen Staatsarchivs*, Vol. XXXIV (1981), pp. 234–71.
2 Quoted in E. R. von Rutkowski, 'Gustav Graf Kalnoky von Köröspatak, Oesterreich-Ungarns Aussenpolitik von 1881–1885', PhD dissertation, Vienna University, 1952, fo. 646.
3 Memorandum by Bülow, 20 Sept 1903, *G.P.*, Vol. 38, pt 1, no. 5609.
4 The following statistics are taken from *Oesterreichisches Statistisches Handbuch* (1900), p. 222; (1913), pp. 232–3.
5 F. R. Bridge, *Great Britain and Austria-Hungary 1906–1914: A Diplomatic History* (London, 1972), pp. 77 ff.
6 Pallavicini to Aehrenthal, dispatch no. 6B, 29 Jan. 1908, PA XII/[Karton] 344; Pallavicini to Aehrenthal, dispatch No. 13B, 26 Feb. 1908, PA XII/339.
7 Aehrenthal Memorandum to the minister-presidents of Austria and Hungary, 14179/I/HP, 28 Feb. 1908, AR, Faszikel 19.
8 Dörte Löding, *Deutschlands und Oesterreich-Ungarns Balkanpolitik von 1912 bis 1914 unter besonderer Berücksichtigung ihrer Wirtschaftsinteressen* (Hamburg, 1969), p. 215.
9 For details, see Bridge, 'Austria-Hungary', pp. 237–8.
10 Cartwright to Grey, telegram 53, 12 Sept. 1910, FO, Series 371, Vol. 828.
11 Elliot to Lansdowne, dispatch no. 147, 15 Oct. 1902, copy, FO 120/790.
12 Franz Ferdinand to Berchtold, private letter, 1 Oct. 1912, PA, Berchtold MSS.
13 Grey to Goschen, dispatch no. 119, enclosing dispatch from Sinaia, 15 Oct. 1906, FO 120/829.
14 See also Kent, below, pp. 184, 200 n. 101.
15 Pallavicini to Burián, dispatch no. 94p/B, 10 Nov. 1915, PA XII/463.
16 See, for instance, Strong to Plunkett, dispatch no. 35, 4 Sept. 1903, FO 7/1345.
17 Goluchowski to Aehrenthal, dispatch no. 393, 15 April 1904, AR 217b, Botschaftsarchiv St Petersburg/9.
18 Macchio to Aehrenthal, private letter, 2 May 1901, PA, Aehrenthal MSS.

19   Plunkett to Lansdowne, dispatch no. 265, 31 Oct. 1902, FO 78/394.
20   Bridge, 'Austria-Hungary', pp. 242–7; and F. R. Bridge (ed.), *Austro-Hungarian Foreign Office Documents on the Macedonian Struggle, 1896–1912* (Thessaloniki, 1976).
21   PA, Mensdorff MSS, Tagebuch, 19 April 1905.
22   Mérey to Aehrenthal, private letter, 15 Sept. 1905, PA, Aehrenthal MSS.
23   Bridge, *Great Britain and Austria-Hungary*, pp. 79 ff.
24   BD, Vol. V, no. 180.
25   W. M. Carlgren, 'Informationsstycken från Abdul Hamids senare regeringsår', *Historisk Tidskrift* (1952), pp. 1–35.
26   Aehrenthal to Berchtold, private letter, 26 June 1908, PA XII/343.
27   Aehrenthal to Szögyeny, dispatch no. 965, 24 June 1908, PA XII/343.
28   F. R. Bridge, 'Izvolsky, Aehrenthal, and the end of the Austro-Russian entente', *Mitteilungen des österreichischen Staatsarchivs*, Vol. XXIX (1976), p. 330.
29   Aehrenthal to Berchtold, telegram 89, 24 July 1908, PA XII/343.
30   Ingrid Raabe, *Beiträge zur Geschichte der diplomatischen Beziehungen zwischen Frankreich und Osterreich-Ungarn, 1908–12* (Vienna, 1971), p. 119.
31   PA, Mensdorff MSS., Tagebuch, 15 Aug. 1908.
32   ibid.
33   Bridge, 'Izvolsky, Aehrenthal', p. 331.
34   Goschen to Grey, telegram 41, 4 Oct. 1908, FO 120/852.
35   Aehrenthal to Thurn, telegram 33, 6 Oct. 1908, PA XV/122.
36   Pallavicini to Aehrenthal, dispatch no. 83C, 9 Oct. 1908, PA XII/556.
37   Aehrenthal to the minister-presidents of Austria and Hungary, nos 2921 and 2922, 28 Dec. 1908, PA XII/351. On the Italian reaction to the annexation, see Bosworth, below, p. 58.
38   Pallavicini to Aehrenthal, dispatch no. 4, 18 Jan. 1909, PA XII/351.
39   Cartwright to Grey, telegram no. 39, 16 Feb. 1909, FO 371/750.
40   Aehrenthal to Pallavicini, dispatch no. 1262, 1 April 1909, PA XII/341.
41   Aehrenthal to Otto, dispatch no. 2006, 27 May 1909, PA XII/341.
42   Cartwright to Hardinge, private letter, 15 April 1909, Cambridge University Library, Hardinge MSS.
43   Cartwright to Hardinge, private letter, 13 May 1909, Cambridge University Library, Hardinge MSS.
44   Aehrenthal to Pallavicini, dispatch no. 2533, 22 July 1909, PA XII/294.
45   Cartwright to Grey, dispatch no. 142, 5 Sept. 1909, FO 371/601.
46   Mensdorff to Aehrenthal, dispatch no. 11F, 17 April 1910, PA VIII/144.
47   Bridge, *Great Britain and Austria-Hungary*, p. 158; see also Kent, below, p. 179.
48   Cartwright to Hardinge, private letter, 6 Jan. 1910, Cambridge University Library, Hardinge MSS.
49   Ministerratsprotokoll, 17 May 1910, PA XL/309.
50   Cartwright to Grey, private letter, 28 Sept. 1910, Public Record Office, London, Grey MSS, Austria.
51   Ministerratsprotokoll, 6 Jan. 1911, PA XL/310.
52   Bridge, *Great Britain and Austria-Hungary*, pp. 169 ff.
53   Cartwright to Grey, dispatch no. 115, 15 July 1911, FO 371/1230.
54   Rubina Möhring, 'Die Beziehungen zwischen Oesterreich-Ungarn und dem osmanischen Reich 1908–1912', PhD dissertation, Vienna University, 1978, fo. 92.
55   Grey to Cartwright, telegram no. 75, 17 July 1911, FO 120/882.
56   Grey to Cartwright, dispatch no. 64, 5 Oct 1911, FO 120/882.
57   Bridge, *Great Britain and Austria-Hungary*, pp. 182 ff.
58   Pallavicini to Aehrenthal, private letter, 16 Jan. 1912, PA XII/374.
59   OUA, Vol. IV, no. 3551; see also Bosworth, below, pp. 60–4, 66–7.
60   Cartwright to Grey, telegram no. 62, 30 July 1912, FO 120/895; see also Bosworth, below, pp. 61, 64–5.
61   Pallavicini to Berchtold, dispatch no. 72B, 25 Aug. 1912, PA XII/206.
62   Möhring, 'Die Beziehungen', fo. 104.
63   Pallavicini to Berchtold, dispatch no. 48G, 21 Aug. 1912, PA XII/206.
64   Bridge, 'Austria-Hungary', p. 259.
65   Löding, *Balkanpolitik*, pp. 197 ff.

66 Pallavicini to Berchtold, dispatch no. 58A, 2 Oct. 1913, PA XII/207.
67 Löding, *Balkanpolitik*, p. 179.
68 ibid., p. 112.
69 ibid, p. 222; see also Ahmad, above, pp. 24–5.
70 Bridge, 'Austria-Hungary', pp. 260–1.
71 Pallavicini to Berchtold, dispatch no. 33C, 10 June 1913; private letter, 28 June 1913, PA XII/463.
72 Pallavicini to Berchtold, dispatch no. 15 Pol-H, 2 March 1914, PA XII/463.
73 F. R. Bridge, '*Tarde venientibus ossa:* Austro-Hungarian colonial aspirations in Asia Minor, 1913–14', *Middle Eastern Studies*, Vol. VI, 1970, pp. 319–30.
74 Berchtold to Pallavicini, dispatch no. 4319, 11 Nov. 1913, PA I/495.
75 Forgách to Mensdorff, 5 Feb. 1914, PA, Mensdorff MSS.
76 Pallavicini to Berchtold, dispatches nos 20 M, 23 March 1914; 28 N, 22 April 1914; 32 G, 4 May 1914, PA XII/207.
77 Pallavicini to Berchtold, telegram no. 333, 16 July 1914, PA I/522.
78 Pallavicini to Berchtold, private letter, 25 July 1914; telegram no. 334, 18 July 1914; dispatch no. 51 Pol, 20 July 1914; dispatch no. 51-Pol-C, 20 July 1914; telegram no. 346, 25 July 1914, PA I/522.
79 Berchtold to Pallavicini, private letter, 1 Aug 1914, PA I/522.
80 Berchtold to Pallavicini, telegram no. 918, 26 Dec. 1914, PA I/521.
81 Pallavicini to Berchtold, dispatch no. 14P, 18 Feb. 1915, PA I/581; dispatch no. 79A, 31 Dec. 1914, PA I/521.
82 Pallavicini to Berchtold, dispatch no. 3P, 7 Jan. 1915, PA I/521.
83 Pallavicini to Berchtold, dispatch no. 22P, 18 March 1915, PA I/581.
84 Pallavicini to Burián, dispatch no. 74A/P, 29 Sept. 1916, PA I/522.
85 Pallavicini to Burián, telegram no. 537, 9 Nov. 1916, PA I/522.
86 Pallavicini to Czernin, dispatch no. 39, 8 May 1917, PA I/522.
87 Pallavicini to Burián, dispatch no. 93P/B, 7 Nov. 1915, PA XII/463.
88 Nadamlenzky to Pallavicini, dispatch no. 95 Pol, 7 Nov. 1915, PA XII/463.
89 Pallavicini to Burián, dispatch no. 94 P-B, 10 Nov. 1915, PA XII/463.
90 Pallavicini to Burián, dispatch no. 22P/D, 17 March 1916, PA XII/463.
91 Trauttmannsdorff to Czernin, dispatch no. 75D, 15 Sept. 1917, PA XII/463.
92 Pallavicini to Czernin, dispatch no. 28P, 23 March 1918, PA I/522.
93 Pallavicini to Burián, dispatch no. 48B/Pol, 1 June 1918, PA I/522.
94 ibid.
95 Bridge, 'Austria-Hungary', pp. 269 ff.
96 K. u. k. KM Marine-Sektion to Armeeoberkommando, Op. geh, Nr 1014, 9 Feb. 1918, PA I/522.
97 Trauttmannsdorff to Burián, Z1.31.933, 16 Aug. 1918, PA I/522.
98 Burián to Trauttmannsdorff, draft, Sept. 1918, with minute: 'entfällt', PA I/522.

3 Italy and the End of the Ottoman Empire

R. J. B. Bosworth, University of Sydney

In June 1938, Galeazzo Ciano, the young, brash, ambitious, but sometimes curiously, even painfully, realistic Italian Foreign Minister, was engaging in that favoured game of Italian Fascist politicians, rhetoric, the spinning words about a future which might or might not come. Listening to him was Count Giuseppe Volpi di Misurata, who had been Giolitti's negotiator at the Treaty of Lausanne in 1912, Mussolini's Governor of Tripolitania and Minister of Finance in the 1920s, and who was President of Confindustria, Italy's big business league, in 1938. He had also, before 1914, been a financier of the royal house of Montenegro and then and later had 'large financial interests in the Levant', notably in the Eregli coalfields. To Ciano's naïve pleasure Volpi guessed without difficulty that Fascism had 'designs on Albania'. And the President of Italy's industrialists added a suggestion of his own. When Albania glistened as a jewel in the Fascist Empire what would be needed was 'a subsequent operation in Anatolia'.[1] With Albania as a bridgehead in the Balkans, an Italy 'on the march' could not stop until its flags were raised in Asia Minor.

Although he was speaking as a Fascist in 1938, Volpi represented the continuity of Italian foreign policy, its ambition, its opportunism and its lack of genuine achievement. In the story of the Great Powers' involvement in the collapse of the Ottoman Empire, Italy finds a place, but also a characteristic place. In the Libyan War, in her Albanian and general Balkan policy, and in her dreams about penetrating Asia Minor, Liberal Italy before 1914 played a major part, on the surface and in the short term, in hastening the demise of the Ottoman Empire. By 1914 no other Great Power was so cynically hopeful that Turkey was about to collapse. Yet, on a long-term or profound level, to ascribe to Italy a major role in the downfall of the Ottoman Empire, or to claim that Asia Minor was the fulcrum of Italian foreign policy, is absurd. In an area where some saw 'oil and empire', Italy aspired to agricultural settlement and government-financed shipping lines, and even these aspirations were usually constructed out of the paperwork of diplomacy rather than built on serious financial or factual bases. In the Dodecanese, in Adalia, even in Albania, Italy meddled in the affairs of the eastern Mediterranean with enthusiasm, with skill and often with apparent success. But the unspoken assumption of most Italian industrialists was that Italy's financial problems and intentions would not be resolved or achieved in Asia Minor. And the unspoken assumption of all but the most recklessly foolish Italian diplomatists was that, strategically and politically, the Habsburg Empire was a greater issue than the Ottoman Empire. Italy participated in the downfall of the Ottoman Empire, but she did so as circumstances allowed, playing any cards offered to her in the game of negotiation, but in an old-fashioned, tactical, almost *ancien régime* style of diplomacy. In any diagnosis of the contribution made by the Great Powers to the death of the Ottoman system, Italy's activities should be seen as a disease of the skin and not of the heart. Italy was an irritant, performing as usual, as before and as after, the task of the least of the Great Powers.

A certain Italian interest in the eastern Mediterranean had long been evident. After unification, Italy had not been behindhand in demanding and acquiring a place in the grave councils which were set up by the Great Powers to guide Hamidian Turkey towards modernity, and to extract for themselves the maximum possible reward – moral, political and financial. In 1881, Italy was one of six foreign states granted a place on the Council of the Ottoman Public Debt Administration.[2] After 1897, Italy joined Britain and France in supervising the agreement between Greece and Turkey for the 'autonomy' of Crete. During the Macedonian troubles of 1903, it was an Italian general, De Giorgis, who was appointed by the Powers to command the *gendarmerie*, which, it was hoped, would prevent further murderous conflicts among the local population. In 1908, on his death, he was replaced by another Italian general, De Robilant. That year, too, Italy was accorded the right, already possessed by the other Great Powers, to organise her own postal system throughout the Ottoman Empire.[3]

At its simplest, Italian policy towards Turkey was therefore one of participation. As Sonnino would later define it disarmingly: 'O tutti, o nessuno' – either a place for Italy, or no Great Power should be warmed in the Ottoman sun.[4] Thus, with the perseverance of the least of the Great Powers, Italian leaders strove to attend every international conference on Balkan or Levantine affairs, to belong to every international commission and, most of all, to be part of any deal which might bring real or apparent advantage. Entirely characteristic of all Italian policy was the scheme of Alessandro Guiccioli, then Italian Ambassador in Constantinople, who in 1892 suggested that the presidency of the Debt Council should rotate among the members. Italy would thus be accorded 'equality', despite the fact that she possessed only a minimal number of Ottoman bonds. Guiccioli was innocent or adroit enough to persuade Germany, Italy's ally since 1882, to back his scheme, which was, however, rejected.[5]

In other, less formal, aspects of the Great Powers' financial involvement in the Ottoman Empire, Italy was equally zealous and adept at claiming her share. Even before the Risorgimento, some Italian states had shown an interest in Asia Minor and north Africa. Naples–Sicily, for example, had long had diplomatic and financial dealings in Tunis, Tripoli and Alexandria. More important for the future was Piedmont, which, having been given Genoa by the peacemakers at Vienna in 1815, inherited the ancient mantle of Genoese

imperialism in the eastern Mediterranean. Piedmont opened diplomatic relations with Turkey in 1819, and in 1823 signed a commercial arrangement with
the Ottoman Empire. In 1824, Piedmont held fourth place, behind only
Austria, Russia and Britain, in international shipping passing through
Constantinople. In 1837, the Rubattino shipping company inaugurated its
lines in the eastern Mediterranean.[6]

The traditions of Piedmont were easily absorbed by United Italy. In
shipping, for example, the Florio company opened a state-subsidised line to
Constantinople in 1879. When, in 1881, Rubattino and Florio were combined,
under government prompting, to form the Società di Navigazione Generale
Italiana, the new company's major formal activity lay in lines which joined
Italy to the Ottoman Empire. Informally, the SNGI's better-rewarded activity
lay in digesting government subsidies, granted because a transport network to
the Levant was 'a national interest'.[7]

More generally, Italian financial involvement in Turkey increased considerably in the two decades before 1914. From 1896 to 1906, for example, Italian
trade with the Ottoman Empire rose by 150 per cent, from 53 to 132 million
lire. In 1914, Italian commerce with Turkey was surpassed only by that of
Britain, Germany and Austria. Italy, although accustomed to having a balance-
of-payments deficit with most states, had a positive trade-balance with the
Ottoman Empire.[8] Hopeful Italian industrialists talked of Asia Minor as the
ideal market for Italian textiles, and some Italian entrepreneurs, notably
Giuseppe Volpi and his Società Commerciale d'Oriente, looked to Turkey as
the ready source of raw materials which Italy lacked (for example, coal from
the mines at Eregli,[9] or Eraclea as classically trained Italians preferred to call
it). A semi-official propagandist bewailed the lack of commercial training
among Italian diplomats, and argued that the Italian Ambassador, the
southern aristocrat, Marchese Guglielmo Imperiali, had been repeatedly out-
witted by his French colleague, Constans, because Constans was interested in
money and Imperiali only in 'snobismo'.[10]

Yet finance was not the basis of Italy's policy in the Ottoman Empire, nor
even of her presence there. Past centuries of 'Italian' history had left 'Italians'
or, rather, Venetians, Genoese, Neapolitans and Sicilians scattered in communities all over the Mediterranean basin. In 1870 it was reported that there
were 10,000 'Italians' in Constantinople, 6,000 in Smyrna, 2,000 in Syria,
2,500 in Greece and the Aegean Islands, 20,000 in Alexandria, 6,000 in Cairo
and 1,000 in Port Said. The most numerous settlement of all was in Tunis
where, by 1915, there were 130,000 Italian emigrants, despite the fact that
Tunis had, in 1881, been taken by France in a most humiliating diplomatic
defeat for Italy.[11]

The ethnic Italians were divided into two main classes. Most were poor –
seamen, labourers, or sometimes, as in Tunis, small landowners or share-
croppers. But some Italians retained the role of what today could be called
technocrats, especially in engineering and medicine where Italy had once led

the world. Some Italians, too, had found positions as merchants and middle-men, notably in Egypt. The new Nationalist *littérateur*, Filippo Tommaso Marinetti, born in Alexandria in 1876, would later recall in the *Futurist Manifesto* the inspiration which he drew from 'the black teat of [his] Sudanese nurse'.[12] Others of his countrymen, in the same golden days of Khedive Ismail, gained their nourishment from posts as diverse as manager of the khedival shipping line, superintendent of the khedival postal service, director of the khedival health system and various important positions in Egyptian banking.[13] There was a particularly close relationship between the khedival dynasty and that of the Savoys. Fuad, who became King of Egypt in 1917, was trained as a soldier in Turin, and his son, Farouk, was eventually to offer Victor Emmanuel III asylum in Alexandria in 1946.[14]

Matching these achievements of the Liberal State, the Roman Catholic Church also had a notable position in the Mediterranean basin. The rivalry between church and state in the Risorgimento, and indeed in many Italian domestic matters prior to the Lateran Pacts of 1929, was always much weaker abroad, where the agents of an Italian Caesar and a Rome-based God often combined against foreigners in the interests of what one missionary organisa-tion called 'religion and fatherland'.[15] The Vatican's quarrel with Republican France led Italy, in 1905, to be admitted, with church approval, to a share in the protection of Catholic organisations in the Holy Places.[16] Church and state also united in sponsoring Italian language schools abroad which, a propa-gandist boasted, in 1904–5 had 15,633 pupils, more than double the figure of a decade before.[17] In the dispute over Palestine during the First World War, it was believed that Franciscan missionaries could be relied on to be 'eminently patriotic Italians' – unlike the rival Dominicans, who were reputed to be pro-French.[18]

More significant still was financial co-operation between the Roman Catholic Church and the Italian State. The Roman Catholic Church had very early begun to play a major part in the finances of Liberal Italy both through small local banks and co-operatives[19] and through major agencies, especially the Banco di Roma. This last by 1910 was a veritable agent, or even propellant, of Italian imperialism, with major interests in Libya and Egypt, and with ambitions to secure more in Asia Minor.[20] The Italian Foreign Minister (1903–5, 1906–9), a Roman named Tommaso Tittoni, was the brother of one of the Banco di Roma's chief officials and, during Tittoni's ministry, there was, naturally, a warm fraternal relationship between government and bank. Similarly, the appointment of the Italian delegate to the Debt Council was made by the Rome Chamber of Commerce, a body which was traditionally vulnerable to the attractions of clericalism. The Italian delegates Alberto Theodoli (1905–12) and Bernardino Nogara (1912–14) were both *persone gratissime* with the highest circles in the Vatican.[21]

Yet, if these financial, popular and religious factors were the unspoken assumptions of Italian policy in the eastern Mediterranean, their connection with actual political decisions was at best ambiguous. Egypt provides a typical enough story. There, after she had turned down a British suggestion, in 1882, for a sort of junior partnership in the protection of Egypt,[22] Italy was left as the most obvious potential patron of anti-British, Egyptian nationalist movements. However, all the evidence shows that Egyptians manipulated the ambitious and gullible Italians, rather than the reverse. The local 'Italian' community was divided over politics, religion and regional loyalties, and its members spent much time intriguing and bickering amongst themselves.[23] Moreover, the laws of extra-territoriality made nationality necessarily vague. One clerical Italian has noted disapprovingly in his memoirs that Levantine 'Italians' owned ninety-four local brothels.[24] Some businessmen made money, and probably the Savoys, too, punted some of their considerable fortune on Egyptian affairs, but perhaps the most successful Italian contact with Egypt remained that made by Giuseppe Verdi in 1871. For the world première of *Aïda* at the Cairo Opera House, the generous Khedive Ismail had paid the always financially careful Verdi 150,000 gold francs, deposited cash down at the Rothschild Bank in Paris.[25]

In the Balkans, Italy's 'patronage' of nationalist movements was similarly equivocal. Balkan newspapers entitled themselves *Piedmont* and proclaimed the example of Italian unification to give precedent for their own campaigns for freedom from the Ottoman or Habsburg empires. There was some Italian trade with the Balkan area, and some individuals did well – notably the ubiquitous Volpi in Montenegro and Serbia.[26] Some Italian money certainly passed to local chieftains in order to buy arms and equipment for their raids – Albania was a special centre of contact,[27] being assisted by a considerable Italo-Albanian community within Italy and, in the 1911 revolt, by the sons of the great Garibaldi.[28] But Italy's European preoccupations were too near and too pressing for her ever to be the masterful director of ethnic revolts in the Balkans. Indeed, in that area, Italy was usually either manipulated or disregarded by the Balkan leaders and, in her own policy, was more timidly anxious than most that the *status quo* in the Balkans should survive.

The timidity was not engendered by a love for the Ottoman Empire but, rather, by a combination of suspicion, jealousy and fear of the Habsburg Empire. Article VII of the Triple Alliance, agreed between Italy and Austria in 1887, spoke of compensation for one if the other gained advantage in the Balkans.[29] Italian policy-makers always hoped, but could never say openly, that this might mean some arrangement whereby Italy regained the *terra irredenta* of Trieste and the Trentino. In the Balkans, and elsewhere, whatever financiers schemed or propagandists boasted, the ultimate fulcrum of Italian policy lay by the Isonzo and in the Alto Adige, in 'completing the Risorgimento' and not in a *Drang Nach Osten*, in nationalism and not in imperialism. Thus, Italian financial dealings in the wider Ottoman Empire remained small beer, the delight and reward of individuals (notably of Volpi) rather than the lubricant of state policy. It was characteristic that Italy, despite her lack of energy resources, such as coal, at home, showed very little interest before 1914 in oil,[30] and, as the owner of Libya from 1911 to the Second World War, actually rejected expert advice that oil might be the one product which could bring a profit from that 'fourth shore'. The Nationalist writer, Enrico Corradini, with his usual grandiloquence, feared lest mineral discoveries in Libya would enfeeble Italians by 'allowing them to grow rich'.[31] In practice poverty was preserved while Italian colonial administrators dreamed of restoring Libya to its position in Classical times as the great grain-producing province of the Roman Empire under the laborious hand of Italian peasants.[32]

Generally, then, the bases of Italian policy in the eastern Mediterranean were traditional, imitative and often quite out of date. It was as though the effort required to be the least of the Great Powers left Italian leaders, both Liberal and Fascist, panting too hard just in order to keep up, to be able to understand too many modern themes of finance or, later, of ideologically 'fascist' imperialism. In the Great Power scramble for influence in Turkey, Italy was not an initiator, but simply the Power which did not wish to be left out.

This essential weakness admitted, it is also ironically true that specific Italian policies, undertaken for traditional reasons, often had a major impact on the unhappy Ottoman Empire. The most drastic example came in 1911 with the Italian invasion of the Turkish provinces of Tripoli and Cyrenaica, which, in November, together with the inland vilayet of Fezzan, were annexed to Italy and became the colony called Libya.[33]

Despite Libya's lack of natural appeal (Turkey herself, despite minimal expense, made a financial loss out of administering it), Italy had long enunciated her special interest in the area. She did so initially on the beggars-can't-be-choosers principle that, after the establishment of the French protectorate in Tunis (1881) and the rejection of British overtures about Egypt (1882), there was no other suitable 'vacant' territory left. For two decades, Italy built up a baroque web of agreements and half-agreements with the other Powers (notably in the Visconti Venosta and Prinetti-Barrère exchanges with France in 1900 and 1902) that, 'should the *status quo* be changed' in north Africa, then Italy must take Libya. After 1905, the doubtful achievements of diplomacy were bolstered by equally doubtful achievements of finance as the Banco di Roma began considerable investment in Libya. The Bank invested in railways, shipping, port developments, and agricultural modernisation in such concerns as olive oil production. Italian commerce with Libya increased – by 1910 imports and exports totalled some 14 million lire, still basically very small-scale but a major increase on the situation five years before.[34]

Italy's politicians, diplomats and businessmen initially greeted the Young Turk revolution with enthusiasm.[35] Abdul Hamid had long been depicted as the epitome of Evil, and Italian publicists had grown accustomed to using the Ottoman system as the most notorious example of corruption and tyranny. One future Italian Foreign Minister, visiting Albania in 1900, briefly defined

Turkish justice as a public danger.[36] An Italian journalist, reporting on the Balkan Wars, thought that Turkish government was in a state of 'putrefaction' and that 'the only . . . excuse' for Turkish military incompetence was 'perhaps that . . . of being Moslem'.[37] The political philosopher Gaetano Mosca, though denying that one race was intrinsically superior to another, none the less argued that, currently, all Moslem systems were inferior.[38]

All this, it was for a time innocently believed, could be changed by revolution. The Young Turks would modernise their Empire and create a Liberal Turkey with whom Liberal Italy could associate with fewer moral inhibitions. But the Young Turks were also nationalists, suspicious of the presence of foreigners. Libya was not the nub of political attention in Constantinople but, in October 1910, Tripoli was sent a new *vali*, Ibrahim Pasha, who at once started to campaign against the most obvious foreign presence, that is, the Italian. Thereupon Italian diplomats began to prophesy gloomily that Tripoli would find the destiny of Tunis and be lost to Italy. Italian publicists shocked their readers with tales of Italian military heroism traduced by the Young Turk rulers, of Italian businessmen hindered, and even of Italian maidens despoiled by dastardly Muslims. Libya, they said, was Italy's 'promised land' and the 'hour was sounding' in which Italy must take it.[39] In particular, the *romanità* of Libya was emphasised and re-emphasised. A typical contemporary cartoon showed a soldier of the 'Third Italy' finding the skeleton of a Roman legionary in the desert, plucking out his still shining sword and raising it aloft to proclaim to Italy and the world the revived Roman destiny which awaited Libya and perhaps other littoral regions of the 'mare nostrum'.

Yet Italy's invasion of Libya on 29 September was not really caused in any direct sense by the misdeeds of Ibrahim Pasha, nor by the rhetorical exhortations of publicists and politicians anxious to make their patriotic mark in 1911 – that year of many celebrations of the fiftieth anniversary of United Italy. Instead, as in many other aspects of Italian policy towards Turkey, the real spur to Italian action was bound to neither internal nor local events, nor even to Italy's particular relationship with Turkey. It came, rather, from Italy's position with regard to the other Great Powers.

In 1908 a decade of relatively passive public policy was undermined by Italy's humiliation during the Bosnia–Herzegovina affair. Then Austria annexed the territory which she had occupied since 1878. This conversion of the *de facto* and the *de jure* carried for Italy the negative accompaniment of being unable to claim compensation despite palpable Austrian advantage. The Italian Foreign Minister at the time, Tommaso Tittoni, was all the more exposed, given his own well-known penchant for intrigue. At home he had to suffer the slings of Nationalist opinion, outraged that he had gained nothing, and abroad the arrows of diplomatic suspicion that his failure did not spring from a want of trying. In London, normally a seat of somewhat condescending benevolence towards Italy, a clerk in the Foreign Office minuted without rebuke that Tittoni was 'a past master in the art of lying'.[40] Tittoni's career never recovered from his failure. In March 1910 a new government was formed in Italy by Luigi Luzzatti, a Jewish financier who was acting as a stop-gap before the return of the accustomed Prime Minister, Giolitti. Luzzatti chose as his Foreign Minister not Tittoni but Antonino di San Giuliano, a Sicilian aristocrat with a markedly nationalist background.[41] When Giolitti himself took over from Luzzatti in March 1911, he kept San Giuliano on at the Foreign Ministry.

The renewed desire for action in foreign affairs was stimulated not merely by the effects of Tittoni's passivity. The Italian economy, after a decade of growth, turned down in 1907 and recovered thereafter only very slowly. Italian businessmen were aware of the 'social peril' and, on the model of their German and French seniors, were beginning to seek some modern solution to obviate the class struggle. In 1910, Italy saw the foundation of a Big Business League, Confindustria, and by 1912 the President of that League, a French citizen named Luigi Bonnefon Craponne, and its secretary, Camillo Olivetti, were praising 'autarky' as the ideal policy for the Italian economy. A certain naïveté always remained – Olivetti called war 'a monstrous phenomenon' – but Italy was beginning to develop, in a minor way and with many internal divisions, what one historian has called an 'industrial–military complex'.[42]

The industrialists' potential interest in imperialism had been preceded, however, by a more defined interest from bureaucrats, politicians and journalists, especially those, including San Giuliano, who, in 1906, had set up the Italian Colonial Institute. The ambition of this body was to spread an enthusiasm for colonialism among the ruling élite, rather as the *parti colonial* was supposed to do in the French Chamber of Deputies. Turkish territory was regarded as especially suitable for a revival of Italian colonialism. In May 1906 an archaeologist writing about 'Antiquity in Tripoli and Cyrenaica' urged blandly: 'Archaeological explorations . . . must follow and not precede the occupation, armed or passive, of the country.' A politician defined Cyrenaica as a 'real Eden' and recalled that Tripoli was 'a land fertile, rich, once a happy and prosperous colony of the Greeks and Romans'. Asia Minor, too, inspired renewed colonialist dreams which prophesied throughout the eastern Mediterranean a great future for Italian demographic colonisation.[43]

Indeed, the emigration figures, especially from the Italian south, were becoming so enormous that it is scarcely surprising that some politicians began to seek anew for colonies which could cope, to some extent, with the flood of expatriation. In Calabria and the Abruzzi, by 1909–13, 3.3 per cent of the population was emigrating annually,[44] and when it is noted that these were young, healthy, adult men the loss was all the more drastic. Italy's existing colonies, Eritrea and the Somaliland, had proved ill suited to settlement. In Eritrea, the better and older of the two, in 1913 the total non-military or bureaucratic personnel was sixty-one.[45] The major activity in such colonies was not a growth in agrarian production but bureaucratic in-fighting between civilians and representatives of the army. One civilian governor of Eritrea wrote back to Rome that the officers of his colony passed their time exclusively between local 'madams and the green baize table'.[46]

In 1910–11 the traditional rhetoric of conservative colonialists was blended with the sharper mixture provided by Enrico Corradini and his fellows of the Nationalist Association and its newspaper, *L'Idea nazionale*. It was Corradini who coined the phrase that Italy was 'a proletarian nation' and who argued a thesis in favour of the primacy of foreign policy. For Italy, he averred, an expansionist, even warmongering, foreign policy was more important and salutary than were any domestic reforms.

But the final and major stimulus to action came from outside Italy. Without the international pressure arising both from the dispatch of the German gunboat *Panther* to Agadir on 1 July 1911 and the subsequent Franco-German crisis and settlement, and from the rumours in September that Austria wanted the Triple Alliance to be renewed prematurely, it is very difficult to imagine Giolitti departing from his cautious principle that an attack on Libya would mean war against the whole Ottoman Empire. Such a grandiose ambition, he feared, could have a result which none could foresee: 'The integrity of what is left of the Ottoman Empire is one of the principles on which is founded the equilibrium and peace of Europe . . . What if, after we attack Turkey, the Balkans move? And what if a Balkan war provokes a clash between the two groups of Powers and a European war?' Italy, he averred with propriety, would be foolish to take on such a terrible responsibility.[47]

Despite this perceptiveness about the ramifications of an Italo-Turkish war, by 17 September, Giolitti and San Giuliano had decided to launch an attack on Libya. At 2.30 p.m. on 29 September a blatant Italian ultimatum to the Turkish government expired. By then, Italian troop-ships were already sailing towards the Libyan coast.

Italy, the least of the Great Powers, thus became the first major state to engage in open war against Turkey since the Congress of Berlin. Italy had loosed the first stone in what for the next decade would turn into the avalanche which would overwhelm the Ottoman Empire.

It was, however, a very curious war in which Italy engaged. Territorially, campaigning was concentrated mainly in Libya itself, where Italian troops under General Caneva soon seized the coastal towns, but were then at a loss to know what to do next. Italian confidence that the local Senussi Arabs would join them in order to throw off their Ottoman overlords proved to be misplaced. Instead, Muslim religious leaders proclaimed a *jihad* against the infidel invaders, and a bitter guerilla resistance began. During the First World War, Italian occupation was reduced to those same few coastal settlements seized in the first days of the Libyan campaign. An Italian 'pacification' was not achieved until 1930 under first Liberal and then Fascist impulse. One commander during the near-genocidal campaign was Giuseppe Volpi, whose chequered career had led him, from 1922 to 1925, to be Governor of Tripolitania.[48] Back in 1911–12 the only solace to Italian nationalists came from the boast that their country was pioneering the use of aeroplanes in combat or that some soldier's letters, blessed with official approval, depicted Libya as a land as rich and fertile as 'America'.[49] A popular song rejoiced that Tripoli was a paradise: 'Tripoli, bel suol d'amore'. Less publicised was the fact that the Italian death-toll soon began to rise, though more from cholera than from Arab bullets. At the same time, the age-old Italian peasant hope for land (and religious hatred of the 'turchi' who, in past centuries had owned Sicily and devastated the Italian coast and who were not 'cristiani')[50] was being perverted by that other age-old peasant comprehension that war brought only trouble and loss. Soldiers on official parades cheerfully sang 'Tripoli, bel suol d'amore', but in the privacy of their camps they learned instead to chant more pessimistic words which had been coined at home:

> Oh iniqua, oh infame Turchia
> L'hai ucciso il mio amato consorte
> ma quando ebbi l'annuncio di morte
> un dolore provai da morir . . .
> Comanda Cristo oppure il padrone
> maledetta sia sempre la guerra
> chi di sangue ha sporcato la terra
> che non possa il sole veder.[51]

'Evil, infamous Turkey/You have killed my loved companion/When I received the death notice/it was a pain equal to death/Christ rules or rather the boss does/ Accursed forever be war/which has so besmirched the earth with blood/that the sun cannot be seen.

For the Italian government (as indeed for the Young Turk administrations in Constantinople), these military and social events in Libya were something of a sideshow. Desultory war might be waged inland from Homs and Benghazi, but the real contest was to find a peace acceptable to both parties without too much loss of face.

The Italian leadership did go on dreaming of a military *coup* which would prove so decisive that Turkey would have abjectly to sue for peace. The problem was that dreaming of a *coup* was easier than carrying it out. In the early days of the war, action was contemplated in the Adriatic, probably against Albania, that perennial object of Italian interest and ambition. But it was made absolutely plain that Austria-Hungary would not tolerate independent Italian action in an area so sensitive for her own interests. Aehrenthal, the Austrian Minister of Foreign Affairs, warned Italy off.[52]

The superior Italian navy was then left in the irritating dilemma that its unquestioned superiority against Turkey could not be utilised except to escort troops across the Mediterranean, or to earn trouble for itself and Italy's politicians by interfering with 'the freedom of the seas' – for example, when arresting the French ships, *Carthage*, *Manouba* and *Tavignano*, in order to ascertain if they were carrying contraband men or material to Libya.[53] In April and July 1912 some release from frustration was found in officially 'accidental', but in fact planned, raids against the Straits. The action in April was particularly effective since Turkey mined the Straits in reply, and thus blocked such important commerce as the Anglo-Russian grain trade. In the following weeks, Turkish delay in removing the mines earned her the opprobrium of Britain and Russia, and Italy, almost unnoticed, was able to occupy first the island of Stampalia on 28 April, and later the rest of the Dodecanese and Rhodes, which, patriotic propagandists soon reminded their readers, had once been the 'friend and ally of the Roman people'.

The Dodecanese soon became a major bargaining-counter in all Italian diplomatic manoeuvring in the Balkans and Asia Minor,[54] but in the spring of 1912 their seizure brought peace no closer since the Turkish government showed no great pain at the loss of such ethnically Greek and economically valueless property. In these circumstances, the Italian Chief of the General Staff, Alberto Pollio, decided, at the end of June, that drastic measures were called for. In a remarkable *pro memoria* he suggested that now was the time for Italy to engage in total war against Turkey and simply to dismantle the Ottoman Empire. An Italian force, landed at Smyrna, would provide the military muscle, but Italy should also excite the Christian people of the Balkans to rise and expel Turkey from Europe. 'The Eastern Question', he argued, had 'lasted for centuries'. It was Italy's task to cut the Gordian knot and to ensure that the collapse of Turkey, which was certain in the immediate future in any case, would happen now at the moment of greatest advantage to Italy.[55]

Pollio's statement thus provides the most serious military 'plan' for a general attack on Turkey made by any of the Great Powers before the First World War. Yet, once again, Italian policy must be seen in context. There is absolutely no evidence that either Giolitti or San Giuliano, the two men who made Italian foreign policy, took Pollio's ideas seriously. Civil–military relations in Italy are a complicated enough story domestically,[56] but in the practice of diplomacy the army leadership had almost no influence at all. It is notorious, but also indicative, that Pollio was never told the terms of the Triple Alliance. In September 1911, San Giuliano and Giolitti planned the Libyan War with only the most desultory contact with the military who would wage it. In July–August 1914, San Giuliano made policy with no reference to the army leadership, which continued to ready itself to fight against the Triple Entente until the very morrow of the Italian declaration of neutrality.

Thus, in the summer of 1911, Pollio's sudden interest in total warfare in Asia Minor provoked little reaction from Giolitti or San Giuliano. The Foreign Minister, indeed, was already gloomy about the war clouds gathering over the Balkans, and advocated peace with Turkey via some sort of strategic retreat[57] – perhaps an abandonment of the outright annexation of Libya proclaimed by Giolitti on 4 November 1911. The Prime Minister was less pessimistic. He had soon decided that peace would not come from military victory, and had also turned from the orthodox channels of diplomacy in seeking reconciliation with

Turkey. Interestingly, and most significantly for Italian policy towards the Ottoman Empire for the last years before the First World War, the world in which Giolitti sought to find the key to the Libyan imbroglio was the financial one.

Italian financial dealings with Turkey pursued a twisted course throughout 1911–12. They began in failure when Theodoli, the clerical conservative who was Italian delegate to the Debt Council, was persuaded to return to Rome in October 1911 with a compromise peace plan, which was then rejected by Giolitti.[58] Theodoli's failure ruined his reputation in Constantinople, and he was soon expelled from the Ottoman Empire.

Other businessmen, however, were ready to step into Theodoli's shoes. Notable was Bernardino Nogara, who directed the Constantinople offices of Volpi's Società Commerciale d'Oriente. Nogara was permitted to remain in Constantinople throughout the war, and his informative dispatches to Volpi were in turn passed on to Giolitti. In June 1912, Volpi himself went on a private mission to Constantinople. In the short term, the mission brought no enlightenment except that Volpi, too, now wrote philosophically to Giolitti that Turkey was 'a country which continues its fatal path towards its end'.[59] However, the contacts made by Volpi were renewed in July 1912, when unofficial Italian and Turkish delegations met in Lausanne to search for mutually acceptable and rewarding peace terms. The Italian delegation consisted of the apposite combination of a politician, Pietro Bertolini, said to be Giolitti's political dauphin, a legal expert, Guido Fusinato, and a businessman, yet again the indestructible Volpi.

For the next three months, parleying continued at various luxurious Swiss hotels. The Turkish delegates, however enriched by their acquaintance with the financial skills of Volpi, proved even more able at procrastination. In the end, it was only the outbreak of the Balkan Wars, on 8 October, which drove Turkey, ten days later, to initial the Treaty of Lausanne with Italy. The chain reaction which Giolitti had predicted before the outbreak of the Libyan War had moved on to its next link.

All in all, Italy's war with Turkey had been an oddly tangential event. It was a war in which experts in warfare were less important than experts in bribery. It was a war in which Italy could not fully utilise her military and, especially, naval superiority, given the tacit restrictions imposed on her by the other Great Powers. This apart, it was also a war towards which all the other Great Powers followed a policy of shutting their eyes and hoping for the best. In 1911–12 neither Britain, France, Russia, Germany nor Austria-Hungary was anxious to adopt too open a stance which might fatally antagonise either Italy or Turkey. The peace of Lausanne in October 1912 was equally paradoxical. For the next twenty months, the ex-combatants, Italy and Turkey, became bosom friends, and Italy became easily the most intrusive newcomer into the strategic and commercial politics of the future of Asia Minor. And the great interest which caused this friendship to blossom was that, by Article 2 of the Treaty of

Lausanne, Italy remained in 'temporary' occupation of the Dodecanese until all Turkish troops had left Libya.

As far as Italy was concerned, it soon became apparent that Turkish troops were readily identifiable with Arab insurgents. Unless there was severe international pressure, Italy would not hand back the Dodecanese until Libya was pacified. Even if that unlikely event happened, it was conceivable that there existed good reasons (for example, the expense occasioned by the onerous task of occupation)[60] which would continue to justify Italian retention of the islands. As the history of Bosnia and Herzegovina and Egypt had already demonstrated, 'temporary' occupation of Ottoman territory by a Great Power could easily become permanent.

The Dodecanese issue was further complicated both for Italy and Turkey because, with the Balkan Wars, or should any principle of ethnic justice be applied, the islands would be delivered not to Turkey but to Greece. The Turkish government readily understood that the Dodecanese in 'temporary' Italian hands had more chance of returning one day to the administration of Constantinople than if they became part of Greek dominion.

Turkish reliance on procrastination was all the greater, since it was plain that, for Italy, Greece was always the most annoying and uppity Small Power. Indeed, the theme of Italo-Greek antagonism runs like a golden thread through the grey cloth of policies and half-policies which made up Italian diplomacy in the eastern Mediterranean from 1912 to the Corfu incident of 1923 and beyond. Partly, the problem was ideological. If Italy was the heir of the First Rome, Greece carried on the traditions of Byzantium, and aimed to regain a *Graecia irredenta* in zones of Turkish territory which were often precisely those which excited most Italian attention. Moreover, where Italian rhetoricians had to justify their case by reference to the redolent ruins of Rome, Venice or Genoa, or to the scattered settlements of ethnic 'Italians', Greek patriots could claim that 6.5 million Greeks lived in the Turkish Empire – enough allegedly to deserve a quarter of the seats in the Chamber set up after the Young Turk revolution of 1908. It was this sort of 'evidence' which encouraged one Italian politician to remark inscrutably, apropos of the Greeks, that one could die of starvation but also of indigestion.[61]

One particular area of dispute was southern Albania, or northern Epirus as the Greeks preferred to call it. Italian strategists, with some prompting from their politicians, had decided that whoever dominated Albania controlled the outlet to the Adriatic and thus potentially possessed a naval stranglehold on Italy's vulnerably flat and harbourless Adriatic coastline.[62]

The Albanian tangle was knotted tighter by Austria-Hungary's ambition in the area. Despite a number of agreements in 1900, 1909 and 1913 between Italy and Austria marking out their interests in Albania, in the decades before 1914 the two fought out a bizarre cold war for the control of the souls and bank accounts of Albanians. Italian naval vessels pointedly made annual calls to Albanian ports, and Italian experts involved themselves as advisers in the hotly disputed question of the ideal Albanian alphabet.[63] However, for Italy, the major problem was that the Albanian issue never clarified sufficiently for her to have one straight policy-line. Thus, before 1912, Italians provided financial and moral sustenance, and sometimes physical asylum for Albanian nationalists who, each spring, threatened to expel Turkish tax-collectors. The Italian government, on the other hand, went on proclaiming its loyalty to the *status quo* in Albania, and occasionally persecuted those of its own citizens who became too fervent enthusiasts for an Albanian nation. In 1912–13, at the London Conference, Italy was an earnest advocate of the recognition of Albania as an autonomous state. But, in the privacy of the Foreign Ministry, officials had little doubt that Albania did not have a future.[64] Thus, while acknowledging that Austria's candidate, William of Wied, was the best prospect as ruler of Albania, Italy provided funds for the chiefs of the rebellious northern, Roman Catholic, tribe of the Mirditi and for Essad Pasha, the main Muslim challenger for the title of Prince of Albania. These inconsistencies were not helped by the collapse of Wied's rule in the summer of 1914. In October 1914 the Italian navy occupied the island of Saseno – the 'Gibraltar of the Adriatic' as Italian propagandists loved to call it. When it turned out that Saseno had no supplies of running water, the port of Valona was also necessarily occupied on Christmas Day, 1914.[65] Italian policy towards Albania was set in the groove which would lead to the request for a mandate at Versailles, to the 'protection' of King Zog in the 1920s, and eventually to the annexation of Albania to the Italian Empire on Good Friday, 1939.

Italy's preoccupations in Albania, and towards Greece on the one hand and Austria on the other, meant that she was no proponent of Balkan nationalism during the Balkan Wars. In any case, while peace between the Great Powers survived, Italian strategic, financial and political attention had shifted to Asia Minor. Turkey-in-Europe had collapsed, and the Small Powers had taken their reward. Turkey-in-Asia would soon follow, but on this occasion the rewards would go to the Great Powers. In those circumstances, 'Italy must be there'.

The detail of Italian policy in Asia Minor bears remarkable similarity to that of her ally and rival, Austria-Hungary, which found only 'tarde venientibus ossa'.[66] Italy in 1913–14 gained more on paper than Austria, was more persistent and cynical, but that had much to do with the personality and ability of San Giuliano compared to the new Austrian Foreign Minister, Berchtold. Any advantage held was soon lost with the outbreak of war and the death of San Giuliano.

But, in 1913–14, Italy busily engaged herself in finding a 'sphere of interest' in Asia Minor, most persistently in the region of Adalia, which lay inland from the Dodecanese islands. Any sphere of interest, it was hoped, would turn into something more substantial in the event of what San Giuliano repeatedly called 'the probable, not far-off, collapse of the Ottoman Empire'.[67] In order to be granted a place in any hypothetical division of Turkey, San Giuliano used all possible means. He worked within the Triple Alliance, both stating his perpetual and total loyalty to his partners, and, more subtly, encouraging Austria to involve herself more in Turkey, and then begging Germany for sympathy and support lest Austria steal a march over Italy and upset the balance within the Alliance. A characteristic San Giuliano memorandum explained, in September 1913, that 'naturally' Italy would favour Austria being granted a sphere of interest for herself but that 'we must search to have the biggest and best part and . . . give Austria-Hungary the zone which would most put her into conflict with the Triple Entente'.[68]

Meanwhile, Italy strove to exploit her own peculiar relationship with France and especially with Britain to get Triple Entente backing for a recognition of her interests in Asia Minor. In this regard, the Dodecanese were especially useful pawns to be played since the British Admiralty had decided that, under continued Italian ownership, they were a potential threat to the imperial naval route to the East. Time and time again, without his bluff being called, San Giuliano pushed into play the promise that he would return the islands. British diplomatists were left to take refuge in wit, one composing a limerick to define Italian policy:

> They mustn't keep Rhodes or Stampalia,
> So they've sent a young man to Adalia,
> Where he's now hard at work
> At cajoling the Turk
> To cry 'viva, evviva Italia!'[69]

By March 1914, through adroit use of the islands, San Giuliano had managed to persuade Sir Edward Grey to admit Italian association in the right to construct a railway in the hinterland of Smyrna. This right conflicted with the previous concession granted by the Turkish government to the British Smyrna–Aidin railway company, whose activities in the area Grey had previously described as those of 'so to say, our ewe lamb'. (It was appropriate that the legal expert for the company was a Mr Slaughter.[70]) San Giulano's negotiating methods continued to be marked by a confident cynicism most unusual in Italian diplomacy. On the Smyrna–Aidin railway, for example, the Ambassador in London was instructed bluntly by San Giuliano: 'Our supreme aim is to obtain fully public concessions in Asia Minor . . . at this moment it is less unfortunate to displease Grey than to [annoy] the Ottoman government.'[71]

To the Turks, as well, San Giuliano behaved with ruthless insincerity. The time was approaching, he hinted over and over again, when the Dodecanese could be transferred not to Greece but to Turkey. This tomorrow, however, would never come, since San Giuliano and his diplomats believed that 'the Ottoman Empire because of its heterogeneous ethnic composition, because of the disorder of its administration, [and] of its inability to reform could not, for much longer, resist disintegration'.[72] It was safe to write cheques to Turkey to be cashed on some future day, because, on that future day, Turkey would not exist.

The major question raised in examining prewar Italian policy towards Turkish Asia Minor is what was its motivation? Sometimes it is alleged that the answer to this question is financial, that Italy looked to Turkey as a potential market for the excess products of her industrialisation process, notably for her textile industries, and as a source of much needed raw materials, from coal to cotton to grain and other foodstuffs. Yet the hard evidence is all to the contrary. Foreign experts, such as those in Britain and Germany, commenting on the Smyrna–Aidin railway question, were quite clear that Italian motivation was 'political' rather than anything else.[73] Even within Italy, whatever evidence there is for pressure by industrialists or bankers in favour of a more forward policy in the East is far outweighed by evidence of the government trying to encourage business to involve itself in Turkey in ways which would be useful to the political ambitions of Italian foreign policy. In January 1913, San Giuliano underlined to Camillo Garroni, his new Ambassador in Constantinople, that it was 'absolutely necessary' for the Italian government and its agents to stimulate 'a network of economic interests' and formal rights in Turkey which could then be utilised both to woo nationalist 'public opinion' behind the cause of Italian expansion, and to be available for the various manipulations of Italian diplomacy. Therefore, San Giuliano explained, economic penetration should begin 'not only in that part of Asiatic Turkey to which we can perhaps one day put forth claims for territorial dominion but also in other parts as eventual objects of exchange'. And it was to be the government which should smooth the path for business by winning Turkish favour with diplomatic finesse.[74]

In practice, therefore, Italian entrepreneurs did not actually construct railways or modernise ports in Adalia, although an improvement in the naval potentiality of the harbour at Rhodes was at least planned. Production from the Eregli coalfields in which Volpi was so interested was scarcely available to Turkey when it entered the First World War as a result of the lack of transport facilities. Indeed, throughout Asia Minor, the Turkish military relied in theory on oxen, mules, camels and horses, and in practice on peasant women, to carry foodstuffs and even arms to the front.[75] Before the war, any new Roman empire in the eastern Mediterranean remained an edifice made solely out of diplomatic papers, out of schemes and deals (often paid for in Rome not in Asia Minor) and not of practice, out of hopes and ambitions and not of treaties. Even Italian trade with Turkey, although it soon returned to normal at the end of the Libyan War and thereafter grew rapidly, was still only some 3 per cent of the national total, well below the figures for Italy's seven major trading partners (Austria, France, Britain, Germany, Switzerland, Argentina and the United States) to which over 60 per cent of all Italian commerce was directed.[76]

San Giuliano was given to speaking about Adalia as a potential part of Italy's colonial dominion. It is not altogether clear whether, in 1913–14, in using such phrases, he was motivated by a desire to solve Italy's demographic problems, that is, one day to settle Italian peasants in Asia Minor. San Giuliano was himself a Sicilian aristocrat, who had once described emigration as the haemorrhage of Italy's best blood, and in his somewhat tortuous mind he probably did nurture his diplomatising in the eastern Mediterranean with the half-expectation that a 'colony' might one day bring not so much financial reward as a satisfaction of the southern peasant longing for land.

In 1917, that is, during the First World War, Leopoldo Franchetti, an old associate of San Giuliano in the colonialist debates of the 1890s about Ethiopia, did openly suggest that Asia Minor would be the ideal venue for Italian peasant colonists. Franchetti overcame his disappointment with the practical results of Italian stewardship in Eritrea, Somaliland and Libya to argue that Italy must aim at the outright possession of most of Anatolia and the littoral of Asia Minor. It was, he averred, only fair that Italy thus be rewarded by her allies since 'alone among the nations of the Entente Italy lives and breathes exclusively in the Mediterranean'. Therefore, he stated, 'the acquisition of Asia Minor is . . . essential for the organic development of our country'. To Anatolia, Italy would carry power and civilisation but, perhaps more important, 'the fecundity and labour of her emigrants'.[77]

Partly, the grandiosity of Franchetti's ideas can be explained by the fact that they were raised in wartime, as a deliberate part, indeed, of the debate within the ruling class about what should be Italian war aims. But what Franchetti said in 1917 probably had also occurred to Italian diplomats, and especially to San Giuliano, before 1914. Then, however, in the circumstance of peace, and given the complex artifice of Italian diplomacy, they preferred to leave such ambitions unspoken and assumed.

Indeed, in the last months before the July Crisis, Italian policy in Asia Minor, as in Albania and elsewhere, was beset by new and perilous challenges. The relief occasioned by the end of the Balkan Wars had allowed the resounding of the natural disharmony between Italy and Austria-Hungary. All San Giuliano's reiterated innocence and attention to detail could not restore a pastoral atmosphere to that relationship. Thus, in April 1914 the meeting in Abbazia between San Giuliano and Berchtold had brought no satisfaction to Italy, and, in the next weeks, Austria continued to make a nuisance of herself in so far as Rome was concerned by complaining that Italian scheming in Asia Minor made it conceivable that Austria would miss out altogether there.[78] Small wonder, then, that San Giuliano was driven, on 14 July 1914, to write a long dispatch openly questioning whether the Triple Alliance still brought sufficient protection and gains for Italy for it to be worth preserving.[79]

Italy's mutual relations with Turkey were also deteriorating, given the end of the Balkan Wars and given the Turkish government's subsequent drift into the tight embrace of Germany. Turkey started to be less courteous towards Italian negotiators for spheres of interest, and even began to wonder when

Clause 2 of the Treaty of Lausanne should be applied. With the outbreak of hostilities in Europe and the Italian declaration of neutrality on 3 August, Italy's position in Asia Minor weakened further. In war, the military feebleness of the least of the Great Powers, evidenced anew by the fact that Italy was the only non-combatant Great Power, made the superficiality of Italian pretensions in the Ottoman Empire quite plain. In war, railways which did not exist, but which might just possibly, one day, materialise, became irrelevant. By 5 August an Italian consul in Anatolia was already glum about any commercial operations during the war, even though Turkish entry still lay two months ahead. 'Here laws or binding treaties no longer exist,' he explained briefly.[80] Italian penetration had certainly not fertilised the womb of Asia Minor sufficiently for Italy, in times of trouble, to father strapping native offspring.

In 1914, Italy, therefore, had few genuine claims to any inheritance in the eastern Mediterranean. But what had Italy contributed to the weakened state of the Ottoman Empire by then? The practical answer to this question is, in substance, very little. However cynical and sometimes almost magically dextrous San Giuliano was in staking out an Italian place in the sun in Adalia, he had not achieved much by 1914. Nor, except by imitation, had Italy done much to damage Turkey. Most Italian investors preferred to invest in state bonds at home, rather than to risk capital in Turkey. Italian diplomatists were willing enough to cut up the corpse of the Ottoman Empire, but they lacked the strength themselves to give the Empire its death-blow. Italy's policy towards Turkey says much about the state of the Ottoman Empire and about the policy and ambition of the other states in Asia Minor. But, in relation to Italy itself, it merely provides additional evidence of the limited nature of that nation's achievements in foreign policy. In the final analysis, Italy involved herself in Turkey only to the extent permitted by the other Great Powers.

Nor was this situation changed much by the war. In the *intervento*, that is, the period from the declaration of neutrality in August 1914 to the entry into the war against Austria on 24 May 1915, ambitions in the eastern Mediterranean were included in all Italian bargaining terms. The Treaty of London, which Italy signed with the Triple Entente on 26 April, offered, in Article 8, Italian retention of the Dodecanese and, in Article 9, somewhat vaguely, an acknowledgement of Italy's special place in the Adalia region should Turkey be dismembered, since Italy was 'interested in preserving the political balance of power in the Mediterranean'.

Italy's new Foreign Minister, Sidney Sonnino, has sometimes been blamed by patriotic Italian diplomatic historians for not extracting a better payment, cash down, from the Allies at the Treaty of London.[81] The fussy, 'principled' and legalistic Sonnino was not a particularly able diplomat, or at least not a diplomat adept at the sort of sleight of hand required if Liberal Italy was going to reconstruct a Roman empire. Yet, with war, it was inevitable that Italian diplomacy would concentrate on what really was central to it, that is, the Adriatic, the Trentino and Venezia Giulia. Sonnino was more interested in having settled as clearly as possible Italy's territorial gains there than in worrying too much about distant prospects in the eastern Mediterranean – all the more so because, in March–April 1915, the Italian negotiators feared that the war would end before they could get a shot in, and thus before an Italian attendance at any peace conference could be justified.[82]

Italian patriotic historians also like to claim that Sonnino and Imperiali, his Ambassador in London, were tricked by Grey into not making more specific demands on Turkey and into not attempting to reconcile Italian ambitions with those of France and Russia. Perhaps, to some extent, Grey sensed that British interests in the eastern Mediterranean might clash with Italian, and therefore was relieved that matters were not defined too closely. Italy would have to work her passage, and circumstances in the eastern Mediterranean might well be changed by victory or defeat at the Front.

In any case, it was the prolongation of the war which revived Italian interest in Asia Minor and which raised the possibility that the other Allies might pay more attention to the division of Turkey. Italy did not even declare war on Turkey until August 1915, and it was not until 1916–17 that her leaders began again to think seriously about territorial acquisition from a defunct Turkish Empire. By then, Franchetti's plans for demographic colonisation had been endorsed by a number of Nationalist propagandists such as Tomaso Sillani[83] and G. A. Rosso. Rosso, for example, declared simply that Anatolia was 'necessary' for Italian emigration and commerce, and demanded that Italy be granted a major port, either Smyrna or Alexandretta. There was no need, he stated, for Italy to be worried by 'empty Hellenic megalomania' about the ethnicity of Smyrna. Italy should simply remember, and make others remember, that she was a Great Power. Another Italian Nationalist, with extraordinary logic, decided that Constantinople was an Italian city since it had been constructed by a Roman emperor and contained important Genoese buildings. These, he opined, implored an Italian presence 'while the cry of the *Muezzin* rocks the Turk in his fatal torpor'.[84]

The ambitions openly expressed by Nationalist propagandists were shared by many Italian officials, especially in the Ministry of Colonies, which had only been established after the Libyan War and which was anxious now to justify its existence. Gaspare Colosimo, Minister of Colonies from 1916 to 1919, had the most extensive ambitions for Italian gains not only in Africa (for example, in Ethiopia and in the German, Portuguese and Belgian colonies), but also in Asia Minor and in Yemen and other Arab lands bordering the Red Sea.[85] Sonnino was more cautious but, in April 1917, at St Jean de Maurienne, he did pressure the Allies, not altogether ingenuously, into offering Italy Konia and Smyrna, an offer irreconcilable with previous Allied distribution in the Sykes–Picot agreement of February 1916.[86] The offer of Smyrna meant that, once again, rather as in the negotiation of the southern Albanian border at the London

Conference in 1913, Italy had had it conceded that her Great Power interests be recognised as superior to those of the Small Power, Greece.

St Jean de Maurienne was another moment, too, in which Italy was scarcely treated with absolute loyalty and frankness by her allies. In Britain, there is some evidence of a deliberate intention to embroil Italy with France.[87] What is absolutely plain, then and later, is that the Great Powers were easily aroused to irritation by Italian pretensions, and could allow themselves a greater insincerity towards Italy with the comfortable justification that it was Italy which was at fault for having any Mediterranean ambitions at all. As Arthur Balfour sighed in lordly fashion in June 1919: 'The Italians must be mollified, and the only question is how to mollify them at the smallest cost to humanity.' Sonnino had scarcely assisted the Italian case by arguing, characteristically, for a special role in Palestine since Italy, he declared, was 'both a Catholic and a Moslem country'.[88]

St Jean de Maurienne was thus a hollow triumph for Sonnino. The extent of the failure was rapidly apparent since the treaty needed Russian ratification, and this Russia did not give. Instead, the Bolshevik government took pleasure, after November 1917, in publishing the various secret agreements made between the Powers over Turkey and elsewhere, and particularly embarrassed the Italian government by revealing how frequently offers made to Italy were irreconcilable with offers made to other states.

By the time the peacemakers assembled at Versailles, both domestic events in Italy and the unsettled situation in Asia Minor, and especially the general crisis of Italian diplomacy combined to force Italy back, once again, into what really mattered most to her, that is, her ambitions in the Adriatic and about her borders with the successor states to the Habsburg Empire. The embattled Turkish leadership also had good reason to regard Italy as the least of their problems. It was entirely predictable that Carlo Sforza, arriving in Constantinople as Italian High Commissioner on 13 November 1918, should find a general ignorance there about Italy's 'victories'.[89]

Italo-Turkish relations were thus only a minor aspect of the complicated treatying of 1919, all the more since Britain and France, in October 1918, had declared that St Jean de Maurienne was invalid, given the lack of Russian ratification.[90] Instead, it was the Greeks who won greater sympathy for their ethnically more justifiable ambitions in Asia Minor, and indeed, in May 1919, they were secretly encouraged to occupy Smyrna to forestall any Italian move there.[91] By 29 July, Italian weakness had become so great that Tittoni, who had returned as Foreign Minister, pledged to hand over all the Dodecanese to Greece. Only Rhodes would be retained, and even that might be ceded after a referendum.

The Treaty of Sèvres, signed on 10 August 1920, still held out the hope for Italy of territorial or economic participation in a mandated Asia Minor, but the Treaty was no sooner initialled than it became a dead letter. The new nationalist Turkey of Kemal Atatürk would not accept destruction by the Great

Powers. In the face of Turkish resistance, Italian troops, which had still been stationed in garrisons on the mainland, withdrew from Adalia in June 1921.[92] By then Italy, somewhat gleefully, could watch the collapse of the Greek Empire in Asia Minor, and the accompanying humiliation of Greece's Franco-British sponsors. The Nationalist, Luigi Federzoni, detected in Asia Minor the reality of 'historic energies' which could not be suppressed as Kemal won over 'Greek pseudo-imperialism'.[93] Italian politicians, too, remembered that Greek weakness meant that the Dodecanese need not be surrendered after all and, in July 1923, Italy's ownership of the islands was finally recognised.[94] By then Italian leaders were already dreaming again, as once had San Giuliano, that the islands would be a 'base for new expansion . . . in the eastern Mediterranean'. Victory would need long planning, but the contest must be engaged in since a Darwinian 'struggle of the peoples' would always continue.[95]

The illusions of Fascism were sillier and more perilous than those of Liberal Italy. But by the time Fascism could lead Italy towards disaster the Ottoman Empire was dead. In its last moment, Italo-Ottoman relations retained a suitably bathetic point of contact. The last sultan, the powerless Mehmed VI Vahdettin, on 16 November 1922, had gone into exile to Malta in a British cruiser. But, shortly after, he transferred himself, for 'the comfortable seat of his permanent exile, to San Remo'.[96] Italy's economy, even under Fascism, gained more from tourism than it did from speculation in the Near East.

Italy had been one of the Great Powers under whose financial, political and even military blows the Ottoman Empire had finally collapsed. Italy by herself was not the cause of the collapse. Rather, that Italy was able and willing to participate in that collapse was symptomatic of the state of the Concert of the Great Powers not only in the eastern Mediterranean but also in Europe as a whole.

Notes: Chapter 3

Abbreviations

ACS   Archivio Centrale dello Stato
AS MAE   Archivio storico, Ministero degli affari esteri
DDI   *I documenti diplomatici italiani*
FO   Foreign Office records, Public Record Office, London
GP   *Die Grosse Politik der Europaischen Kabinette, 1871–1914*, ed. Johannes Lepsius, A. Mendelssohn-Bartholdy and Friedrich Thimme, 40 vols (Berlin, 1922–7)

1   C. Ciano, *Ciano's Diary, 1937–1938*, ed. A. Mayor (London, 1952), p. 129.
2   D. C. Blaisdell, *European Financial Control in the Ottoman Empire* (New York, 1929), p. 2. See also Ahmad, above, p. 24.
3   Stanford and E. K. Shaw, *History of the Ottoman Empire and Modern Turkey*, Vol. II (Cambridge/New York, 1977), p. 229.
4   F. E. Manuel, 'The Palestine Question in Italian diplomacy, 1917–1920', *Journal of Modern History*, Vol. XXVII, no. 3 (1955), p. 274.
5   Blaisdell, *European Financial Control*, pp. 121–2.

6   J.-L. Miège, *L'Imperialisme colonial italien de 1870 à nos jours* (Paris, 1968), pp. 16–17; C. Masi, 'L'Italia e il Levante nella storia politica e diplomatica contemporanea (1815–1934)', in T. Sillani (ed.), *L'Italia e il Levante* (Rome, 1934), p. 45.

7   U. Spadoni, 'Linee di navigazione e costruzioni navali alla vigilia dell'inchiesta parlamentare sulla marina mercantile italiana (1881–2)', *Nuova Rivista Storica*, Vol. LVII, nos. 3–4 (1973), pp. 319–21, 371; R. Webster, *L'imperialismo industriale italiano 1908–1915* (Turin, 1974), pp. 296–300, notes that in July 1913 over 18 million lire out of a total state subvention of almost 20 million went on lines to the Adriatic and eastern Mediterranean.

8   Miège, *L'Imperialisme*, pp. 81–2; R. Bachi, *L'Italia economica nell'anno 1915* (Città di Castello, 1916).

9   V. Mantegazza, *Italiani in Oriente: Eraclea* (Rome, 1922).

10 V. Mantegazza, *L'altra sponda* (Milan, 1906), pp. 21, 513–14; and *La Turchia liberale e le questioni balcaniche* (Milan, 1908), pp. xiv–xxi.

11 Masi, 'L'Italia', p. 64; R. F. Foerster, *The Italian Emigration of Our Times* (Cambridge, Mass., 1919), pp. 210–16.

12 A. Lyttelton (ed.), *Italian Fascisms from Pareto to Gentile* (London, 1973), p. 211.

13 Masi, 'L'Italia', p. 70.

14 For further detail, see R. J. B. Bosworth, *Italy, the Least of the Great Powers* (Cambridge, 1979), pp. 344–6.

15 L. Ganapini, *Il nazionalismo cattolico* (Bari, 1970), pp. 55–62; G. B. Scalabrini, *Trent'anni di apostolato: memorie e documenti*, ed. A. Scalabrini (Rome, 1909).

16 R. Tritonj, 'La questione dei Luoghi Santi', in Sillani, *L'Italia e il Levante*, pp. 119–120.

17 Masi, 'L'Italia', p. 78.

18 Manuel, 'The Palestine Question', p. 272.

19 A. Caroleo, *Le banche cattoliche dalla prima guerra mondiale al Fascismo* (Milan, 1976); M. Degl'Innocenti, *Storia della cooperazione in Italia* (Rome, 1977).

20 R. Mori, 'La penetrazione pacifica italiana in Libia dal 1907 al 1911 e il Banco di Roma', *Rivista di studi politici internazionali*, Vol. XXIV, no. 1 (1957), pp. 102–18; A. D'Alessandro, 'Il Banco di Roma e la guerra di Libia', *Storia e Politica*, Vol. VII, no. 3 (1968), pp. 491–509.

21 Bosworth, *Italy*, pp. 139–41, 340–3.

22 It was Britain which, at the time, encouraged Italy to take what was legally Turkish territory around the Horn of Africa, notably at Massawa and Assab, and thus plant the seeds of the eventual colonies of Eritrea and Somaliland. See A. Ramm, 'Great Britain and the planting of Italian power in the Red Sea, 1868–1885', *English Historical Review*, Vol. LIX, no. 2 (1944), pp. 211–36; A. Del Boca, *Gli italiani in Africa Orientale* (Bari, 1976), pp. 171–92.

23 e.g. see P. Levi, *Missione nell'Africa settentrionale, giugno-luglio 1908* (Rome, 1908).

24 G. Licata, *Notabili della Terza Italia* (Rome, 1968), p. 317.

25 J. Wechsberg, *Verdi* (London, 1974), pp. 144–5.

26 Bosworth, *Italy*, pp. 346–52.

27 e.g. see the exotic story of one deal in R. J. B. Bosworth, 'The Albanian forests of Signor Giacomo Vismara', *Historical Journal*, Vol. XVIII, no. 3 (1975), pp. 571–86.

28 AS MAE, Archivio riservato, 5/205, 23 April 1911, San Giuliano to Avarna; Politica (hereafter P), 671/844, 9 June 1911, San Giuliano to Avarna.

29 A. F. Pribram, *The Secret Treaties of Austria-Hungary 1879–1914* (Cambridge, Mass., 1921–2), Vol. I, pp. 106–11.

30 Italy was a major importer of Romanian oil in 1913, holding fifth place behind Britain, France, Germany and Egypt. M. Pearton, *Oil and the Romanian State* (London, 1971), p. 44.

31 E. Corradini, *Discorsi politici* (Florence, 1925), p. 176.

32 D. Mack Smith, *Mussolini's Roman Empire* (London, 1976), p. 122; C. G. Segrè, *Fourth Shore* (Chicago, Ill., 1974).

33 The standard studies in Italian are F. Malgeri, *La guerra libica (1911–1912)* (Rome, 1970); P. Maltese, *La terra promessa: la guerra italo-turca e la conquista della Libia, 1911–1912* (Milan, 1968). In English see W. C. Askew, *Europe and Italy's Acquisition of Libya* (Durham, NC, 1942), and Bosworth, *Italy*, pp. 127–95.

34 ibid., p. 140.

35 e.g. L. Luzzatti, *Memorie* (Milan, 1966), Vol. III, p. 309.

36 F. Guicciardini, 'Impressioni d'Albania', *Nuova antologia*, no. 708, 1 July 1901, p. 25.

37 C. Zoli, *La guerra turco-bulgara* (Milan, 1913), pp. 13, 26.

38 e.g. G. Mosca, *The Ruling Class* (New York, 1939), pp. 140, 181.

39   e.g. see G. Piazza, *La nostra terra promessa* (Rome, 1911); E. Corradini, *L'ora di Tripoli* (Milan, 1911).
40   Minute on 5 October 1908, Egerton to Grey, FO 371/551/35042. On Bosnia and Herzegovina see also Bridge, above, pp. 37–8.
41   For biographical details, see Bosworth, *Italy*, pp. 68–94.
42   M. Abrate, *Ricerche per la storia dell'organizzazione sindacale dell'industria in Italia* (Turin, 1966), p. 151; Webster, *L'imperialismo*, pp. 102–7, 271.
43   Bosworth, *Italy*, pp. 60–2; L. Vannutelli, 'Nella Turchia Asiatica', *Bollettino della Società Geografica Italiana*, 4th series, Vol. 8, March 1907, pp. 201–29.
44   C. Seton-Watson, *Italy from Liberalism to Fascism* (London, 1967), p. 314.
45   Segrè, *Fourth Shore*, p. 14.
46   A. Del Boca, *Gli italiani*, p. 752.
47   Cited by Malgeri, *La guerra libica*, pp. 98–9.
48   Mack Smith, *Mussolini's Roman Empire*, p. 37.
49   S. Bono, 'Lettere dal fronte libico (1911–1912)', *Nuova antologia*, no. 2052, December 1971, pp. 530–1.
50   F. Grassi, *Il tramonto dell'età giolittiana nel Salento* (Bari, 1973), pp. 17–20. It is reported also that in the 1950s local villagers in Apulia hated and detested the sea-shore, because they still feared, somewhere in their souls, the return of Turkish or Barbary raiders. A. L. Maraspini, *The Story of an Italian village* (Paris, 1968), p. 56.
51   See recorded collection on disc, O. Profazio, *L'Altra Spoleto* (Turin, 1975).
52   ACS, Carte Giolitti, 15/25, 2 October 1911, Avarna to Giolitti; 20/47, 8 October 1911, San Giuliano to Avarna. See also Bridge, above, pp. 41–2.
53   Bosworth, *Italy*, pp. 181–3.
54   ibid., pp. 299–399; see also R. J. Bosworth, 'Britain and Italy's acquisition of the Dodecanese 1912–1915', *Historical Journal*, Vol. XIII, no. 4 (1970), pp. 683–705.
55   ACS, Carte Giolitti, 22/59, C/5, 29 June 1912, Pollio *pro memoria*.
56   For some comment in English, see J. Whittam, *The Politics of the Italian Army* (London, 1977).
57   ACS, Carte Giolitti, 21/48/2, 6 August 1912, Giolitti to San Giuliano.
58   Bosworth, *Italy*, p. 342; A. Theodoli, 'La preparazione dell'impresa di Tripoli: ricordi di una missione in Turchia', *Nuova antologia*, no. 1496, 16 July 1934, pp. 239–249.
59   ACS, Carte Giolitti, 18/43/9, 20 June 1912, Rodd to Grey.
60   e.g. FO 371/2112/2179, 11 January 1914, Rodd to Grey.
61   Shaw, *History of the Ottoman Empire*, Vol. II, p. 278; C. Sforza, *L'Italia dal 1914 al 1944 quale io la vidi* (Milan, 1944), p. 109.
62   ACS, Presidenza del consiglio, gabinetto, atti, 9/2, 1 April 1913, Chief of General Staff, *pro memoria*.
63   S. Skendi, *The Albanian National Awakening* (Princeton, NJ, 1967), pp. 274–7. See also Bridge, above, pp. 40–1.
64   AS MAE, P, 3 August 1913, P. Levi memorandum.
65   For the mud content of that town, see A. I. Sulliotti, *In Albania: sei mesi di regno* (Milan, 1914), pp. 5, 144.
66   F. R. Bridge, '*Tarde venientibus ossa*: Austro-Hungarian colonial aspirations in Asia Minor, 1913–14', *Middle Eastern Studies*, Vol. VI (1970), pp. 319–30.
67   e.g. AS MAE, Archivio di gabinetto, 16/97 ter, 14 February 1913, San Giuliano memorandum.
68   ACS, Carte Giolitti, 22/59/D, 10 September 1913, San Giuliano to Garroni.
69   Cited in Michael Llewellyn Smith, *Ionian Vision: Greece in Asia Minor 1919–22* (London, 1973), p. 68.
70   See D. McLean, 'British finance and foreign policy in Turkey: the Smyrna–Aidin railway settlement 1913–14', *Historical Journal*, Vol. XIX, no. 3 (1976), pp. 521–30.
71   AS MAE, Archivio di gabinetto, 17/106, 3 February 1914, San Giuliano to Imperiali.
72   ibid., P, 160/17, 24 June 1913, Garroni to San Giuliano.
73   *GP*, Vol. 37, pt 2, no. 15049, 1 June 1913, Flotow to Bethmann Hollweg; McLean, 'British Finance', p. 527.
74   ACS, Presidenza del consiglio, gabinetto, atti, 9/1, 21 January 1913, San Giuliano to Giolitti; AS MAE, Archivio di gabinetto, 29/402, 23 January 1913, San Giuliano to Garroni.
75   Ahmed Emin, *Turkey in the World War* (New Haven, Conn./Oxford, 1930), pp. 86–9.

76 R. Bachi, *L'Italia economica nell'anno 1913* (Città di Castello, 1914), p. 37.
77 L. Franchetti, *Mezzogiorno e colonie*, ed. U. Zanotti-Bianco (Florence, 1950), p. lxxxii; 'L'Italia e L'Asia Minore', *Nuova antologia*, no. 1087, 1 May 1917, pp. 109–13.
78 Bosworth, *Italy*, pp. 249–51, 369–92.
79 *DDI*, 4s, xii, 225, 14 July 1914, San Giuliano to Bollati.
80 AS MAE, P, 168/17, 5 August 1914, Carletti to Garroni. Italian trade (e.g. in textile exports and food imports) was soon feeling the pinch. See R. Bachi, *L'Italia economica nell'anno 1915* (Città di Castello, 1916), pp. 23–5, 46.
81 e.g. M. Toscano, 'Le origini diplomatiche dell'art. 9 del patto di Londra relativo agli eventuali compensi all 'Italia in Asia Minore', *Storia e Politica*, Vol. IV, no. 3 (1965), pp. 339–84; 'Imperiali e il negoziato per il patto di Londra', *Storia e Politica*, Vol. VII, no. 2 (1968), pp. 177–205.
82 Toscano, 'Le origini diplomatiche dell'art. 9', p. 364.
83 Masi, 'L'Italia', pp. 88–9.
84 G. A. Rosso, *I diritti d'Italia oltremare* (Rome, 1916), p. 113; L. Medici Del Vascello, *Per l'Italia* (Bari, 1916), p. 185.
85 G. Colosimo, *Opera* (Naples, 1959), pp. 95–120, 127–8.
86 See M. Toscano, *Gli accordi di San Giovanni di Moriana* (Milan, 1936).
87 Jukka Nevakivi, *Britain, France and the Arab Middle East 1914–1920* (London, 1969), pp. 54–5.
88 Manuel, 'The Palestine Question', pp. 265–70, 275.
89 *DDI*, 6s, i, 142, 13 November 1918, Sforza to Sonnino.
90 R. Albrecht-Carrié, *Italy at the Paris Peace Conference* (Hamden, Conn., 1966), p. 207.
91 Llewellyn Smith, *Ionian Vision*, p. 79.
92 Masi, 'L'Italia', p. 103.
93 L. Federzoni, *Presagi alla nazione* (Milan, 1924), p. 340. See also Kent, below, pp. 191–3.
94 Britain was far from reconciled to the event. Harold Nicolson explained in a minute that, however, nothing could be done 'until that remote day when Italian public men learn the meaning of self-respect', FO 371/8822/C13383/4/19, 4 August 1923.
95 Federzoni, *Presagi*, pp. 340–1.
96 Shaw, *History of the Ottoman Empire*, Vol. II, p. 365.

4 Russia and the End of the Ottoman Empire

Alan Bodger, University College of Swansea

For Russia the Congress of Berlin plunged the Eastern Question into a diplomatic stalemate that lasted until 1907. During that time Russia's military, economic and political difficulties compelled her to pursue a conservative policy towards the Ottoman Empire. From the renewal of the Three Emperors' League in 1881, through the alignment with France in the 1890s, down to the Anglo-Russian *rapprochement* of 1907, Russia worked in harmony with the Concert Powers – especially Austria – to preserve the *status quo* in the Ottoman Empire. The active focus of her foreign policy switched from the Balkans and the Near East to Persia and the Far East, with the war against Japan and the subsequent revolution absorbing most of her attention between 1904 and 1906.[1]

Not that the traditional 'historic tasks' of the Eastern Question had been forgotten or forsworn. Control over the Straits, national statehood for the Balkan Christian peoples, and ascendant political influence throughout the region remained the ultimate goals of Russian policy.[2] But these very long-term, elusive – even utopian – targets had to be stalked with ever greater caution and patience. Broadly speaking, Russia could pursue these ends in three ways: by the use of force, by diplomatic combination with the Powers, or by alliance with the Porte itself. The events of 1877–8 had emphasised once again, and with unparalleled clarity, that the issues involved were inextricably intertwined, of general European concern and incapable of solution simply by Russian pressure against the Porte. Successive diplomatic alignments, first with the Central Powers, then with France, brought some security but no unequivocal or lasting support for Russia's eventual aims in a region where all the Powers cherished important interests.[3] Bismarck's acknowledgement of Russia's right to seize Constantinople and the Straits should Turkey collapse ended with the demise of the Reinsurance Treaty in 1890. From then on Germany was concerned to deflect Russian ambition to the Far East.[4] From 1894, Russia's new ally, France, sought to strengthen Russia's presence on Germany's eastern borders, rather than to encourage her ambitions in the Near East.[5] By the end of the century Britain, Russia's traditional opponent in the Eastern Question, may no longer have considered the Ottoman Empire as worthy and capable of indefinite preservation or that the Royal Navy could prevent a Russian descent on the Bosporus, but this implied no slackening of Anglo-Russian hostility as Russian expansionism gained momentum in Persia and China.[6] The third stratagem, a Russo-Turkish *rapprochement* as briefly achieved against Napoleon in 1797 and 1805, or at Unkiar Skelessi in 1833, was kept alive by the sultan's resentment of Western tutelage and his natural desire to play off Power against Power, but remained highly unlikely on account of ineradicable and well-founded Turkish russophobia. Russia's determined hostility to all schemes for Ottoman economic and military rejuvenation also inevitably hampered close Russo-Turkish understanding.[7]

For the time being Russia had to prevent any reopening of the Eastern Question until she was strong enough to secure her own interests against the encroachments of third parties should the Ottoman Empire fall. This entailed maintaining the sultan's shaky authority while obstructing all serious measures of reform and attempting to counter the growing influence of other Powers at the Porte.[8] Early in the nineteenth century it had already become an axiom of Russian policy that the preservation of a weak Turkey under predominantly Russian influence would be preferable to its dissolution and partition.[9] With the growth of foreign financial and political intervention in Ottoman affairs since Berlin, the emergence of Austria-Hungary as a Balkan power, the strengthening of the British presence in the Near East, the dramatic awakening of German interests in Turkey, and the expanding national pretensions of the Balkan states this axiom now commanded special respect.[10]

Commitment to the Slav Christian cause in the Balkans still stirred strong emotions among sections of the Russian public and officialdom, but after Berlin strains and tensions appeared between Russia and her Balkan clients, and following the rift with Bulgaria in the mid-1880s the Balkans took a decidedly subordinate place in Russia's Turkish policy.[11] Russia was content to co-operate with Austria in maintaining the *status quo* and in urging moderate reforms on the sultan so as to lessen the risk of upheavals and inevitable outside intervention. This policy found its expression in the Muraviev–Goluchowski agreement of 1897 which also affirmed the 'eminently European character of the question of the Straits and Constantinople', thus placing the Balkans 'on ice' for the next decade.[12] Russia helped to keep Serbia and Bulgaria out of the Greco-Turkish war over Crete in 1896–7 and worked with the Powers to bring the belligerents to a negotiated settlement. During the Armenian crisis of 1896, Russia backed the authority of the sultan against attempts by Britain to extend international intervention on behalf of the Armenians and refused to coerce the sultan into radical reforms, such as the establishment of an autonomous Armenian region in eastern Anatolia. In this question Russian concern to underwrite the Ottoman Empire was fortified by the fear of Armenian revolutionary activity in her own Transcaucasian territories.[13]

Without doubt, the real focal point of Russian economic, political and strategic interests in the Ottoman Empire lay at the Straits. These 'keys and gates to the Russian house' lay on the axis of the overland communications between Europe and Asia, commanded the approaches to the shores of Russian possessions around the Black Sea, gave access to the Mediterranean for

Russian commerce, and formed a natural pivot for the exercise of potential political influence in the Balkans. They guarded Constantinople, the cradle of Russian culture and the object of dreams of reconquest among Russians as for Greeks and Bulgars. They were open to all genuine commercial shipping, but closed by international agreement to all non-Turkish warships in time of peace.[14]

In theory, possession of the Straits and the right for Russian warships to pass the Straits was Russia's undisputed goal.[15] In practice, however, it was her policy after Berlin to abide by and uphold the principle of the closure of the Straits to warships. The Russian government interpreted this as a mutually binding obligation of all the Concert Powers and not – as Lord Salisbury claimed for Britain – a set of bilateral agreements with the sultan.[16] Closure was of great value to Russia in view of her military and naval weakness on the Black Sea. Banned after the Crimean War from maintaining a Black Sea Fleet and shore fortresses, Russia did not regain this right until 1871 and only began the slow reconstruction of her Black Sea Fleet from 1883. Although committed to this clearly defensive view of the Straits Question, the Russian government was nevertheless adamant that under no circumstances could it permit the Straits to pass under the control of a third state.[17] Consequently, whenever Ottoman collapse seemed imminent and unavoidable it was natural that contingency plans for a pre-emptive seizure of the Straits, or at least the Bosporus, should be discussed in St Petersburg. In 1882, 1892 and 1896, A. I. Nelidov, the Russian Ambassador in Constantinople, initiated such discussions. Although in 1896 he received imperial authority to summon a Russian strike-force from Sevastopol and Odessa in an emergency, Russia's forces – troops, transports and warships – were so clearly inadequate for the task that no serious preparations could be made.[18] It cannot be argued that such contingency plans signified any real change in Russia's determination to prevent premature Ottoman disintegration and partition or to uphold the current Straits regime. In 1897, Foreign Minister Muraviev reminded his new Ambassador in Constantinople, I. A. Zinoviev, that, while he should not lose sight of Russia's 'great mission' in the Near East and the extreme importance of the Straits, this was 'no longer the issue of the moment' and had to be 'postponed until Russia was in a position to concentrate all her energies upon it'.[19]

Early in 1900 the principal Russian ministers, reviewing Russia's foreign-policy prospects throughout Asia, agreed with the War Minister, General A. N. Kuropatkin, that seizure of the Bosporus was 'Russia's most important task in the twentieth century', but clearly took to heart the grave warning of the Finance Minister, Count S. Y. Witte, that this was inconceivable outside the context of a general European war – the last thing for which Russia was prepared in view of her internal political and economic difficulties and her imperial commitments. The Navy and War Ministers stressed Russia's total inability to mount any kind of action against the Bosporus in the foreseeable future.[20]

In this exchange of views the feature of the Near Eastern scene which most disturbed the ministers was the rapid development of German interests in the Ottoman Empire, specifically the Baghdad Railway scheme.[21] It was Russia's policy to prolong the backwardness and isolation of the eastern Anatolian plateau as a defensive glacis covering her volatile and vulnerable Trans-caucasian territories, as a barrier to European economic and political competition in Persia (which Russia at that time hoped to convert into a satellite), and – optimistically – as an exclusive highway for future economic penetration to the Levant. The railway, then, threatened Russia's economic, strategic and political aims throughout the region, as well as offering a clear German challenge to Russian influence at the Straits. Germany was warned that she 'could never be allowed to play a dominant role on the banks of the Bosporus', but that Russia would have no objection to Germany's purely economic interests in Anatolia.[22] The German government declined to con-clude a formal agreement with Russia along these lines, but persuaded the Turks to direct the route of the line southwards, away from the Russian frontier and the eastern Black Sea coast. Zinoviev then obtained the sultan's agreement not to grant concessions for railway construction north of a line between Kaiseri, Diarbekir, Sivas and Kharput to any foreign company. This agreement, similar to one imposed on the Shah of Persia in 1890 and valid for ten years, effectively 'sterilised' this buffer zone against the encroachments of railways for more than a decade.[23]

For the next six years Russia was preoccupied with events in the Far East and with revolution at home. She maintained her co-operation with Austria in Macedonia, but the programme of moderate reforms drawn up at Mürzsteg in 1903 was only dilatorily implemented by the Turks.[24] The Straits Question was not seriously raised during those years. The sultan gave occasional *firmans* (edicts or special licences of the sultan) for the passage of the Straits by vessels of the Russian Volunteer Fleet – dual-purpose privateer transports – but, even at the height of the war against Japan, Russia continued to observe the closure of the Straits. The Black Sea Fleet was thus penned in and condemned to inactivity, but also saved from virtually certain destruction.[25] In 1905, Russian Straits policy was expressed in a memorandum by Baron Taube, a member of the Council of the Foreign Ministry, who argued that Russia's interests called for the closure of the Straits 'for many years yet'. When the time was ripe for change he recommended that Russia should work to combine the principle of closure with the exclusive right of passage for her own warships. The opening of the Straits to all could only be countenanced were Russia to possess a really powerful Black Sea Fleet, if foreign naval bases were banned from the Black Sea, and if the Straits were unfortified.[26]

Russia's humiliating defeat by Japan was followed by the revolution of 1905, which compelled the Tsar to set up a consultative quasi-parliament, the Duma, and also dictated a radical realignment in foreign policy. The new Minister of Foreign Affairs, A. P. Izvolskii, insisted that Russia settle her rivalry with

Britain and Japan for ascendancy in Central Asia and the Far East in order once again to devote her full attention to the area of real importance to Russia – the Near East, where the *status quo* seemed gravely imperilled by German expansion, by Austro-Serbian friction following the Karageorgevich *coup* in 1903 and by the upsurge of Greek, Serbian and Bulgarian terrorism in Macedonia.[27] An agreement with Japan settling spheres of influence in the Far East in July 1907 was followed in August by the convention with Britain covering Persia, Afghanistan and Tibet.[28] Izvolskii's move towards Britain, following the intensification of Franco-Russian relations by a big loan secured in 1906 to tide the government over the aftermath of revolution, was strongly resisted by influential circles in the court, the military and civil bureaucracy and the more conservative landowning nobility. These groups believed that a restoration of the alliance of the three east European monarchies would lead to a more effective suppression of revolutionary and liberal forces.[29] The sheer impossibility of carrying on the old struggle with Britain, however, the encroachments of the Central Powers on Russia's traditional interests, the need for French and British support if this menace were to be countered, and the increased financial dependence on France all carried the day for Izvolskii in the Special Conference set up to debate this decision.[30] The pro-Entente orientation was also strongly supported by public opinion, expressing the interests of the broad landowning nobility, the commercial, industrial and professional middle classes represented in the Duma by the moderate right Octobrist Party and the Constitutional Democrats.[31] It is important to note that Izvolskii gambled heavily on being able to placate the pro-German lobby and maintain good relations with Germany despite this drift towards the Entente. He hoped to regain the freedom to manoeuvre between Berlin, Vienna, Paris and London and not to be forced into an encirclement of Germany – Russia's strongest and most dangerous neighbour, her first trading partner and a country whose military and political traditions and values had such influential admirers in Russia.[32] He hoped to arrive at a new understanding with Austria-Hungary over the Balkans which would reflect the changes in the political situation there since 1897. His plan thus to restore Russia to the ranks of the Great Powers was frustrated by the increasing polarisation of the two alliance systems which found Russia too weak and dependent on her Entente partners to avoid being drawn into their orbit.[33] It is as a not fully independent power that we must see her policies affecting the Porte in this period, but before considering the fate of these policies something must be said about the way Russian foreign policy and diplomacy were determined and executed, and the nature of Russian interests in the Ottoman Empire between 1907 and 1914.[34]

Since Russia remained an autocracy after the introduction of the Duma the Tsar was still theoretically the sole arbiter of foreign policy. Article 12 of the new Fundamental Laws affirmed the emperor's prerogative as the 'supreme director of the external relations of the Russian state'.[35] The Minister of Foreign Affairs was the executor of the Tsar's will. Having no formal responsibility to the Council of Ministers and the Council of State, and providing he enjoyed the Tsar's confidence, he had, in fact, considerable freedom in the initiation of policy.[36] The favourite way of arriving at decisions in a difficult case, however, was by the Tsar's convening an *ad hoc* Special Conference comprising interested ministers and other relevant specialists.[37] The Duma was allowed to discuss foreign policy only once a year, when reviewing the annual budget. Less than 1 per cent of the Duma's time was spent on foreign affairs, and the two Foreign Ministers of the period, A. P. Izvolskii (1906–10) and S. D. Sazonov (1910–16), were authorised to report to the Duma on only five occasions between 1906 and 1914.[38] This absence of formal constitutional control over foreign policy gives the impression that policy was formulated arbitrarily, reflecting not the 'national interest' but the narrow concerns of state and dynasty. However, in most states foreign policy differed from that of domestic policy by being more arcane and less under constitutional control. Russia differed mainly in degree. The Tsar and his ministers operated within a framework of historical, geographical, economic, military and political constraints, and pursued objectives related to what they perceived as the 'national interest' in much the same way as other governments.[39] With the hindsight of history some of their perceptions may seem to have been misguided – for example, the obsession with naval power, the emotional attachment to the south Slav cause, the yearning for the Straits and Constantinople, Russia's estrangement from the Central Powers, even her general pretensions to Great Power status – but there is no evidence that these errors would have been avoided if the Duma and public opinion had played a more active formal role in foreign policy. On the contrary, these policies would most probably have been pursued more enthusiastically.[40] In practice the ministers managed the Duma by balancing between the extreme Right on the one hand and the moderate Right, Octobrist and Constitutional Democrat parties on the other. These last represented the interests and views of the broad landowning, commercial, industrial and professional classes. Without their political support the government would have been trapped between the forces of reaction and revolution; peaceful economic progress would have been impossible.[41] More harmful was the lack of formal collaboration and collective responsibility among ministers and ambassadors.[42] Izvolskii, energetic, creative and strong-minded, used his freedom to the full, even concluding the agreement at Buchlau with his Austrian counterpart Aehrenthal behind his fellow-ministers' backs.[43] Sazonov's character made its mark on Russian policy by the vacillations and contradictions with which he tried to solve the Balkan tangle.[44] I. A. Zinoviev, the ambassador at the Porte between 1897 and 1909, played a very important part in the actual formulation of policy in the Near East, especially in Macedonia.[45] His successor, N. V. Charykov (1909–12), was notable for his pro-Turkish sympathies, his scheme for a Turco-Slav Balkan alliance and his attempt to open the Straits in 1911 by a Russo-Turkish *rapprochement*.[46] M. N. Giers, on the other hand, who succeeded him and was the Russian minister at the Porte from 1911 to 1914, was more conservative and *protocollaire*, and could hardly make any impression on the growth of German influence at the Porte, let alone create policy.[47] The scope for independent action a vigorous, self-willed ambassador could enjoy was clearly demonstrated by Hartwig's activities in Belgrade during the period. He identified himself with Serbian aims and made and carried out Serbian rather than official Russian policy, completely sabotaging Sazonov's efforts to preserve the Balkan alliance.[48] Russian consuls in the Ottoman Empire, on the other hand, played a very small role. It was their unenviable lot to try to reconcile the conflicting responsibilities of the official Russian policy of support for the integrity of the Ottoman Empire with their role as protectors of the subject Christian population. They were rarely kept informed of current negotiations and played no economic role owing to the paucity of Russia's commercial interests in the Empire.[49]

Such lack of cohesion and consistency in Russian policy was disastrous, but the range of virtually irreconcilable problems facing Russia would have defied the ingenuity of a government far more sophisticated, well articulated and far-sighted than that of the backward, ill-co-ordinated and almost ungovernable Russian Empire.[50]

In the twentieth century Russia's basic interests in the Ottoman Empire underwent considerable modification. In the previous century the problem of the Straits and Constantinople was mainly a political and strategic one. The economic aspect resided in the growing importance to the Russian economy of the exports of agricultural produce to Europe, the beginnings of industrialisation in the Ukraine, and the appearance of the oil industry in Baku. But this interest had been more or less adequately protected by the international treaties safeguarding free commercial navigation through the Straits in time of peace, and by the general stability in the Near East following the Congress of Berlin. The automatic closure of the Straits to Russian trade was the known price Russia would have to pay for any seriously hostile action against the Porte. The matter was thus largely in Russia's own hands. But with renewed instability throughout the region from the 1890s navigation through the Straits was increasingly put at risk. The Straits might now be closed owing to a variety of circumstances quite beyond Russia's control. It was this that helped to convince Izvolskii (and indeed his predecessor Lamsdorff) and most Russian opinion representing the industrial and commercial agricultural interest that Russia had to abandon the principle of the closure of the Straits and try to find ways of having them opened to Russian warships for the protection of trade.[51] To solve this problem became the definitive aim of Russian foreign policy down to the war.[52] Initially, Izvolskii hoped to achieve it by diplomatic means, first with the support of Britain following the Anglo-Russian *rapprochement* of 1907, then via the bilateral agreement with Austria arranged at Buchlau in 1908.[53] These having failed, Charykov tried to secure the opening of the Straits via a direct Russo-Turkish *rapprochement* in 1911.[54] When this, too, failed it was not perhaps surprising that the initiative passed into the hands of the navy, with their close connections with the interested sections of Russian industry and agriculture, and led to their grandiose plans for outright conquest of the Straits and even the creation of a Russian High Seas Fleet capable of protecting Russian commerce throughout the world.[55]

As the security of commercial navigation through the Straits became more precarious, so their economic importance to Russia grew. Grain exports had begun to be important from the second half of the nineteenth century, but by the end of the century they had come to be one of the key elements in the desperate drive for modernisation and industrialisation inaugurated by Finance Minister Vyshnegradskii in the 1880s and brought to a coherent, self-conscious grand strategy by his successor, Count S. Y. Witte, in the following decade.[56] For Russia to elevate herself from the status of a semi-colonial appendage of Europe and become an independent Great Power she had to change from a backward agrarian country to a modern industrial one.[57] This could only be done by importing foreign capital, principally from her ally France, in the form of loans and investments. These depended on Russia's financial stability, which in turn depended largely on her ability to maintain a positive balance on her foreign trade account. This surplus would also contribute to the formation of Russian domestic capital and lead eventually to a lessening of dependence on foreign investments.[58] Russia's chief marketable resource was grain and other agricultural products. Thus, the forced export of grain became a major plank of the government's economic strategy: 'We must export even if we starve,' decreed Vyshnegradskii, and this policy continued under Witte and in a milder form down to 1914. Between 1900 and 1913 grain comprised about a half of all Russian exports, and between 75 and 90 per cent of all grain, varying annually, went through the Straits.[59] An additional impulse to Black Sea grain exports lay in the growing obstacles to the expansion of Russian grain exports to Germany and the hopes of finding 'an almost limitless' market in Britain and western Europe. This was an important factor in the growing pro-British orientation of the bulk of Russian grain-producers.[60]

As grain exports brought the indispensable foreign capital flowing in, the extractive and metallurgical industries of the Caucasus and the Ukraine began also to export their products (coal, manganese, oil) through the Straits.[61] All in all, between a half and a third of all Russian exports passed through the Straits between 1900 and 1909.[62] Machinery for these new industries was also imported by sea from the Mediterranean. By 1913 the volume of shipping passing the Straits came to about two-thirds of the tonnage using the Suez Canal.[63] Furthermore, as Germany came to dominate Russian trade, with 47.5 per cent of her total foreign trade by 1913, and became also Russia's most dangerous commercial rival in the Near East, the value of the Straits as an independent access to the markets of the world and her Entente partners grew accordingly.[64]

The developing southern regions of Russia supplied 87 per cent of her coal (excluding Polish production), 74 per cent of her pig iron, 63 per cent of her steel, 66 per cent of her sugar, 60 per cent of her flour and 90 per cent of her oil by 1913. Georgia was one of only three sources of manganese in the world.[65] Almost a third of the whole population of the Empire was concentrated around the Black Sea basin on the eve of the war.[66] It was therefore not surprising that Russia's government, industrial and landowning interests should have been so impressed by the extreme vulnerability of this whole region to a blockade of the Straits. The very existence of Russia's key economic factors was at risk.[67] Their fears were confirmed in 1911 and again in 1912 when the Straits were briefly closed during the Italo-Turkish war. On the first occasion grain began to pile up rapidly at Russian ports, prices fell by 15–20 per cent, freight charges rose accordingly. The banks stopped handling bills of exchange, and the Ministry of Trade and Industry was flooded with panic appeals for help from local authorities and merchants. The second closure was more serious and led to the reduction of the trade balance of 1912 by 100,000,000 roubles and a 1–1½ per cent increase in the bank rate.[68] In a report to the Tsar of November 1913, Sazonov pointed to the potential gravity of a seizure of the Straits by a state less responsive to Russian pressure than Turkey.[69]

Compared with the 300,000,000–400,000,000 roubles' worth of exports passing the Straits annually between 1908 and 1913, Russian trade in the Ottoman Empire itself was minuscule.[70] Between 1901 and 1913, Russian exports to Turkey rose from 21,000,000 to 35,000,000 roubles, or to about 2½ per cent of all Russian exports. Turkish exports to Russia were only 18,000,000 roubles in 1913.[71] In 1910–11 Russia had only 6 per cent of the foreign trade of Turkey, behind Britain (22 per cent), Austria (16 per cent), France (13 per cent), Germany (9 per cent) and even Italy (8½ per cent). By 1913, Russia had managed just to overtake Italy (8.3 per cent against 6 per cent).[72] Russia's share of Balkan trade was even smaller. In 1909 she provided only 2.7 per cent of Romanian, 3.9 per cent of Bulgarian and 2.4 per cent of Serbian imports.[73]

There was, then, a startling disproportion between the insignificance of Russia's actual trade with the Ottoman Empire and the Balkans and the magnitude of her sense of 'historic mission'. Her main economic interest in the Ottoman Empire was a life-line which could be cut with ludicrous ease and was therefore a source of great weakness rather than a source of political power or influence. It also revealed Russia's backwardness as a Great Power. Her chief exports were those of an undeveloped agrarian country for which there was not much of a market in the equally agrarian lands of the Near East. Witte and the other advocates of industrialisation aimed at transforming Russia into an industrial country capable of exporting manufactured goods which would dominate her natural markets along her Asiatic frontiers, but by 1913 manufactures still comprised only 5.6 per cent of all her exports, and their price and quality made them competitive only in markets naturally or artificially isolated from European competition.[74] The Baghdad Railway scheme and other plans for Turkish railway concessions eliminated Russian chances of creating such a market in Anatolia, but Russia was forced to come to terms with these developments between 1910 and 1913 owing to the pressures of her general international situation. The absence of real commercial interests in the Ottoman Empire had been frequently held up as a grave weakness in Russia's influence at the Porte by I. A. Zinoviev, but nothing positive was done until after the Russo-Japanese War.[75] In 1907 a branch of the Russian Foreign Trade Bank opened in Constantinople and commercial committees were set up at the consulates in Constantinople and Smyrna.[76] In the next few years criticism of the backwardness of Russia's trade in the Near East came from many quarters, including the navy, who were strongly influenced by modern ideas of economic imperialism and the struggle for foreign markets. One of the founder members of the Naval General Staff, A. N. Shcheglov, naval attaché in Constantinople in 1909, complained that 'now, when more than ever firm economic ties are the best conductors and bases of a realistic and genuinely national policy', there were in Turkey 'absolutely no Russian chambers of commerce, no commercial attachés, no trade exhibitions, no knowledge of the market or trade routes etc.'[77] The Russian government began slowly to awaken to the need for action. In 1909 a floating exhibition of Russian goods spent several days in Constantinople. It was visited by 70,000 people and attracted big orders for footware, railway sleepers and preserves.[78] In 1911 a joint commission of officials and business representatives toured the major coastal cities of the Ottoman Empire. Their report repeated the general criticism of Russian trade: poor credit, advertising, quality and knowledge of the market, and high prices (15–20 per cent above those of her rivals). Even established Russian exports were losing ground to German and Austrian goods. The only bright spot was the subsidised Russian Steamship Company, which dominated the carrying trade along the Black Sea coast.[79] The lack of correlation between Russia's political, strategic and economic interests was particularly glaring in the Armenian vilayets of eastern Anatolia. Both Russia and Turkey had done all they could in the past to retard the development of this remote and inhospitable plateau. There were no roads crossing the frontier, but a very small quantity of Russian goods were beginning to appear in Van vilayet from the Black Sea coast.[80]

Russia was uniquely handicapped among the Great Powers in having no capital investments, railway interests or concessions in the Ottoman Empire. She needed her meagre resources for her own vast backward land, and political and strategic considerations did not permit the application of the techniques of 'peaceful economic penetration' applied by Witte in Persia and Manchuria at the turn of the century. Russia was not represented on the Ottoman Public Debt Administration.[81] As a result, between 1881 and 1909 Russia had but one financial lever of influence at the Porte, the 1878 War Indemnity of 802,000,000 francs, which Turkey had to pay off at the rate of 8,000,000 francs a year. Russian ambassadors Nelidov and Zinoviev had allowed arrears to build up and then used these to block foreign loans to Turkey, to reduce the kilometric guarantee on the Baghdad Railway and to secure the Black Sea 'sterilisation' agreement of 1900. Witte successfully resisted French efforts to get the Indemnity merged into the Ottoman Public Debt, preferring to keep it as an independent lever. The Indemnity was finally used by Izvolskii to smooth the path of Bulgarian independence in 1909. Forty Turkish annuities were waived, thus reducing the debt by 125,000,000 francs, more than enough to compensate Turkey for the loss of the Bulgarian tribute, east Rumelian taxes and the loss of the Oriental Railway Company. In return Russia received the Bulgarian tribute, 85,000,000 francs over eighty-five years. Russia forwent 40,000,000 francs in what turned out to be a vain attempt to increase her influence in the Balkans.[82]

Just before the war Russia, under strong French pressure, was forced to modify her negative attitude to Turkish economic development in the hope of salvaging at least some crumbs of political influence. Gulkievich, councillor of the Russian embassy in Constantinople, wrote to Sazonov in 1913 that it was simply no longer possible to exert influence at the Porte by political pressure alone. Russian prestige could only be restored by developing her 'material interests' in Turkey.[83] In October 1913, the Russian government agreed to the 4 per cent tariff increase, to the revision of the 1900 railway agreement, and to the establishment of Turkish state monopolies in goods traditionally imported from Russia in return for a seat on the board of the Ottoman Public Debt Administration and the participation of the Russo-Asiatic Bank in the Anglo-French purchase of one of Turkey's biggest banks, the Salonika Bank. This agreement, thought Giers, gave Russia 'for the first time a chance to establish her economic influence in Turkey, without which she would not be able to realise her historic tasks' there.[84] Following this agreement the Russian Ministry of Foreign Affairs showed some interest in the efforts of Russian capitalists to participate in international banking and mining concessions in Anatolia. These tentative explorations, delicate because of the involvement of Armenian businessmen, were cut short by the outbreak of war.[85]

The belated interest shown by the Russian government in commerce, finance and concessions in the Ottoman Empire certainly indicated a growing awareness in St Petersburg of the importance of economic levers of policy, but could not conceal the fact that this was a defeat for Russia's traditional means of exerting pressure on the Porte. Increasingly in the tow of the Entente, she had been forced by the pressure of her allies' interests to surrender her few in-dependent levers of influence for the role of a nominal, junior partnership in enterprises dominated by Anglo-French interests. This was yet another mark of the fatal gap between Russia's Great Power aspirations and her real resources.[86]

Russian strategic interests in the Ottoman Empire hinged on two specific military problems: command of the Black Sea, with a minimum goal of defending Russia's coasts and a maximum task of seizure of the Straits, and the defence of the Caucasian frontier. The condition of Russia's armed forces in

1907 was appalling. The Pacific and Baltic Fleets had been annihilated, the army disordered and demoralised in three years of war and revolution. All sections of official and public opinion agreed that the resurrection of her armed forces was a matter of life or death for Russia as an independent power. She simply would not survive another Tsushima or Mukden.[87] Between 1907 and 1913 the ordinary army grant went up from 406,000,000 roubles to 581,000,000 and the navy's from 88,000,000 roubles to 245,000,000. Together this came to roughly 35 per cent of the total ordinary budget. In addition a total of 2,301,000,000 roubles' worth of extraordinary credits were assigned to the armed forces, of which the navy received the most.[88] Rearmament was paid for partly by loans, but more by increases in indirect taxation. But despite this huge expenditure Russia would still be unprepared for war until 1917–19 and had still to avoid war at all costs, relying on the 'arts of her diplomacy'.[89]

The most remarkable feature of this rearmament was the stress on navalism. The Tsar, court, Ministries of the Navy and Foreign Affairs, industry, banking and commerce and public opinion were intoxicated with the fashionable *mariniste* doctrines of the age. Russia, it was argued, had to have a Great Fleet to be a Great Power. With a powerful navy she would develop overseas trade, dominate the balance of sea-power between Britain and Germany, and thus be able to exact whatever political price she cared to name in return for her favours.[90] Such delusions of grandeur hardly matched her economic, financial and institutional backwardness and dependence.

The Black Sea Fleet at the end of the Russo-Japanese War was completely unbattleworthy. It consisted of six outdated battleships, three ancient cruisers and a motley collection of smaller vessels. Bases and yards were run down; the establishment was 50 per cent below strength and politically suspect. Over the past twenty years it had been adequate to meet its minimum tasks, thanks only to the closure of the Straits and the even weaker state of the Turkish fleet. In the new era of instability, and with Izvolskii's ambition to open the Straits, its tasks would be immense.[91] Admiral Dikov, Head of the Naval General Staff, saw it as a major instrument of Russian power, not only commanding the Black Sea itself, but also controlling the access to the high seas, ensuring the development of the whole of southern Russia and spreading Russian influence in the Balkans. Izvolskii agreed that the fleets of Russia had to be free to go wherever policy decided. He hoped that the *rapprochement* with Britain, a new understanding with Austria and the support of France would neutralise German opposition to a great Black Sea Fleet and leave Turkey isolated.[92] In the lengthy interministerial debate during 1907, however, on how the huge sums demanded by the armed forces were to be distributed, the needs of the Baltic Fleet were given priority. The navy was given preference over the army, but their demands were cut down to the so-called 'Little Programme', which envisaged the construction of eight 'Dreadnoughts' on the Baltic (for 660,200,000 roubles) but only thirteen destroyers and six submarines on the Black Sea (for 70,000,000 roubles). Even these last were not built owing to lack of finance and the belief that the closure of the Straits and the weakness of the Turkish navy were still adequate guarantees of Russian security.[93]

Over the next few years Russia's position deteriorated. The Young Turk revolution, Turco-Persian border clashes, Austrian railway schemes in the Balkans and finally the Annexation crisis of 1909 found Russia still with no military or naval presence in the Near East. Izvolskii's plans for opening the Straits by diplomacy had been dashed; there could be no question of any Russian action at the Straits.[94] Extra credits assigned to the armed forces as a result went to the army and the Baltic Fleet. Nothing was done to strengthen the Black Sea Fleet until the news reached St Petersburg of the Turkish decision to create a powerful navy almost overnight by the purchase of three dreadnoughts being built in Britain for Brazil. Dreadnought-type battleships rendered all other battleships obsolete; one such battleship could send the whole of the Russian Black Sea Fleet to the bottom. This event, then, completely overturned all Russian calculations.[95] It was all the more serious in Russian eyes by coinciding with a period of mounting pressure on Russia to abandon her 1900 moratorium on Anatolian railway construction, by growing Turkish nationalism after the honeymoon period of the Young Turk revolution and by continued German involvement in Turkish rearmament. From the spring of 1910, Charykov protested to Hakki Pasha about this build-up, and Sazonov informed the Turkish Ambassador in St Petersburg, Turkhan Pasha, that 'Russia will never allow the domination of the Black Sea by any other fleet'.[96] In this the Tsar, navy, army and public opinion concurred. In August 1910 an ambitious programme was announced which included the construction of three dreadnoughts – *Yekaterina II*, *Emperor Alexander II* and *Empress Maria*. In May 1911 the necessary credits of 150,000,000 roubles were granted by the Duma. The three dreadnoughts would enter service between 1915 and 1917. Since the Turkish battleships were expected to come into service between 1913 and 1915 there would be a two-year period of great danger for Russia, when the Turks would enjoy a crushing superiority.[97] During 1911 the Russian government debated how this gap could be reduced and what Russia's Straits policy should now be. The appearance of a strong Turkish fleet would completely deprive Russia of the protection offered since the Congress of Berlin by the closure of the Straits. The Ministry of Foreign Affairs argued that Russia should now renew her efforts to have the Straits opened to allow her to bring into the Black Sea vessels built abroad or transferred from the Baltic, but the Naval Minister, Admiral I. K. Grigorovich, insisted that Russia must give up all thought of opening the Straits and must build a powerful fleet in her own Black Sea yards at Nikolaevsk in preparation for a seizure of the Straits in five or six years' time.[98]

The potential danger of Turkish naval superiority between 1913 and 1915 was increasingly and paradoxically coupled with the even greater danger of the 'premature' collapse of the Ottoman Empire. The Italo-Turkish War presented the Ministry of Foreign Affairs with its last chance to solve the Straits

Question by diplomacy before the First World War. Charykov's offer in the autumn of 1911 of a guarantee of Turkish territorial integrity and revision of the 1900 railway agreement in exchange for the opening of the Straits, was turned down by the Turks owing to the pressure of Germany and Britain.[99] During the recurring crises of the next few years – the brief closures of the Straits to commerce, the Balkan Wars and the Liman von Sanders affair – Russia was still impotent to take any independent naval action. As she could not bring warships into the Black Sea owing to the closure of the Straits, she was obliged to build the new capital ships in her own Black Sea yards, with massive foreign, financial and technical help, at double the cost and time of construction abroad.[100] Meanwhile Turkey was negotiating for the purchase of two or three more dreadnoughts, and ordered destroyers and cruisers from Germany, France and Britain and a dockyard from Britain. In November 1913 the navy called for a dreadnought programme that would enable Russia by 1919 to concentrate eleven dreadnoughts and supporting ships in the Aegean.[101]

Sazonov reported Russia's predicament to the Tsar in late November 1913 and called for further naval increases.[102] In December the navy suggested Russia should try to hamper Turkish naval construction by buying up four dreadnoughts currently under construction in America which might go to Turkey. But the cost – about 35,000,000 roubles each – was prohibitive. The Liman von Sanders crisis spurred the Russian government to action. In March 1914 the Tsar approved the laying down of a fourth dreadnought, *Emperor Nicholas I*, and two light cruisers in Nikolaev at a cost of 110,000,000 roubles. This was passed by the Duma and became law in June.[103]

The creation of a Black Sea Fleet commensurate with the magnitude of what Kuropatkin had called in 1900 'Russia's main task in the twentieth century' – control over the Straits – began too late to be of any use for such an ambitious task. At the outbreak of war *Empress Maria* was only 65 per cent ready, and two other dreadnoughts 53 and 33 per cent ready. *Admiral Nakhimov* and the cruiser *Admiral Lazarev* were only 14 per cent ready. The Russian war plans of 1914, marked 'Secret. Known to four people only!', laid down only defensive tasks: mining the approaches to the Bosporus and the protection of Russian bases. Russia, it admitted, 'not having increased her army parallel with the German and Austrian expansion of 1913, and not having either a powerful fleet or adequate means for carrying a large landing force, and also fearing internal upheavals, will not start war herself. War on the Black Sea in 1914 can only be an aggressive one by Turkey with Russia on the defence.'[104]

In contrast to the problems of the role of the Black Sea Fleet, the strategic requirements of the Vice-Regency of the Caucasus were purely defensive as far as the Ottoman Empire was concerned and aimed more at internal security and the furtherance of Russian influence over north Persia. Transcaucasia was an economically important region supplying in 1913 about 80 per cent of all Russia's oil products. The port of Baku was the busiest in the whole Empire, including St Petersburg. The population of the Caucasus of 6½ million was ethnically and confessionally mixed, with Christian Georgians and Armenians, Muslim Azeris and mountain tribes. These last, pacified only in the middle of the last century, were presumed to be pro-Turkish and vulnerable to pan-Turkic and pan-Islamic propaganda, and were under special military administration. The loyalty of the Georgians and Armenians was also suspect, owing to their highly developed sense of nationalism and to the wide spread of socialist ideas among them. The whole region had been deeply affected by the revolution of 1905. The authorities were specially hostile to Armenian nationalist and revolutionary groups – a policy which began to change only from 1911 owing to the need for Armenian support in a possible Russo-Turkish clash. Railways in the Caucasus reflected the Russian preoccupation with internal security and expansionism in northern Persia. The region was linked by rail with Russia and the Persian border, but there was no line along the Black Sea coast nor any line to the Turkish frontier.[105]

As mentioned earlier, Russian policy at the turn of the century was to try to shield the Caucasian frontier from the approach of outside influences. The Baghdad Railway posed a general threat to Russian interests throughout the region, but once its final route had been determined Russian hostility stemmed predominantly from its menace to Russian interests in Persia.[106] If Germany could guarantee those, then Russia would have no objection to ending that hostility. This was made clear by Izvolskii in February 1907.[107] Russian interests in northern Persia were recognised by the Anglo-Russian convention of 1907, and an agreement along these lines was reached with Germany in August 1911. In return for German recognition of Russia's special interests in Persia, Russia undertook to build a line from Tehran to join up with a branch line of the Baghdad Railway at Khanekin, on the Perso-Ottoman border.[108] Sazonov, explaining the arrangement at a Special Conference in October 1910, admitted that the link-up might not be to Russia's advantage, but that she could not prevent the Baghdad Railway, or branch lines, from being built and would at least have ten to fifteen years to prepare for the connection by strengthening her political and economic grip on northern Persia. It was hoped that improved relations with Germany would lead to greater German sympathy for Russian aims in the Near East generally.[109]

The only real instrument Russia possessed for maintaining the defensive isolation of the Armenian plateau was the 1900 railway 'sterilisation' agreement. In the 1911 Baghdad Railway agreement with Russia, Germany secretly agreed not to build branch lines into the Caucasus, but by then Russia's grip on railway development in this zone was beginning to come under pressure.[110] The Young Turk government were determined both to free Turkey from the various instruments restricting her sovereignty and to modernise the Empire.[111] They wanted railways, and from at least September 1909 began talks with the American Chester syndicate to build railways in Anatolia linking Samsum, Sivas, Trebizond and Erzerum, in the so-called 'forbidden zone'.

When the Russian embassy protested they announced that they would build the lines themselves with the help of foreign loans; this was not excluded in the 1900 agreement. The Russian government realised at once that the game was up; French capitalists were also angling for concessions in Anatolia, and Turkey would probably get the finance without much difficulty.[112] In June 1910 a Special Conference held in the royal yacht *Standard* decided that Russia would have to retreat and try to negotiate a new agreement which would preserve the ban on railways east of the Samsum–Sivas–Diarbekir–Mosul line while permitting the construction of lines between these points. The Ministry of War was dismayed at the crumbling of Russian influence in such a vital part of Turkey and insisted that under no circumstances could railways be allowed in the direction of Erzerum.[113]

During 1911, Izvolskii, now Ambassador in Paris, made the Russian position known to Poincaré and tried to enlist the support of the French by pointing out that if Russia's Caucasian frontier were to be exposed she would need to transfer forces from European Russia to strengthen the Caucasian army. The French were not particularly sympathetic since they felt that Russia's agreement with Germany undermined their plans for the internationalisation of the Baghdad Railway and possibly weakened the Entente. In June 1911 the Chester concession was acquired by the French Régie Générale des Chemins de Fer and a draft agreement drawn up for concessions on lines in eastern Anatolia.[114]

The Ministry of Foreign Affairs, now also deeply disturbed by the Turkish naval programme and the closure of the Straits in the Italo-Turkish War, cast around for some way to extract the maximum compensation for the collapse of the 1900 agreement. It occurred to Izvolskii, Neratov and Charykov to link the renegotiation with the offer of a guarantee of Turkish integrity in return for the opening of the Straits to Russian warships. Charykov had worked hard for better Russo-Turkish relations and appeared to have some support in Turkish government circles, but the scheme collapsed.[115] From then on Russia really had very little leverage on the question. Various devices were thought of: Russian agreement to the 4 per cent increase of the Turkish customs; the representation of railways parallel to the coast as unprofitable; plans to offer concessions to the Régie to build railways in the Caucasus. But in the end too much pressure on France and Turkey would be counter-productive. The Turks might turn to Germany or the Régie sell out to the German company. In September 1913, Russia agreed to the granting of a concession to the French syndicate for the Samsun–Sivas–Kharput–Diarbekir line including a spur to Pekeridj in the direction of Erzerum, but demanded that lines to Erzerum, Trebizond and the frontier be built only by a Russian firm. These conditions were included in the general Russo-Turkish economic agreement of October 1913.[116] Russian efforts to retard railway construction in eastern Anatolia had not been entirely unsuccessful. It is doubtful that Russia could have resisted further encroachments on her zone of interest, but her stubborn rearguard action ensured that when war came the Turkish offensive would be seriously handicapped by poor communications.[117]

Ultimately, even in the new age of diesel engines, dreadnoughts and discount rates, Russia's interest in the Near East – specifically in the Straits – cannot be explained solely in terms of rational self-interest or strategic requirements. Deeper, emotional forces were still at work: the instinctive drive of a land-locked people to the seas; the instincts of an empire to expand the domain of its power; the old religious dream of 'setting the Cross back on St Sophia'; the pan-Slav utopia of a happy, free fraternity of Balkan peoples basking in the sun of their beloved Elder Brother and protector; the image of a Russia resurrected at last from centuries of suffering and humiliation to her full stature in the world; dreams of glory, fears also of insecurity, isolation and impotence. The new strains, hopes and imperatives of the struggle for modernisation, added to the dangers of an increasingly insecure environment, flowed into and intermingled with these older impulses, complicating the choices to be made, rendering solutions more difficult rather than easier, yet creating a broad spectrum of patriotic feelings and a general consensus on the tasks of foreign policy between government and society. The pan-Slav traditions carried on by ambassadors Neklyudov and Hartwig in Sofia and Belgrade; Izvolskii's aim of agreement with Britain and Austria over the heads of the Slavs; Sazonov's efforts to build a Slav Alliance against Austria; Charykov's hopes for a *rapprochement* with the Porte; the army, the navy, industrial interests, grain-exporting interests, the Tsar and the extreme Right – all presented varying solutions to Russia's 'Historic Tasks', yet all believed that somehow the very key to Russia's future still lay in the Near East on the territory of the Ottoman Empire. A cautious official like Baron Rosen might argue that it was high time to abandon the dream of pocketing the key to the Russian house – 'it is one of those phrases which convey no precise meaning, but being thoughtlessly repeated by millions of people, end by acquiring an hypnotic influence over men's minds' – but he was fighting against the tide.[118] From whichever way one looked at Russia's problems the answer still seemed to lie at and around the Straits. It was difficult to agree what that answer was, but circumstances seemed to conspire to leave Russia very little option but to fall back, finally, to the old aim of seizing the Straits by force, even though this was conceivable only in the context of a European war, which Russia, more than any of the Powers, wished to avoid, and would be quite beyond Russia's strength for many years.[119]

Izvolskii's failure to reassert Russia's grip on the Balkans and Near East was foreshadowed from the start. The 1907 Anglo-Russian Convention over spheres of influence in Asia did not touch the Straits Question or the Ottoman Empire directly. Grey made sympathetic noises about Russia's legitimate interests, but he indicated that Britain was not yet ready to make any exclusive concessions to Russia at the Straits. The British view was that if there were to be any changes, then the Straits would have to be opened to all navies. This was quite unacceptable to Russia in view of her special interests and naval weakness. Izvolskii was unable to press the point. He had to think of German susceptibilities and the domestic pro-German lobby. Russia could not afford to adopt insistent tones in European diplomacy.[120]

This was borne home in 1908 when he suggested at a Special Conference that Russia might take some action against Turkey, using a Turkish occupation of Persian border territories as pretext, in order to obtain compensation for Austria's unwelcome Mitrovitsa railway concession. The Prime Minister, P. A. Stolypin, firmly stated that such adventurism would be 'the delirium of a government that had lost its reason'. The Foreign Minister, like others before him, would have to rely on diplomatic skill alone, or, as Izvolskii put it, on 'un levier sans point d'appuis'.[121] In Macedonia in 1907, Russia and Austria had kept up their common opposition to partition in the face of renewed fighting between Greco-Serb and Bulgarian bands, but the Mitrovitsa concession was an ominous sign of the beginning of the end of Austro-Russian co-operation. In the summer of 1908, Izvolskii had some success in gaining British support for his plan of new reforms to improve the Turkish administration in Macedonia, and the Young Turk revolution brought temporary relief while the Powers hoped the new constitutional regime would solve the Macedonian question for them.[122]

The full weakness of Izvolskii's 'diplomatic lever' was brutally revealed only in 1909 by the disastrous Buchlau deal whereby he thought he had achieved the miracle of securing the opening of the Straits in exchange for Russia's accept-ance of the Austrian annexation of Bosnia and Herzegovina. International recognition for the Russian demand was not forthcoming. This was, in the words of the leader of the Constitutional Democratic Party, a 'diplomatic Tsushima'. Izvolskii's reputation was thoroughly, if unfairly, discredited and Russian pro-Slav opinion incensed by what was seen as a callous betrayal of Serbian interests.[123] Finally, Izvolskii, in desperation to get some sort of agreement with someone over the Balkans, concluded an agreement with Italy at Racconigi in October 1909, which gained Italian support for Russia's interests in the Straits and for the preservation of the *status quo* in the Balkans in return for Russia's recognition of Italy's interest in Tripolitania. This only helped clear the decks for Italian aggression against the Ottoman Empire, which in turn precipitated a chain reaction in the Balkans.[124] The Italo-Turkish War gave the Russian Foreign Ministry a chance to test the success of Charykov's policy of friendliness towards the Porte. Its plan for a Russo-Turkish *rapprochement* which would open the Straits to Russia in return for a revision of the 1900 railway agreement and a Russian guarantee of Turkish European possessions failed. It smacked too strongly of the 1833 Unkiar Skelessi arrangement to be acceptable either to Turkey or to the Powers.[125]

After Izvolskii's failures and the collapse of the Charykov *démarche* Russia's only resource seemed to be to lend her support to the idea of a Balkan alliance to contain possible Austrian expansion. Initially, it was hoped to include

Turkey, but this had no chance of success, given that the 'sacred goal' of the Balkan states was to drive the Turks out of Europe and apportion their territories amongst themselves.[126] This is not the place to catalogue the many disasters that befell this ill-fated venture. Sazonov's aim was to create a Serbo-Bulgar bastion against Austria, to preserve the *status quo* and protect the Straits. He thought it was possible to reconcile their mutual animosities and contain their restless urge for southward expansion. This would hardly have been possible even if Russian policy had been single-minded, consistently applied in all the Balkan capitals and backed up by force. It was none of these. Sazonov vacillated between supporting one state then the other. He was systematically sabotaged by his own ambassadors, above all by N. G. Hartwig in Belgrade. Hartwig, indeed, helped bring about the First Balkan War in which Serbia, Bulgaria, Montenegro and Greece seized Macedonia, and he was the driving force behind the Second Balkan War, when Romania, Serbia and Greece fought Bulgaria to redivide the spoils. Sazonov also had not the means to prevent Austria from blocking Serbian expansion westwards to the Adriatic. The thrust of the Slavo-Greek drive could not be diverted from the region of the Straits.[127] When the Bulgarian advance in the first war threatened the Straits, Russia was helpless to halt it by force. When the Turks reoccupied Adrianople in January 1913, in the second war, Sazonov found himself forced for diplomatic reasons to defend the Bulgarian claim to the city but was unable to mount a naval demonstration independently to force the Turks to withdraw.[128] Russia proved impotent to halt that which she least desired – the progressive destruction of Ottoman power in the region of the Straits. Throughout the crisis she received only moderate support from her allies. Sazonov preferred a temporary Bulgarian occupation of Constantinople to Grey's plan for international control of the city.[129]

The crisis sharply exposed the need to define exactly what kind of Russian presence at the Straits was required. Prince G. N. Trubetskoy, head of the political division of the Ministry of Foreign Affairs, argued that defensive considerations were paramount. The aim must be to deny an enemy fleet access to the Black Sea and might be facilitated by acquiring a base on the Bosporus together with the neutralisation or demilitarisation of the Dardanelles. Given the still feeble state of the Black Sea Fleet, it was not clear how such measures might be effected.[130] Admiral Lieven, head of the Naval General Staff, on the other hand, thought that the navy must be able to guarantee access to the Mediterranean in time of war. This task would require not just political hegemony in the Balkans and possession of the Straits themselves – conditions demonstrably utopian under the circumstances – but also, he argued, the occupation of all the islands of the Greek archipelago, including Crete. The Admiral had the honesty to conclude that Russia really should develop a strong Black Sea Fleet more to stiffen her diplomacy than to attempt to solve the Straits question by force.[131]

The appointment of the German General Liman von Sanders as commander of the Turkish First Army Corps at the end of 1913 was another grave blow for Russian policy. It was assumed in St Petersburg that this was a deliberate German move to dominate the Straits and to outflank Russia by converting the Turkish army into an instrument of German aggression.[132] In a dismal report to the Tsar early in December, Sazonov reaffirmed his determination that the Straits must remain in the hands of a Turkey 'not too strong, nor yet too weak' and that the 'keys to the Black Sea and Mediterranean' must never be allowed to fall into the hands of a third state. He deplored the wasted decades of talk and extravagant naval expenditure that had still not borne fruit. Now, he reported, the Turkish fleet, re-equipped and trained by Russia's ally, Britain, would achieve superiority over the Black Sea Fleet within the next few years. This was 'intolerable', and he demanded that construction of the Black Sea Fleet be speeded up immediately.[133] A Special Conference met on 31 December to decide how to compel Germany and Turkey to modify Liman von Sanders' appointment. The Conference agreed that neither military nor financial pressure could be exerted. For this complete Entente unanimity was required, but was hardly to be hoped for in the light of French and British economic interests in the Ottoman Empire and their known reluctance to risk war for Russia's interests.[134] The general furore over Liman von Sanders' appointment induced Germany to modify her stance, but the transfer of the General to a non-field command – inspector-general of the Turkish army – was an empty victory for Russia. It hardly lessened the potential of German influence at the Porte.[135]

The Special Conference of 8 February 1914, reviewing the Straits Question and the technical requirements for the re-establishment of Russian power on the Black Sea, once again aired the 'hallowed doctrines'. But the army Chief of Staff echoed Witte's warnings of 1900 that the Straits Question could only be solved as part of a general European war. The navy's spokesman, Captain Nemits, made the even more telling point that even so Russia would have to rely solely on her own efforts. An Entente victory in Europe would not necessarily give the Straits to Russia: 'others might seize them while we are fighting on our western front'. But as the Conference surveyed yet again the state of Russia's armed forces it was clear that there could be no question of an active policy until 1917 at the earliest. No plans were made for the seizure of the Straits; the mood was 'wholly defensive'.[136]

Following upon the Balkan Wars and the Liman von Sanders affair, there appeared, during 1913 and 1914, other challenges to Russia's policy of trying to postpone the partition of the Ottoman Empire. The Franco-German and Anglo-German agreements over the Baghdad Railway divided much of Asiatic Turkey into spheres of economic influence. Even Austria and Italy presented claims, although these were not formally recognised owing to the outbreak of war. Seen through Russian eyes these agreements were a further step towards a future political partition.[137] It is doubtful that the Russian economic and railway agreement with Turkey would have been as effective as those of the western Powers in creating a zone of special privilege, even though it was fortified in February 1914 by the signing of a Russo-Turkish convention concerning the Armenian vilayets of eastern Anatolia. This convention gave Russia a certain authority in supervising reforms providing for the appointment of foreign inspector-generals and for elected assemblies of Christian and Muslim community representatives. The reforms had been drawn up by the very influential first dragoman at the Russian embassy, A. A. Mandelstam, as a response to the outbreaks of anti-Armenian activity after Muslim refugees from European Turkey had settled in the region, but they had been considerably watered down owing to German and Austrian pressure.[138] Russo-Turkish relations worsened as a result of the Armenian question but, in May, Talat Bey (Pasha), leading the annual Ottoman courtesy visit to Livadia, the Tsar's summer palace in the Crimea, actually proffered Sazonov an alliance. It was done, according to Sazonov, in such a furtive manner that he left the offer open pending clarification by Giers in Constantinople. Nothing further happened and it was assumed that the German embassy had succeeded in squashing the idea.[139]

In August the First World War erupted. On 2 August, one day after the German declaration of war on Russia, Turkey signed a fateful alliance with Germany. On learning that Britain had joined the war Enver Pasha offered Russia an alliance which would place the Ottoman army at Russia's disposal in return for the cession of the Greek islands of Lemnos and Chios with some Bulgarian territory in Thrace. 'The Straits Question – Enver evasively promised – would fall of its own weight.'[140] Giers wanted Sazonov to accept this surprising offer. Although Sazonov was indeed desperate to keep Turkey out of the war in order to prevent closure of the Straits, the concessions required by Enver (which came to include abolition of the Capitulations) were not acceptable to Britain. Negotiations broke down by the end of August, Turkey remained in the camp of the Central Powers, and Sazonov instructed the Viceroy of the Caucasus to prepare for war with Turkey.[141]

Russia had not entered the war in order to seize the Straits or to destroy the Ottoman Empire. The Straits Question, nevertheless, was bound to surface once Russia found herself embroiled in a war which seemed to omit what General Kuropatkin had called in 1900 her 'most important task in the twentieth century'. On 7 August, Prince G. N. Trubetskoy, the Head of the Near Eastern Section of the Ministry of Foreign Affairs, wrote to Giers that, 'involuntarily, one's first thoughts are of the Straits'. If Turkey stayed neutral, he wrote, she would have to be forced to open the Straits after the war to warships of the Black Sea states. If Turkey implemented her alliance with Germany, Russia would have to try to seize the minimum territory necessary to secure free passage of the Straits. Constantinople should not be touched, he warned, nor any other move made which might put Russia at cross-purposes with the Entente or their potential allies.[142]

Russia's war aims, revealed by Sazonov on 14 September, contained no claims against Turkey, but on the 16th the French Ambassador in Petrograd, Paléologue, managed to extract from Sazonov the statement that Russia was determined to open the Straits to her warships 'once and for all', and to obtain a naval base on the Bosporus. Constantinople might remain in Turkish hands, he thought, but the Sea of Marmara would have to be demilitarised and placed under some form of international control, whether Turkey were to enter the war or not.[143] The following day the Germans and Turks closed the Straits. Russia was now 'fatally isolated' from all contact with her allies except through Scandinavia, and her Black Sea exports – one half of all her exports – came to a halt. Precisely to prevent this had been possibly the most persistent aim of Russian foreign policy for almost a decade.[144]

Hostilities began with the attack by the cruisers *Goeben* and *Breslau* (now *Yavus* and *Midilli*) on Russian shipping and ports on 29 and 30 October. Russia declared war on Turkey on 2 November. For the tenth time in just over two hundred years Turkey and Russia were again at war, but this time Turkey's traditional allies and protectors were on the Russian side. Britain and France declared war on Turkey on 5 November. In Russia the Duma, press and general public were jubilant. The Tsar's manifesto declaring war spoke predictably of the 'fulfilment of Russia's historic tasks on the shores of the Bosporus'. Pressed by Paléologue, Sazonov mentioned 'tangible guarantees on the Bosporus', while Constantinople 'with a decent-sized kitchen garden' might remain in Turkish hands.[145]

For the time being the Russian army envisaged only a strategy of 'active defence' along the Caucasian frontier, including deploying Russian troops based in northern Persia. It was while discussing the possibility of enticing Persia into the war against her old religious rival that the Russian Ambassador in London, Count Benckendorff, heard Grey's astonishingly casual promise that after victory the fate of the Straits and Constantinople could be settled only in conformity with Russian desires. This was followed on 13 November by King George's even more laconic aside to the Russian minister that 'as far as Constantinople is concerned, it is clear that it must be yours'. Thus, the goal that had shimmered tantalisingly through all the frustrations of Russian policy in the Near East, and which had seemed quite beyond Russian ambitions even at the start of the war with Turkey, now appeared to be miraculously within reach. Even so, the British Ambassador's written confirmation of the offer still left the details open; they were to be left until after the defeat of Germany.[146]

On 21 November the Tsar acquainted the French ambassador with Russia's initial response to the British offer. He spoke of expelling the Turks from Europe, of dividing Thrace between Bulgaria and Russia along the Enos–Midia line, of the neutralisation of Constantinople and the annexation of Armenia, or possibly its autonomy under Russian protection. Paléologue gave his guarded support for these aims in return for Russian acceptance of French claims to Syria and Cilicia.[147] Meanwhile Sazonov sought once more to clarify Russia's real aims by convening yet another Special Conference. The resulting memorandum strongly reflects the navy's predilection for an 'active solution' to the Straits Question as opposed to a more narrowly defensive version. Either way, the solution would require the occupation of the Bosporus and a strip of land on both sides of the Straits, and participation in Allied control of the Dardanelles. Free access to the Mediterranean, on the other hand, could only be guaranteed by the seizure of Gallipoli and the Greek islands and the partition of Thrace with Bulgaria. Sazonov was opposed to the annexation of Constantinople, but in the end agreed that outright acquisition could not be avoided. Turkey would be too weak to maintain her independence, and international control would be tantamount to control by the western Powers.[148]

Some weeks later Captain Nemits followed this up with a long and emotional appeal for immediate preparations for an attack on the Straits. Russia, he argued, should be under no illusion that the Allies would simply hand over the Straits at the conference table; Russia must seize them herself to be sure of her gains. The expansion of the Black Sea Fleet was now under way, but the army warned Sazonov that it could not take part in an attack on the Bosporus until victory had been won in Europe. Until then Russia would have to rest content with the Entente promises.[149]

Implementing their strategy of active defence in the Caucasus, Russian forces in November occupied the Alashkirt valley and the approaches to Köprüköy and Karakilisse on the Aras river. Turkish forces moved across the frontier in the north, seizing Artvin and Ardanuch. In December the Turkish Third Army, under Enver himself, launched its disastrous offensive against Sarykamysh.[150] At the height of the battle, Grand Duke Nicholas, the Russian Commander-in-Chief, requested an Allied diversionary operation to relieve the pressure on Sarykamysh. The Russians had in mind something along Turkey's southern frontiers, and the Allied Dardanelles campaign was not at all to their liking. Were it to succeed, the immediate economic and strategic advantages of direct communication with the Allies would have ultimately to be weighed against the violation of the 'golden rule' of Russian policy that under no circumstances could Russia allow the Straits to fall into the hands of a third state. To Sazonov's chagrin, Russia could not take part in the operation owing to the situation on her western front. Nevertheless, the opening of the Dardanelles campaign and the eventual Russian victory at Sarykamysh at the beginning of the New Year greatly excited Russian opinion. In the Duma all parties except the Social Democrats agreed that acquisition of the Straits and Constantinople must be Russia's main war aim.[151]

On 4 March 1915, Sazonov presented Russia's demands to the Allies. She wished to annex Constantinople, the western shore of the Sea of Marmara and the Dardanelles, southern Thrace up to the Enos–Midia line, part of the Asiatic coast between the Sakaria river and the Gulf of Ismid, and the islands of Tenedos and Imbros. By early April the Allies had accepted these demands on condition that Constantinople remain a free port, that the Straits remain open to commercial navigation, that Britain absorb the neutral zone between the Russian and British zones of influence in Persia, and that France take Syria, Palestine and Cilicia from the Mediterranean to the Taurus mountains.[152] Thus was the November promise formalised, but in quite different circumstances from those ideally desired by Russia. The Straits would be conquered by foreign forces; there would be no unified Armenian state under exclusively Russian influence; a formal partition of Asiatic Turkey was foreshadowed; Russia's horizons in the Near East would be clouded by the gathering encroachments of her allies' interests. Many Russians doubted that the Allies would honour their promises. This apparently historic settlement, then, 'hardly signified the achievement of ancient hopes'.[153] It contained the seeds of future conflicts with the Entente and the Balkan states, not to mention Turkey itself, were it to be implemented.

As victory seemed to recede during 1915, with the fall of Poland and Serbia, the collapse of the Dardanelles campaign and Bulgaria's adherence to the Central Powers, Russia could do little but mount limited – but moderately successful – naval engagements against strategic and economic targets on the Black Sea coast and press on in eastern Anatolia. By mid-May, Russian and Armenian forces were in control of Van and were preparing for a big winter offensive.[154] At the start of the war the Russian government had encouraged Armenians to hope for the creation, after the war, of a united and independent Armenian state, but it was adamant that Russian interests would determine the fate of Armenia.[155] Already in the spring of 1915, when Cilicia (western Armenia) had been included in the French sphere of influence, Armenian aspirations had been sacrificed to Russian and French requirements.[156] In the wake of the advancing Russian forces officials were now planning the postwar settlement of peasants and Cossacks on the abandoned Armenian and Kurdish farmsteads along the border.[157]

By midsummer 1916 the Russians were in possession of Erzerum, Trebizond and Erzinjan. The Turkish army, with losses of almost a third of a million men, was quite disorganised. Russian forces were poised to drive into the heartland of Anatolia but were restrained by communications problems (to which Russia's prewar railway policy had contributed), by war-weariness and the onset of revolutionary discontent. During the winter months military activity almost ceased, but had the offensive been resumed, and the Tsarist regime not fallen in March 1917, there can be little doubt that the Turkish armies in the east would have collapsed completely.[158]

Throughout the war the Tsarist government stuck to its agreements with the Allies and rejected all suggestions of a separate peace.[159] For the army the Turkish front, despite Russian successes, was an almost irrelevant sideshow, but the navy still nursed the idea of an attack on the Bosporus, and both the Tsar and the Foreign Minister remained determined to 'make an end of Turkey' at any cost.[160] Between March and September 1916, Russia adhered to the so-called 'Sykes–Picot agreement', which disposed of the Turkish Asiatic possessions. She was to annex the regions of Erzerum, Van, Bitlis and part of Kurdistan, but their full integration into the Russian Empire was to be subject to the protection of the 'existing rights of navigation and development' of British subjects in those regions.[161]

But by now the Russian government, Duma and public had far greater concerns to occupy them than the 'historic tasks' in the Near East or anywhere else. Prime Minister Trepov's revelation of the existence of the secret treaties in the Duma on 2 December, intended to raise morale, met only with general indifference.[162] In February the Tsar abdicated and the regime was replaced by the unstable diarchy of the Provisional Government and the Soviets. The new Foreign Minister, Paul Milyukov, the leader of the Constitutional Democrat Party, whose devotion to Russia's war aims rivalled that of Sazonov himself, fought in vain to hold Russia in the war until he, too, was replaced in May.[163] In October the Bolsheviks seized power and proclaimed the dawn of a new era, the construction of the socialist order. Among their first acts were the denunciation of Tsarist war aims, the demand for peace without annexations or indemnities, and the publication of the secret treaties.[164] On 18 December, Russian and Turkish commanders signed an armistice at Erzinjan and Russian forces withdrew, leaving mainly Armenian units facing the Turks, who temporarily recovered their ground in the east and embarked on their short-lived pan-Islamic crusade into Transcaucasia.[165] At the Brest-Litovsk peace negotiations between Soviet Russia and the Central Powers early in 1918 the former Tsarist Empire was dismantled and the Russian state thrust back to the frontiers of seventeenth-century Muscovy.[166] By the end of October the Ottoman Empire itself ceased to exist as an independent power.

Throughout the period under review the overwhelmingly predominant interest of the Russian government in the Ottoman Empire was to prevent the Straits from falling into the hands of a third power, or the Porte succumbing to the dominant influence of a third power. In either case not only the security of Russia's Black Sea possessions would be put at risk, but also her vital commerce through the Straits could be blockaded. Other Russian interests in the Empire – the fate of the Christian subjects of the sultan, missionary activity,[167] commercial and financial interests – were only secondary and were seen as possible instruments for the attainment of the main task. The existence of the Ottoman Empire was not *per se* incompatible with Russian interests; Russia's struggle was to assert the validity of her interests as a Great Power against the opposition of the Powers, friend and foe alike. Russia was on the defensive throughout the period and wished to maintain the territorial integrity of the Empire at least until she had overcome her domestic economic, political and military problems. Seizure of the Straits was never seriously contemplated before 1913. Whenever it was mentioned it was always as a last desperate expedient, and the resources for its implementation were always lacking. Russia had few effective levers with which to slow down the accelerating pace of Ottoman decline, Austrian expansionism, Balkan nationalism and – most important – German activity in the Near East. She did not dispose of enough influence with her Entente partners to get them to address themselves seriously to her interests. Neither was Russia strong enough to be able to balance between the two alliance systems and thereby enhance her bargaining power. Her very efforts to achieve this leverage by military and naval rearmament only served to highlight her dependence on foreign technology and finance and to alarm her immediate neighbours. Russia's practical aim of preserving stability in the region of the Straits was complicated and contradicted by the powerful pro-Slav currents in public opinion and officialdom. The government, in its uneasy co-operation with the Duma, not only could not afford to ignore these currents, but was also always exposed to the temptation to manipulate them for its own political advantage. Russia was a prisoner of her own prestige and sense of 'historic mission', both in the Balkans and at the Straits, and her very real interests in the region were shrouded in emotions deriving from past history and religio-nationalist feelings.

The discrepancy between Russian ambitions and resources was vast. This is clearly seen in the failure to develop a strong Black Sea Fleet despite the primacy accorded to the Straits Question. In times of crisis Russia could not even mount a credible naval demonstration at the Bosporus, not to mention a seizure of the Straits. The 'maximum' goal of securing the free egress from the Black Sea under all conditions was in fact insoluble. Its apparent attainment in April 1915 was illusory, the result of skilful Allied manipulation of Russian desires. It would eventually have ranged all Europe against Russia.

In competition with the more advanced Powers for influence and prestige within the Ottoman Empire, Russia lacked the powerful levers of capital, concessions and commerce. Even if she had possessed abundant capital, strategic considerations would have inhibited its export to Turkey. Given the legacy of Russo-Turkish hostility deriving from two centuries of conflict, and the exposure of the Empire to outside influences, Russia could not automatically welcome her transformation into a strong state. But what actually was Russia's contribution to the decline and demise of the Ottoman Empire? In our period we can see very little, active, Russian contribution apart from the war itself, which was precipitated by Turkish, not Russian action. Russia's contribution lay rather in the history of her expansionism at Ottoman expense, dating from the end of the seventeenth century, culminating in the Crimean War and the Russo-Turkish war of 1877–8 which destroyed Ottoman finances and launched Turkey on the slippery slope of financial dependence on European capital. In the actual institutions of that financial control Russia played no part at all and was only tentatively preparing to play a junior role on the eve of the war. Russia was always seen in Turkey as the instigator of Slav and Armenian revolt, despite the Russian government's efforts to contain such movements in order to uphold the *status quo* and to ensure tranquillity in the Caucasus. Russia certainly contributed to the general growth of nationalism within the Ottoman Empire, but here, as we have seen, the Russian government was as much the puppet as the puppet-master. Probably Russias most significant contribution to the fall of the Ottoman Empire lay in the Turks' perception of Russia as the Power most implacably dedicated to the destruction of the Empire. This conviction played an important part in disposing the Turks to join the war on the side of Germany and hence in their subsequent defeat. If, however, we were to view the Russian influence on Turkey outside the framework of foreign-policy interests, we should have to consider the increasingly subversive effect on Ottoman institutions exerted by the picture of the progressive collapse of autocracy witnessed in Russia. The flowering of Russian secular culture, the rise of political radicalism, the defeat of Russia by Japan and the revolution of 1905 all had profound repercussions throughout the East, undermining the mystique of imperialism and fanning the sparks of indigenous nationalism.[168]

Notes: Chapter 4

Western students of Russian foreign policy in the decades preceding the October Revolution have not yet been given access to Soviet archives; they are dependent on selective material published in the Soviet Union between the wars, on the works of ex-Tsarist officials and scholars in emigration, and on material published in the diplomatic document collections of the other Powers. The two most valuable Soviet collections of documents concerning Russian policy towards the Ottoman Empire are: E. A. Adamov (ed.), *Evropeiskie derzhavy i Turtsiia vo vremia mirovoi voiny: Konstantinopol' i prolivy. Po sekrenym dokumentam byvshego Ministerstva inostrannykh del (The European Powers and Turkey during the World War: Constantinople and the Straits. From the Secret Documents of the Former Ministry of Foreign Affairs)*, 2 Vols (Moscow, 1925–6); and E. A. Adamov (ed.), *Razdel aziatskoi Turtsii po sekretnym dokumentam Biblioteki Ministerstva inostrannykh del (The Partition of Asiatic Turkey from the Secret Documents of the Library of the Ministry of Foreign Affairs)* (Moscow, 1924). The biggest Russian collection of diplomatic correspondence concerning Turkey is in *Mezhdunarodnye otnosheniia v epokhu imperializma. Dokumenty iz arkhivov tsarskogo i vremennogo pravitel'stv 1878–1917 (International Relations in the Age of Imperialism. Documents from the Archives of the Tsarist and Provisional Governments, 1878–1917* (Moscow, 1930–). The first series was never published, the second and third series cover the period from 1 May 1911 to 31 March 1916. There is a German translation edited by O. Hoetzsch called *Die internationalen Beziehungen im Zeitalter des Imperialismus* (Berlin, 1930–). Considerable material is also to be found in the journal *Krasnyi arkhiv (The Red Archives)*, published by Tsentrarkhiv in Moscow and Leningrad between 1922 and 1941. These publications of the interwar period still provide the main sources for the various Western studies mentioned below as for the chief work of Turkish scholarship on the subject, A. N. Kurat, *Türkiye ve Rusya: XVIII yüzyıl sonundan Kurtuluş savaşına kadar Türk-Rus ilişkileri (1798–1919) (Turkey and Russia: Russo-Turkish Relations from the Eighteenth Century to the War of Liberation)* (Ankara, 1970).

1   For general surveys of Russian foreign policy, see: Barbara Jelavich, *St Petersburg and Moscow: Tsarist and Soviet Foreign Policy, 1814–1974* (Bloomington, Ind., 1974); Barbara Jelavich, *A Century of Russian Foreign Policy, 1814–1914* (New York, 1964); G. Bolsover, 'Aspects of Russian foreign policy, 1815–1914', in R. Pares and A. J. P. Taylor (eds), *Essays Presented to Sir Lewis Namier* (London, 1956); T. Hunczak (ed.), *Russian Imperialism from Ivan the Great to the Revolution* (Rutgers, NJ, 1974); A. J. P. Taylor, *The Struggle for Mastery in Europe* (London, 1954). On the Eastern Question see: M. S. Anderson, *The Eastern Question, 1774–1923* (London, 1966); B. H. Sumner, *Russia and the Balkans, 1870–1880* (London, 1962); Charles Jelavich, *Tsarist Russia and Balkan Nationalism* (Berkeley, Calif., 1958). For the involvement in the Far East, see: A. Malozemoff, *Russian Policy in the Far East, 1880–1904* (Berkeley, Calif., 1958); B. H. Sumner, 'Tsardom and imperialism in the

Far East and the Middle East, 1880–1914', *Proceedings of the British Academy*, Vol. XXVII (1941), pp. 25–65. For interpretive studies, see: Hunczak, *Russian Imperialism*; I. J. Lederer (ed.), *Russian Foreign Policy: Essays in Historical Perspective* (New Haven, Conn., 1962); G. Katkov and M. Futrell, 'Russian foreign policy, 1880–1914', in G. Katkov *et al.* (eds), *Russia Enters the Twentieth Century* (London, 1971), pp. 9–33; R. E. McGrew, 'Some imperatives of Russian foreign policy', in T. G. Stavrou (ed.), *Russia under the Last Tsar* (Minneapolis, Minn., 1969), pp. 202–52.

2 I. J. Lederer, 'Russia and the Balkans, in Lederer, *Russian Foreign Policy*, pp. 417–53; C. E. Black, 'The pattern of Russian objectives', in ibid., pp. 4–16; Y. Zakher, 'Konstantinopol' i prolivy', *Krasnyi arkhiv*, Vol. VI (1924), p. 48; Charles Jelavich, *Tsarist Russia*, p. 3.

3 See: W. M. Medlicott, *The Congress of Berlin and After*, 2nd ed (London 1963); W. L. Langer, *European Alliances and Alignments, 1871–1890* (New York, 1950); Sumner, *Russia and the Balkans*; W. L. Langer, *The Diplomacy of Imperialism, 1890–1902* (New York, 1968).

4 ibid., p. 184.

5 Anderson, *Eastern Question*, p. 258; W. L. Langer, *The Franco-Russian Alliance, 1890–1899* (Cambridge, Mass., 1929), pp. 394–400.

6 Anderson, *Eastern Question*, pp. 257–9. See also: F. Kazemzadeh, *Russia and Britain in Persia, 1854–1914* (New Haven, Conn., 1968); D. Gillard, *The Struggle for Asia, 1828–1914: A Study in British and Russian Imperialism* (London, 1977): Kent, below, pp. 172–3.

7 Langer, *Diplomacy of Imperialism*, pp. 337, 646; A. I. Novichev, *Ocherki Ekonomiki Turtsii do mirovoi voiny* (Moscow, 1937); D. C. Blaisdell, *European Financial Control in the Ottoman Empire* (New York, 1929), p. 44; M. R. Milgrim, 'The 1878 War Indemnity', PhD thesis, University of Pennsylvania, 1974. By the terms of the treaty of Unkiar Skelessi (8 July 1833) Russia would provide armed assistance to the Turks, if requested, in return for a Turkish promise to close the Straits to all foreign warships if asked to do so by Russia. It was from the Russian point of view essentially defensive, but gave Russia a uniquely privileged position at the Porte. It lapsed with the conclusion of the Straits Convention of 1841 between all five European Powers and the sultan. See Anderson, *Eastern Question*, pp. 84–6.

8 Langer, *Diplomacy of Imperialism*, pp. 336–7.

9 'Report of a Special Committee on the Affairs of Turkey, 16 September, 1829', English translation in M. S. Anderson, *The Great Powers and the Near East, 1774–1923* (London, 1970), pp. 35–9.

10 Anderson, *Eastern Question*, chs viii and ix; Langer, *Diplomacy of Imperialism*, chs v, vi, x, xix.

11 Charles Jelavich, *Tsarist Russia*, p. 3; A. Popov, 'Ot Bosfora do Tikhogo Okeana', *Istorik Marksist*, Vol. XXXVII (Moscow, 1954), pp. 3–28.

12 Langer, *Diplomacy of Imperialism*, pp. 373–7; Anderson, *Eastern Question*, pp. 261–3; Bridge, above, pp. 31–3.

13 Anderson, *Eastern Question*, pp. 253–7, 262–3; Langer, *Diplomacy of Imperialism*, chs v, vii, x, xi; A. O. Sarkissian, 'Concert diplomacy and the Armenians, 1890–1897', in A. O. Sarkissian (ed.), *Studies in Diplomatic History and Historiography in Honour of G. P. Gooch* (London, 1962), pp, 48–75.

14 On the history of the Straits Question, see: C. Phillipson and N. Buxton, *The Question of the Bosphorus and Dardanelles* (London, 1917); Barbara Jelavich, *The Ottoman Empire, the Great Powers and the Straits Question, 1870–1887* (Bloomington, Ind., 1973); B. A. Dranov, *Chernomorskie prolivy* (Moscow, 1948); Z. Zechlin, 'Die Türkischen Meerengen – ein Brennpunkt der Weltgeschichte', in *Geschichte in Wissenschaft und Unterricht*, Vol. XVII, no. 1 (Stuttgart, 1966), pp. 1–31.

15 For Russian Straits policy, see: A. A. Mandelstam, 'La Politique russe d'accès a la Méditerranée au XXe siècle', *Academie de Droit International. Receuil des cours*, Vol. I (Paris, 1934), pp. 597–802; see also the very competent unpublished MA thesis: R. J. J. Mulligan, 'Great Britain, Russia and the Turkish Straits, 1908–1923', University of London, 1953.

16 Mandelstam, 'La politique russe', pp. 615–16; Barbara Jelavich, *The Ottoman Empire*, pp. 109–26.

17 Mandelstam, 'La politique russe', pp. 616–20; 'Zapiska A. I. Nelidova v 1882 o zakhvate Prolivov', *Krasnyi arkhiv*, Vol. XLVI (1931), pp. 179–87.

18 French opposition was also decisive. See: Anderson, *Eastern Question*, pp. 258–9; Mandelstam, 'La politique russe', pp. 617–27; V. Khvostov, 'Proekt zakhvata Bosfora v 1896 g.',

Krasnyi arkhiv, Vols XLVII–XLVIII (1931), pp. 50–70; Langer, *Diplomacy of Imperialism*, ch. x, gives an optimistic assessment of Russian strength at the time.

19   A. Popov, 'Ot Bosfora do Tikhogo Okeana', p. 15; 'Tsarskoe pravitel'stvo o probleme Prolivov, 1898–1911', *Krasnyi arkhiv*, Vol. LXI (1933), pp. 135–40.

20   Mandelstam, 'La politique russe', pp. 632–6; 'Tsarskaia diplomatiia o zadachakh Rossii no vostoke v 1900', *Krasnyi arkhiv*, Vol. XVIII (1926), pp. 3–29.

21   Langer, *Diplomacy of Imperialism*, pp. 640–7; Novichev, *Ocherki Ekonomiki Turtsii do mirovoi voiny*, pp. 135–46; G. L. Bondarevskii, *Bagdadskaia doroga i proniknovenie Germanskogo imperializma na Blizhnii Vostok (1883–1903)* (Tashkent, 1955), pp. 209–12; E. M. Earle, *Turkey, the Great Powers and the Baghdad Railway: A Study in Imperialism* (New York, 1924), pp. 65–6, 147–53; J. B. Wolf, *The Diplomatic History of the Baghdad Railway* (Columbia, Miss., 1936), p. 64; Trumpener, below, pp. 115–16. For the French reaction to Russian hostility to the Baghdad Railway, see Fulton, below, pp. 149–50.

22   'Tsarskaia diplomatiia o zadachakh Rossii na vostoke v 1900', pp. 3–29; Bondarevskii, *Bagdadskaia doroga*, p. 220.

23   Langer, *Diplomacy of Imperialism*, p. 646; Bondarevskii, *Bagdadskaia doroga*, pp. 222–4; Wolf, *Baghdad Railway*, p. 28; Earle, *Turkey*, p. 149; Anderson, *Eastern Question* pp. 264, 265.

24   ibid., pp. 271–3; Mandelstam, 'La politique russe', pp. 643–7; D. Dakin, *The Greek Struggle in Macedonia, 1897–1913* (Thessalonika, 1966), pp. 112–16, 146–62; see also below, p. 93, and Kent, pp. 183–4, and n. 101, and Bridge, above, pp. 36–7.

25   Mandelstam, 'La politique russe', pp. 636–40; M. Grishina, 'Chernomorskie prolivy vo vneshnei politiki Rossii, 1904–1907', *Istoricheskie zapiski*, Vol. XCIX (Moscow, 1977), pp. 145–8; 'Tsarskoe pravitel'stvo o probleme Prolivov, 1898–1911', pp. 137, 138.

26   ibid., pp. 138–40; Grishina, 'Chernomorskie', p. 151.

27   F. Stieve, *Izvolsky and the World War* (London, 1926), p. 12; I. B. Bestuzhev, *Bor'ba v Rossii po voprosam vneshnei politiki, 1908–1910* (Moscow, 1961), p. 25; G. A. Hosking, *The Russian Constitutional Experiment: Government and Duma, 1907–1914* (Cambridge, 1973), pp. 228, 229. For a close examination of the evolution of this realignment, see Beryl J. Williams, 'The revolution of 1905 and Russian foreign policy', in C. Abramsky and Beryl J. Williams (eds), *Essays in Honour of E. H. Carr* (London, 1974), pp. 101–25.

28   R. P. Churchill, *The Anglo-Russian Convention of 1907* (Cedar Rapids, Iowa, 1959); Kazemzadeh, *Russia and Britain in Persia*, pp. 482–500. See also n. 120 below.

29   Bestuzhev, *Bor'ba v Rossii*, pp. 44–46.

30   ibid., pp. 140–53.

31   ibid., pp. 46–50; Hosking, *Russian Constitutional Experiment*, pp. 215–29.

32   Bestuzhev, *Bor'ba v Rossii*, pp. 145, 180–98; B. O. Schmitt, *The Annexation of Bosnia, 1908–1909* (Cambridge, 1937), pp. 8, 9.

33   Williams, 'The revolution of 1905 and Russian foreign policy', p. 118.

34   For a many-sided discussion of the forces moulding Russian foreign policy, see: Lederer, *Russian Foreign Policy*; Katkov and Futrell, 'Russian foreign policy'; McGrew, 'Some imperatives'; Hunczak, *Russian Imperialism*, passim.

35   R. C. Tucker, 'Autocrats and oligarchs', in Lederer, *Russian Foreign Policy*, p. 172; Bestuzhev, *'Bor'ba v Rossii*, p. 52.

36   ibid., p. 195; Hosking, *Russian Constitutional Experiment*, pp. 226–8.

37   Bestuzhev, *'Bor'ba v. Rossii*, pp. 53, 54.

38   R. E. Pipes, 'Domestic politics and foreign affairs', in Lederer, *Russian Foreign Policy*, pp. 145–56; F. W. Ermath, *Internationalism Security and Legitimacy: The Challenge to Soviet Interests in Eastern Europe, 1964–1968* (Santa Monica, Calif., 1969), p. 6.

39   Most commentators have stressed that the concept of 'national interest' is hardly applicable in the case of Tsarist Russia. See Adam B. Ulam, 'Nationalism, panslavism, communism', in Lederer, *Russian Foreign Policy*, pp. 41–5; Pipes, 'Domestic politics', pp. 147–9. The concept is, nevertheless, notoriously elusive and ultimately highly subjective. The general official and public concern with Russia's influence in the Balkans and the Near East between 1907 and 1914 must be considered as reflecting a sense of 'national interest' in the region. See the views of Hosking (*Russian Constitutional Experiment*, pp. 241, 242) on the role played by the idea of the 'people' or 'nation' in the politics of the Duma period.

40   This conclusion is based on my reading of ibid., and Bestuzhev, *Bor'ba v Rossii*, passim.

41   ibid., pp. 382–8; Hosking, *Russian Constitutional Experiment*, pp. 1–55, 243–6.

42   R. M. Slusser, 'The role of the Foreign Ministry', in Lederer, *Russian Foreign Policy*, pp. 209, 210; Katkov and Futrell, 'Russian foreign policy', pp. 10, 11.
43   A. D. Kalmykov, *Memoirs of a Russian Diplomat* (New Haven, Conn., 1971), pp. 174–6; Baron M. Taube, *Der Grossen Katastrophe Entgegen* (Leipzig, 1937), pp. 183, 222, 223, V. N. Kokovtsov, *Iz moego proshlogo*, 2 vols (Paris, 1933), Vol. I, pp. 331–6.
44   Kalmykov, *Memoirs*, pp. 211–16; Slusser, 'Foreign Ministry', pp. 210–11; N. V. Charykov, 'Sazonov', *Contemporary Review*, Vol. CXXXIII, no. 3 (1928), pp. 284, 288; A. Rossos, *Russia and the Balkans, 1909–1914* (Ann Arbor, Mich., 1971), p. 451.
45   Dakin, *Greek Struggle*, p. 343.
46   E. C. Thaden, *Russia and the Balkan Alliance of 1912* (University Park, Pa, 1965), pp. 192, 193.
47   Kalmykov, *Memoirs*, pp. 250–2.
48   Rossos, *Russia and the Balkans*, p. 177; Anderson, *Eastern Question*, p. 295.
49   Kalmykov, *Memoirs*, p. 253; Bestuzhev, *Bor'ba v Rossii*, pp. 59, 60.
50   Deficiencies of institutions and personalities were real enough, but the peculiar complexity of Russia's Near Eastern problems cannot be denied. See Anderson, *Eastern Question*, pp. 392, 393; H. L. Roberts, 'Introduction' in A. Dallin *et al*. (eds), *Russian Diplomacy in Eastern Europe, 1914–1917* (New York, 1963), pp. xii, xiii.
51   W. L. Langer, 'Russia, the Straits Question and the European Powers, 1904–1908', *English Historical Review*, Vol. XLIV (1929), p. 65. The main motive, however, was to open the Straits in order to be able to use the Black Sea Fleet in support of Russian influence in the eastern Mediterranean. See Grishina, 'Chernomorskie', p. 132; Zinoviev's memorandum of 25 August 1906, in 'Ob istorii anglo-russkogo soglasheniia 1907' ogo goda', *Krasnyi arkhiv*, Vols LXIX–LXX (1935), pp. 5–18; Williams, 'The revolution of 1905 and Russian foreign policy', p. 16.
52   Zakher, 'Konstantinopol' i prolivy', p. 49.
53   Mandelstam, 'La politique russe', pp. 656–91.
54   ibid., pp. 692–708; Anderson, *Eastern Question*, pp. 289–90; E. C. Thaden, 'Charykov and Russian foreign policy at Constantinople in 1914', *Journal of Central European Affairs*, Vol. XVI, no. 1 (1956), pp. 23–44.
55   Zakher, 'Konstantinopol' i ptolivy', pp. 50–65; K. F. Shatsillo, *Russkii imperializm i razvitie flota* (Moscow, 1968), pp. 148–62.
56   On the industrialisation of Russia, see: R. Portal, 'The industrialization of Russia', in H. J. Habakkuk and M. M. Postan (eds), *The Cambridge Economic History of Europe*, Vol. VI, pt 2 (Cambridge 1965), pp. 801–72; T. von Laue, *Sergei Witte and the Industrialization of Russia* (New York, 1963); M. E. Falkus, *The Industrialization of Russia, 1700–1914* (London, 1972).
57   T. von Laue, 'A secret memorandum of Sergei Witte on the industrialization of Russia', *Journal of Modern History*, Vol. XXVI, no. 1 (1954), pp. 60–74.
58   Portal, 'Industrialization', p. 815, concludes, 'The development of industrial life depended very largely, in the end, on sales of grain abroad . . .'. See also P. I. Liashchenko, *A History of the National Economy of Russia to the 1917 Revolution*, trans. L. M. Herman (New York, 1949), pp. 718–38; P. A. Khromov, *Ekonomicheskoe razvitie Rossii v XIX–XX vekakh* (Moscow, 1950), p. 361; A. Kahan, 'Government policies and the industrialization of Russia', *Journal of Economic History*, Vol. XXVII, no. 4 (1967), pp. 460–77; Margaret Miller, *The Economic Development of Russia, 1905–1914* (London, 1926), pp. 50–6; A. Raffalovich, *Russia: Its Trade and Commerce* (London, 1918), pp. 306, 307. For an argument that Russia's indebtedness did not lead to foreign control over her foreign policy, see J. P. Sontag, 'Tsarist debts and Tsarist foreign policy', *Slavic Review*, Vol. XXVII, no. 4 (1968), pp. 529–41.
59   Miller, *Economic Development*, pp. 44, 74; M. Kholisher, 'Ekonomicheskoe znachenie Dardanell', in F. Rotshtein (ed.), *Prolivy. Sbornik statei* (Moscow, 1924), pp. 64–9; Khromov, *Ekonomicheskoe*, p. 492.
60   Bestuzhev, *Bor'ba v Rossii*, pp. 48, 49.
61   V. A. Gurko-Kriazhin, *Blizhnii Vostok i derzhavy* (Moscow, 1925), pp. 44, 45.
62   Raffalovich, *Russia*, p. 304.
63   Gurko-Kriazhin, *Blizhnii Vostok*, p. 49.
64   ibid., p. 50.
65   Portal, 'Industrialization', p. 857.

66 F. Lorimer, *Population of the Soviet Union: History and Prospects* (Geneva, 1946), pp. 17–23.
67 'At a whim, with a stroke of the pen, the master of Constantinople can disrupt both the agricultural life of Russia and the supply of food to many European countries': Kholisher, 'Ekonomicheskoe', p. 64.
68 Shatsillo, *Russkii imperializm*, pp. 98, 99.
69 'Report of S. D. Sazonov on Russia's Near Eastern policy, 23 November 1913', in Zakher, 'Konstantinopol' i prolivy', pp. 69–76.
70 Calculated from Khromov, *Ekonomicheskoe*, pp. 452–5, 468–71, and Raffalovich, *Russia*, p. 504.
71 Novichev, *Ocherki Ekonomiki Turtsii do mirovoi voiny*, p. 287.
72 ibid., p. 284; F. Courdoglu, *La Turquie économique* (Anvers, 1928), pp. 66, 67.
73 E. Zaleski, *Les Courants commerciaux de l'Europe danubienne au cours de la première moitié du XX siècle* (Paris, 1952), p. 43.
74 Miller, *Economic Development*, p. 46.
75 'The limited extent of our material interests in Turkey has long been recognised as a serious obstacle to strengthening our influence there: memorandum by Zinoviev cited by Novichev, *Ocherki Ekonomiki Turtsii do mirovoi voiny*, p. 227.
76 ibid., p. 228.
77 Shatsillo, *Russkii imperializm*, pp. 93, 94.
78 ibid., p. 94.
79 V. K. Lisenko, *Blizhnii Vostok kak rynok sbyta russkikh tovarov*, 2 vols (St Petersburg, 1913), Vol. I, pp. 1–26, 168–276.
80 Gurko-Kriazhin, *Blizhnii Vostok*, pp. 28, 29; Adamov, *Razdel aziatskoi Turtsii*, pp. 26–8.
81 ibid., pp. 9–15; Blaisdell, *European Financial Control*, p. 44.
82 Novichev, *Ocherki Ekonomiki Turtsii do mirovoi voiny*, p. 225; Milgrim, 'The 1878 War Indemnity', passim.
83 Novichev, *Ocherki Ekonomiki Turtsii do mirovoi voiny*, p. 227, citing Gulkievich to Sazonov, 10(23) February 1913, *Mezhdunarodnye otnosheniia v epokhu imperializma* (hereafter *MOVEI*), 3rd series, Vol. I, no. 199, pp. 240–1.
84 Novichev, *Ocherki Ekonomiki Turtsii do mirovoi voiny*, p. 228; also Giers to Sazonov, 21 June (4 July) 1914, *MOVEI*, 3rd series, Vol. I, no. 83, p. 127. For the general background to the agreement see Novichev, *Ocherki Ekonomiki Turtsii do mirovoi voiny*, Gurko-Kriazhin, *Blizhnii Vostok*, H. Howard, *The Partition of Turkey: A Diplomatic History, 1913–1923* (Norman, Okla., 1931), pp. 52–9; Blaisdell, *European Financial Control*, pp. 231–3.
85 Novichev, *Ocherki Ekonomiki Turtsii do mirovoi voiny*, 235–40; Gurko-Kriazhin, *Blizhnii Vostok*, pp. 18–30, *MOVEI*, 2nd series, Vol. XX, pt 2, and 3rd series, Vols I–IV, contain documents on Russian commercial and economic policy in Turkey between 1912 and 1914. Russian railway policy, being largely a strategic interest, is dealt with above, pp. 89–92.
86 D. Geyer, *Der Russische Imperialismus* (Göttingen, 1977), p. 258. See also Marian Kent, 'Constantinople and Asiatic Turkey, 1905–1914', in F. H. Hinsley (ed.), *British Foreign Policy under Sir Edward Grey* (Cambridge, 1977), pp. 148–64.
87 See: K. F. Shatsillo, *Rossiia pered pervoi mirovoi voiny* (Moscow, 1974); K. F. Shatsillo, 'O disproportsii vooruzhennykh sil Rossii nakanune pervoi mirovoi voiny (1906–1911)', *Istoricheskie zapiski*, Vol. LXXXIII (1969), pp. 123–36.
88 Khromov, *Ekonomicheskoe*, pp. 524–9.
89 For a discussion of the economic aspects of Russian military preparations, see Geyer, *Der Russische Imperialismus*, pp. 192–220.
90 Shatsillo, *Russkii imperializm*, chs 1 and 2. Typical is the view of the Chairman of the Council of Ministers, P. A. Stolypin, that 'Every world power cannot but take part in world politics, cannot but take part in political combinations or renounce her right to have a voice in the solution of world events. A fleet is a lever to implement that right. It is the attribute of a Great Power' (p. 24).
91 ibid., pp. 121–4.
92 ibid., pp. 92–6.
93 ibid., pp. 124–7; M. Petrov, *Podgotovka Rossii k mirovoi voine na more* (Moscow, 1926), pp. 133–8.
94 Shatsillo, *Russkii imperializm*, pp. 97, 98.
95 ibid., pp. 109–21; Petrov, *Podgotovka Rossii*, pp. 138, 139.

96 Shatsillo, *Russkii imperializm*, pp. 117, 118.
97 ibid., pp. 130–6; Petrov, *Podgotovka Rossii*, pp. 139–45.
98 P. Mosely, 'Russian policy in 1911–12', *Journal of Modern History*, Vol. XII, no. 1 (1940), pp. 69–86; Thaden, 'Charykov and Russian foreign policy', pp. 25–44.
99 ibid., passim.
100 Shatsillo, *Russkii imperializm*, pp. 100–9, 144–6; Petrov, *Podgotovka Rossii*, pp. 163–7.
101 Shatsillo, *Russkii imperializm*, pp. 151, 152; Zakher, 'Konstantinopol' i prolivy', pp. 67–9.
102 ibid., pp. 69–76; Shatsillo, *Russkii imperializm*, pp. 152, 153.
103 ibid., pp. 153–9.
104 ibid., pp. 161, 162.
105 Geyer, *Der Russische Imperialismus*, pp. 218–30. See F. Kazemzadeh, 'Russian imperialism and Persian railways', *Russian Thought and Politics*, Harvard Slavic Studies, 4 (The Hague, 1957), pp. 355–63; A. T. Sagretyan, *Istoriia zhelezhykh dorog Zakavkaz'ia* (Erevan, 1970), passim.
106 Kazemzadeh, *Russia and Britain in Persia*, pp. 488–90.
107 'K istorii Potsdamskogo soglasheniia 1911 g.', *Krasnyi arkhiv*, Vol. LVIII (1933), pp. 52–7.
108 I. I. Astaf'ev, 'Potsdamskoe soglashenie 1911 g.', *Istoricheskie zapiski*, Vol. LXV (1970), pp. 142–58. See also Trumpener, below, p. 120, and for the French reaction, Fulton, below, pp. 157–8.
109 'K istorii Potsdamskogo soglasheniia 1911 g.'; Kazemzadeh, *Russia and Britain in Persia*, pp. 395–7.
110 ibid., p. 396.
111 Adamov, *Razdel aziatskoi Turtsii*, pp. 38–44; Ahmad, above, pp. 11–12.
112 Adamov, *Razdel aziatskoi Turtsii*, pp. 40–4; Fulton, below, pp. 157–9.
113 Novichev, *Ocherki Ekonomiki Turtsii do mirovoi voiny*, pp. 231–4; *MOVEI*, 2nd series, Vol. XIX, pt 1, no. 637, p. 298.
114 Adamov, *Razdel aziatskoi Turtsii*, pp. 40–4; *Materialy po istorii franko-russkikh otnoshenii za 1910–1914 gg.* (Moscow, 1922), pp. 24, 25, 52–4.
115 Thaden, 'Charykov and Russian foreign policy', pp. 25–44.
116 For the discussions between Russian officials on this subject, see *MOVEI*, 2nd series, Vol. XVIII, pts 1 and 2; Vol. XIX, pts 1 and 2; Vol. XX, pts 1 and 2. The text of the notes exchanged is in Adamov, *Razdel aziatskoi Turtsii*, pp. 184–6.
117 W. R. Stanley, 'Review of Turkish Asiatic railways to 1918: some political–military considerations', *Journal of Transport History*, Vol. VII, no. 3 (1966), pp. 180–204.
118 Baron R. Rosen, *Forty Years of Diplomacy*, 2 Vols (London, 1922), Vol. II, p. 101.
119 On the spread and potency of nationalist sentiments (Neo-Slavism and Great Russianism), and their effect on foreign policy, see ibid., pp. 96–143; McGrew, 'Some imperatives', pp. 206, 209, 210; Geyer, *Der Russische Imperialismus*, pp. 220–37; Hosking, *Russian Constitutional Experiment*, pp. 215–26.
120 For the text of the Convention, see J. C. Hurewitz, *Diplomacy in the Near and Middle East*, 2 vols (Princeton, NJ, 1956), Vol. I, pp. 266, 267. For recent analyses, see: O. Hauser, 'Die Englisch-Russisch Konvention von 1907 und die Meerengenfrage', *Geschichtliche Kraefte und Entscheidungen: Festschrift zum Otto Becker* (Wiesbaden, 1954), pp. 233–65; Beryl J. Williams, 'Great Britain and Russia, 1905 to the 1907 Convention', in Hinsley, *British Foreign Policy*, pp. 133–48. For the British attitude, see also Kent, below, pp. 184–5, and Kent, 'Constantinople and Asiatic Turkey', in Hinsley, *British Foreign Policy*, pp. 156–9. Izvolskii is reported as assuring the Tsar that the Convention 'restored to Russia her full freedom of action and returned her to a fitting place among the European Powers', Grishina, 'Chernomorskie prolivy vo vneshnei politike Rossii', p. 176.
121 Mandelstam, 'La politique russe', pp. 657–62; Anderson, *Eastern Question*, p. 280.
122 Dakin, *Greek Struggle*, pp. 320–3, 340–59, 397–401. See also Bridge, above, p. 37. At the Reval meeting between Edward VII and Nicholas II in June 1908 the discussion centred on Macedonia. There was no formal mention of the Straits Question. Izvolskii was at pains to point out his concern to maintain good relations with two Germanic Powers; Bestuzhev, *Bor'ba v Rossii*, pp. 153, 154. See also Ahmad, above, p. 5.
123 For a full examination of the attitudes of the various sections of the Duma and the press to the annexation crisis, see Bestuzhev, *Bor'ba v Rossii*, pp. 199–293. See also Bridge, above, pp. 37–8.
124 Anderson, *Eastern Question*, pp. 287–8.
125 ibid., pp. 289, 290; Mandelstam, 'La politique russe', pp. 692–707; Thaden, 'Charykov and

Russian foreign policy', pp. 25–44. Owing to a misunderstanding between Charykov and the Acting Foreign Minister, A. A. Neratov, Charykov handed his draft agreement to the Porte before the response of the Powers, or the Turks, had been properly elucidated. The fault was with Neratov, rather than Charykov. See also W. L. Langer, 'Russia, the Straits Question and the origins of the Balkan League, 1908–1912', *Political Science Quarterly*, Vol. XLIII, no. 3 (1928), pp. 321–63.

126   Thaden, *Russia and the Balkan Alliance*, passim; Anderson, *Eastern Question*, p. 290; Langer, 'Russia, the Straits Question and the origins of the Balkan League'. For the scathing comments of Hartwig and Nekliudov on the idea, see *MOVEI*, 2nd series, Vol. XVIII, pt 2, no. 806, pp. 309–11; Vol. XIX, pt 1, no. 97, pp. 93 and 94, and no. 98, p. 95. See also Bridge, above, p. 42.

127   See E. C. Helmreich, *The Diplomacy of the Balkan Wars* (Cambridge, Mass., 1938); Rossos, *Russia and the Balkans*, passim.

128   Shatsillo, *Russkii imperializm*, pp. 101, 102, points out that the Black Sea Fleet in the autumn of 1912 had only two transport ships available and could land only 5,000 men at the Bosporus. In January 1913 only one ship was to hand and it was only capable of ferrying 750 men. See also Rossos, *Russia and the Balkans*, pp. 212, 477–81. Sazonov also dared not act lest the Turks close the Straits and cut off Russian grain exports in a critical harvest period.

129   ibid., p. 212.

130   G. Zotiades, 'Russia and the question of the Straits and Constantinople during the Balkan Wars', *Balkan Studies*, Vol. II, no. 2 (Thessaloniki, 1970), pp. 285–98. For Prince Trubetskoy's memorandum of 30 Oct. (12 Nov.) 1912, see *MOVEI*, 3rd series, Vol. IV, pt 1, no. 227, pp. 232–3.

131   For Admiral Lieven's memorandum of 15 (28) Nov. 1912, see Zakher, 'Konstantinopol' i prolivy', pp. 58, 59. In this collection are also other memoranda by Sazonov, the representative of the Naval General Staff, Captain Nemits and Admiral Grigorovich which illustrate their common determination to uphold the *status quo* at the Straits and to create a Black Sea Fleet capable of seizing the Bosporus in the event of final Ottoman collapse.

132   R. J. Kerner, 'The mission of Liman von Sanders', *Slavonic Review*, Vol. VI, nos 16–18 (1927–8), pp. 12–27, 344–63, 543–60; Vol. VII, no. 19 (1928–9), pp. 90–112. The Russians were bound to regard the appointment as a grave threat, even though the extent of German influence at the Porte may have been less than they imagined. See U. Trumpener, *Germany and the Ottoman Empire, 1914–18* (Princeton, NJ, 1968), p. 368; also Trumpener, below, pp. 114–120, and his article 'Liman von Sanders and the German–Ottoman alliance', *Journal of Contemporary History*, Vol. I, no. 4 (1966), pp. 179 ff.

133   Zakher, 'Konstantinopol' i prolivy', pp. 69–76; Kerner, 'Mission of Liman von Saunders', pp. 93–4.

134   Stieve, *Izvolsky*, pp. 219–29; Kerner, 'Mission of Liman von Sanders', pp. 97–102.

135   ibid., pp. 102–4. See also n. 132 above.

136   Zakher, 'Konstantinopol' i prolivy', pp. 51–4. For an accurate depiction of the mood of the conference, see M. T. Florinsky, *Russia: A History and an Interpretation*, 2 vols (New York, 1947), Vol. II, p. 1308; S. D. Sazonov, *Fateful Years* (New York, 1928), pp. 126, 127.

137   Howard, *Partition of Turkey*, pp. 50–9; Kent, 'Constantinople and Asiatic Turkey', pp. 153–4. See also Kent, below, p. 182; and, for the French policy, Fulton, below, pp. 159–61.

138   The plan would probably have satisfied the Russian interest in maintaining political stability in the region without giving her the dominance to which she aspired. See R. H. Davison, 'The Armenian crisis, 1912–14', *American Historical Review*, Vol. LIII, no. 3 (1948), pp. 481–505; R. Hovannisian, *Armenia on the Road to Independence* (Berkeley, Calif., 1967), pp. 31–9.

139   Howard, *Partition of Turkey*, pp. 72–5; Sazonov, *Fateful Years*, pp. 133–8. Was there a real chance of a Turko-Russian *rapprochement* in May 1914? Both Sazonov and the Turkish Ambassador in Berlin, Muhtar Pasha, seem to have thought so; Howard, *Partition of Turkey*, pp. 71–5. See also Ahmad, above, p. 15.

140   *MOVEI*, 3rd series, Vol. VI, pt 1, no. 94, pp. 85–90.

141   C. J. Smith, *The Russian Struggle for Power, 1914–1917: A Study of Russian Policy during the First World War* (New York, 1956), pp. 69–76; Adamov, *Razdel aziatskoi Turtsii*, pp. 56–66; A. Cunningham, 'The wrong horse?', *St Antony's Papers*, Vol. XVII (Oxford, 1965), pp. 56–76. See also Trumpener, below, pp. 120–1, and his *Germany and the Ottoman Empire*, pp. 15 ff.; Ahmad, above, pp. 15–17.

142 Adamov, *Evropeiskiederzhavy i Turtsiia*, Vol. I, p. 155; Smith, *Russian Struggle*, pp. 72–4.

143 ibid., pp. 76–8; Howard, *Partition of Turkey*, pp. 119–20; M. Paléologue, *La Russie des Tsars pendant la grande guerre*, 3 vols (Paris, 1921), Vol. I, pp. 135–6.

144 Sazonov, *Fateful Years*, pp. 227–31. For the economic effects of Russia's isolation in the war, see Baron B. E. Nolde, *Russia in the Economic War* (New Haven, Conn., 1928), pp. 22–44.

145 Smith, *Russian Struggle*, pp. 76–82; Paléologue, *La Russie des Tsars*, pp. 181–2.

146 Smith, *Russian Struggle*, pp. 84–8; See also: W. A. Renzi, 'Great Britain, Russia and the Straits, 1914–1915', *Journal of Modern History*, Vol. XLII, no. 1 (1970), pp. 1–20; C. J. Smith, 'Great Britain and the 1914–1915 Straits agreement with Russia: the British promise of November 1914', *American Historical Review*, Vol. LXX, no. 4 (1965), pp. 1015–54; R. J. Kerner, 'Russia, the Straits and Constantinople, 1914–1915', *Journal of Modern History*, Vol. I, no. 3 (1929), pp. 400–15. See also Kent, below, pp. 185–6.

147 Smith, *Russian Struggle*, pp. 97–110.

148 ibid., pp. 110–14; Adamov, *Evropeiskei derzhavy i Turtsiia*, Vol. I, pp. 156–81.

149 Smith, *Russian Struggle*, pp. 128–34; Adamov, *Evropeiskie derzhavy i Turtsiia*, Vol. I, pp. 181–95; Florinsky, *Russia*, Vol. II, pp. 1350–1, n. 12.

150 For the war in the Caucasus, see W. E. D. Allen and P. Muratoff, *Caucasian Battlefields: A History of Wars on the Turko-Caucasian Border, 1828–1921* (Cambridge, 1953), pp. 239 ff. The authors believe that Russia's most vital political and economic interests were centred in Asia Minor and that she should have driven through Armenia to secure an outlet to the eastern Mediterranean at Alexandretta. They imply (p. 231) that Russia's 'strangely defensive' strategy was due solely to her obeisance to French war plans.

151 Howard, *Partition of Turkey*, pp. 121–7; Smith, *Russian Struggle*, pp. 186–216.

152 Howard, *Partition of Turkey*, pp. 127–36; Smith, *Russian Struggle*, pp. 217–38; Kerner, 'Russia, the Straits and Constantinople', pp. 400–15. See also Kent, 'Asiatic Turkey, 1914–1916', pp. 442–3, and Fulton, below, pp. 162–3.

153 Roberts, 'Introduction to Dallin, *Russian Diplomacy*, p. xii; R. J. Kerner, 'Russia and the Straits Question, 1915–1917', *Slavonic and East European Review*, Vol. VIII, no. 24 (1930), pp. 589–600; Adamov, *Evropeiskie derzhavy i Turtsiia*, Vol. I. pp. 251–2.

154 Allen and Muratoff, *Caucasian Battlefields*, *op. cit.*, pp. 239 ff; Adamov, *Razdel aziatskoi Turtsii*, pp. 77–80; Smith, *Russian Struggle*, pp. 352–3. For summaries of the activities of the Black Sea Fleet during the war, see D. Mitchell, *A History of Russian Sea Power* (London, 1974), pp. 311–21; D. Woodward, *The Russians at Sea* (London, 1965), pp. 173–9.

155 Smith, *Russian Struggle*, pp. 124–8; F. Kazemzadeh, *The Struggle for Transcaucasia, 1917–1921* (Oxford, 1951), p. 26.

156 Smith, *Russian Struggle*, pp. 234–8; Adamov, *Razdel aziatskoi Turtsii*, pp. 127–36.

157 Hovannisian, *Armenia*, p. 67.

158 Allen and Muratoff, *Caucasian Battlefields*, pp. 437–9; A. Emin, *Turkey in the World War* (Oxford, 1930), pp. 261–5.

159 Howard, *Partition of Turkey*, pp. 132–5; Florinsky, *Russia*, Vol. II, pp. 1351–2.

160 Howard, *Partition of Turkey*, p. 135. Among those who wanted a separate peace with Turkey were the Chief of the Army Staff, General M. V. Alekseev, and Sazonov's representative at army HQ, Prince N. A. Kudashev. They held that Russia's survival in the war depended on her abandoning the utopian and dangerous dreams of domination at the Straits and throwing all her forces against Germany; Adamov, *Evropeiskie derzhavy i Turtsiia*, Vol. I, pp. 103–9.

161 Howard, *Partition of Turkey*, pp. 184–7; Smith, *Russian Struggle*, pp. 358–82; Adamov, *Razdel aziatskoi Turtsii*, pp. 154–235. In the Franco-Russian agreement of 26 April 1916, Sazonov had to sanction French control over all Cilician Armenia and the preservation of French concessionary interests in the Russian zone in order to prevent the French from approaching too closely to the north Persian frontier. The 'existing rights' mentioned in the Anglo-Russian agreement were in the Black Sea coastal trade, mining at Kersund, port and wharf construction concessions at Samsun and Trebizond; Adamov, *Razdel aziatskoi Turtsii*, pp. 161–235. See also Kent, 'Asiatic Turkey', pp. 443–51, and below, pp. 186–7, and Fulton, below, pp. 163–4.

162 For the economic and social disintegration resulting from the war, see Florinsky, *Russia*, Vol. II, pp. 1353–79.

163 ibid., pp. 1426–7.

164 ibid., p. 1452.

165   Kazemzadeh, *Struggle for Transcaucasia*, pp. 85–144.
166   For the peace negotiations, see J. W. Wheeler-Bennett, *Brest-Litovsk: The Forgotten Peace, March 1918* (London, 1938), passim.
167   Russian religious interests in the Ottoman Empire were in the care of the Russian Orthodox Palestine Society, a voluntary, philanthropic body founded in 1881 and supported mainly by private contribution. Its aim was to spread information about Russian Orthodoxy and culture, to support the many thousands of Russian pilgrims visiting the Holy Land annually and to maintain schools and clinics. In 1906 it owned 2,000,000 roubles' worth of property, eight hostels for pilgrims, a hospital, six clinics and a hundred schools with 10,400 registered pupils. Its educational and spiritual influence was small compared with that of the similar British, German, French and Italian bodies, and declined steadily with the fall in Russia's prestige following the defeat by Japan and the revolution of 1905. It was regarded with suspicion by Greek Orthodox and French religious interests, and for that reason was never allowed by the Russian Foreign Ministry to play any political role, although practically the entire personnel of the Ministry were society members. Its activities had to be subordinated to the wider aims of Russian foreign policy. See D. Hopwood, *The Russian Presence in Syria and Palestine, 1843–1914* (London, 1969); T. G. Stavrou, *Russian Interests in Palestine, 1882–1914* (Thessaloniki, 1963), and Sazonov, *Fateful Years*, p. 257.
168   See I. Spector, *The First Russian Revolution: Its Impact on Asia* (Englewood Cliffs, NJ, 1962) and Ahmad, above, passim.

5 Germany and the End of the Ottoman Empire

Ulrich Trumpener, University of Alberta

By the end of the nineteenth century, only three decades after its unification under Prussian leadership, the German Reich had become one of the most powerful states in the world – economically, technologically and militarily. For the Germans themselves 'the rate of change was stupefying, for foreign observers alarming'.[1] The population of the Reich was growing by over half a million each year, despite the continued emigration of thousands of people to the United States and other overseas areas.[2] The Kaiser's army (a composite force made up of 'royal contingents' from Prussia, Bavaria, Saxony and Württemberg) was rated by many contemporaries as the most formidable in the world, even though it was significantly smaller than the Russian army and only slightly larger than the army of the French Republic.[3] Following the appointment of Admiral Alfred Tirpitz as Secretary of State of the Imperial Naval Office in 1897, construction of a big fleet had begun as well, leading eventually to concern and alarm in Britain. By 1910 over twenty new battleships and many other warships had been commissioned.[4]

The naval construction programme contributed significantly to the economic boom in Germany. The iron and steel industries were growing steadily, and such newly established chemical companies as Bayer, Hoechst and BASF, as well as firms producing electrical equipment, like AEG and Siemens, were already well on their way to dominant positions in the world.[5] Likewise, the transportation system of Germany was rapidly expanding, with total railway trackage in 1900 exceeding 50,000 kilometres and the merchant marine having almost 1,300 steamships with a total tonnage of over 1 million.[6]

Since 1890, when Kaiser Wilhelm II had sent Bismarck into retirement, Germany's foreign policy had become increasingly erratic and fumbling. Faced with Berlin's refusal to renew the Reinsurance Treaty, Russia had moved closer to France and eventually concluded a defensive alliance with her. Germany's relations with Britain had not really improved, as Bismarck's successors had initially hoped; on the contrary, from about 1895 onwards friction between London and Berlin had increased.[7] While Bismarck had picked up sizeable pieces of colonial property in the mid-1880s, mostly in Africa but also in the Pacific, nationalistic pressure-groups and some segments of the German business community remained dissatisfied and called for further imperial acquisitions and a greater voice in world affairs. Partly in response to these pressures, and partly in an effort to deflect socialist and radical demands for sweeping changes in the political system and social structure of the country, the Kaiser and his government in the latter half of the 1890s indulged in a number of speeches, gestures and expansionist moves (particularly in East Asia and the Pacific) which caused annoyance or outright concern among some of the other Great Powers.[8] Simultaneously, German involvement in the affairs of the Ottoman Empire grew steadily, highlighted by rising investments in, and trade with, the sultan's realm.[9] To top it all, Wilhelm II in 1898 made an official visit to Abdul Hamid in Constantinople (his second in nine years) and then went on to the Holy Land. On 31 October, Reformation Day, he personally dedicated a new Protestant church in Jerusalem, the Erlöserkirche (Church of the Redeemer). Two days earlier, to placate the large Roman Catholic minority in Germany, he had also turned over a historic lot, La Dormition de la Sainte Vierge, to the Deutsche Verein vom Heiligen Lande (German Association in the Holy Land) for its use. A week later, the Kaiser appeared in Damascus, where the local ulema welcomed him in the name of the 'three hundred million Muslims' of the world (a rather inflated figure) and where Wilhelm, in response, assured his listeners that Muslims everywhere could always count on his friendship.[10]

Contrary to what has sometimes been said on that subject, German interest and involvement in the Ottoman Empire went back a long way. Already in the 1830s several Prussian officers, among them the future Field-Marshal von Moltke, had worked as advisers or instructors in the sultan's army.[11] Between 1868 and 1875 about 750 Swabian religious dissidents, the *Templers*, had moved to the Holy Land and built up several prosperous settlements.[12] The Prussian consulate in Jerusalem, opened in 1842, had soon attained a fairly important position in Palestine, with the support and protection of both the *Templers* and the local Jewish communities forming an integral part of its activities.[13] And, of course, German engineers and surveyors had been quite active in the sultan's realm since the 1870s, followed in due time by companies interested in railway construction. The first major concession in Asiatic Turkey granted to a German group was signed in 1888, calling for the construction of a line from the Bosporus (actually from Izmit) to Angora. In the very same year, traffic on a trans-Balkan line from Constantinople to central Europe finally began.[14]

Before attempting an assessment of German policies and activities in the Ottoman Empire after the turn of the century, a few words must be said about the institutions and some of the individuals who were involved in the direction of Germany's Turkish policies.

While Wilhelm II and his imperial chancellors – Bernhard, Prince von Bülow (1900–9), Theobald von Bethmann Hollweg (1909–17), Georg Michaelis (1917), Georg Count von Hertling (1917–18) and Prince Max von Baden (1918) – were officially in charge of German foreign policy, a host of other institutions and individuals participated in, and influenced, its formulation and implementation. Like most other countries, the Reich had a Foreign

Office (Auswärtige Amt) and a network of embassies, legations and consular offices abroad. The secretary of state in charge of the Auswärtige Amt, like all other department heads of the imperial government, was constitutionally and in practice a subordinate of the Chancellor (rather than his colleague). He was, thus, often little more than an executor of policies decided elsewhere, but some strong-willed individuals in that post did at times manage to shape these policies themselves. It is also clear that certain officials in the Auswärtige Amt, especially Baron Friedrich von Holstein (senior counsellor in the Political Division until 1906) wielded far more influence than most contemporaries realised.[15]

In Constantinople, the Reich was represented by both an embassy and a consular office. In addition, a growing number of German consuls and vice-consuls were stationed in the various regions of the sultan's realm. By 1912, German consular posts in Asiatic Turkey alone numbered close to twenty, including three in the Mesopotamian region (Mosul, Baghdad, Basra), over half a dozen in 'Syria' and Lebanon (Aleppo, Damascus, Tarabulus, Beirut, Haifa, Jaffa and Jerusalem), two in Cilicia (Adana and Mersin), and two on the Black Sea coast (Samsun and Trabzon).[16]

Though it ranked below London, Paris, Vienna, or St Petersburg, a diplomatic posting in Constantinople nevertheless carried considerable prestige and influence with it.[17] From 1897 onwards, the German embassy in Pera was headed by a succession of very capable men, namely Baron Adolf Marschall von Bieberstein (to 1912), Baron Hans von Wangenheim (to 1915), Count Paul von Wolff-Metternich (to 1916), Richard von Kühlmann (to 1917), and Count Johann Heinrich von Bernstorff (to 1918).

Marschall von Bieberstein, an energetic Badenese lawyer with extensive experience in the courtroom, had been named secretary of state of the Auswärtige Amt after Bismarck's fall, but eventually he had incurred the dislike of Wilhelm II and his entourage. Sent off to Turkey in 1897, he soon regained the Kaiser's favour and gradually transformed his position at the Bosporus into a very important outpost of the Reich; indeed, some students of the period regard him as the true architect of Germany's Middle Eastern policies prior to the war. During his long tenure in Constantinople the Baron was also used for other diplomatic missions; thus, he headed the German delegation to the Second Hague Conference. Just before his death, in 1912, he was transferred to the embassy in London, a posting he had wanted for a long time.[18]

Wangenheim, his successor, was likewise rated as one of the most capable among Germany's diplomats. He, too, would at times manifest considerable independence of spirit and even pursue a course at variance with Berlin's wishes.[19] Upon his death in 1915, the embassy was taken over by a distinguished older member of the diplomatic corps. Wolff-Metternich had represented Germany at the Court of St James for eleven years (1901–12), trying in vain to heal the growing rift between the two countries. Pulled out of retirement, he found the rough political climate in wartime Turkey (and particularly the anti-Armenian programme of the Porte) little to his liking and had to be recalled within less than a year.[20] His place was taken by Richard von Kühlmann, a Bavarian born in Constantinople (his father had been the first director of the Anatolian Railway Company). Kühlmann was called back to Berlin to take over the Auswärtige Amt in 1917.[21] The last imperial ambassador accredited to the sultan's government, Bernstorff, had previously served for nine years in Washington.[22]

To assist the Ambassador in his work, there were usually two or three counsellors on his staff, plus several dragomans and one military attaché. After the outbreak of war in 1914, further personnel were added, and a naval attaché was appointed as well.

Among the embassy counsellors, several rose to prominence in later years (among them Baron Konstantin von Neurath, a Württemberger, who served as Foreign Minister under Papen, Schleicher and Hitler in the 1930s). Among the military attachés, Major Curt Morgen, who was stationed in Constantinople from 1897 to 1901, was the most successful in later years: he was ennobled in 1904 and became a highly decorated corps commander in the First World War.[23] Several of his successors were less fortunate in their careers. Erich von Leipzig, after six years in Constantinople, was given a regimental command and then retired. He was sent back to Turkey as military attaché in 1915, but died of a bullet wound a few months later in a railway station under rather mysterious circumstances.[24] Walter von Strempel played a very important role during his tenure in Constantinople (1907–14), but ran foul of the new German military mission chief, General Liman von Sanders, and was eventually packed off to Germany as 'governor' of some Ottoman princes who were going there for military training.[25] His successor, Major Karl von Laffert, likewise ran into trouble with Liman and was sent back to Germany early in 1915. Undaunted, he later submitted a memorandum to the Crown Prince in which he advocated drastic postwar reforms, including the replacement of civilian diplomats by military men in many foreign capitals. During the 1930s, Herr von Laffert attained a rank in the SS and sat as a member of the notorious People's Court.[26] The last military attaché in Turkey, soon raised to general's rank and given the title of military plenipotentiary, was the Bavarian staff officer Otto von Lossow. He had previously served as an adviser in the sultan's army and even commanded an Ottoman division during the First Balkan War. General von Lossow later rose to command of the Reichswehr's Bavarian division and played a key role in Munich before and during Hitler's beer-hall *putsch* in 1923.[27]

Several German consulates in the Ottoman Empire were routinely staffed by 'non-professional' local residents, usually businessmen, who sometimes had little interest in their official duties. Rudolf Wönckhaus, for instance, a hard-working and increasingly prosperous German trader in the Persian Gulf area, accepted his appointment as 'honorary consul' in Basra around 1910 with great reluctance and apparently never wrote any reports to his superiors.[28]

Among the career consuls serving in the Ottoman Empire after 1900, many were well trained in Middle Eastern affairs and languages. A few of them were expected to serve in that part of the world for the rest of their days; others were eventually posted elsewhere and subsequently rose to some prominence. Wilhelm Stemrich, for instance, after long service as consul-general in Constantinople and a brief stint in Tehran, became the under-secretary of state in the Auswärtige Amt (1907–11). Friedrich Rosen, who had worked in consular positions in Baghdad and Jerusalem around the turn of the century, later headed imperial legations in several European capitals and briefly served as German Foreign Minister after the First World War. Another man of some prominence who had extensive consular experience in and around the Ottoman Empire (Erzerum, Damascus and Tiflis) was Count Friedrich Werner von der Schulenburg. He would later serve as German ambassador to Moscow (from 1934 until Hitler's invasion of the Soviet Union) and was executed in 1944 for his opposition to the Nazi regime.[29]

At least two other individuals must be mentioned. One was Paul Weitz, a newspaperman who represented the *Frankfurter Zeitung* at the Golden Horn from 1895 to the end of the First World War. His work as an intelligence-gatherer and contact man for the embassy appears to have been highly successful.[30] Another valuable contact, particularly to Enver Pasha, was provided by Lieutenant-Commander Hans Humann of the German Imperial Navy. Born to an archaeologist in Smyrna, Humann had spent part of his youth in the Ottoman Empire and knew Enver since those days. He was posted to Turkey in the autumn of 1913 with rather vaguely defined functions (including command of the ageing ambassadorial stationnaire *Loreley*), and it was only in 1915 that his *de facto* role as naval attaché was formally acknowledged. In any event, until his recall in 1917, Humann was probably the most valuable contact man to the CUP regime the Germans had.[31]

As previously mentioned, some Prussian officers had been serving in the sultan's army since the early nineteenth century. From 1882 onwards, German involvement in the military affairs of Turkey had increased with the arrival of a small group of officers under Generalmajor Otto Kaehler. Following Kaehler's death in 1885, the group had been taken over by Lieutenant-Colonel Baron Colmar von der Goltz, who worked with great energy and enthusiasm during the next ten years, advising the Turks on general staff matters, military organisation and training procedures. Late in 1895, Goltz returned to active service in the Prussian army, first as a divisional commander and later as a 'commanding general' (corps commander), but he kept in touch with his Ottoman pupils and some members of his mission remained in Turkey. One of them, Louis Kamphövener, ennobled in 1900, served as inspector-general of the sultan's infantry for a number of years; several others officiated as inspectors of the Ottoman cavalry, artillery and engineering corps. Among the inspectors who were sent to Turkey in later years was Erich Weber, a colonel in the engineers, who rose to divisional command during the war and headed one of the Reichswehr's military districts afterwards. (Weber's daughter subsequently married another veteran of military service in Turkey, Karl Dönitz, the later grand admiral and Hitler's successor as head of state.)[32]

In 1913, following the Balkan Wars, a much larger contingent of German army officers was invited to Turkey. Headed by Generalleutnant Otto Liman von Sanders, a recently ennobled cavalry officer of partially Jewish ancestry, this new German 'mission' would take over additional training functions in the sultan's realm.[33] Its appearance in Constantinople late in 1913 caused grave diplomatic tension with Russia.[34]

Probably as important as the presence of German military experts in the Ottoman Empire was the secondment of impressionable young Ottoman lieutenants to German regiments for extended period of training. During the 1890s, on average fifteen to twenty such trainees were annually involved in this programme, with some of them also being posted to the Prussian general staff. Thereafter, the number of trainees fluctuated wildly from year to year, with up to fifty being listed in the German army rolls in some years and practically none in others.[35] Among the early trainees were several prominent Ottoman generals of later years, including Ahmed Izzet Pasha, who served as War Minister in 1913–14, as an army group commander in 1917 and as Grand Vezir in 1918. Another important Ottoman general, Mahmud Şevket Pasha (assassinated while Grand Vezir, in June 1913), had spent almost ten years on duty in southern Germany supervising the delivery of Mauser rifles to the Ottoman army; in consequence he spoke German fluently, but with a pronounced Swabian accent.[36]

The special position German 'reformers' were able to carve out in the Ottoman army was paralleled prior to 1914 by growing British involvement in the Ottoman navy, and French and Italian involvement in the Ottoman *gendarmerie*. However, it is probably fair to say that, thanks to the sheer size and manifold functions of the army in the sultan's realm, the Germans had a considerable advantage over the other European Powers in terms of exerting their influence.

The steady expansion of German economic activity in the Ottoman Empire after the turn of the century was spearheaded by the Deutsche Bank of Berlin. This largest of all German banks was involved particularly in sponsoring various railway enterprises, including the so-called Bagdadbahn, and in organising loans to the Porte. Otherwise the Deutsche Bank remained quite inconspicuous, having no branch offices in the Ottoman Empire until 1909. By contrast, the Deutsche Palästinabank, established in 1899, opened branches in Jerusalem, Jaffa, Haifa, Beirut, Damascus and Tarabulus, as well as harvest-season agencies in Nazareth and Gaza. From 1906 onwards, it also started to co-operate with the Deutsche Orientbank, newly founded by some of the chief competitors of the Deutsche Bank (that is, the Dresdner Bank, the National-bank für Deutschland and the Schaafhausenscher Bankverein). The Deutsche

Orientbank eventually maintained twelve branch offices in the sultan's realm (plus seven in Egypt). The branch in Bursa was managed from 1907 on by Mahmud Celâl (Bayar) who ended his career, in the 1950s, as President of Turkey.[37]

Until the outbreak of the First World War, the most visible and the most controversial aspect of Germany's *pénétration pacifique* of the sultan's realm was the construction of a rail line which would, when finished, link Constantinople, and Europe in general, with Baghdad and the Persian Gulf. During the 1890s a German-controlled syndicate had already built rail connections from the Bosporus to Angora (completed late in 1892) and Konya (completed in 1896), both lines being since operated under German management by the Société du Chemin de Fer Ottoman d'Anatolie (commonly known simply as the Anatolie). As a result of concessions obtained between 1899 and 1903 the same German-controlled syndicate secured the right to build and operate an extension of the line, running from Konya south-eastwards, through Adana, Mosul and Baghdad, to Basra. Financing problems, which were in turn largely caused by political objections from the British, French and Russian governments, as well as some very difficult terrain, especially in the Taurus and Amanus ranges, led to long delays and pauses in the actual construction work (which was handled by the Philipp Holzmann Company of Frankfurt). In 1911 the German sponsors of the railway agreed to some modifications of the concession. Perhaps the most important change was that Baghdad was accepted, at least temporarily, as the terminus of the line.[38] By August 1914 the whole line was still in a badly truncated state. Through train service operated from the vastly expanded terminus on the Asiatic side of the Bosporus, Haydar Pasha, via Konya to an obscure village at the foot of the Taurus Mountains. On the other side of that range the track continued through Cilicia to the foot of the Amanus Mountains. Beyond that second gap, which was almost 100 kilometres wide, trains ran to Aleppo and on to the almost finished Euphrates bridge at Jarabulus, with improvised service possible as far as Tall Abyad. There was also a stretch from Baghdad northwards to Samarra in service.[39]

Despite its truncated condition, the Baghdad Railway on the eve of the war carried close to 600,000 passengers and 116,000 tons of freight annually, though most of the freight, especially between Konya and the Bosporus, moved in one direction only, from the interior to the sea.[40] The rolling stock of both the Anatolie and its Baghdad subsidiary came almost wholly from German firms, notably Henschel, Borsig and Maffei, and by 1914 included approximately 200 steam locomotives and about 3,500 freight or passenger cars.[41]

German rolling stock was also used almost exclusively on the narrow-gauge Hejaz Railway, built under government auspices from Damascus to Medina between 1900 and 1908. The selection of German equipment (nearly 100 locomotives and over 1,100 cars by 1913) was largely due to the fact that the technical management of the entire construction project had been entrusted to Heinrich August Meissner, a graduate engineer from Saxony who had first come to Turkey in 1885. After completing the Hejaz line Meissner directed work on a section of the Baghdad line, built a military railway into the Sinai desert during the First World War, and concluded his career in the 1930s as a technical adviser and academic teacher in Istanbul.[42]

Like the manufacturers of rolling stock, German companies making steel rails benefited considerably from the construction projects in the Ottoman Empire. Between 1910 and 1913, for instance, the value of rails and cross-ties shipped from Germany to Turkey amounted to over 19 million Goldmark, and some German shipping lines derived much of their business from transporting bulky railway supplies. Among these lines the Deutsche Levante-Linie, created in 1889, was for a while the most prominent. From 1906 on, the HAPAG Company of Hamburg maintained a regular service to ports on the Persian Gulf and likewise became involved in supplying the Baghdad Railway enterprise.[43]

Next to German banks and railway interests, several major armaments firms of the Reich were particularly active and visible in prewar Turkey. From the 1880s on, Germany's biggest artillery producer, the Krupp Company of Essen, sold hundreds of heavy and light guns to the sultan's armed forces, sometimes with the active assistance of German officers stationed in Turkey. Baron von der Goltz's efforts in that context in the 1880s and 1890s have often been noted.[44] Major Morgen, when he was serving as military attaché around the turn of the century, likewise did his best to keep the purchase orders coming. As he recalled many years later, the orders going to the Krupp Company were 'on such a scale that its sales representatives in Constantinople, the Huber brothers, became multi-millionaires solely through the commissions they earned thereby'.[45]

Other beneficiaries of Turkish arms purchases were Heinrich Erhardt's Rheinische Metallwaren- und Maschinenfabrik of Düsseldorf (Krupp's principal German competitor in the artillery sector),[46] the Ludwig Loewe Company of Berlin and the Mauser Company of Oberndorf in Swabia, the last two later merged in the Deutsche Waffen- und Munitionsfabriken. Loewe and Mauser supplied large quantities of rifles and carbines to the Turks, while a number of other German firms sold them bullets, cartridges and various other types of hardware.[47]

From the 1880s on, the sultan's navy also bought some of its ships from German yards, but until the outbreak of the First World War the German role in Ottoman naval procurement remained quite small. True, the Ottoman fleet by 1914 included several small destroyers built by the Schichau Company of Elbing as well as *Torgut Reis* and *Heireddin Barbarossa*, two obsolete battleships (launched in 1891) which had been purchased from the Kaiser's navy in 1910, but compared to Turkish orders placed in Britain, which included three dreadnoughts and two cruisers, or even in France, which included six destroyers and two submarines, the German share was very modest indeed.[48] German interest in the exploration and future development of the Mesopotamian oilfields prior to 1914 likewise remained at a fairly low level, in part at least because of limited capital reserves available to the Germans. After much vacillation, the Deutsche Bank agreed in March 1914 to accept a junior position in a British-dominated consortium.[49]

If one looks at trade statistics of the prewar decades, it becomes obvious that the Germans were making headway in that field, but by 1914 they were still far from having a dominant position in the Ottoman Empire. In 1913, Germany ranked fourth (behind Britain, France and Austria-Hungary) as a market for Turkish exports and was in third place (behind Britain and Austria-Hungary) as a source of Turkish imports. Moreover, even though it was growing, trade with the Ottoman Empire still constituted only a very modest segment of Germany's worldwide commercial activities. In 1912, for instance, only about 1.3 per cent of all German exports went to Turkey, and only 0.7 per cent of all German imports came from that country. The figures for 1913 were quite similar: German exports to Turkey, worth 98.4 million Goldmark, consisted (in order of value) of woollen cloth, cotton cloth, cartridges, machinery, wheat flour and other items. Imports from Turkey consisted mainly of tobacco, raisins, woollen rugs, nuts, raw cotton and the like.[50]

While the traditional literature on international relations prior to 1914 has usually, and with some justification, focused on governmental policies and the activities of economic-interest groups, an assessment of Germany's relations with the Ottoman Empire must include at least a number of German religious, cultural and other special-interest groups which were active in the sultan's realm during that period.

Both the Protestants and the Roman Catholics of Germany were represented in the Ottoman Empire by numerous missionaries, nurses, social workers and teachers. The Kaiserswerth Deaconesses, for instance, had been active in the Holy Land since the mid-nineteenth century, and the Jerusalems-Verein (Jerusalem Association) by 1902 maintained eight schools with over 400 pupils. Schools, orphanages, dispensaries and hospitals, both in the Holy Land and in other parts of the Ottoman Empire, were also supported by the Evangelischer Bund (Protestant League), the Deutsche Orient-Mission (German Orient Mission), which was particularly active among the Armenians, the Roman Catholic Palästinaverein (Palestine Association) and a number of other religious organisations.[51]

To many German Jews the affairs of the Ottoman Empire took on new significance as well. Following the creation of the Zionist movement in the 1890s, several German citizens of Jewish background would soon play major roles in the promotion of the cause. Indeed, following Theodor Herzl's death in 1904, the central office of the World Zionist Organisation (WZO) was moved to Cologne (where its new president, Lithuanian-born David

Wolffsohn, was active in the timber business) and later, in 1911, to Berlin, where Professor Otto Warburg, a botanist, carried on as chairman of the organisation.[52] In 1908 the WZO sent a young Prussian lawyer, Arthur Ruppin, to Jaffa as director of its Palestine office. His labours there were difficult but also very successful;[53] indeed, Jewish settlement in Palestine probably owes more to him than to anyone else.[54] Also active in the Holy Land was the Hilfsverein der deutschen Juden (Aid Association of German Jews), founded in 1901 by the cotton magnate James Simon and the prominent journalist Paul Nathan. A willing instrument of German cultural propaganda in Eastern Europe and the Middle East, the Hilfsverein sponsored educational programmes among Jews in which at least part of the instruction would be conducted in the German language. Support of that medium of instruction eventually, in 1912, led the Hilfsverein into a nasty confrontation with Palestinian Zionists over the use of Hebrew in the new technical college in Haifa (the Technikum) – a dispute in which both the German and the Ottoman authorities ultimately became involved.[55]

Ever since Herzl had first approached Kaiser Wilhelm II and other German dignitaries, the small but dedicated group of German Zionists periodically attempted to secure official government support for their cause. For a long time the results were very limited. Until the outbreak of the war the German government did occasionally lend its assistance to Jewish educational and charitable organisations in Palestine and elsewhere in the Ottoman Empire, and some high-ranking German figures did express great sympathy with the concept of further Jewish settlement in the Holy Land, but no one in Berlin was prepared to endanger the Reich's relations with the Ottoman government by any kind of overt support of political Zionism.[56]

While Zionists were dreaming of large-scale Jewish migration to Palestine, the ultra-nationalistic Pan-German League, founded in 1891, dreamed, at least for a while, of using Anatolia as a settlement area for German farmers. From the turn of the century onwards, though, the League increasingly fell into line with official government policy, which emphasised Germany's desire to see the Ottoman Empire preserved and strengthened. Besides, as one of the leading propagandists of the Baghdad Railway project, Paul Rohrbach, repeatedly reminded the German public, the Turks were in no mood to permit large numbers of Germans, or any other foreigners, to settle among them.[57]

Rohrbach, a Baltic German with theological training, had started in the late 1890s to explore and write about the Ottoman Empire. The other prominent 'Orient propagandist' in prewar Germany, Ernst Jäckh, began his advocacy of closer ties with the Turkish realm only in 1908. Aside from writing numerous articles and pamphlets on the subject this enterprising Swabian journalist-scholar also found time to drum up private and government support for the creation of a German–Turkish Association (Deutsch-Türkische Vereinigung).[58] Officially launched in March 1914, the Vereinigung began with about 500 members, but grew about tenfold within the next four years. Dedicated to a variety of programmes, especially the promotion of German educational and cultural influence in the Ottoman Empire, the Vereinigung boasted of a large number of prominent bankers in its governing body, including Arthur von Gwinner of the Deutsche Bank and Hitler's future Economics Minister, Hjalmar Schacht. As the Vereinigung informed the German public at the time of its formation, Germany had a long way to go to catch up with the French, the Americans, the British and the Italians, all of whom had more schools, with more pupils, in the Ottoman Empire than the Reich. Indeed, out of about one thousand foreign schools operating in the sultan's realm, a mere twenty-three were presently offering instruction in German; and only about 3,000 pupils (out of 90,000 attending foreign schools) were being taught in the German institutions.[59] This situation, as Major Theodor Kübel pointed out at about the same time in the Prussian General Staff's military quarterly, was reflected also in the way the German-built Baghdad Railway was run: though the top management was German, most of the employees – Ottoman Turks, Greeks, or Armenians – knew no German at all, but used French instead for all business transactions.[60]

Finally, a few words must be said about Baron Max von Oppenheim, who served on the staff of the German consul-general in Cairo from 1896 to 1910. Oppenheim was highly knowledgeable about Islamic and Arab matters as well as being a successful archaeologist. He has sometimes been depicted as a key figure in the conduct of Germany's Middle Eastern policies before and during the First World War, particularly as regards subversion and the incitement of a Holy War against the Entente Powers. It appears, however, that his influence was actually quite limited.[61] Indeed, as Cecil has recently pointed out, the Baron, because of his Jewish name and ancestry, found it difficult to advance in the foreign service, and there is some evidence in the wartime records of the Germany embassy in Constantinople that his views were not rated very highly there.[62]

In recent years, Wilhelmian Germany has often been depicted as a country with a woefully defective constitutional system, an outmoded social order, a distorted system of values, and a host of inadequate leaders.[63] Some historians have, furthermore, charged that (probably because of these very shortcomings) the foreign and defence policies of the Reich (highlighted by a turn to *Weltpolitik*, rampant navalism, and the adoption of an overly ambitious and politically dangerous campaign plan by the army) were singularly maladroit and, in the final analysis, largely responsible for the outbreak of the First World War in 1914.[64]

Wilhelmian Germany's growing involvement in Turkish affairs – ranging from the promotion of the Baghdad Railway project to overt diplomatic support of the Hamidian regime on some occasions – has likewise often been criticised. Indeed, Berlin's Turkish policies from the 1890s onwards, according to some historians, constitute a major example of German bungling (or provocativeness). They have charged, in particular, that several other European powers (notably Russia, but also Britain and France) had traditional rights and interests in that region and could therefore hardly be expected to welcome yet another competitor in the Middle East.[65]

A British historian of pronounced anti-imperialist views suggested some time ago that in the years leading up to the First World War the Entente Powers 'were each tugging at the best portions of the [Ottoman] Empire from outside', while the Germans were 'endeavouring to hold it together by capturing the whole from within'.[66] Those pithy observations contain an element of truth, but they also exaggerate both the rapaciousness of the Entente and the consistency of Berlin's Turkish policies.

As far as the Germans are concerned, their dedication to the preservation of the Ottoman Empire and their hope of ultimately turning it into a pliable junior partner or outright satellite of the Reich were not nearly as pronounced as has often been claimed. While Kaiser Wilhelm II had a strong personal interest in the sultan's realm and recognised its potential usefulness to the Reich, his feelings on those subjects were shared by only a handful of other senior men in the government. Moreover, the Kaiser himself repeatedly changed his mind on the value of Turkish 'friendship'. Likewise, throughout the prewar years most senior men in the German army and navy did not consider the Ottoman armed forces sufficiently trained and equipped to make much of a contribution in a major European war, although they were all aware of the potential geopolitical advantages of an alliance with Turkey. Altogether it may be concluded that, prior to 1914, Germany's Turkish policies had only one discernible constant, namely the advancement (and protection) of German investments in, and trade with, the Ottoman Empire, while on all other issues Berlin's position was and remained flexible.[67]

From the mid-1890s down to 1908, Germany's official relations with Sultan Abdul Hamid II's regime were usually friendly and at times even cordial. Pushed by Ambassador Marschall in Constantinople and by Wilhelm II at home, the Wilhelmstrasse increasingly thought of the Baghdad Railway project as a matter of national (as distinct from private, capitalistic) concern, and accordingly supported the enterprise to the best of its ability. Since the goodwill of Abdul Hamid was deemed essential in that context, the German government also dissociated itself repeatedly from collective action by some of the other Great Powers which aimed at forcing internal reforms on to the sultan's government.[68]

The Young Turk revolution in the summer of 1908 caught the Germans, like everyone else, by surprise. Ambassador Marschall was on holiday in Germany, several dragomans and other staff members of the embassy were likewise on leave, and the senior man on duty in Pera, Alfred von Kiderlen-Wächter, temporarily found himself in a rather difficult situation.[69] Although most military men among the revolutionaries could be counted on to favour a continuation of friendly relations with the Reich, some leading figures among the Young Turks resented Germany's previous support of the Hamidian regime and tended to look with favour on the liberal principles of the Western Powers and, more particularly, on Britain.[70]

Austria-Hungary's decision later the same year to convert its 'administration' of Bosnia and Herzegovina into outright annexation jeopardised Germany's standing in Constantinople even further, for the Turks, quite understandably, held Berlin at least partially responsible for the objectionable policies of its principal ally. However, through very astute diplomatic manoeuvring, particularly in connection with the Cretan and Macedonian Questions, the Wilhelmstrasse gradually restored its position in the Turkish capital, and British diplomatic blunders, particularly during the April events in 1909, did the rest. By May, following the suppression of the mutinies in Constantinople and the replacement of Abdul Hamid by his brother Mehmed, the Young Turks manifested their new, much more friendly, attitude towards Germany by proposing greater German involvement in the reorganisation of the Ottoman army and inviting Baron von der Goltz, by now a colonel-general and army inspector in the Reich, to come back to Turkey for that purpose.[71]

In the summer of 1910, Kiderlen-Wächter, a strong-willed Swabian with long experience both in Constantinople and in Bucharest,[72] took over the Auswärtige Amt as secretary of state. Unlike Chancellor Bülow, who had stepped down in 1909, Kiderlen-Wächter did not regard Germany's alliance with the Habsburg Empire as quite so central to Berlin's diplomacy; he also was more intent on loosening up the Entente through bilateral agreements. The first major agreement was concluded in 1910–11 with the Tsarist government: Berlin recognised Russia's sphere of interest in northern Persia and promised not to support Austro-Hungarian ambitions in the Balkans, while the Russians formally abandoned their opposition to the Baghdad Railway and agreed to support the establishment of a connecting rail-link to Tehran.[73] The Porte was, understandably, annoyed by this arrangement behind its back, but with new challenges facing the Ottoman Empire – particularly the Italian invasion of Libya – the Turks were ultimately thrown back into Germany's arms. Since Italy was a formal ally in the *Dreibund*, Berlin's efforts to bring the two belligerents together were difficult and for a long time quite unsuccessful, but the Turks recognised the goodwill.[74]

While the Ottoman army and navy had held their own quite well against the Italians, at least for a while, the Balkan War which started in October 1912 revealed very serious flaws in the Turkish military establishment. Pushed back very quickly to the Chatalja Lines, the Turks signed an armistice on 3 December. The rout of their armies and the loss of most of their European possessions (only a few fortresses still held out) produced great political tension among the Turks. The military defeat also gave rise to accusations, particularly in foreign newspapers, that the Germans had evidently not done a very good job in training and equipping the Turkish army.[75]

Baron von der Goltz, by now a field-marshal, responded to this criticism with a treatise entitled *Der jungen Türkei Niederlage und die Möglichkeit ihrer Wiedererhebung*. In it he asserted that decades of mismanagement under Abdul Hamid II simply could not be wiped out in a few years, and that the Ottoman officer corps in particular needed further reform.[76] In a private memorandum to Wilhelm II and Chancellor Bethmann Hollweg, the Field-Marshal also pointed out that Turkey's defeat and the new situation in the Balkans would put a further strain on the Habsburg Empire. Henceforth, Austrian help in a war with the Entente would be very limited at best, and the Reich must therefore prepare itself for such a war much more thoroughly and vigorously than it had done hitherto.[77]

The *coup d'état* of 23 January 1913, which removed Kamil Pasha's cabinet and brought a more militant group of Young Turks to power, among them Colonel Enver Bey,[78] led to a resumption of hostilities with the Balkan states. However, once again the Ottoman army suffered setbacks, and the fortresses still holding out fell one after the other, with Adrianople (Edirne) capitulating on 24 March.[79]

The new Grand Vezir, Mahmud Şevket Pasha, reacted to these developments by proposing even greater German involvement in the reform of the Ottoman army. Negotiations with Berlin, started by Şevket, were carried on after his assassination by the new war minister, Ahmed Izzet Pasha, and resulted eventually in the dispatch of a new, enlarged 'mission' headed by General Liman. Starting with about forty officers, including several colonels, Liman's mission subsequently grew by another thirty men (by August 1914), and by hundreds more during the war years. Many of the German officers arriving in 1913–14 were immediately given important staff positions, both in the War Ministry and out in the field, but since the Turks retained practically all command positions it is simply not true that Liman's mission controlled the Ottoman army and hence the country at large.[80]

Although both France and Britain in 1913 and the first half of 1914 concluded a number of agreements with Germany concerning the Baghdad Railway and related questions, tensions between the Entente Powers and the German–Austrian bloc continued unabated.[81] The assassination of Archduke Franz Ferdinand in Sarajevo late in June 1914 brought the latent conflict between Serbia and the Dual Monarchy to a head and quickly drew most of the European Powers into a major confrontation.[82] On 22 July, Enver Pasha (who had replaced Izzet Pasha as War Minister at the beginning of the year) proposed to Ambassador Wangenheim that the Ottoman Empire join the Triplice as a formal ally, pointing out, quite bluntly, that he and many of his colleagues believed that the Triplice 'was stronger than the Entente and would be victors in a world war'. Wangenheim, well aware of Turkey's military unpreparedness, initially rejected the proposal, but on the Kaiser's personal instructions negotiations were opened a few days later, and on 2 August a formal treaty of alliance was secretly signed in Constantinople.[83]

Inasmuch as several members of the Ottoman cabinet had neither wanted nor even known about the alignment of their country with Germany, but also because the Allied coalition arrayed against the Central Powers proved to be both larger and stronger than expected, the Porte adopted a posture of armed neutrality early in August and clung to it for several months to come. While Enver Pasha and some of his subordinates worked hard at preparing the Ottoman Empire for war and made several major concessions to the Central Powers – particularly by allowing the ships of the German Mediterranean Squadron to enter, and stay in, the Turkish Straits[84] – neither Ambassador von Wangenheim nor General Liman von Sanders was able to stir the Porte out of its policy of *attentisme*. Attempts by Admiral Wilhelm Souchon, the commander of the German Mediterranean Squadron, to secure a free hand likewise ran into spirited opposition from members of the Ottoman cabinet, including the Grand Vezir, Prince Said Halim Pasha, despite the fact that he had personally signed the alliance treaty with Germany earlier in the month. The German position in Constantinople was somewhat strengthened late in August, when a task force of German coast-defence specialists under the command of Admiral Guido von Usedom arrived at the Straits and began to prepare for the closure of the Dardanelles, but the advocates of *attentisme*, together with the outright opponents of intervention, continued to prevail in the Ottoman cabinet. General Liman von Sanders, headstrong as ever, reacted to this situation by requesting that he and his entire mission be recalled to Germany. His impatience with the Turks was not shared by Wangenheim, who repeatedly reminded Berlin that the Turks needed time to get their armed forces and their chronically empty treasury ready for a big war like this. The ambassador's apparent willingness to wait was not appreciated in Berlin, which eventually sent Richard von Kühlmann as a special emissary to Constantinople to stir both Wangenheim and the Porte into some action. Finally, after several carloads of gold had been transferred from the German to the Ottoman treasury – a difficult operation since the shipments had to go through two neutral states, Romania and Bulgaria – Enver, with the reluctant support of some of his colleagues at the Porte, authorised Admiral Souchon to open hostilities against Russia.[85] The Admiral's Black Sea raid, late in October, promptly provoked a major political crisis in Constantinople. About half a dozen ministers, including the Grand Vezir, threatened to resign, and four of them actually did so early in November. Among them was Cavid Bey, the capable and wily Finance Minister. Officially, he would not return to that portfolio until February 1917 but, whether he was in or out of the Cabinet, the Germans would have to contend with him and his spirited defence of Ottoman economic and financial interests throughout the war years.[86]

For almost a year following their intervention on the side of the Central Powers, that is, until the defeat of Serbia in the autumn of 1915, the Turks were geographically isolated from their German and Austro-Hungarian allies. While the Germans managed to smuggle some military supplies and small groups of soldiers through neutral Romania before and during the Gallipoli campaign, the Turks found themselves left largely to their own devices until November 1915, when the first major shipments of ammunition and weapons were dispatched to them on the Danube. Two months later, in mid-January 1916, the first train from Germany reached Constantinople via the restored Serbian sections of the traditional trans-Balkan line.[87]

The secret alliance treaty signed on 2 August 1914 had stipulated that General Liman von Sanders and his mission would be given 'an effective influence on the general direction' of the Ottoman army. The Germans soon found out that neither Enver Pasha nor anyone else in the upper echelons of the Ottoman army was prepared to surrender control of the war effort to them. Liman von Sanders himself was given command of a number of Ottoman field armies – first in the Constantinople region, then on Gallipoli, and finally, in 1918, in Palestine – but all of his efforts to participate in the strategic direction of the Ottoman war effort, to serve as a mentor or at least as a senior adviser at Enver's general headquarters, were resolutely turned aside by the Turks. Field-Marshal von der Goltz did not fare any better. Invited back to Turkey in December 1914, he spent a few months in Constantinople as a 'special adviser' to the Ottoman High Command, but Enver soon tired of him, calling him too old, too soft, and a poor judge of men. After six months as a unit commander in the Constantinople region, the elderly German field-marshal eagerly accepted a front-line assignment in Mesopotamia, taking charge of the Sixth Ottoman Army, but he died there of spotted fever shortly before his troops captured General Townshend at Kut-el-Amara. Another prominent German general who was transferred to Turkey during the war years, Erich von Falkenhayn, was likewise kept on a short leash. Though he had previously served both as Prussian War Minister and as Chief of the General Staff, General von Falkenhayn found it very difficult to establish effective control over the Ottoman forces assigned to him, the so-called Army Group F in Palestine, and returned to a more congenial command, in eastern Europe, within nine months.[88]

While most Ottoman senior commands, at the army and corps level, remained in the hands of Ottoman generals, German field-grade officers were entrusted with many important staff positions and also served quite frequently as regimental or even divisional commanders in some of the more important theatres of war. Particularly noteworthy in this regard were the Bavarian colonel Baron Friedrich Kress von Kressenstein, who held a number of important posts on the Sinai Front until 1917, and the Prussian major Felix Guse, who served as chief of staff to the commander of the Ottoman Third Army in eastern Anatolia until Russia's withdrawal from the war.[89] Another Prussian major who ended up as chief of staff to an Ottoman army commander was Franz von Papen. Later, in the 1930s, after serving as Chancellor of the Weimar Republic and as Vice-Chancellor in Hitler's first Cabinet, he would once again appear in Turkey, this time as the ambassador of the Third Reich.[90]

Although Enver was unwilling to let any senior German general on to his headquarters staff, he had no reservations about surrounding himself with German staff officers of lower rank. Until December 1917 he used a German colonel (later Generalmajor), Friedrich Bronsart von Schellendorff, as his chief of staff, and many of the technical sections at Ottoman headquarters were likewise headed by German field-grade officers. When Bronsart was called back to Germany, his place was taken by Generalmajor Hans von Seeckt, a first-rate staff officer who would demonstrate his talents again in the 1920s when he rebuilt the German army. It should be emphasised, though, that neither Bronsart nor Seeckt was able to push the Turks very far in any given direction; that is, whenever Enver Pasha disagreed with their advice or views he blithely went his own way.[91]

In the Ottoman fleet, reinforced since August 1914 by the modern German battle-cruiser *Goeben* (officially renamed *Yavus Sultan Selim*) and the small cruiser *Breslau* (*Midilli*), the Germans enjoyed somewhat more latitude during the war years. However, given the ill-assorted collection of obsolete Turkish ships they had under their command, neither Admiral Souchon nor his successor, Hubert von Rebeur-Paschwitz, could actually do very much by way of bold manoeuvres. Suffice it to add that in January 1918 *Midilli* was lost in an Allied minefield and *Yavus Sultan Selim* severely damaged. Refurbished after the war, the erstwhile German battle-cruiser was turned into the flagship of the new Turkish navy and served in that capacity for many years. She was finally scrapped in the 1970s.[92]

From the moment the Turks threw in their lot with the Central Powers, the German High Command (OHL) did its best to direct the military energies of the Ottoman Empire towards tasks which would most effectively supplement the Central Powers' own operations in the various European theatres of war. Much of the time Enver Pasha proved co-operative in this respect and eventually, in 1916, even loaned half a dozen Ottoman divisions to his allies for use in Galicia and the Balkans.[93] However, whenever he disagreed with the views or plans of the German High Command he went his own way without fail, and even the imperious first quartermaster-general at the OHL, General Erich Ludendorff, was unable to budge the Ottoman vice-generalissimo from a given position. Enver's independence of mind became particularly evident in 1918, when he sent far more Ottoman troops into Transcaucasia than the Germans, for military and political reasons, wanted him to.[94]

Throughout the war period, most political and military leaders in Germany thought of the Ottoman Empire primarily in military–strategic terms. Berlin's prime concern was to keep the Ottoman armies in the field and to have them tie down as many Allied troops as possible. Hence, German policies after August 1914 were often characterised by a reluctance to say or do anything which might be offensive to the Porte. When the Turks unilaterally abolished the capitulatory system in October 1914, the Germans were highly annoyed but swallowed their anger.[95] When, in the following month, the Porte demanded a new alliance treaty which would offer the Ottoman Empire more tangible benefits and guarantees, Chancellor von Bethmann Hollweg initially would not hear of it. As he reminded his subordinates, 'the exaggeration and spread of the system of alliances' had contributed to the outbreak of the current war, and 'we decided only with great reluctance to conclude a formal alliance with Turkey'. A further extension of this alliance was therefore 'basically undesirable'.[96] However, as soon as the Porte pointed out that the issue might cause a split in the CUP regime, Berlin's opposition caved in and the Turks got exactly what they wanted.[97]

Berlin's reluctance to become embroiled with its prickly ally became even more evident in the spring and summer of 1915, when the Ottoman authorities began a massive, and often very brutal, programme of deportations among the Armenians in the eastern vilayets. While some German officials openly voiced their concern (and disgust) to the Turks, the leading men in Berlin were determined not to risk a break with the Porte over this issue and consequently adopted a policy of 'diplomatic restraint'.[98] Official German efforts to protect the Jewish community in Palestine against harassment and deportations were a bit more vigorous, and also much more effective in the long run.[99] It must be emphasised, though, that the stakes in the second case were not nearly as high; that is, to the CUP regime repressive measures against the Yishuv were not nearly as important as the 'pacification' of the Armenian districts, and Berlin could thus be more 'daring' in its suggestions and comments regarding the maltreatment of Jews.[100]

Berlin's concern about keeping the Porte in a co-operative mood also manifested itself in the sphere of financial and commercial transactions. As the war progressed, the Porte demanded more and more subsidies and loans from its allies but turned a deaf ear to various German suggestions for Ottoman reforms in the fiscal and monetary systems. In the end, the Porte usually got what it wanted. Indeed, by 1918 it had collected close to 5 billion marks in German loans and credits, and many German experts were by then convinced that most of these advances would never be paid back.[101]

German efforts, both at the official level and by private groups, to secure a stronger economic position in the Ottoman Empire likewise proved largely futile. Attempts to obtain adequate compensation for the services of the German railway companies in the Ottoman Empire brought few tangible results, nor did the Germans fare any better when they tried to have the Porte contribute financially to the completion of the Baghdad line. Most of the construction carried out during the war years, in the Taurus, the Amanus, and the Syrian desert, was thus ultimately paid for by the German government.[102]

Berlin's attempts, starting in 1917, to secure the liquidation of French and British economic enterprises in the sultan's realm and open up new investment opportunities for German capital likewise ran into spirited opposition from the Porte, with Cavid Bey leading the fight against the Germans.[103] In the light of the CUP regime's attitudes, some German officials eventually came to the conclusion that a really close long-term relationship with the Ottoman Empire, particularly in the economic sphere, was probably not possible and perhaps not even desirable. As Ambassador von Kühlmann pointed out to Chancellor von Bethmann Hollweg in June 1917, demands by General Ludendorff and others for greater German participation in the economic development of the Ottoman Empire should not necessarily be accepted. Whether in the future German capital should be given an exclusive role in the construction of the Ottoman railway system, as Ludendorff had suggested, was also in question; indeed, 'whether we should really, beyond the absolutely necessary, place German capital on the Turkish card (which, if viewed *sub specie aeterni*, will always be a risky card), these are questions which in my opinion should not be decided without the most careful deliberation . . .'[104] Kühlmann also thought that there was no point in trying to prevent or hamper 'the resumption of economic relations between Turkey and our current enemies' once the war had ended. The revival of their commercial and financial influence was unlikely to jeopardise Germany's 'political position at the Golden Horn'. The ambassador concluded that, though he did not share 'the view of certain pessimists who would like us to drop Turkey after the war like a squeezed-out lemon, I would not wish to recommend on the other hand that we put more national assets into Turkey than is required for maintaining our previous political position there . . .'.[105]

Kühlmann kept faithfully to these views throughout the following months and carried them back to Berlin when he was appointed State Secretary of the Auswärtige Amt in August 1917. His succcessor in Constantinople, Count von Bernstorff, initially took a much harder line. Annoyed by the unco-operative attitude of the Porte on a number of issues, and increasingly sceptical about the value of Ottoman military assistance to the Central Powers, the ambassador in January 1918 advised Chancellor Georg Count von Hertling that 'the moment has come for a last attempt to bind Turkey economically to us', and he made it clear that such an attempt should certainly be made:

> Only if Turkey is willing to let herself be economically dominated by us in the future will the great sacrifices be worthwhile which we must presently make for her in military, financial, and diplomatic terms as a result of her deplorable condition. If Turkey does not accept our economic predominance, she has nothing more to offer to us . . .[106]

Predictably, given Kühlmann's views, Bernstorff's advice was ignored in Berlin, though Ludendorff and some other influential figures in the Reich continued to dream of, and to push for, a 'closer' economic relationship with the Ottoman Empire, and some civil servants wrote studies and memoranda on that subject practically right down to the end of the war.[107] Altogether it may be said that the efforts of German government agencies and private-interest groups to advance German economic influence in the sultan's realm during the war years were generally unsuccessful – largely because the CUP regime put up effective obstacles of various sorts, but also because there never was any agreement in German official circles on just how desirable and important a closer link with the Ottoman Empire would actually be.[108]

While the German authorities were haggling with the Turks over their respective spheres of interest in Transcaucasia and a number of other issues, the military situation of the Central Powers deteriorated steadily. From July 1918 on, the overextended German armies on the Western Front were being pushed back slowly but surely. In September a successful Allied offensive on the Macedonian front induced Bulgaria to quit the war, and the Turks themselves were being routed in Palestine by General Allenby's forces. Like Germany and the Dual Monarchy, the Ottoman Empire officially notified President Wilson early in October that it was prepared to make peace. Simultaneously, the Ottoman Cabinet was thoroughly restructured. By mid-October a fresh team under General Izzet Pasha had taken over the reins of government, and armistice talks were shortly thereafter opened. To the relief of the Germans, Izzet and some of his colleagues at the Porte proved quite co-operative – they kept Berlin posted on their plans and allowed the Germans to start the evacuation of their military personnel from the Ottoman Empire. Moreover, in the Armistice of Mudros, signed on 30 October, the Turks secured formal British agreement that all German and Austro-Hungarian troops still in the Ottoman Empire would be given ample time to withdraw.[109]

The good relationship between Berlin and the Porte was strained considerably early the next month when it became known that German ships ferrying evacuees across the Black Sea to Russian ports had also provided transportation to many prominent figures of the deposed CUP regime, including Enver, Talât and Cemal Pashas. The Kaiser's government, during the last week of its existence, refused to return these 'fugitives' to Turkey, and most of them eventually made their way to the Reich – some of them in disguise since they were wanted both by their own country and by the Allies.[110]

Since the Armistice of Mudros obligated the Ottoman government to sever relations with the Central Powers, the German diplomatic and consular offices in the Empire were gradually closed down. By the end of the year most of the diplomatic personnel had departed, while General Liman von Sanders stayed on in the Straits region until late January 1919 to supervise the evacuation of German and Austro-Hungarian soldiers who were coming in from the more remote theatres of war.[111]

Faced with manifold domestic problems and stiff peace terms from the Allies, the German government during the next few years had little time or opportunity to concern itself with Turkish affairs, and it was only in 1924 that formal diplomatic relations were restored between the two countries.[112] One year later, several retired German army officers, including Colonel Willi von Klewitz (one of the most highly decorated staff officers of the defunct Royal Prussian Army), arrived in Turkey to serve as instructors at various military academies. In 1926 a number of retired naval officers, among them Vice-

Admiral Baron Ernst von Gagern, likewise took over teaching positions in Turkey.[113] Though much strained during the war – by tactless conduct by individual German officers and a variety of other problems – the special relationship between the German and the Turkish military establishments thus survived into the new era. Indeed, by the 1930s that relationship was tightened with the arrival of additional, and even more senior, military instructors from the Reich, including Hilmar Ritter von Mittelberger, a retired three-star general of the Reichswehr, and Lieutenant-General Max Schindler, who had served as German military attaché in Warsaw until 1935.[114] Even today the comradeship-in-arms during the First World War is not entirely forgotten.[115]

It has long been customary for Marxist historians, both in the Soviet Union and elsewhere, to depict the foreign policy of Wilhelmian Germany as 'particularly aggressive' and to view its relationship with the Ottoman Empire as one of the worst examples of imperialist exploitation in that age. Several Marxist–Leninist authors have suggested that by 1914 'German imperialism' had won a dominant position in the sultan's realm, and that during the war years the Germans succeeded, with the help of corrupt or misguided elements of Ottoman society, in increasing their control of the country even further, turning it into a satellite and a source of cannon fodder pure and simple.[116]

The verdict that 'German imperialism' in the early twentieth century was particularly bad – certainly worse than that of any other country – has lately received fresh support from various other quarters, including a number of West German historians following in the footsteps of Professor Fritz Fischer of Hamburg University. According to their reading of the available evidence, the government of Wilhelm II, catering to or responding to pressures from important segments of German society, deliberately provoked a great war in 1914 to turn the Reich into a 'world power'. It is further held that the prewar ambitions of Germany's ruling circles, including the expansion of German power and influence into the Middle East, continued to hold sway in Berlin during the war years, and that certain disagreements on war aims among German politicians, military figures, diplomats and civil servants were of a minor nature, revolving almost exclusively around questions of tactics and methods rather than around final objectives.[117]

While the expansionist–imperialist mood of Wilhelmian society and the provocative nature of some of Berlin's policies before and during the First World War are beyond doubt, the picture of rampant German imperialism presented by Marxist writers as well as the Fischer school appears to be badly overdrawn in some respects, certainly in regard to the Ottoman Empire. Both before and after the outbreak of the First World War, there was much less agreement in Germany's ruling circles on questions of foreign policy than most Marxist authors and the Fischer school have suggested. German financial and industrial tycoons frequently disagreed quite emphatically with the

Auswärtige Amt or the military authorities on what should be done in, or with, the sultan's realm. Moreover, within the Kaiser's government itself unanimity on Turkish policies was very rare indeed. Before 1914 some Germans in high places thought of the Ottoman Empire primarily as the sick man who was unlikely to recuperate and whose possessions would soon be up for grabs; many others saw it as an exciting area for profitable economic activity; still others imagined that the Turks might some day become important helpmates in a military conflict with the Entente. However, German ideas and estimates as to what the Turks had to offer varied considerably from time to time, leading in turn to further disagreements among those most concerned. During the July Crisis of 1914, for instance, the German Ambassador in Constantinople was very reluctant to respond to the alliance overtures of the Turks, the Kaiser was eager to line them up on his side, and the Chancellor was lukewarm on the whole issue. Nobody in the German navy had given much thought to co-operation with the Turks, and the army was similarly unprepared. While the Chief of the General Staff, Helmuth von Moltke, optimistically thought that the Turks would intervene very soon and therefore formulated all kinds of ambitious projects for them, General Liman von Sanders had so little confid-ence in the CUP regime that he desperately tried to get out of the Turkish backwater. Indeed, throughout the war period, various German dignitaries had so many different views on the subject of Turkey that a coherent policy development was practically impossible.[118]

With the Germans badly divided amongst themselves and often at odds with their Austro-Hungarian ally as well, it was relatively simple for the CUP regime to resist or deflect various pressures from Berlin and to maintain control over the internal affairs of the country. The CUP regime has often been blamed for entering the First World War on the 'wrong' side – the side that would lose in the end – and for ruining their country in the process. That is all very true, but it should be added that the leading men of the regime were never subservient tools of 'German imperialism', and acted the way they did because they wished to revive and strengthen the Empire.[119] If they miscalculated disastrously, it is only fair to add that others did not do very much better, among them the Tsarist regime, the House of Habsburg, and the German Kaiser himself.

If one looks at the record of Germany's policies towards the Ottoman Empire from the 1880s to 1918, it becomes clear why so many prominent political and military figures in the sultan's realm regarded a close relationship with the Reich as desirable, or at least as less problematical than one with any of the other Great Powers. From the 1880s on, albeit for very selfish reasons, Imperial Germany did provide considerable political support to the sultan's realm on many occasions and tried sincerely to help in the modernisation and training of the Ottoman army. Moreover, at least some of the economic projects in the Ottoman Empire that were financed and managed by German firms – from railway building to agricultural reclamation schemes – were of definite benefit to the Turks. Finally, it must be stressed that the deterioration and ultimate collapse of the Ottoman Empire during the First World War can only partially be blamed on the Germans. To be sure, some of the advice the Germans gave to their Turkish allies was bad, and some of the demands they made on them were excessive, but the CUP regime itself certainly contributed more than its share to the problems which ultimately brought the Ottoman Empire down. Against German advice, and sometimes against strenuous objections from Berlin, the CUP regime repeatedly embarked on political and military ventures which were harmful to the Ottoman war effort and thereby hastened the demise of the Empire. The Turkish 'pacification' programme against the Armenians, for instance, was not only far more sweeping, and brutal, than the Germans thought necessary, but it was also economically disastrous, pushing the already overstrained economy of the sultan's realm closer to total collapse. Likewise, it should be recalled that in the last year of the First World War the CUP regime launched an expansionist drive in Transcaucasia, in defiance of German wishes, which diverted important military resources from theatres of war where they were urgently needed to stem further Allied advances, that is, both in Palestine and in Mesopotamia. The Turkish march to Baku in the summer of 1918, which was carried out against the wishes of the German High Command, constituted, as it were, the last fling of Ottoman 'imperialism'. That operation should also remind us that German power and influence in the sultan's realm had very definite limits.

Notes: Chapter 5

Abbreviations

AA	Auswärtige Amt, Bonn. Microfilmed files of the German Foreign Office
BA-MA	Bundesarchiv-Militärarchiv, Freiburg
DBJ	*Deutsches Biographisches Jahrbuch*
GGH	*Gothaischer Genealogischer Hofkalender nebst Diplomatisch-statistischen Jahrbuch*
GP	*Die Grosse Politik der Europäischen Kabinette, 1871–1914*, ed. Johannes Lepsius, A. Mendelssohn-Bartholdy and Friedrich Thimme, 40 vols (Berlin, 1922–7)
JdIfDG	*Jahrbuch des Instituts für Deutsche Geschichte, Tel Aviv University*.
JfGO	*Jahrbücher für Geschichte Osteuropas*
MES	*Middle Eastern Studies*
MGM	*Militärgeschichtliche Mitteilungen*
MR	*Marine-Rundschau*
VfTuH	*Vierteljahreshefte für Truppenführung und Heereskunde*
WA	*Weltwirtschaftliches Archiv*

1 Jonathan Steinberg, 'The German background to Anglo-German relations, 1905–1914', in F. H. Hinsley (ed.), *British Foreign Policy under Sir Edward Grey* (Cambridge, 1977), p. 193; cf. David Calleo, *The German Problem Reconsidered* (Cambridge, 1978), ch. 4 and passim.

2 The total population of the Reich rose from 49.5 million in 1890; to 56.4 million in 1900, to nearly 64 million by 1910. German emigration, about 400,000 between 1890 and 1895, sharply declined thereafter, with the annual emigration rate remaining below 30,000 during most years until the First World War. For further details, see the prewar editions of *GGH*

(1871–1919). See also Gerd Hohorst *et al.*, *Sozialgeschichtliches Arbeitsbuch: Materialien zur Statistik des Kaiserreichs 1870–1914* (Munich, 1975), ch. 1.

3　On the organisation and growth of the German army prior to 1914, see especially Curt Jany, *Die Königlich Preussische Armee und das Deutsche Reichsheer 1807–1914* (Berlin, 1933), and Wiegand Schmidt-Richberg *et al.*, *Von der Entlassung Bismarcks bis zum Ende des Ersten Weltkrieges* [*Handbuch zur deutschen Militärgeschichte*, Vol. V] (Frankfurt am Main, 1968). On the determination of France to keep up with German military strength despite its much smaller population-base, see also Henry Contamine, *La Revanche, 1871–1914* (Paris, 1957).

4　See Jonathan Steinberg, *Yesterday's Deterrent – Tirpitz and the Birth of the German Battle Fleet* (London, 1965); Volker R. Berghahn, *Der Tirpitz-Plan* (Düsseldorf, 1971); and Holger H. Herwig, *'Luxury' Fleet: The Imperial German Navy 1888–1918* (London, 1980), chs 3–6 and passim.

5　For convenient surveys of German industrial developments prior to 1914, see Gustav Stolper *et al.*, *The German Economy, 1870 to the Present* (New York, 1967), chs 3 ff.; and Helmut Böhme, *An Introduction to the Social and Economic History of Germany* (Oxford, 1978), ch. 7. See also Lutz Graf Schwerin von Krosigk, *Die grosse Zeit des Feuers: Der Weg der deutschen Industrie*, 3 vols (Tübingen, 1957–9), Vols II and III; John J. Beer, *The Emergence of the German Dye Industry* (Urbana, Ill., 1959); and Friedrich-Wilhelm Henning, *Die Industrialisierung in Deutschland* (Paderborn, 1973), pp. 203 ff.

6　See *GGH* (1902), pp. 488 ff.

7　cf. J. Alden Nichols, *Germany after Bismarck* (Cambridge, Mass., 1958), chs 4, 8 and passim; Norman Rich, *Friedrich von Holstein: Politics and Diplomacy in the Era of Bismarck and Wilhelm II*, 2 vols (Cambridge, 1965), pts III ff.; and the classical older study by William L. Langer, *The Diplomacy of Imperialism, 1890–1902*, 2nd edn (Cambridge, Mass., 1951), passim.

8　On the interrelationship of Germany's domestic problems and her foreign policy during the Wilhelmian era, cf. Winfried Baumgart, *Deutschland im Zeitalter des Imperialismus (1890–1914): Grundkräfte, Thesen und Strukturen* (Frankfurt am Main, 1972); Hans-Ulrich Wehler, *Das Deutsche Kaiserreich 1871–1918* (Göttingen, 1973); and Gordon A. Craig, *Germany 1866–1945* (New York, 1978), chs 7–9. See also the editor's introduction in Richard J. Evans (ed.), *Society and Politics in Wilhelmine Germany* (London, 1978); and Wolfgang J. Mommsen, 'Die latente Krise des Wilhelminischen Reiches', *MGM*, Vol. 15 (1974), pp. 7–28.

9　On German economic activities in the Ottoman Empire in the 1880s and 1890s, cf. Langer, *Diplomacy*, p. 632 ff.; E. M. Earle, *Turkey, the Great Powers, and the Baghdad Railway: A Study in Imperialism* (New York, 1924), chs 2–3; and Lothar Rathmann, *Berlin–Baghdad: Die imperialistische Nahostpolitik des kaiserlichen Deutschlands* (Berlin, 1962), pp. 12–56 passim. See also A. S. Silin, *Ekspansiya Germanii na Blizhnem Vostoke v kontse XIX veka* (Moscow, 1971), pp. 121 ff., 170 ff. and passim.

10　cf. Langer, *Diplomacy*, pp. 637 ff.; Michael Balfour, *The Kaiser and His Times* (New York, 1972), pp. 216 ff.; and the contemporary account in Karl Wippermann, *Politische Geschichte der Gegenwart: Das Jahr 1898* (Berlin, 1899), pp. 138–56. For a comparison of Wilhelm's two visits, see also Joan Haslip, *The Sultan: The Life of Abdul Hamid II* (London, 1958), chs 24–5, 29; and Alex Carmel, 'Die deutsche Palästinapolitik 1871–1914', *JdIfDG*, Vol. 4 (1975), pp. 233 ff.

11　See Jehuda L. Wallach, *Anatomie einer Militärhilfe: Die preussisch-deutschen Militärmissionen in der Türkei 1835–1919* (Düsseldorf, 1976), pp. 17–29. For detailed assessments of Moltke's work in Turkey, see W. Bigge, *Feldmarschall Graf Moltke*, 2 vols (Munich, 1901); and Eberhard Kessel, *Moltke* (Stuttgart, 1957).

12　See Alex Carmel, *Die Siedlungen der württembergischen Templer in Palästina, 1868–1918* (Stuttgart, 1973); and his 'The political significance of German settlement in Palestine, 1868–1918', *JdIfDG*, Beiheft 1 (1975), pp. 45–71.

13　See Mordechai Eliav (ed.), *Die Juden Palästinas in der deutschen Politik: Dokumente aus dem Archiv des deutschen Konsulats in Jerusalem, 1842–1914*, 2 vols (Tel Aviv, 1973).

14　The literature on the development of the Ottoman railway system and the involvement of German and other foreign companies in it is enormous. For the early phases, see especially Earle, *Turkey*; Hermann Schmidt, *Das Eisenbahnwesen in der asiatischen Türkei* (Berlin, 1914); Carl Mühlmann, 'Die deutschen Bahnunternehmungen in der asiatischen Türkei, 1888–1914', *WA*, Vol. 24 (1926), pp. 121–37, 365–99; Reinhard Hüber, *Die Baghdadbahn* (Berlin, 1943), pp. 9–43; and E. R. J. Brünner, *De Bagdadspoorweg* (Gröningen, 1957). See also Jean Ducruet, *Les Capitaux européens au Proche-Orient* (Paris, 1964), pp. 180 ff., and the works listed in n. 38 below.

15 See Lamar Cecil, *The German Diplomatic Service 1871–1914* (Princeton, NJ, 1976), passim. See also Rich, *Friedrich von Holstein*, pts II ff.; and Holstein's recently published letters in Gerhard Ebel (ed.) *Botschafter Paul Graf von Hatzfeldt: Nachgelassene Papiere*, 2 vols (Boppard, 1976).

16 See *GGH* (1912), p. 1110.

17 See Cecil, *German Diplomatic Service*, pp. 14, 158 ff.

18 cf. ibid, pp. 260 ff. and passim; John Röhl, *Germany without Bismarck: The Crisis of Government in the Second Reich, 1890–1900* (Berkeley and Los Angeles, Calif., 1967), passim; Erich Lindow, *Freiherr Marschall von Bieberstein als Botschafter in Konstantinopel 1897–1912* (Danzig, 1934); and AA, Nachlass Hans von Miquel, essay on 'Freiherr Marschall von Lieberstein [sic]'.

19 cf. Joseph Pomiankowski, *Der Zusammenbruch des Ottomanischen Reiches* (Vienna, 1928), pp. 49 ff. and passim; Frank G. Weber, *Eagles on the Crescent: Germany, Austria, and the Diplomacy of the Turkish Alliance 1914–1918* (Ithaca, NY, 1970), pp. 18 ff.; and Isaiah Friedman, *Germany, Turkey, and Zionism 1897–1918* (Oxford, 1977), pp. 187 ff. and passim. See also Ulrich Trumpener, *Germany and the Ottoman Empire 1914–1918* (Princeton, NJ, 1968), passim, for his role during the war.

20 See ibid., pp. 90 ff., 125 ff., 229 ff.; and Eberhard von Vietsch (ed.), *Gegen die Unvernunft: Der Briefwechsel zwischen Paul Graf Wolff Metternich und Wilhelm Solf 1915–1918* (Bremen, 1964).

21 While Kühlmann's *Erinnerungen* (Heidelberg, 1948) are unreliable and badly garbled in places, they hardly warrant the abuse heaped on him in Sir Lewis Namier, *Vanished Supremacies* (New York, 1963), pp. 95 ff. On his role in Turkey, see Trumpener, *Germany*, pp. 46, 128, 244 ff., 326 ff., and passim; on his work as Secretary of State, cf. Fritz Fischer, *Griff nach der Weltmacht* (Düsseldorf, 1961), passim; Gerhard Ritter, *Staatskunst und Kriegshandwerk*, 4 vols (Munich, 1954–68), Vol IV, passim; and Winfried Baumgart, *Deutsche Ostpolitik 1918* (Vienna, 1966), passim.

22 On Bernstorff's efforts to keep the United States neutral, cf. Ritter, *Staatskunst*, Vol. III, passim; Ernest R. May, *The World War and American Isolation, 1914–1917* (Cambridge, Mass., 1959), passim; and Arthur S. Link, *Wilson*, 5 vols (Princeton, NJ, 1947–65), vols III–V, passim. On his work in Turkey, see Trumpener, *Germany*, pp. 161 ff. and passim; and ch. 4 of his own *Erinnerungen und Briefe* (Zurich, 1936).

23 On Morgen's service in Turkey, cf. Martin Reymann's obituary in *DBJ*, Vol. X (1931), 176 ff.; George W. F. Hallgarten, *Imperialismus vor 1914*, 2nd edn, 2 vols (Munich, 1963), Vol. I, pp. 478 ff.; and his own account, 'Meine Lebenserinnerungen' (typescript, *c.* 1927), in BA-MA, Nachlass Curt von Morgen, N227/11.

24 Data on Colonel Leipzig (known as Leipziger until 1905) are sparse. I have reconstructed his career on the basis of the annual *Ranglisten* of the Prussian Army. See also Karl-Heinz Janssen (ed.), *Die graue Exzellenz . . . Aus den Papieren des kaiserlichen Gesandten Karl Georg von Treutler* (Frankfurt, 1971), pp. 50 ff.; Pomiankowski, *Zusammenbruch*, pp. 56, 143; and Trumpener, *Germany*, pp. 82 ff.

25 cf. Hallgarten, *Imperialismus*, Vol. II, pp. 370 ff., 430 ff.; and Wallach, *Anatomie*, pp. 145 ff. and passim.

26 See Trumpener, *Germany*, pp. 77 ff.; AA, Deutschland 122 No. 2, Treutler to AA, 5 Nov. 1915, Lyncker to Treutler, 27 Nov. 1915; and Cuno Horkenbach, *Das Deutsche Reich von 1918 bis Heute*, 2 vols (Berlin, 1930–5), Vol. II, p. 975. Pomiankowski's statement (*Zusammenbruch*, p. 56; repeated in Wallach, *Anatomie*, p. 147) that Laffert was removed from his Turkish post in August 1914 is incorrect. He actually played a very important role in Constantinople until the end of that year.

27 See Wallach, *Anatomie*, passim; Trumpener, *Germany*, pp. 88 ff. and passim; and Harold J. Gordon, *Hitler and the Beer Hall Putsch* (Princeton, NJ, 1972), pp. 142 ff. and passim. See also Bernd F. Schulte, *Vor dem Kriegsausbruch 1914* (Düsseldorf, 1980), pp. 30 ff., 47, 133 ff., 154.

28 See Eugene Staley, 'Business and politics in the Persian Gulf: the story of the Wönckhaus firm', *Political Science Quarterly*, Vol. XLVIII, no. 3 (1933), pp. 367–85.

29 On Rosen, see his memoirs, *Aus einem diplomatischen Wanderleben*, 2 vols (Berlin, 1931). On Schulenburg's consular activities in wartime Turkey, see especially Wolfdieter Bihl,

Die Kaukasus-Politik der Mittelmächte, pt I (Vienna, 1975), pp. 68 ff. and passim.
30   For a partial résumé of his services to the embassy, see AA, Deutschland 135 No. 1 secreta, Weitz to Zimmermann, 15 Dec. 1916. See also his Nachlass in the AA archives; Rudolf Vierhaus (ed.), *Das Tagebuch der Baronin Spitzemberg* (Göttingen, 1960), passim; John G. Williamson, *Karl Helfferich* (Princeton, NJ, 1971), pp. 89 ff.; and Weber, *Eagles*, pp. 9, 82, 133, 204.
31   See ibid., pp. 25 ff. and passim; Trumpener, *Germany*, pp. 41 ff. and passim; and Klaus-Volker Giessler, *Die Institution des Marineattachés im Kaiserreich* (Boppard, 1976), pp. 189 ff. See also Humann's letters in the Ernst Jäckh papers (Yale University Library), and 'Unterredung mit Professor Lepsius am 4. Oktober . . . [1915]', in the Kanner Papers (Hoover Library, Stanford University), Vol. II.
32   See Ulrich Trumpener, 'German officers in the Ottoman Empire, 1880–1918', *JdIfDG*, Beiheft 1 (1975), 32 ff.; and Wallach, *Anatomie*, pp. 34 ff.
33   cf. Trumpener, 'German officers', pp. 37 ff.; Ulrich Trumpener, 'Liman von Sanders and the German–Ottoman alliance', *Journal of Contemporary History*, Vol. I, no. 4 (1966), 179 ff.; and Wallach, *Anatomie*, pp. 126 ff.
34   cf. Luigi Albertini, *The Origins of the War of 1914*, 3 vols (London, 1952–7), Vol. I, pp. 540 ff.; Fritz Fischer, *Krieg der Illusionen* (Düsseldorf, 1969), pp. 483 ff.; and Akademiya Nauk SSSR, *Istoriya pervoi mirovoi voiny*, ed. I. I. Rostunov, 2 vols (Moscow, 1975), Vol. I, pp. 88 ff. See also Bodger, above, pp. 94–5.
35   See Wallach, *Anatomie*, pp. 60 ff., 88 ff. and passim; and the reminiscences of one of the early trainees, General Pertev Demirhan, in his book on *Generalfeldmarschall Colmar Freiherr von der Goltz* (Göttingen, 1960), pp. 30 ff. In the German (Prussian) army rolls (*Ranglisten*), the Turkish trainees were normally listed under the rubric of 'Offiziere à la suite der Armee'.
36   Hallgarten, *Imperialismus*, Vol. II, pp. 169, 430 and passim, depicts both men in very dark colours: Izzet as 'terribly corrupt and brutal', Şevket as 'energetic' and pro-German but 'personally, it appears, hardly less corrupt than the other Turks'. For a very different picture of Şevket, see Field-Marshal von der Goltz's 'Erinnerungen an Mahmud Schewket Pascha', *Deutsche Rundschau*, Vol. CLVII (1913), 32–46, 184–209; cf. Ahmad, above, p. 14.
37   cf. Walter Hoffmann, 'Deutsche Banken in der Türkei', *WA*, Vol. VI (1915), 410–21; Raymond Poidevin, *Les Relations économique et financières entre la France et l'Allemagne de 1898 à 1914* (Paris, 1969), pp. 64 ff., 242, 253 ff., 567 ff. and passim; and Kurt Grunwald, '*Pénétration pacifique* – the financial vehicles of Germany's "Drang nach dem Osten" ', *JdIfDG*, Beiheft 1 (1975), 85–103. On Bayar, see Metin Tamkoç, *The Warrior Diplomats* (Salt Lake City, Utah, 1976), pp. 313 ff.
38   In addition to the literature listed in n. 14, see J. B. Wolf, *The Diplomatic History of the Bagdad Railroad* (Columbia, MO, 1936); Maybelle K. Chapman, *Great Britain and the Bagdad Railway 1888–1914* (Northampton, Mass., 1948), Helmut Mejcher, 'Die Bagdadbahn als Instrument deutschen wirtschaftlichen Einflusses im Osmanischen Reich', *Geschichte und Gesellschaft*, Vol. I, no. 4 (1975), pp. 447–81, and below, Kent, pp. 181–2, and Fulton, passim.
39   cf. Richard Hennig, *Die deutschen Bahnbauten in der Türkei* (Leipzig, 1915), p. 9; AA, Türkei 152, Bd 79, Rössler to Bethmann Hollweg, 20 Oct. 1914; Memorandum by Otto Riese 23 Nov. 1914. The information given in Fischer, *Krieg*, p. 646 (Map 6), is thoroughly garbled.
40   See Hennig, *Die deutschen Bahnbauten*, p. 28 and passim; and Mühlmann, 'Die deutschen Bahnunternehmungen', pp. 366 ff., 388 ff.
41   See ibid., pp. 369 and 385. For an excellent description of the rolling stock used, see Derwent G. Heslop, 'The Bagdad Railway', *The Engineer*, 3 Dec. 1920, pp. 552 ff.
42   See Herbert Pönicke, 'Heinrich August Meissner-Pascha und der Bau der Hedschas- und Bagdadbahn', *Welt als Geschichte*, Vol. XVI (1956), pp. 196–210; and Walter Pick, 'Der deutsche Pionier Heinrich August Meissner-Pascha und seine Eisenbahnbauten im Nahen Osten 1901–1917', *JdIfDG*, IV (1975), 257–300.
43   See Mejcher, 'Die Bagdadbahn', p. 480; Rathmann, *Berlin–Bagdad*, pp. 34 ff.; Earle, *Turkey*, pp. 107 ff.; and N. Honig, 'Schiffahrt und Schiffahrtspolitik der Türkei', *WA*, Vol. VII (1916), pp. 79–92; also Kent, below, pp. 179–80, 182–3, 199 nn. 82–4, 200 n. 94.
44   See Hallgarten, *Imperialismus*, Vol. I, pp. 267, 307, 478 and passim; Rathmann, *Berlin–Bagdad*, pp. 16 ff.; and Wallach, *Anatomie*, pp. 105 ff.
45   Morgen, 'Meine Lebenserinnerungen', p. 207.
46   On the competition between Krupp and the technologically much more progressive Ehrhardt

firm, cf. Eckart Kehr, *Der Primat der Innenpolitik: Gesammelte Aufsätze* . . ., ed. Hans-Ulrich Wehler (Berlin, 1965), pp. 223–30; and Willi A. Boelcke, *Krupp und die Hohenzollern in Dokumenten* (Frankfurt am Main, 1970), pp. 106 ff., 183 and passim.

47 See Wallach, *Anatomie*, pp. 105 ff.

48 cf. Hermann Lorey, *Der Krieg in den türkischen Gewässern*, 2 vols (Berlin, 1928–38), Vol. I, 32 ff.; Paul G. Halpern, *The Mediterranean Naval Situation 1908–1914* (Cambridge, Mass., 1971), pp. 314 ff.; and Djemal Pasha, *Memories of a Turkish Statesman, 1913–1919* (London, 1922), pp. 83 ff.

49 See Marian Kent, *Oil and Empire: British Policy and Mesopotamian Oil, 1900–1920* (London, 1976), pp. 59 ff., 170 ff.; Fischer, *Krieg*, pp. 434 ff.; and Kent, below, p. 183 and especially p. 199 n. 92.

50 cf. Osman Nebioglu, *Die Auswirkungen der Kapitulationen auf die türkische Wirtschaft* (Jena, 1941), p. 64 and passim; M. L. Flanigam, 'German eastward expansion, fact and fiction: a study in German–Ottoman trade relations 1890–1914', *Journal of Central European Affairs*, Vol. XIV (1955), pp. 321–33; Mejcher, 'Die Bagdadbahn', pp. 478 ff.; and Antoine Fleury, *La Pénétration allemande au Moyen-Orient 1919–1939* (Leiden, 1977), pp. 22 ff.

51 See Earle, *Turkey*, pp. 132 ff.; Gotthard Jäschke, 'Die christliche Mission in der Türkei', *Saeculum*, Vol. VII (1956), pp. 68–78; and the relevant entries in Kurt Galling *et al.* (eds), *Die Religion in Geschichte und Gegenwart: Handwörterbuch für Theologie und Religionswissenschaft*, 6 vols (Tübingen, 1957–62). See also the government memorandum on German schools in Turkey, drafted April 1914, in Kurt Düwell, *Deutschlands Auswärtige Kulturpolitik 1918–1932* (Cologne, 1976), pp. 268 ff.

52 See Friedman, *Germany, Turkey, and Zionism*, chs 1, 4 ff.; Egmont Zechlin, *Die deutsche Politik und die Juden im Ersten Weltkrieg* (Göttingen, 1969), pp. 59 ff., 310 ff. and passim; and Richard Lichtheim, *Rückkehr: Lebenserinnerungen aus der Frühzeit des deutschen Zionismus* (Stuttgart, 1970), chs 1–11.

53 See ibid., pp. 153 ff.; and Friedman, *Germany, Turkey, and Zionism*, pp. 132 ff.

54 Walter Laqueur, *A History of Zionism* (New York, 1972), p. 152.

55 See Friedman, *Germany, Turkey, and Zionism*, pp. 156 ff., 171 ff.; Zechlin, *Deutsche Politik*, pp. 302 ff.; and the documents reprinted in Eliav, *Juden Palästinas*, nos 203–4, 210, 213–26.

56 In addition to the literature cited in n. 52, see also the contributions by Peter Pulzer, Lamar Cecil, Yehuda Eloni and others in Werner E. Mosse and Arnold Paucker (eds), *Juden im Wilhelminischen Deutschland, 1890–1914* (Tübingen, 1976).

57 See Alfred Kruck, *Geschichte des Alldeutschen Verbandes, 1890–1939* (Wiesbaden, 1954), pp. 38 ff.; and Paul Rohrbach, *Die Bagdadbahn*, 2nd edn (Berlin, 1911), pp. 7 ff., 10 ff.

58 See Henry Cord Meyer, *Mitteleuropa in German Thought and Action 1815–1945* (The Hague, 1955), pp. 96 ff.; Walter Mogk, *Paul Rohrbach und das 'Grössere Deutschland'* (Munich, 1972), passim; and Ernst Jäckh, *Der Goldene Pflug* (Stuttgart, 1954), pp. 120 ff.

59 See *WA*, 'Chronik und Archivalien', Vol. III (1914), p. 389; Jäckh, *Goldene Pflug*, pp. 130 ff.; Meyer, *Mitteleuropa*, pp. 219 ff.; and Lothar Rathmann, *Stossrichtung Nahost 1914–1918: Zur Expansionspolitik des deutschen Imperialismus im ersten Weltkrieg* (Berlin, 1963), pp. 184 ff. See also the statistical data on various German schools in Düwell, *Deutschlands Auswärtige Kulturpolitik*, pp. 323, 326 ff.

60 Major Kübel, 'Die Eisenbahnen der Türkei und ihre militärische Bedeutung', *VfTuH*, Vol. X (1913), pp. 344 ff. Kübel, a Bavarian officer, subsequently joined Liman's new mission in Turkey as head of the Railway Section and promptly became embroiled in a bitter dispute with the German directors of the Anatolie. On this political 'scandal' and Kübel's ultimate recall, see Hallgarten, *Imperialismus*, Vol. II, pp. 441 ff., 561 ff.; and Wallach, *Anatomie*, pp. 147 ff.

61 cf. Fischer, *Griff*, pp. 136 ff. and passim; R. L. Melka, 'Max Freiherr von Oppenheim: sixty years of scholarship and political intrigue in the Middle East', *Middle Eastern Studies*, Vol. IX (1973), 81–93; and Wilhelm Treue, 'Max Freiherr von Oppenheim: Der Archäologe und die Politik', *Historische Zeitschrift*, Vol. CCIX, no. 1 (1969), pp. 37–74.

62 See Cecil, *German Diplomatic Service*, pp. 101 ff.; and AA, Deutschland 122 No. 2, Wangenheim to Zimmermann, 30 Jan. 1915, No. 260; same to same, 5 Feb. 1915, No. 302.

63 In addition to the previously cited works by Wehler (n. 8) and Röhl (n. 18), see also Erich Eyck, *Das Persönliche Regiment Wilhelms II* (Zurich, 1948), and some of the essays in Michael Stürmer (ed.), *Das kaiserliche Deutschland: Politik und Gesellschaft 1870–1918* (Düsseldorf, 1970).

64   See particularly the works of Fritz Fischer, cited in nn. 21 and 34. See also Imanuel Geiss, *German Foreign Policy 1871–1914* (London, 1976), pts I, IV and V.
65   cf. Fischer, *Griff*, pp. 36 ff.; Fritz Klein *et al.*, *Deutschland im Ersten Weltkrieg*, 3 vols (Berlin, 1968–9), Vol. I, pp. 83 ff.; and Rathmann, *Berlin–Bagdad*, pp. 8 ff.
66   W. W. Gottlieb, *Studies in Secret Diplomacy during the First World War* (London, 1957), p. 32.
67   cf. Alfons Raab, *Die Politik Deutschlands im Nahen Orient von 1878 bis 1908* (Vienna, 1936), chs 2 ff.; Meyer, *Mitteleuropa*, pp. 72 ff. and passim; and Charles D. Sullivan, 'Stamboul crossings: German diplomacy in Turkey, 1908–1914', PhD thesis, Vanderbilt University, Nashville, Tenn., 1977, pp. 2, 5 ff., 26 ff., 34 ff. and passim. See also Herbert Feis, *Europe the World's Banker 1870–1914* (New Haven, Conn., 1930), passim, and the recent reassessment in Schulte, *Vor dem Kriegsausbruch*, passim.
68   See Langer, *Diplomacy*, pp. 318 ff., 362 ff. and passim; Raab, *Politik Deutschlands*, passim; Lindow, *Freiherr Marschall*, pp. 33 ff.; and Sullivan, 'Stamboul crossings', pp. 51 ff.
69   See *GP*, Vol. XXV, pt 2, nos 8875 ff.; AA, Nachlass Bernhard von Bülow, Marschall to Schoen, 27 July 1908; Wilhelm II to Bülow, 25 July and 29 July 1908; cf. Lindow, *Freiherr Marschall*, pp. 101 ff.
70   cf. Sullivan, 'Stamboul crossings', pp. 57 ff.; A. S. Silin, *Ekspansiya Germanskogo Imperialisma na Blizhnem Vostoke nakanunye pervoi mirovoi voiny* (Moscow, 1976), pp. 15 ff.; and Ernest E. Ramsaur, Jnr, *The Young Turks: Prelude to the Revolution of 1908* (Princeton, NJ, 1957), passim; cf. Ahmad, above, pp. 12 ff.
71   See Sullivan, 'Stamboul crossings', pp. 82 ff.; Wallach, *Anatomie*, pp. 91 ff.; and A. S. Silin, 'Fon der Goltz i ego voennaya missiya v Turtsii', in Akademya Nauk SSSR, *Germanskii imperializm i militarizm* (Moscow, 1965), pp. 64 ff; cf. Ahmad, above, pp. 12 ff.
72   For assessments of his career and influence, cf. Gordon A. Craig, *From Bismarck to Adenauer: Aspects of German Statecraft*, rev. edn (New York, 1965), pp. 39 ff.; and Cecil, *German Diplomatic Service*, pp. 309 ff. and passim.
73   See *GP*, Vol. XXVII, pt 2, chs 218 and 219; Bradford G. Martin, *German–Persian Diplomatic Relations 1873–1912* ('s-Gravenhage, 1959), pp. 172 ff.; and I. I. Astaf'ev, *Russko-germanskie diplomaticheskie otnosheniya 1905–1911 gg.* (Moscow, 1972), ch. 5; cf. Bodger, above, p. 90.
74   See Martin, *German–Persian*, pp. 189 ff.; Albertini, *Origins*, Vol. I, pp. 342 ff.; and Sullivan, 'Stanboul crossings', pp. 194 ff.
75   See ibid., pp. 296 ff.; Wallach, *Anatomie*, p. 119; cf. Silin, 'Fon der Goltz', pp. 89 ff.
76   See Generalfeldmarschall Freiherr von der Goltz, 'Der jungen Türkei Niederlage', *Deutsche Rundschau*, Vol. CLIV (1913), pp. 161–96. For similar criticisms, see also the article by the Bavarian general staff captain Count Hans von Podewils, 'Taktisches vom thrazischen Kriegsschauplatz', in *VfTuH*, Vol. X (1913), pp. 176 ff.; and von Lossow's secret report of 19 May 1913, in: Schulte, *Vor dem Kriegsausbruch*, pp. 133–7.
77   BA-MA, Nachlass Bruno von Mudra, N80/1, memorandum by Goltz, 17 Nov. 1912, entitled 'Betrachtungen über die politische Lage Europas nach dem Zusammenbruch der türkischen Herrschaft', with annotations by General Mudra. Presumably the Field-Marshal's warnings had some influence on subsequent deliberations in Berlin, on which cf. Fischer, *Krieg*, pp. 226 ff.; John Röhl, 'An der Schwelle zum Weltkrieg: Eine Dokumentation über den "Kriegsrat" vom 8. Dezember 1912', *MGM*, Vol. XXI (1977), pp. 77 ff.; and Konrad H. Jarausch, *The Enigmatic Chancellor: Bethmann Hollweg and the Hubris of Imperial Germany* (New Haven, Conn., 1973), pp. 134 ff.
78   The *Babiâli* incident, and particularly the shooting of War Minister Nazim Pasha, shocked Wilhelm II and put a severe strain on his relationship with Enver (whom he knew well from Enver's previous service as Ottoman military attaché in Berlin). See Trumpener, *Germany*, pp. 18 ff.; Kanner Papers, Vol. II, 'Unterredung mit Professor Lepsius am 4. Oktober . . . (1915)'; and the *Tagebuch der Baronin Spitzemberg*, p. 562. See also AA, Deutschland 138, Bd 51, Souchon to Wilhelm II, 28 May 1914.
79   As in the first round of the war, some German officers again participated actively in the operations of the Ottoman armed forces. See Wallach, *Anatomie*, pp. 114 ff.; and the amusing reminiscences of Major Franz Karl Endres, 'Maritime Erlebnisse einer Landratte: Aus meinen türkischen Tagebüchern 1913', *MR*, Vol. XXIX (1924), pp. 82 ff. (On Endres, who later took out Swiss citizenship, see Trumpener, 'German officers', p. 36; and Friedman, *Germany, Turkey and Zionism*, passim.) See also 'Tätigkeit türkischer Flugzeuge im Kriege 1912–13', *Militär-Wochenblatt*, Vol. XCVIII (1913), pp. 2236–40.

80 See Wallach, *Anatomie*, pp. 126 ff.; Trumpener, *Germany*, pp. 13, 69 ff. and passim; cf. Silin, *Ekspansiya Germanskogo Imperializma*, pp. 207–18, 229 ff.

81 See Poidevin, *Les Relations*, pp. 689 ff.; R. T. B. Langhorne, 'Great Britain and Germany, 1911–1914', in Hinsley, *British Foreign Policy*, pp. 313 ff.; Chapman, *Great Britain*, ch. 10; and Fischer, *Krieg*, pp. 431 ff. See also Ducruet, *Les Capitaux*, pp. 217 ff.

82 For recent assessments of the July Crisis, cf. Fischer, *Krieg*, pp. 663 ff.; V. R. Berghahn, *Germany and the Approach of War in 1914* (London, 1973), ch. 10; Dwight E. Lee, *Europe's Crucial Years* (Hanover, NH, 1974), ch. 13; and L. C. F. Turner, *Origins of the First World War* (London, 1970), chs 5–6. See also Ulrich Trumpener, 'War premeditated? German intelligence operations in July 1914', *Central European History*, Vol. IX (1976), pp. 58–85.

83 See Trumpener, *Germany*, pp. 15 ff.; cf. Weber, *Eagles*, pp. 61 ff., and Ahmad, above, p. 15.

84 See Trumpener, *Germany*, pp. 25 ff.; and his 'The escape of the *Goeben* and *Breslau*: a reassessment', *Canadian Journal of History*, Vol. VI (1971), pp. 171–87.

85 cf. Trumpener, *Germany*, pp. 32 ff.; Ahmad, above, pp. 15 ff.

86 See Trumpener, *Germany*, pp. 55 ff., 71, 274 ff. and passim.

87 cf. Carl Mühlmann, *Oberste Heeresleitung und Balkan im Weltkrieg 1914–1918* (Berlin, 1942), pp. 52 ff., 80 ff.; Karl-Heinz Janssen, *Der Kanzler und der General: Die Führungskrise um Bethmann Hollweg und Falkenhayn, 1914–1916* (Göttingen, 1967), pp. 41 ff.; and Gerard E. Silberstein, *The Troubled Alliance: German–Austrian Relations 1914–1917* (Lexington, Ky, 1970), pp. 114 ff. On the background to the supply problem, see also Ulrich Trumpener, 'German military aid to Turkey in 1914', *Journal of Modern History*, Vol. XXXII (1960), pp. 145 ff.

88 See Carl Mühlmann, *Das Deutsch-türkische Waffenbündnis im Weltkriege* (Leipzig, 1940), pp. 285 ff. and passim; Trumpener, *Germany*, pp. 68 ff. and passim; and Wallach, *Anatomie*, pp. 170 ff.

89 On Baron Kress, see ibid., pp. 133 ff., 192 ff and passim; and his memoirs, *Mit den Türken zum Suezkanal* (Berlin, 1938). On Guse, see his recollections of *Die Kaukasusfront im Weltkrieg bis zum Frieden von Brest* (Leipzig, 1940).

90 See Papen's memoirs, *Der Wahrheit eine Gasse* (Munich, 1952); Lothar Krecker, *Deutschland und die Türkei im zweiten Weltkrieg* (Frankfurt am Main, 1964), passim; and Frank G. Weber, *The Evasive Neutral* (Columbia, Mo., 1979), pp. 28 ff.

91 See Trumpener, *Germany*, passim; Wallach, *Anatomie*, chs 6–8 passim; and Hans Meier-Welcker, *Seeckt* (Frankfurt am Main, 1967), passim.

92 See Lorey, *Krieg in den türkischen Gewässern*, Vol. I; R. I. Lusar, 'Die Verluste der türkischen Kriegsmarine im Weltkriege', *MR*, Vol. XLI (1936), pp. 498 ff.; Şemsi Bargut, 'Die türkische Marine von 1945–1974', *MR*, Vol. LXXII (1975), pp. 65 ff.; and Martin-Christoph Wanner, 'Verbleib türkischer Kriegsschiffe', Vol. LXXII (1975), pp. 418 ff.

93 See Trumpener, *Germany*, pp. 62 ff. and passim; Mühlmann, *Waffenbündnis*, pp. 241 ff.; and Reichsarchiv *et al.*, *Der Weltkrieg 1914 bis 1918: Die militärischen Operationen zu Lande*, 14 vols (Berlin, 1925–44), Vol. XIII, pp. 445 ff.

94 cf. Trumpener, *Germany*, ch. 6; Werner Zürrer, *Kaukasien 1918–1921* (Düsseldorf, 1978), pp. 28 ff.; and Winfried Baumgart, 'Das Kaspi-Unternehmen: Grössenwahn Ludendorffs oder Routineplanung des deutschen Generalstabs?' *JfGO*, NS, Vol. XVIII (1970), pp. 47–126; 231–78. On the background, see also Bihl, *Die Kaukasus-Politik*, Vol. I, passim.

95 See Trumpener, *Germany*, pp. 38 ff.; cf. Ahmad, above, pp. 17 ff.

96 AA, Deutschland 128 No. 5 secreta, Bd 5, Bethmann Hollweg to Auswärtige Amt, 5 November 1914, No. 97.

97 See Trumpener, *Germany*, pp. 60 ff., 108 ff.; cf. Gerard E. Silberstein, 'The Central Powers and the Second Turkish Alliance 1915', *Slavic Review*, Vol. XXIV (1965), pp. 77 ff., and Bridge, above, pp. 42–3.

98 See Trumpener, *Germany*, pp. 204 ff. For similar behaviour by the Austro–Hungarian government, cf. Bridge, above, p. 46. On the whole Armenian issue, see also Gwynne Dyer, 'Turkish "falsifiers" and Armenian "deceivers": historiography and the Armenian massacres', *MES*, Vol. XII (1976), 99 ff.

99 See Zechlin, *Deutsche Politik*, pp. 316 ff.; Friedman, *Germany, Turkey, and Zionism*, pp. 191 ff.

100 See Ahmed Emin, *Turkey in the World War* (New Haven, Conn., 1930), chs 17–18; and Yusuf Hikmet Bayur, *Türk inkilâbi tarihi*, 3 vols in 10 pts (Ankara, 1940–67). Vol. III, pt 3, pp. 6 ff., 33 ff. and 44.

101 See Trumpener, *Germany*, ch. 8 and passim.
102 See ibid., ch. 9.
103 See ibid., pp. 330 ff. and passim.
104 AA, Türkei 152, Bd 94, Kühlmann to Bethmann Hollweg, 22 June 1917.
105 ibid.
106 AA, Weltkrieg, 15, Bd 25, Bernstorff to Hertling, 26 January 1918, No. 27.
107 See Trumpener, *Germany*, pp. 342 ff.
108 These conclusions conflict with the interpretations advanced by Fritz Fischer, Lothar Rathmann and a number of other authors; cf. below, pp. 131 ff.
109 See Trumpener, *Germany*, pp. 352 ff.; and Gwynne Dyer, 'The Turkish armistice of 1918', *MES*, Vol. VIII (1972), pp. 143 ff., 313 ff.
110 See Trumpener, *Germany*, pp. 359 ff.
111 On the withdrawal of German personnel from Turkey, see the documents in AA, Deutschland 135 No. 1, Bd 6; Türkei 158, Bd 21; and [Otto] Liman von Sanders, *Fünf Jahre Türkei* (Berlin, 1920), pp. 398 ff.; cf. Wallach, *Anatomie*, pp. 246 ff.
112 See Gotthard Jäschke and Erich Pritsch, 'Die Türkei seit dem Weltkriege: Geschichtskalender 1918–1928', *Die Welt des Islams*, Vol. X (1927–9), pp. 1 ff.; Krecker, *Deutschland und die Türkei*, pp. 11 ff.
113 See BA-MA, N239/66, 'Deutsche Marineberaterschaft in der Türkei 1925–26'; and BI78, 'Deutsche Offiziere in der Türkei', pp. 45, 47. On Klewitz, see also Hanns Möller, *Geschichte der Ritter des Ordens pour le mérite im Weltkrieg*, 2 vols (Berlin, 1935), Vol. I, pp. 581 ff.
114 See 'Deutsche Offiziere in der Türkei', pp. 46 ff.; and BA-MA, Nachlass Hilmar Ritter von Mittelberger, N40/12 and passim.
115 It is noteworthy that the pictures of hundreds of German military advisers of the nineteenth and twentieth centuries are still prominently displayed in the War Museum in Istanbul. According to press reports, not long ago a West German delegation was welcomed by the Turkish Minister of Finance with words to the effect that just 'as our fathers' had stood side by side in the trenches 'our sons' were now standing side by side at the workbenches.
116 cf. A. F. Miller, *Pyatidesyatiletye mladoturetskoi revolutsii* (Moscow, 1958), pp. 44 ff.; M. S. Lazarev, *Kruchenye turetskogo gospodstva na Arabskom vostoke 1914–1918 gg.* (Moscow, 1960), pp. 54 ff., 66 and passim; E. M. Shukov (editor-in-chief), *Vsemirnaya istoriya*, 10 vols (Moscow, 1955–65), Vol. VII, pp. 360 and 572; G. Z. Aliev, *Turtsiya v period pravlenya mladoturok 1908–1918 gg.* (Moscow, 1972), p. 261 and passim; and Klein *et al.*, *Deutschland im ersten Weltkrieg*, Vol. I, pp. 83 ff. and passim. See also Rathmann, *Berlin–Bagdad*, passim; and his *Stossrichtung Nahost*, pp. 19 ff. and passim.
117 In addition to the works by Fischer and Geiss cited in nn. 21, 34 and 64 above, see Hartmut Pogge von Strandmann and Imanuel Geiss, *Die Erforderlichkeit des Unmöglichen: Deutschland am Vorabend des ersten Weltkrieges* (Frankfurt am Main, 1965); Klaus Wernecke, *Der Wille zur Weltgeltung: Aussenpolitik und Oeffentlichkeit am Vorabend des Ersten Weltkrieges* (Düsseldorf, 1970); and Adolf Gasser, 'Der deutsche Hegemonialkrieg von 1914', in I. Geiss and B. J. Wendt (eds), *Deutschland in der Weltpolitik des 19. und 20. Jahrhunderts* (Düsseldorf, 1973), pp. 307 ff.; cf. L. L. Farrar, Jnr, *Divide and Conquer: German Efforts to Conclude a Separate Peace, 1914–1918* (New York, 1978), pp. 109 ff. and passim.
118 See Trumpener, *Germany*, passim. See also Ritter, *Staatskunst*, Vols III and IV; Wolfgang Steglich, *Die Friedenspolitik der Mittelmächte 1917–1918* (Wiesbaden, 1964); and Baumgart, *Deutsche Ostpolitik*, passim.
119 cf. Ahmad, above, pp. 17–18.

6 France and the End of the Ottoman Empire

L. Bruce Fulton, University of Sydney

During the years 1898 to 1918, France made a vigorous attempt to strengthen her influence in the Ottoman Empire. Her expansionism, which involved a thorough exploitation of the imbalance of power between the two states, was primarily a response to the impact of German *Weltpolitik* on the Near East. For much of the period, French governments were convinced that a far-reaching ambition lay behind Germany's growing activity in the Ottoman Empire, and their reaction was intensified by a broader Franco-German rivalry in which the chief arena, prior to 1914, was the Mediterranean and, thereafter, western Europe.

In 1898, France was very much an established power in the Ottoman Empire, where she had long possessed important interests. These were interests associated primarily with Catholic religious orders, whose work was declining in importance, and an economic action whose significance was rapidly increasing. France, whose protection of the church dated back to the sixteenth century, provided diplomatic support to Catholic missionaries and to such Ottoman Christian communities as the Maronites of Lebanon. The missionary orders, with the aid of the protecting power, had acquired substantial congregations and created an extensive network of schools and hospitals. In return, ecclesiastical personnel had made an important contribution to the diffusion of the French language and provided a Catholic clientele which numbered about 750,000 in the Asiatic portion of the Ottoman Empire.[1]

At the end of the nineteenth century, the proselytising activity of the Catholic orders had lost some of its earlier effectiveness and was encountering stiffer Greek Orthodox competition. To the further disadvantage of France, nationalist sentiment was intensifying among Italian and German missionaries. Hence, France's influence was becoming more dependent on economic interests. Since the 1860s, French investors had shown so sustained an interest in Turkish securities that, by 1898, they held at least 50 per cent of the Ottoman Debt. As a result of this large movement of capital, French bankers had come to occupy a predominant place in Ottoman financial affairs and in the administration of the Imperial Ottoman Bank, an institution of vital importance to the economic life of the Ottoman Empire. At the time of its founding, in 1863, the IOB had been very much a Franco-British venture. But British investors had ceased to welcome Ottoman securities, and by the late 1890s the operations of the IOB were largely controlled from Paris.

France's financial preponderance did not extend to the commercial realm. Her share of Ottoman imports, a modest 11.63 per cent in 1895, was 9.3 per cent in 1911.[2] By 1898, however, French industrialists were making their presence felt. French railway companies, in particular, had achieved a prominent situation. Successful lines were operated by the Salonika–Constantinople Junction and Smyrna–Cassaba companies. An important Syrian network had been started by the Beyrouth–Damas–Hauran Company. The short, but strategically placed line between Mersina and Adana was directed by a French businessman. The chief harbour works of the Ottoman Empire, located in Constantinople, Beirut, Smyrna and Salonika, were French-owned. On the shores of the Black Sea, the Société d'Héraclée was beginning to work the coal mines of the Heraclea Basin, which it proposed to link by rail to the port of Zonguldak. Finally, the lighthouses of the Ottoman Empire were administered by a French company, while French-controlled firms supplied Beirut with gas and Constantinople with water.[3]

French governments considered Syria and the area of Constantinople and the Straits as zones of maximum political importance. Constantinople was thought of as both the Ottoman capital city and the business centre of the Turkish Empire. France quietly favoured the continued closure of the Straits and the preservation of the existing distribution of naval power in the Mediterranean. In Syria (including Lebanon and Palestine) there was a marked concentration of French interests. The Syrian region, moreover, was a traditional sphere of action for French diplomacy and a territory accessible to French naval expeditions. Hence, French policy-makers were inclined to think of Syria as an area of exceptional political significance, where France might one day have territorial claims and where, therefore, it was essential to maintain the primacy of French influence.

In 1898 the defence of French interests and, ultimately, the formulation of French policy were still left largely to the Foreign Ministry. The power of Foreign Ministers was sometimes circumscribed by the composition and the parliamentary weakness of the government to which they belonged. Yet, in dealing with Ottoman affairs, they were spared the interministerial rivalry which had arisen in such areas of policy-making as the Far East and north Africa. The French press published little on the Ottoman Empire. Parliament, especially the Chamber of Deputies, was less indifferent. The traditional Right, with its clerical sympathies, was much attached to France's religious protectorate. The extreme Left, comprising socialist deputies for the most part, favoured vigorous diplomatic intervention on behalf of Ottoman minorities. Yet parliamentary interpellations on issues relevant to the Ottoman Empire were infrequent. Moreover, the influential colonial party, headed by the Algerian deputy, Eugène Etienne, was interested primarily in Morocco. Its Asian enthusiasts were limited in number and more strongly attracted by the Far East than the Near East.

As French influence in the Ottoman Empire became identified with economic action, bankers and industrialists acquired a greater say in the making of policy. At the same time, Ministers of Finance were involved more frequently in the decision-making process by virtue of their relations with French banking houses and their responsibility for the listing of foreign securities on the Paris Stock Exchange. But, in 1898, France's Ottoman policy still emanated largely from the Foreign Ministry. The Foreign Minister was obviously of fundamental importance, but the Constantinople embassy, the consular service and the Political and Commercial Sections of the Quai d'Orsay all had some part in deciding policy. French Ambassadors, who traditionally did long service in Constantinople, possessed a large measure of authority which was strengthened by their proximity to Ottoman affairs and the considerable latitude they were allowed in applying policy directives. Consuls fulfilled several important functions. They intervened on behalf of Frenchmen and French protégés; presided over consular courts which heard both civil and penal cases; and provided French businessmen and the Commercial Section with detailed information. The Political and Commercial Directors, leading advisers of the Foreign Minister, spent an important portion of their time on Ottoman affairs. Their work was occasionally unco-ordinated, however, and tended to overlap in a manner which contributed to the appointment of a single Political and Commercial Director in 1907.[4]

By 1898, French politicians and diplomats, many of whom were drawn from a liberal, middle-class background, were inclined to view with distaste the regime of Sultan Abdul Hamid II. For the most part, they disliked the autocratic nature of the Hamidian regime, its treatment of Macedonian and Armenian minorities and its responsiveness to a well-placed bakhshish. Some French diplomats clearly shared the mentality of a colonialist era and viewed Ottoman politicians with a decided sense of superiority. However, the importance of French interests in the Ottoman Empire did much to restrain such antipathies. Abdul Hamid, though frequently reproached with throwing himself into German arms, was formally regarded as a friendly sovereign, and Turkish political exiles in Paris were treated in somewhat inhospitable fashion. Those known to be Young Turks were put under police surveillance and given no opportunity to organise demonstrations.[5]

For much of the 1890s, French governments had made but limited use of the diplomatic resources at their disposal. Little was done to control the flow of French capital to the Ottoman government. In the early 1890s the Ottoman Bank experienced no difficulty in having its loan participations quoted on the Bourse, and it was able to negotiate the important 1896 loan without consulting the French embassy in Constantinople. Meanwhile, France's promotion and protection of Catholic interests had rather slackened. The Constantinople embassy complained that the French government had failed to match the zeal displayed by Russia on behalf of Greek Orthodoxy. Even so, French Foreign Ministers were generally more concerned to second the work of religious orders than to strengthen French industrial enterprises.[6]

During 1898, German diplomatic activity did much to bring about a change in French official attitudes. For some years, French governments had been uneasy about the progress of German influence in Constantinople. They had been disturbed by the extension of German railways from Izmit to Angora and Konia, and by the cordiality of relations between Sultan Abdul Hamid II and the German government. Only in 1898, however, did it seem as though Germany was making a systematic bid for diplomatic preponderance. French apprehensiveness was aroused by the installation of Baron Marschall von Bieberstein, a diplomat of exceptional competence, as German Ambassador to Constantinople; by reports that Germany was seeking a lease on the Mediterranean port of Alexandretta; and by a revival of German interest in the Baghdad Railway. Moreover, France's religious protectorate was under German attack. The German emperor had decided to visit the Holy Land, and his government was encouraging the establishment of diplomatic relations between the Ottoman Empire and the Vatican.

An energetic reaction was initially forthcoming from Gabriel Hanotaux, French Foreign Minister in the years 1894 to 1898. But he had vacated the Foreign Ministry by June of 1898 and the reshaping of France's Ottoman policy was left largely to his successor, Théophile Delcassé. A hard-working and intensely patriotic individual, Delcassé quickly established himself as an able Foreign Minister. His objectives were carefully conceived and pursued with a formidable perseverance. Soon after his arrival in office, he developed a preoccupation with the Mediterranean and its shores. Hence, though primarily interested in north Africa, he was disturbed by the growing involvement of Germany in Ottoman affairs.[7] As early as July of 1898, he made clear his determination to defend France's religious protectorate. In a speech of considerable firmness, he informed both the Chamber of Deputies and, less directly, the German Foreign Ministry of his intention to maintain French prerogatives. By late August the Vatican had issued assurances that it would not establish diplomatic relations with the Ottoman Empire.[8]

This initial achievement did not lead Delcassé to relax his vigilance. Three years later, the Franco-Ottoman dispute known as the Lorando–Tubini affair enabled him to reaffirm France's attachment to its Catholic protégés. During this conflict, France demanded not only a settlement of the financial claims of its citizens, Lorando and Tubini, but additional privileges for Catholic establishments in the Ottoman Empire. A French naval expedition to the island of Mitylene in November 1901 achieved the desired results. In the Chamber of Deputies, Delcassé described the subsequent strengthening of French moral interests as 'the consolidation of our place in the Eastern sun'.[9] Such enthusiasm was hardly justified by the Mitylene concessions, but Delcassé had clearly given substance to the promises made in 1898.

Though Delcassé's initial concern with religious and cultural expansion persisted, his attention was increasingly diverted to economic questions as the

Baghdad Railway project took shape. By early 1899, the Germans were prepared to bid for a concession whose economic, political and strategic importance the French were quick to recognise. The proposed line would extend from Germany's Anatolian railway network through the heart of Asia Minor, reduce the Constantinople–Baghdad journey from twenty-three days to two and cost about 600 million francs. Few neighbouring railways would be capable of surviving its commercial competition.

Initially, German planning encountered the hostility of French diplomacy. In seeking a concession for port works at Haydar Pasha, which would eventually serve the Baghdad Railway, German diplomats met with stubborn opposition from the French Ambassador to Constantinople, Paul Cambon. The French engineer, Cotard, a director of the Smyrna–Cassaba Company, announced his intention of competing with the Germans for a Baghdad Railway concession. However, France's resistance ceased in April 1899, when Delcassé began to envisage the Baghdad Railway as a joint Franco-German undertaking. He had come to believe that French businessmen could obtain an equal share in the venture and that, as a result, France's influence would be strengthened at least as much as Germany's.[10]

Delcassé adopted this view after discussions with Ernest Constans, who replaced Cambon as French Ambassador in December 1898. Constans, no career diplomat, was none the less a politician of skill and stature. In 1889 he had provided French Republicans with leadership in their struggle against the Boulangist movement and, thereafter, he had been powerful enough to bid for the Presidency of the Republic. He was still a prominent parliamentarian at the time of his departure for Constantinople. He retained his seat in the Senate, a sizeable parliamentary following and supporters in the French press. His private means, adroitness and eminence enabled him to be an exceptionally independent ambassador.

Constans' diplomacy was strongly influenced by his realism and financial acquisitiveness. He was sceptical of schemes for reforming the Ottoman Empire and put rather more show than substance into his defence of Catholic establishments. Instead, he gave priority to economic interests and was primarily concerned with the safeguarding of French investments. To some extent, he was both businessman and ambassador. He was in search of personal enrichment – an aim which had figured prominently in his political career.[11] It was probably with his personal finances in mind that he brought with him to Constantinople Léon Pissard, who had been an employee of the French penitentiary service before joining Constans' private cabinet. Sponsored by Constans, Pissard acquired the important post of Director–General of the Ottoman Public Debt Administration and was added to the *conseil d'administration* of the Salonika–Constantinople Junction Company.

Constans was enthusiastic about French participation in the Baghdad Railway scheme. He was impressed by the strength of German influence in Constantinople and convinced that Germany could ultimately build the

Baghdad line herself. Also, it may well be, as the British Foreign Office thought, that he had acquired a speculative interest in the Baghdad venture.[12] The eventual appearance of Pissard on the *conseil d'administration* of the Baghdad Railway Company certainly suggests as much. In the early months of 1899, Constans pressed his views strongly on Delcassé and clearly had some success in shaping his superior's attitude to the Baghdad Railway.[13]

Delcassé's response to the Baghdad project was very much to the liking of the Imperial Ottoman Bank and the Régie Générale des Chemins de Fer, the chief representatives of French capitalism in the Ottoman Empire. The IOB had had its ups and downs, but was in a solid position at the close of the 1890s. Since 1863 it had much extended the range of its activities. Its initial preoccupation with state loans had been somewhat moderated by the expansion of its commercial operations and the creation of a network of agencies. During the 1880s it had been attracted by industrial investment. It had made an important loan to the Beyrouth–Damas–Hauran company and purchased shares in the Smyrna–Cassaba Company, La Compagnie du Port de Beyrouth, and La Compagnie du Gaz de Beyrouth. It appointed a delegate to the Debt Council, which enabled it to participate directly in the management of Ottoman revenues. Finally, it was strongly backed by the Paris Haute Banque,[14] and was able to obtain capital for Turkish financial and industrial ventures a good deal more readily than its international competitors.[15]

Count Vitali, founder of the Régie Générale, did business on a large scale in the Ottoman Empire. A specialist in the management and construction of railways, he had built, or helped to build, both the Smyrna–Cassaba line and the German line from Izmit to Angora. He owned about two-thirds of the shares of the Smyrna–Cassaba Company and enjoyed good relations with Paris banking houses. His business associates included Léon Berger who, until 1909, was France's chief representative on the Debt Council. Vitali's political connections were equally good. His allies included high-ranking Ottoman officials and Eugène Etienne, leader of the French colonial party.[16]

By 1898 the IOB and the Régie Générale were closely associated. They represented a powerful grouping, which tended to be singleminded in its pursuit of profit. Vitali was expensive to hire, as the Anatolian Railway Company discovered during construction of its Izmit–Angora line. The IOB, which had speculated heavily and unwisely in South African gold shares in 1895, retained its eagerness for the large commissions which could be earned from Turkish loans and loan conversions. Neither Vitali nor the financiers of the IOB gave much thought to the political consequences of their business dealings. Baron Marschall, after some years as German Ambassador, described them as people 'avid for money', whose outlook on international affairs was entirely that of the businessman.[17]

It required no urging on Delcassé's part to persuade Vitali and the IOB to co-operate with German capitalists in the Baghdad Railway enterprise. What was no less important, the German government, in its desire to avoid the hostility of France, was prepared to make a place in the venture for French capitalists. The Baghdad Railway would be difficult to finance without access to the French money-market. To obtain a Baghdad concession without lengthy delay, Germany needed the goodwill of the French government. Above all, the French-owned Beyrouth–Damas–Hauran company was entitled to build a railway from Rayak through Aleppo to Biredjik on the Euphrates and, when required, to construct branch lines to the Gulf of Alexandretta. The BDH's concession represented a serious obstacle for German planners, who were eager to bring the important trading place of Aleppo within the Baghdad Railway system and who regarded a link with the Gulf of Alexandretta as essential to the economic viability of the projected line.

By April of 1899, both French and German governments favoured a co-operative approach to the Baghdad Railway. But they did so with quite different aims in mind. Germany, supported by the Ottoman government, wanted the enterprise to be controlled by German capitalists. On the other hand, Delcassé's policy was to internationalise the line by obtaining an equal participation for French capitalists.[18] Had subsequent Franco-German negotiations taken place at an official level this incompatibility would speedily have become apparent. But Delcassé wanted the Baghdad venture to be considered a purely private affair involving the co-operation of capitalists rather than governments. Official detachment much simplified the task of explaining French participation to the Russian government and to the Chamber of Deputies.[19] Hence, French capitalists, discreetly supervised by the Constantinople embassy and the Commercial Section of the Quai d'Orsay, were allowed to negotiate directly with their German counterparts.

This procedure depended heavily on the Ottoman Bank, Vitali and Constans, all of whom were prepared to accept a participation on terms less rigorous than those laid down by Delcassé.[20] Indeed, after negotiations with a German group headed by the Deutsche Bank, the IOB and Vitali signed an accord on 6 May 1899 which was not in conformity with Delcassé's wishes. The French group accepted a participation of 40 per cent while agreeing that 60 per cent, 'in proportions to be determined', should be reserved for the Deutsche Bank's group.[21]

Delcassé was not made aware of this departure from his doctrine of equality. Ambassador Constans, aided by compliant Paris newspapers, successfully gave the impression that something like parity had been achieved.[22] And, in the months which followed the May agreement, French businessmen continued to behave with remarkable indifference towards France's general interests. The Ottoman Bank–Vitali combination allowed the German-owned Anatolian Railway Company to seek both the preliminary and definitive concessions from the Ottoman government. What was more serious, the French negotiators surrendered most of the privileges of the Beyrouth–Damas–Hauran company. The BDH, which had reached the verge of bankruptcy by 1899, was unable to act independently of the IOB's wishes. By early 1900, when the Germans decided definitively on a southerly route for the Baghdad Railway, the Ottoman Bank saw little financial advantage in extending the BDH's network beyond Hama. Consequently, to the astonishment of German negotiators, the Bank abandoned most of the BDH's Rayak–Biredjik concession. The BDH ceded to the Anatolian Railway Company not only the right to extend its line beyond Hama, but the priority it possessed for branch lines to the Gulf of Alexandretta.[23]

The co-operation which the Germans obtained from the IOB and Vitali extended to Constans. During the German–Ottoman negotiations for the preliminary concession, which lasted from May until December of 1899, he sometimes followed his instructions, which were to remain neutral. On other occasions, however, he provided German diplomacy with what Baron Marschall described as 'effective support'.[24] Constans clearly had some knowledge of the compromising agreements accepted by French businessmen, but he expressed no opposition prior to 1903.[25]

Long before the granting of a definitive concession in January 1902, the Baghdad Railway consortium was grappling with the problem of financing the projected line. It was evident that Baghdad Railway bonds issued by the Ottoman Empire could not be successfully floated unless backed by a solid guarantee. But, to provide such a guarantee, the Turkish government required an additional source of income. Given the difficulties involved in raising the Ottoman tariff, the German government and the Deutsche Bank decided to seek the necessary revenue through a unification of the Ottoman Debt.

This operation, because of France's majority holding in the Debt, depended heavily on the co-operation of French bankers and diplomats. Thus, a French financier, Maurice Rouvier, was chosen by Abdul Hamid to formulate a unification proposal. This was a shrewd move. Rouvier, the founder of La Banque Française pour le Commerce et l'Industrie, was strongly in favour of French participation in the Baghdad Railway and did not share Delcassé's concern for equality.[26] Though primarily a businessman, Rouvier was also an experienced and influential parliamentarian. His success in combining the two roles was demonstrated anew in June 1902 when he became French Finance Minister. His return to office prevented him from completing his work on unification, but the scheme eventually accepted by the Ottoman government owed much to his expertise.

In its final form, unification involved an amalgamation of the various bonds comprising the Ottoman Debt.[27] A fixed annuity, drawn from revenues ceded to the Ottoman Public Debt Administration, was to be set aside to service the newly unified Debt. If income from the ceded revenues exceeded this sum, 25 per cent of the surplus would be turned over to the Debt Administration while the remainder would be put at the disposal of the Ottoman government. Most diplomats agreed that under relatively prosperous conditions the Ottoman share would soon be large enough to permit the issuing of a substantial state loan.

Rouvier's return to the Finance Ministry offered encouragement to those who were willing to allow French capitalists to participate in the Baghdad Railway venture on a less-than-equal footing. Initially, no doubt, proponents of this view hoped that Delcassé could be brought to accept something less than complete equality or that he and his doctrine of equality would disappear amidst a ministerial crisis. But the realisation of such hopes was made much more difficult in March 1902, when, in a speech to the Chamber of Deputies, Delcassé laid it down that official approval of French participation in the Baghdad Railway venture would be dependent on the achievement of complete equality. He made his determination still clearer by rejecting the business accords of February 1903, which stopped well short of parity. As a result, some effort was made by the Germans, at the suggestion of Constans and the Ottoman Bank, to give the newly formed Baghdad Railway Company an egalitarian façade.[28] But the ensuing agreement, dated 13 June, failed to deceive or to satisfy Delcassé.

Admittedly, he continued to think of equality as something which Germany had initially accepted[29] and which remained attainable. This was surely a mistaken belief, but there was no doubt that the French government could seriously obstruct the projected Baghdad Railway by opposing unification of the Ottoman Debt. This was the course which Delcassé decided to follow, and the result was a collision with Rouvier. The Finance Minister, backed by the Ottoman Bank, represented unification as a *fait accompli*, evoked the interests of French bondholders and – what was decidedly suspect for someone of his financial acumen – argued that there was no connection between unification and the Baghdad Railway.[30] The dispute between Rouvier and Delcassé was resolved at an important cabinet meeting held on 28 July 1903. The outcome was not particularly satisfying for either man. The French government decided not to oppose or to delay unification. At the same time, it agreed, very much against Rouvier's wishes, to support Delcassé's insistence on Franco-German equality within the Baghdad Railway Company.

Following the cabinet meeting of 28 July, negotiations resumed between French and German capitalists. With unification assured, the Germans were less inclined than ever to grant France an equal participation. The Brussels agreement of 1 October met none of the requirements laid down by the French government. Though Constans and Rouvier favoured acceptance,[31] Delcassé disagreed and, in late October 1903, Baghdad Railway bonds were officially denied a quotation on the Paris Stock Exchange.

Explanations of this decision, which was virtually inevitable after the cabinet meeting of 28 July, have often emphasised Russian hostility to the Baghdad Railway.[32] But Delcassé, for all his devotion to the Russian alliance, was unwilling to see French interests in the Ottoman Empire subordinated to those of Russia. In late 1898, he had been congratulated by Paul Cambon for his readiness to follow an independent policy in the Near East,[33] while, three years later, he had braved Russian displeasure in concluding the Lorando–

Tubini affair. Much of the press campaign by which the Russian government manifested its dislike of the Baghdad venture had had little or no effect upon him.[34] His speech to the Chamber in March 1902, which clearly foreshadowed his later stand, had been made at a time when he thought Russia favourably disposed to the Baghdad enterprise. At bottom, it was Delcassé's attachment to the principle of an equal participation which determined his attitude to the Baghdad Railway. He had asked for equality at the beginning of Franco-German negotiations, insisted upon it before the Chamber and refused to see it violated in the ministerial debate of 1903.[35]

On balance, the Baghdad Railway negotiations of the period 1899 to 1903 had been decidedly damaging for French interests in the Ottoman Empire. To begin with, the Rayak–Biredjik concession of 1893 had been lost. Germany was entitled to link both Aleppo and the Gulf of Alexandretta to the main line of the Baghdad Railway. France's Syrian railway network, truncated and denied branch lines to the sea, was threatened by a bleak economic future. Ultimately, France's traditional preponderance in northern Syria, and perhaps Syria as a whole, had been placed in jeopardy. Moreover, the business group headed by the Ottoman Bank had developed ties which it refused to sever. It chose to remain in the Baghdad Railway consortium and to accept a 30 per cent share along with six places on the *conseil d'administration* of the Baghdad Railway Company.

Delcassé's decision to seek an equal share of the Baghdad Railway had been made without an adequate understanding of German and Ottoman intentions. Even so, this initial misjudgement would have had limited consequences had he not entrusted negotiations to Constans and French financiers. Looking back, he understandably regretted that, after all, he had not sought to reach agreement at a governmental level.[36] Not only had French interests suffered, but also France had squandered diplomatic resources substantial enough to have forced an indefinite postponement of the Baghdad venture. It was doubtful that Germany could have proceeded without the privileges of the Beyrouth–Damas–Hauran company. A successful unification of the Ottoman Debt would have been unlikely without French co-operation, and Arthur Gwinner, head of the Deutsche Bank, admitted in 1906 that but for the revenue provided by unification Germany would have been unable to finance the difficult second section of the Baghdad line.[37]

By the end of 1903, the prospect of a German-controlled Baghdad Railway had been brought considerably nearer and the French government, as a result, had begun to reconsider its policy towards the Ottoman Empire.

During the period 1903–10 there were times when France's Ottoman policy lacked coherence. A measure of confusion resulted from Delcassé's departure from office in 1905, the importance attached by French governments to their *entente cordiale* with Britain, and the Young Turk revolution of 1908. Yet, apart from the first two years of the Young Turk regime, there was a consistency to French policy which owed much to the Baghdad Railway. Near the end of 1903 the French government decided that the line could still be effectively internationalised. This aim was pursued throughout the period 1903–10 at the same time as a more positive response took shape: the reinforcement of France's economic interests in the Ottoman Empire.

Assuredly, these were not the sole objectives of French policy in the years after 1903. French governments sought to maintain the religious protectorate and to further the cause of Macedonian reform. Yet both objectives were of secondary importance. The political value of the protectorate was clearly diminishing. This trend was stubbornly resisted by French Foreign Ministers, but it gained much added momentum when relations with the Holy See were broken off in July 1904. Still further damage was done by Italian competition and by the numerical decline of French missionaries, whose recruitment had been much hampered by the anti-clerical Associations Law of 1901.[38]

Macedonian reform was an important issue during the years 1903–8, but France's contribution was decidedly modest. The French government, anxious to concert with Russia in the Balkans, was content with an effaced role in the elaboration of reforms involving the Macedonian *gendarmerie* and financial administration. To some extent, moreover, the reformist inclinations of French Foreign Ministers were tempered by France's economic interests. In 1905, when the process of financial reform began, the French government objected to experimentation which would reduce the return on Macedonian tithes assigned to the Debt Administration. This revenue was used to subsidise two French-owned railway companies: the Salonika–Constantinople Junction and the Smyrna–Cassaba.[39]

To realise a policy which aimed primarily at internationalising the Baghdad Railway and encouraging economic expansion, the French government relied heavily on its control of the official money-market. It maintained the exclusion of Baghdad Railway bonds and dealt in much more demanding fashion with Ottoman loans. Since the reorganisation of Turkish finances in 1881, the French government had not systematically interfered with the flow of capital from France to the Ottoman Empire. In December of 1903, however, Delcassé declared that the days of *laissez-faire* were over.[40] Henceforth the Ottoman government would be expected to fulfil precise conditions in return for access to the official money-market. This decision was not wholly to the liking of the Ottoman Bank, which worried about displeasing the sultan and losing important loan contracts. But French diplomats pointed out, in reply, that the Ottoman government could obtain a regular satisfaction of its financial needs only by appealing to French investors.

In addition to their financial power, French governments possessed a further source of diplomatic strength in the Franco-British *entente cordiale*. As France moved towards the acquisition of Morocco, and as Franco-German relations deteriorated, Delcassé became the architect of this understanding. He was succeeded by Foreign Ministers no less anxious to work with Britain.

Stephen Pichon, a Radical politician, was the most notable, if only because he retained office from late 1906 until early 1911. An experienced diplomat, of rather less vision and fixity of purpose than Delcassé, he was under the direct influence of the Radical chieftain, Georges Clemenceau. Like his patron, who was Premier in the years 1906–9, Pichon thought that French influence in the Ottoman Empire could be considerably strengthened by the *entente cordiale*.

For Near Eastern purposes, French governments valued the *entente* primarily as a means of internationalising the Baghdad Railway. France welcomed the prospect of Britain's diplomatic support and also the assistance of Britain's representative on the Council of the Ottoman Public Debt Administration. Though British investment in the Ottoman Empire had been in retreat, it was still of sufficient importance to enable Britain to share with France the presidency of the Debt Council. Given an effective co-operation between French and British delegates, there was some chance that important financial obstacles could be raised to the continuation of the Baghdad line.

Though the French government could call on substantial diplomatic means, the implementation of its policy continued to suffer from the independent action of both the Ottoman Bank and Constans. The Bank was strongly inclined to work with the Germans. It remained attached to its participation in the Baghdad Railway. It feared the competition of the Deutsche Bank and the power of the German embassy and, as a result, it was reluctant to co-operate with British capitalists. Constans, while on occasion prepared to compete with Baron Marschall, was fundamentally as desirous as the Ottoman Bank of an understanding with Germany. He remained well disposed towards the Baghdad Railway and appreciated the advantages of German support in his dealings with the Ottoman authorities.[41]

To Constans' dissatisfaction, France redefined her Baghdad Railway policy at the end of 1903. Thereafter, it was the intention of French governments to do what they could to impede construction of the line. At times they envisaged recovery of the Syrian railway privileges ceded by French financiers in 1900–1. But their ultimate aim was to put an end to German control of the Baghdad Railway and to transform the Baghdad Railway Company into an international corporation in which France, Britain, Germany and Russia were equally represented. This was clearly an ambitious policy, but much faith was placed in the support of Britain and Russia.

During the years 1904–6, following completion of the first section of the Baghdad Railway, from Konia to Bulgurlu, French diplomats were inclined to wait on events. There was some wishful thinking at the Quai d'Orsay, where it was generally held that Germany would require financial assistance in order to build through the Taurus mountains. However, in June 1906, French complacency was shaken when Alfred von Gwinner, head of the Deutsche Bank, on a visit to Paris, let it be known that Germany was capable of resuming construction without outside assistance.[42] The French government was quick to realise that the necessary funds could be raised only if backed by the surplus of ceded revenues, 75 per cent of which had been given to the Ottoman government by the unification of the Ottoman Debt. Unless German financiers could be denied use of this vital source of revenue, a continuation of the Baghdad Railway would be virtually inevitable.

Opponents of the railway took hope from the growing financial difficulties of the Ottoman Empire. By 1906, Macedonian disorder and Macedonian reforms were making serious inroads on the Ottoman treasury. The Ottoman government, with strong German support, proposed to meet the bulk of its monetary needs by a 3 per cent customs surcharge. However, it was generally recognised that a 3 per cent surcharge would not fully erase the sultan's Macedonian deficit. The British government was quick to seize on this point. It demanded, in return for approval of the proposed surcharge, a balanced Macedonian budget. The Ottoman government responded by calling on the Debt Administration to cover the anticipated deficit in Macedonia. The result, in early December of 1906, was an important debate within the Debt Council. The British delegate, Adam Block, argued that, in order to balance the Macedonian budget, it would be necessary to have recourse to the surplus of the ceded revenues. As the Germans were well aware, this was a serious threat to their plans to continue the Baghdad Railway. Once the ceded revenues surplus was committed, however partially, to the payment of an annual subsidy, once it became subject to the claims of a power other than Germany, it would cease to have value as a guarantee for Baghdad Railway loans. Thus, the German delegate, Baron Testa, insisted that the Macedonian budget should be balanced by employing income obtained from the management of tithes and from certain lesser revenues.

The French government was capable of providing Block's thesis with powerful, even decisive, support. The delegate of the French bondholders, Commandant Berger, was President of the Debt Council. To be sure, as one of the select few who possessed shares in the Baghdad Railway Company, he sympathised with the German delegate. But, on a matter of such considerable political significance, he would normally have been obliged to respect the wishes of the French government. The Block–Testa conflict represented the kind of opportunity which France had long been seeking.

Understandably, the Clemenceau ministry strongly favoured the Block thesis and was desirous of Franco-British co-operation on the Debt Council. Yet the wishes of Clemenceau and Pichon were thwarted by Constans. The French government was not informed by its ambassador that Commandant Berger was working with the Germans. Prior to the crucial meeting of the Debt Council on 10 December, Berger assisted Baron Marschall and the Ottoman government in preparing a statement favourable to the German position.[43] At a private meeting of the Debt Council on 7 December, he openly opposed Block's proposal. The French government learned of this Franco-British divergence only on 9 December and only when told by the British ambassador in Paris. Pichon then sent an urgent telegram to Constans, who was instructed to see Berger and to ask him to concert with Block at the meeting of the 10th. Though Constans conveyed this message, he obviously did not do so in a forceful manner. When the Council met, very much as a political forum, Berger took the lead in opposing the British delegate. Block sought an adjournment but was outvoted five to one, with the official representative of the Ottoman Bank abstaining.[44] The Council proceeded to endorse the German–Ottoman proposal.

Inevitably, this remarkable episode aroused much ire in London, where Constans became highly unpopular.[45] In Paris, too, there was ire, though less than might have been expected. Berger was rather strongly taken to task, but Constans received but a mild rebuke. His longstanding friendship with Clemenceau was unimpaired, and within a few months he was dining amicably with Pichon.[46] There could be no doubt, however, that the affair of the Macedonian deficit represented a severe setback for French policy. Thereafter, France's insistence on internationalisation of the Baghdad Railway seemed decidedly unrealistic. The maintenance of a three-power alignment against the Baghdad project had become a much more difficult exercise. As early as February 1907, Izvolskii, the Russian Foreign Minister, informed Germany of his willingness to end Russian hostility to the Baghdad Railway in exchange for a large freedom of action in northern Persia. Several months later, the Quai d'Orsay received a British memorandum which envisaged the division of the Baghdad railway into a northern section controlled by Germany and a southern section controlled by Britain. The Russian and British initiatives were not immediately acceptable to Germany, but they foreshadowed the frustration of French aims.

As the Baghdad Railway project advanced, the French government increasingly placed its weight behind French enterprises in the Ottoman Empire. This policy was at its most pronounced in Syria, where France's traditional preponderance seemed endangered. French governments were primarily concerned to strengthen the railway network of the Beirut–Damas–Hauran company, which had been reconstituted as the Damas–Hama et Prolongements. The Foreign Ministry, anxious to regain as much as possible of the old Rayak–Biredjik concession, pressed the Ottoman government for a retrocession of the Hama–Aleppo line. It also sought an indemnity for the DHP's Damascus–Muzerib extension, which was threatened by competition from the sultan's Hedjaz Railway.[47] Abdul Hamid was forced to satisfy both these demands in order to have his 1905 loan quoted on the Paris Stock Exchange.

The vigilance of the Quai d'Orsay extended to the Société des Quais de Constantinople. This sizeable enterprise, set up in 1891, had constructed quays at both Stamboul and Galata as well as docks and warehouses. However, it had had a troubled existence. Its formative period had been prolonged by the earthquake of 1894. Thereafter, it had encountered the systematic hostility of the Ottoman government, which wanted to buy it back. By 1901, the Société's managing director, Félix Granet, was ready to sell.[48] Fears soon arose at the

Quai d'Orsay that German capitalists would buy the company. French diplomats were increasingly convinced that Germany wanted to control an unbroken line of communications between Vienna and the Persian Gulf.[49] Thus, Delcassé decided on a diplomatic action which would deliver the Société des Quais from economic stagnation. In November 1903 he obtained an imperial *iradé* which ordered a complete and immediate fulfilment of the French concession. But Ottoman officials refused to put this decree into effect. As in the case of the Syrian railways, Ottoman resistance was broken only by France's financial power. When settlement of the quays question was linked to the French loan of 1905, the Société des Quais received a large measure of satisfaction.

The bolstering of this firm was accompanied by official support for French commerce. The Quai d'Orsay had long been concerned about the relative decline of France's trade with the Ottoman Empire, and French industrialists had frequently been criticised for lack of initiative.[50] Ambassador Constans was particularly emphatic about the need to improve France's commercial performance. In late 1903, as the failure of Franco-German negotiations over the Baghdad Railway drew near, he put forward the argument that, in future, a portion of all French loans to Turkey should be earmarked for industrial purchases in France. He was more precise in June of 1904, when he proposed that in forthcoming loan negotiations France should demand a substantial order of French-made artillery and warships.[51] With Delcassé's approval, he asked the Porte to buy both guns and destroyers from Schneider's Le Creusot establishment. Constans worked closely with the French firm, which agreed to provide him with what was euphemistically described as a 'participation' and to hire his protégé, Pissard, as one of its local representatives.[52] By late 1904 the Porte had agreed to purchase four destroyers. An artillery sale, however, was much more difficult to arrange. Germany had monopolised Ottoman artillery orders for almost thirty years, and Constans' demand provoked a vigorous response from German diplomats, who insisted on the integral maintenance of their country's monopoly. Nevertheless, by a mixture of threats and cajolery, Constans kept the issue in doubt. In late March of 1905 it was resolved by Delcassé. A more serious Franco-German conflict had developed in Morocco, and he decided that France should be content with the purchase of industrial goods other than artillery.[53] Consequently, the loan agreement of 1905 simply stipulated that 17 million francs, out of a total of 60 million, should be used to pay for French industrial goods. Schneider ultimately delivered ships worth about 13,500,000 francs.

Finally, during the period 1903–8, the French government accorded a vigorous support to the Société d'Héraclée. This important mining company controlled valuable coal mines in the Heraclea Basin, the nearby port of Zonguldak, and railways linking the two operations. It had failed to achieve a solid prosperity, however, and by 1906 had entrusted its fate to the willing hands of Count Vitali and the Ottoman Bank. Vitali and the leadership of the

IOB had quickly formulated plans to absorb the Heraclea company and to monopolise the coalfields of the Heraclea Basin. But, first, they wanted the Porte to settle the demands of the Heraclea company, which included a clarification of property titles, the introduction of a customs service at Zonguldak and, above all, the payment of a large indemnity. The IOB and Vitali would then buy out Italian claimants and form a new company to consolidate the coalfields of Heraclea.[54]

The Porte was in no mood to satisfy the claims of the Heraclea company. In fact, Vitali and the IOB could have made little progress without official support, which took on generous proportions in 1907. For a full year Constans, who was quite won over to the IOB–Vitali scheme, put intense pressure on the Ottoman government to satisfy the demands of the Heraclea company. Pichon clearly supported him, though, during the acute phase of the Heraclea negotiations, in April and May of 1908, the initiative was taken by the ambassador. Thus, Pichon learned from reading the Paris press that Constans, on 21 April, had given the Porte an ultimatum demanding immediate settlement of the Heraclea company's grievances.[55] On 5 May, without consulting Pichon or the Ministry of Marine, Constans sent the ambassadorial ship with a contingent of marines to Zonguldak. These strong-arm tactics and a liberal distribution of bakhshish were undoubtedly effective. Even so, Ottoman resistance was not overcome without further recourse to France's financial power. The IOB refused advances to the needy Ottoman treasury and, in early May, Pichon threatened the sultan's ambassador with an indefinite closure of the French money-market.[56] On 18 May 1908 the Ottoman government agreed to satisfy the demands of the Heraclea company.

Before this decision could be given practical effect, the Young Turk revolution of July 1908 had brought about important changes in Constantinople: the emergence of an Ottoman leadership with liberal inclinations and the diminution of German influence. In the following months French expectations were high. Pichon, who saw in the Young Turk revolution 'a general movement of sympathy for liberal and republican France', was convinced that the French government could achieve a privileged position in Constantinople.[57] As a gesture of goodwill towards the new regime, he agreed to an unconditional loan of 25 million francs.

He was soon disappointed. During the first year of Young Turk rule, Franco-Ottoman relations steadily deteriorated. The Committee of Union and Progress came to power with a strong dislike of the Ottoman Bank and Constans, both of whom had been intimately involved with the palace intrigues and financial transactions of the *ancien régime*.[58] Moreover, Young Turk patriotism conflicted with Pichon's aspirations. The leaders of the CUP resented their economic dependence. They were highly critical of the Régie des Tabacs, in which French capital was predominant and which managed the lucrative tobacco revenue. Much consternation was aroused in Paris when the Ottoman Finance Minister publicly attacked the Régie and proceeded to set up

a committee of inquiry into its activities. In April 1909, Pichon feared expro-
priation and instructed Constans to make an energetic protest.[59] At the same
time, Joseph Caillaux, French Finance Minister, spoke of an acute crisis and
threatened a complete closure of the French money-market if Ottoman hostility to the Régie persisted.[60] France's wishes were largely respected, but at
considerable cost to Franco-Ottoman relations.

France had clearly failed to become the Young Turks' favourite power and,
as early as the middle of 1909, she was becoming concerned about the revival of
German influence.[61] Temporary differences with the British were smoothed
out, and the French government proceeded to take a firm stand during the loan
negotiations of 1910.[62] The Porte was asked to place a substantial order for
French artillery and naval equipment, and to accept the financial supervision
of French functionaries. The Ottoman government was rescued from this
uncomfortable situation in late 1910, when German and Austrian financiers
agreed to take the loan. Though the IOB was disappointed, the loss of the 1910
loan was by no means a complete defeat for French policy. In the course of loan
negotiations, the Porte granted a new concession to the Smyrna–Cassaba
Company and, what was more remarkable, promised to order French artillery
and naval equipment. The fulfilment of these engagements represented a
further acknowledgement of France's financial power, which, since 1903, had
done much to strengthen French economic interests in the Ottoman Empire.

At Potsdam, in December 1910, Russia and Germany concluded a Baghdad
Railway agreement. This accord was a decisive defeat for France's internationalisation policy, and French decision-makers recognised that they had
little choice but to follow the Russian example and to come to terms with
Germany. However, the French government was determined to extract substantial concessions in return for a renunciation of its hostility to the Baghdad
project. Pursuit of a compensatory agreement therefore became a central
concern for French diplomats. But this diplomatic effort was complicated by
factors both external and internal to the Ottoman Empire. Externally, intensified Franco-German hostility and the resultant tightening of France's links
with Russia and Britain inevitably weighed on the making of Near Eastern
policy. Internally, the Balkan Wars of 1912–13 gave rise to annexationist
thinking in France which, while it had a considerable impact on French policy
before August 1914, came into its own only after the Ottoman Empire entered
the First World War at the side of Germany.

Following the Potsdam accord, the question of French compensation was
clearly posed. A Homs–Baghdad concession, while attractive to some diplomats, was clearly an inadequate answer. It was disliked by the Ottoman
government and economically unsound in the absence of a kilometric guarantee. Thus, in the years 1911 to 1914, French governments sought to realise a
more substantial programme. They decided upon the acquisition of a railway
network in northern Anatolia, the strengthening of French railways in Syria

and the construction of ports on the Black Sea and Syrian coasts. Ultimately, France desired an agreement with the German government which would ratify her gains and lead to the creation of zones of industrial influence in which competition between French and German capitalists would be discouraged.

France's economic separatism owed much to the thinking of Maurice Bompard, who replaced Constans as French ambassador in Constantinople in July 1909. Bompard was an experienced diplomat who had headed the Commercial Section of the Quai d'Orsay and spent five difficult years as ambassador in St Petersburg. Unlike Constans, he was opposed to co-operation with the Germans. As a native of Metz, he remembered the lost provinces of 1871. He was convinced, furthermore, that French interests in the Ottoman Empire had suffered as a result of Franco-German co-operation.[63] Therefore, he favoured the establishment of separate zones of industrial activity. French industrial action would be excluded from the area of the Baghdad Railway network, while the Germans would refrain from competing in Syria, in the hinterland of the Black Sea and even, perhaps, in south-western Anatolia.[64]

Bompard's policy of 'chacun chez soi' was in keeping with the troubled state of Franco-German relations. And it had become acceptable to the Ottoman Bank, which was moving away from co-operation with German capitalists. As early as May 1911 the IOB was reconsidering its role in the Baghdad Railway Company. It had been asked by the Deutsche Bank to supply in full its financial participation of 30 per cent. The IOB was unwilling to comply unless Delcassé's closure of the official money-market could be undone. The French government, though surprisingly hesitant at times, refused to take this step.[65] By late 1912 the IOB was prepared to withdraw from the Baghdad enterprise, and its relations with the Deutsche Bank were becoming increasingly less friendly.[66]

The principle of 'chacun chez soi' commanded the assent of most French policy-makers, but there was widespread disagreement about what should first be done to strengthen French interests. Bompard, for his part, proposed the construction of a large railway network which would extend inland from the Black Sea and penetrate the so-called Armenian vilayets. He regarded the Baghdad line as the world's most prestigious railway, and was eager to establish French lines which would be the equivalent in size, if not in importance.[67] Other diplomats, however, argued that priority should be given to a northwards extension of the French railway network in Syria. They were concerned for the future of French influence in northern Syria, where the Baghdad Railway was making its presence felt. By late 1910, it was clear that the main line would pass through Aleppo, the chief city of northern Syria. Construction from Aleppo towards Mesopotamia and the Amanus Mountains was underway. Concessions obtained in March 1911 enabled the Germans to begin work on a port at Alexandretta and to link Alexandretta to the Baghdad line at Osmanie. Such activity was thought highly disquieting by both French diplomats and the French colonial party. The full import of the Syrian railway agreements of 1900–1 was, for the first time, generally recognised. Paul Cambon, from his London embassy, spoke of 'inexplicable capitulations . . . profoundly damaging for French interests in Syria'.[68] The Comité de l'Asie Française, through its monthly bulletin, denounced the 'scandalous surrenders' of 1900–1 and demanded renegotiation.[69]

Bompard's thesis prevailed during the years 1911–12, and France concentrated on the acquisition of a viable Black Sea railway network.[70] But his thinking was questioned anew when the Balkan Wars deprived the Ottoman Empire of much of its European territory. So damaging a blow to the cohesion of the Ottoman state made a considerable impression on French opinion, both official and unofficial. Doubts about the Empire's capacity to survive led to renewed debate between French policy-makers. Few participants desired a partitioning of Imperial Turkey. A redistribution of power in the Mediterranean, whether to the advantage of Germany or of Russia, was not to French liking. A territorial partition would be ill-suited to the dispersed character of French business activity and to the special status of the Ottoman Bank. There was no assurance, moreover, that the powers who carved up the Ottoman Empire would be prepared to repay a debt held largely by French investors. Finally, there were fears that a partition would lead to unrest among the Muslims of French North Africa.

Yet a scramble for Asia Minor might well develop in spite of French wishes. Consequently, the advocates of a more vigorous Syrian policy gained added support. They held that, unless more was done to strengthen the French presence in Syria, France would not be suitably rewarded in the event of a partition. This determination to reserve a place in Syria was not unanimous. Bompard pointed out that France was heavily involved in Morocco and that Syria would be costly to occupy and defend.[71] To some extent, Bompard's argument was supported by Delcassé, who had returned to government service as ambassador to St Petersburg. In Delcassé's opinion, France's natural sphere of expansion was north Africa, and he was inclined to regard the occupation of Syria south of Alexandretta as an unprofitable diversion.[72] Gaston Doumergue, who became Foreign Minister in early 1914, agreed with Delcassé.[73] For the most part, however, French diplomats, politicians and journalists thought Syria a valuable acquisition or, at least, a necessary compensation. Greater diplomatic activity in the area was urged by the influential brothers Cambon and by the colonial party.[74] They were joined by another pressure-group, the Comité de Défense des Intérêts Français en Orient. This organisation, set up in late 1911 under the presidency of a former Foreign Minister, Alexandre Ribot, was dedicated to 'maintaining and developing France's moral, political and economic situation in the Orient'. Its membership included Pichon and such leading politicians as Raymond Poincaré and Louis Barthou.[75]

For much of 1913, Foreign Minister Pichon resisted the 'Syrians', but eventually a ministry headed by Barthou and supported by Poincaré, who had become President of the Republic, decided to change the emphasis of French policy. An important meeting of diplomats and cabinet ministers was held at the presidential palace on 6 November 1913. This conference decided that negotiations would be resumed at an official level and that France's chief objective would be to regain railway privileges in northern Syria. French representatives would seek to extend the zone of action of the Damas–Hama company northwards to a line drawn from Alexandretta through Aleppo to Meskene. They would be authorised to sacrifice the Black Sea network, or a part of it, in order to achieve the desired strengthening of French influence in northern Syria.[76]

France now wanted a good deal more from Germany. But she had built up a strong bargaining position. The Balkan Wars had been damaging to Ottoman finances. The income which the Debt Administration derived from ceded revenues was no longer sufficient to guarantee Baghdad Railway loans.[77] A tariff increase, which would make possible a reconstitution of the guarantee, would require French consent. The Ottoman government, which might have obstructed France's railway ambitions, urgently required French financial aid. Finally, Britain had agreed to slow down her parallel discussions with Germany so as to facilitate the task of French negotiators.[78]

The new round of Franco-German negotiations, in which France was represented primarily by two high-ranking functionaries and Ambassador Jules Cambon, proved both lengthy and difficult. An atmosphere of hostility was inevitable given the tense relations which prevailed between the two countries. In late January of 1914, the irritation of the German government was explicitly conveyed by Chancellor Bethmann Hollweg. In a lengthy conversation with Cambon, he spoke of the disparity between French and German colonial empires, of Germany's desire for 'a place in the sun', and of her inherent right to expand, which was that of 'every growing being'. He complained of French opposition to the grand design which Germany was pursuing in Asia Minor and warned that, if such hostility continued, France could expect competition elsewhere. 'Believe me,' he concluded, 'it will be dangerous unless we take account of the facts and set aside what divides us.'[79] Cambon, a perceptive observer of German affairs, was deeply impressed. He recalled that Bethmann had employed similar language shortly before the onset of the Second Moroccan Crisis in 1911. On 5 February the Kaiser himself appeared at the conference table where he proceeded to harangue French delegates.[80] But, by then, the French government had heeded Bethmann's warning and decided to moderate its demands.

The ensuing agreement brought France some advantages. In Syria, the Hama–Aleppo and Tripoli–Homs lines were conceded large protective zones. Germany accepted much of France's proposed Black Sea railway network and agreed to the delimitation of zones of industrial influence.[81] However, France had not obtained what she desired most: an agreement allowing French capitalists to link the Hama–Aleppo line to the sea and to build a northwards extension.

On balance, France had realised the programme originally proposed by Bompard. In addition, the financial needs of the Ottoman government, which exceeded the capacity of the German market, enabled France to obtain during 1914 a large industrial order including artillery, submarines and destroyers. While these were substantial gains, they did not offset German control of the Baghdad Railway, which had compromised French influence in Cilicia as well as northern Syria. The French-owned Mersina–Adana line had been purchased by the Deutsche Bank in 1906. The Baghdad Railway had reached Aleppo and, unlike the Hama–Aleppo line, could be linked to the sea. At Alexandretta, Germany was building a substantial port and had planned a harbour to accommodate warships. It remained doubtful whether, in the long run, the Syrian network of the Damas–Hama company could withstand German competition. Finally, possession of the Baghdad Railway network would allow Germany to claim a large portion of Asia Minor in the event of a territorial partition.

Continuation of the Baghdad Railway, for all its importance, had not enabled Germany to regain quite the diplomatic influence she had enjoyed in late Hamidian times. The Young Turk leadership was divided,[82] and some leaders of the Committee of Union and Progress appear to have envisaged a *rapprochement* with the Powers of the Triple Entente. France, which possessed vital financial resources and some capacity to restrain Russian ambition, received her share of attention. Cemal Pasha, Ottoman Minister of Marine, visited the Quai d'Orsay in July 1914, where he was received by Pierre de Margerie, Director of Political and Commercial Affairs. Cemal stated that in exchange for French support in the Aegean, where Greece and Turkey were embroiled, his government would 'orientate its policy towards the Triple Entente'.[83] This proposal was made at a time when French diplomats were seeking improved relations with the Ottoman Empire. A Franco-Ottoman 'friendship committee' had been set up with Bompard's approval in early 1914. Cemal's trip to France had been undertaken at the invitation of the French government.[84] It is unlikely, therefore, that he received, as he later claimed, 'a veiled refusal' from Margerie. Besides, no considered reply could have been expected from the French government. Cemal's visit to the Quai d'Orsay took place on 13 July, two days before René Viviani, French Premier and Foreign Minister, departed for Russia. By the time Viviani returned, the First World War was but three days off. Hence, it would be surprising if Cemal's conversation with Margerie did much to bring about the German–Ottoman military alliance of 2 August 1914.[85]

Following the conclusion of this pact, which was known in Paris by 9 August, the Entente powers sought actively to maintain Ottoman neutrality. Though they offered to guarantee the territorial integrity of the Empire, there was probably much in Bompard's view that the Young Turks would have chosen neutrality only if the course of the European war had been clearly favourable to the Triple Entente. It was difficult to combat that faith in German military prowess which underlay both the prewar privileges accorded German officers and the alliance of 1914.[86] The Ottoman public could be reached only by official communiqué – a means of publicity which the Entente did not employ successfully. The statements issued by the French Ministry of War were much briefer and less skilfully drafted than those which originated in Berlin. Thus, Ottoman readers were better informed about Russia's defeat at Tannenberg in late August than about France's successes on the Marne in early September.[87] As September advanced, French diplomats thought the Young Turk leadership increasingly confident of German victory.[88] Closure of the Straits of the Dardanelles on 26 September indicated that the days of Ottoman neutrality were numbered. By the end of October, the Ottoman Empire was definitively involved in the First World War and, in an ultimate sense, its fortunes had become heavily dependent on the war effort of the German Reich.

For a time France was hopeful of winning the Young Turks back to peace. The magnitude of French interests in the Ottoman Empire served as a powerful impediment to belligerent action. French ministries took the view that their war with the Ottoman Empire was strictly defensive in character and directed essentially against the Young Turk government.[89] No formal declaration of war was made. Nor was there any marked upsurge of colonialist sentiment. In December 1914 the Comité de l'Asie Française was content to demand a revision of existing railway arrangements in Cilicia and northern Syria.[90]

The French government was unable to maintain its initial moderation. It was persuaded by closure of the Straits, British pressure and, above all, stalemate on the Western Front to participate in a Dardanelles offensive. France wanted this to be a limited operation. Delcassé, who was again Foreign Minister, explained that the Franco-British objective was to pierce the Dardanelles and to occupy Constantinople without extending military action to Asia Minor.[91] He certainly did not desire the complete disintegration of the Ottoman Empire. Yet, in the event of victory, he foresaw the need for a provisional Allied regime in Constantinople. And, on 9 February 1915, some ten days before the Anglo-French naval offensive began, he discussed the allocation of 'zones of interest' with the British Foreign Secretary.[92]

A month later, France's conservatism was further weakened when Russia demanded Constantinople. Russia's famous note claiming the Ottoman capital and territory on both sides of the Bosporus was received by Delcassé on 6 March. This claim, though not entirely unexpected, aroused considerable consternation. Delcassé expressed immediate opposition and took the exceptional step of persuading the President of the Republic to write directly to Petrograd.[93] Poincaré, in turn, asserted in his letter that France could not be expected to sacrifice her interests in Constantinople to satisfy Russian aspirations. Russia's acquisition of so vital a place would imply a partition of the Ottoman Empire which France had 'no good reason to desire'.[94] Poincaré's protest was in vain. Two days after it was sent, Britain accepted Russia's demand. Delcassé, though highly displeased,[95] decided he would have to follow suit. He did not do so, however, until Russia had agreed to allow a victorious Franco-British force to set up a provisional wartime regime in Constantinople. Under the umbrella provided by this administration, he hoped, France's financial, industrial and cultural interests could be solidly re-established.[96]

The awarding of Constantinople to Russia led Delcassé to think more seriously about a general dislocation of the Ottoman Empire. As compensation for Constantinople, he asked the Russian government for complete freedom of action in Cilicia and Syria. He was interested primarily in the central portion of the Baghdad Railway network, and he envisaged a French colony which, while including Syria, would have as its real centre of gravity the coastal region of the Gulf of Alexandretta.[97] Even so, Delcassé and his colleagues had not fully given up on the Ottoman Empire. On 28 April 1915, after France's acceptance of Russia's territorial claims, he sharply reminded the Minister of War that the French government did not want a general disorganisation of the Ottoman Empire.[98]

This opposition to radical change was not finally abandoned until the summer of 1915, when Franco-Ottoman warfare intensified. Two French divisions, numbering some 40,000 men, participated in the Gallipoli landings of late April and early May. The heavy fighting which ensued took its toll, and French casualties were eventually estimated at 26,500 men. These losses and the defeat inflicted on Allied forces much hardened French attitudes towards the Ottoman Empire. By July 1915 the Comité de l'Asie Française was calling openly for the annexation of Cilicia and of a Syria inclusive of Palestine.[99] The Comité was supported by the Lyon and Marseilles Chambers of Commerce and, in late August, by the Foreign Affairs Commission of the Chamber of Deputies.[100]

Under these internal and external pressures, the French government adopted an annexationist policy which aimed at the acquisition of Cilicia and a greater Syria.[101] France was given the opportunity to reach a territorial settlement with Britain in October 1915. The British government wanted to open a new theatre of military operations in the Near East and, by creating an Arab kingdom in Asia Minor, to bring about an Arab revolt against Ottoman rule.[102] In exchange for French consent, Britain agreed to negotiate over Syria and Cilicia. In November, France's representative, Georges-Picot, a professional diplomat active in the colonial party, arrived in London to establish the boundaries of a new imperial possession. When negotiations concluded, Picot had not obtained as much as he and the new Foreign Minister, Aristide Briand, had originally desired. Picot was led to accept an international administration of much of Palestine. The Syrian interior, though recognised as a zone of French influence, was placed under the sovereignty of the Sharif of Mecca. On the other hand, Picot obtained concessions largely in accord with the colonial design worked out by Delcassé. France was promised a direct administration of Cilicia, Alexandretta and the coast of northern and central Syria.

The Franco-English settlement or, as it was more commonly known, the Sykes–Picot agreement, was ratified in February 1916. The French government had committed itself to the destruction of the Ottoman Empire, but with more resignation than enthusiasm. This attitude was soon justified by both the fortunes of war and the postwar settlement. In the final two years of the First World War, France was so heavily committed in Western Europe that she could offer but minimal assistance to Britain's military effort in Palestine and Mesopotamia. The French force which accompanied the British into Palestine and central Syria in 1918 was unimposing. In addition to 3,000 Senegalese and 3,000 Armenians, it included 800 French who had been assured that they would not be used for combat purposes.[103] In late October of 1918, when the Ottoman government requested an armistice, the French were decidedly thin on the ground. Though France landed marines at Beirut on 8 October, Syria and Palestine were controlled by British occupation forces. As a result, the British government was in no mood to allow an international administration in Palestine or to facilitate the assertion of French authority in Syria.

In late 1918, the Turkish Empire was at an end, a casualty of the First World War. The subsequent reordering of Near Eastern affairs proved to be a kind of epilogue for France, in which French governments unsuccessfully tried to realise French war aims and to recover influence lost during the years 1914–18. More specifically, France set out to achieve an integral application of the Sykes–Picot agreement and to re-establish and win compensation for prewar economic interests. But, despite the exclusion of Germany, a satisfactory fulfilment of these objectives was prevented by the diminished power of French governments, which could no longer call on substantial financial reserves, by the revival of the Turks and by the re-appearance, in much more vigorous form, of Franco-British rivalry.

France achieved but a limited implementation of the Sykes–Picot agreement. Palestine was conceded to the British in late 1918, while Delcassé's imperial vision was destroyed by a resurgent Turkey. In late 1921, when the French government came to terms with the national movement headed by General Kemal, it ceded Cilicia, which, in economic terms, was the choicest territory acquired by Picot in 1916. No doubt France had been more successful in Syria where, by 1920, she had acquired a direct control over both coastal and interior zones. Yet, in the Franco-Turkish accord of 1921, the French government had yielded a substantial portion of northern Syria, much of which now followed the Baghdad Railway line. Syria stopped short of the track, which was declared to be on Turkish soil. Moreover, while it lasted, France's domination of Syria was seriously troubled by Arab nationalists and given juridical limits by the League of Nations.[104]

The economic settlement which followed the collapse of the Ottoman Empire was still less in conformity with France's aims. French bondholders received a slender compensation. Admittedly, that part of the Ottoman Debt allocated to the successor states under French and British rule was promptly repaid. But the Allies declared two-thirds of the Debt to be Turkey's responsibility. Only a small percentage of this sum was collected. In 1928, after prolonged negotiations, the Turkish share of the prewar debt was reduced by about 52 per cent. Repayment then began but was cut short by the depression of the 1930s. In 1933 it was agreed that Turkey should pay about 12 per cent of the figure originally set by the Allies.[105] Meanwhile, outside Syria, French enterprises were in retreat. At the Lausanne Conference of 1923 the Turks agreed in principle to maintain prewar concessions, but few of these ventures regained their earlier prosperity. While the Ottoman Bank succeeded in getting its statute renewed in 1925, it was obliged to accept a large measure of Turkish control. The Smyrna–Cassaba and Heraclea companies resumed operations but under less favourable conditions than they had enjoyed before the war. A notable venture was never re-established: Bompard's Black Sea railways. Turkish hostility to this concession was intense and France, despite some energetic protests at Lausanne, came away with no solid commitments.[106] The intense diplomatic effort of 1911–14 had been largely in vain. Construction of the Black Sea network had been interrupted by the First World War, and the final result consisted of a single line thirty-five kilometres in length.

Between 1898 and 1918, France's Ottoman policy was undoubtedly shaped by a variety of forces and pressures. Yet a concern at the progress of German *Weltpolitik* was never far from the minds of French policy-makers. France's established position in the Ottoman Empire was challenged by the Baghdad Railway, by the influence which Germany possessed with Ottoman military and civilian leaders and, ultimately, by a German–Ottoman military alliance. As a result, there was often a defensive, or counter-offensive, character to French policy, with France responding to German initiatives or German successes.

The Baghdad Railway project, as the principal manifestation of *Weltpolitik*, preoccupied French governments for much of the period. During the years 1899–1903, Delcassé sought to establish the enterprise as a joint venture in which France and Germany would co-operate on an equal basis. But the unsuccessful conclusion of Franco-German negotiations in late 1903 ushered in an era of competition. Thereafter, France sought to obstruct the Baghdad project and to compensate for it by pursuing new concessions and strengthening existing enterprises. Inevitably, this policy did damage to Franco-German relations and, at the beginning of 1914, may nearly have led to a major diplomatic crisis.

France's financial strength enabled her to become a successful expansionist power in the years 1903–14. On balance, however, she had not dealt at all successfully with the challenge of the Baghdad Railway. While her failure to do so stemmed initially from an error of judgement on Delcassé's part, it owed far more to a lack of policy co-ordination. During the vital negotiations of 1899–1903, French businessmen and the French government frequently worked at cross-purposes. No doubt some divergence between the two was inevitable, but the Ottoman Bank and its associates seem to have made much less effort than their German counterparts to reconcile business with patriotism. Even so, French policy would have been much more effective had it not been for the highly independent course followed by Ambassador Constans. Had he followed his instructions and exercised the supervision of which he was capable, the negotiations of the Ottoman Bank and Vitali would surely have conformed more closely to the wishes of the French government. If, as instructed, he had worked for Franco-British unity on the Debt Council in late 1906, a serious financial obstacle could have been raised to the continuation of the Baghdad Railway. Instead, he facilitated the task of German diplomacy in a manner which suggested that in this, as in other important affairs, he expected financial reward. In 1909, on the subject of Constans' extraordinary embassy, the socialist Jean Jaurès wrote that France was represented in Constantinople by a man who had been involved in 'the most repugnant operations of the Hamidian *ancien régime*' and whose maintenance in Constantinople was 'one of the scandals of our history'.[107] Paul Cambon, though of much different political persuasion than Jaurès, wrote in early 1909 to a friend: 'I do not want to tell you – it is too sad – about the lamentable surrenders of that sceptical old brigand who represents France in Turkey.'[108]

Until 1915, France was strongly in favour of preserving the Ottoman Empire, and she was reluctant to bring about a further reduction in the authority of the Ottoman government. Yet the expansionist character of her policy often had this effect. French governments consistently supported business interests whose conduct enfeebled Turkish rule. For example, the IOB's preoccupation with loan operations and the reliance of the Damas–Hama railway company on its kilometric guarantees were difficult to square with the economic welfare of the Ottoman Empire. Also, France increased Ottoman financial difficulties by temporarily withholding funds and by linking loans to large industrial orders. Given the continued protection which French diplomats extended to their Catholic protégés, France clearly contributed, though in a relatively modest way, to the decline of the Ottoman Empire between 1898 and 1914. The ambivalence of France's policy became more pronounced after the Balkan Wars, but there remained a large gulf between her prewar ambitions and her wartime radicalism. This gulf was bridged only by the struggle in Europe and military defeat at the Dardanelles. It was not until the summer of 1915 that France finally resigned herself to a policy of partition and undertook a determined pursuit of territorial and financial compensation. Her subsequent military endeavours in the Near East were of little significance. Yet the war which France fought against Germany in western Europe had important consequences for the Ottoman Empire, whose collapse in 1918 owed much to the military defeat of the Central Powers.

Notes: Chapter 6

Abbreviations

DDF   *Documents diplomatiques français, 1871–1914* (Paris, 1929–55)
AMAE   Archives du Ministère des Affaires Étrangères
FO   Archives of the British Foreign Office
GP   *Die Grosse Politik der Europaïschen Kabinette, 1871–1914*, ed. Johannes Lepsius, A. Mendelssohn-Bartholdy and Friedrich Thimme, 40 vols (Berlin, 1922–7). (The French translation of *Die Grosse Politik*, entitled *La Politique extérieure de l'Allemagne, 1871–1914*, was also consulted in the preparation of this chapter.)

1   On the religious protectorate, see W. I. Shorrock, *French Imperialism in the Middle East: The Failure of Policy in Syria and Lebanon, 1900–1914* (Madison, Wis., 1976), pp. 11–64.
2   J. Thobie, *Intérêts et impérialisme français dans l'Empire Ottoman, 1895–1914* (Paris, 1977), p. 515.
3   On French economic interests in the Asiatic portion of the Ottoman Empire, there is a wealth of material in ibid.
4   On the French decision-making process, see C. Andrew, *Théophile Delcassé and the Making of the Entente Cordiale* (London, 1968), pp. 53–77; C. Andrew and A. S. Kanya-Forstner, 'The French "colonial party": its composition, aims and influence, 1885–1914', *Historical Journal*, Vol. XIV, no. 1 (1971), pp. 99–128; P. G. Lauren, *Diplomats and Bureaucrats* (Stanford, Calif., 1976); F. L. Schuman, *War and Diplomacy in the French Republic* (Chicago, Ill., 1931), pp. 18–45; Thobie, *Intérêts*, pp. 22–34, 70–1.
5   On French policy towards Ottoman political exiles, see AMAE, Turquie, NS 3, 4, 5.
6   For example, Gabriel Hanotaux, Foreign Minister in the years 1894–1898, thought it more important to legitimise the degrees of the Beirut Medical Faculty than to extend the Mersina–Adana Railway (annotation of dispatch from P. Cambon, ambassador in Constantinople, to Hanotaux, 27 April 1898, *DDF*, 1st ser., Vol. 14, no. 173).
7   On Delcassé and his policies, see Andrew, *Théophile Delcassé*; P. Guillen, 'La politique de Delcassé et les relations Franco-Allemandes', *Revue d'Allemagne*, Vol. IV, no. 3 (1972), pp. 455–64.
8   Andrew, *Théophile Delcassé*, pp. 84–6; Delcassé to Montebello (ambassador in St Petersburg), 30 July 1898, *DDF*, I, 14, no. 271.
9   *Journal officiel, Chambre des Députés*, 22 January 1902. On the Lorando–Tubini affair, see Shorrock, *French Imperialism*, pp. 23–32.
10 On Delcassé's thinking: AMAE, Papiers Delcassé, Vol. 15; Delcassé to Constans, 5 Feb. 1901, DDF, II, 1, no. 65; Delcassé to Bompard (ambassador in St Petersburg), 11 Feb. 1903, *DDF*, II, 3, no. 76; *Journal officiel, Chambre des Députés*, 25 March 1902.
11 On Constans: Archives de la Préfecture de Police, Ba 1018, 1019; AMAE, Papiers Constans; Bibliothèque Nationale, NAF 24327 (Étienne papers).
12 Note by Hardinge (Permanent Under-Secretary), 16 Dec. 1906, FO 371/144. Articles printed in the Russian official press indicated that the Russian Foreign Ministry shared this opinion.
13 Constans to Pichon (French Foreign Minister), 13 Dec. 1906, AMAE, Turquie, NS 339.
14 In 1908 there were seven regents of the Bank of France on the IOB's Paris Committee.
15 On the IOB the only work remains A. Biliotti, *La Banque Impériale Ottomane* (Paris, 1909). There is much helpful material, however, in Thobie, *Intérêts*, Pt I, chs. 3 and 6; Pt II, ch. 7.
16 On Vitali: private letter from P. Cambon to Gout (Sous-Directeur des Affaires Commerciales), 24 July 1907, *DDF* II, 11, no. 91; Marschall to Bülow (German Chancellor), 17 March 1907, *GP*, no. 8582; letter from Adam Block (British representative on Debt Council) to Hardinge, 28 May 1908, FO 371/340.
17 Marschall to Bülow, 17 March 1907, *GP*, no. 8582. Adam Block was of a similar opinion and remarked in 1908 that 'The French financiers have no patriotism' (letter from Block to Hardinge, 28 May 1908, FO 371/538). Ambassador Paul Cambon wrote of Vitali in 1907 that he 'in no way preoccupied himself with the interests of French policy' (private letter from Cambon to Gout, 24 July 1907, DDF, II, 11, no. 91).
18 Thobie (*Intérêts*, pp. 550–5) suggests that Delcassé was originally prepared to sanction a

minority participation and decided to insist on equality only after reading Constans' dispatch of 17 June 1900. Yet Delcassé on several occasions declared that his commitment to equality went back to the inception of Franco-German negotiations. See AMAE, Papiers Delcassé, Vol. 15 (Delcassé's annotation of Finance Minister Rouvier's letter of 1 Aug. 1903); confidential letter from Delcassé to Rouvier, 13 July 1903, *DDF*, II, 3, no. 347 (in which Delcassé said 'J'ai, dès le début, posé le principe de l'égalité'). Several of Constans' dispatches acknowledge an initial commitment to equality: Constans to Delcassé, 21 Jan. 1902, AMAE, Turquie, NS 334; Constans to Delcassé, 4 June 1903, AMAE, Turquie, NS 356; Constans to Pichon, 30 Aug. 1907, *DDF*, II, 11, no. 156.

19   Note the explanation which Delcassé offered the Russian government in December 1899 (Delcassé to Bapst, French chargé d'affaires in Constantinople, 21 Dec. 1899, *DDF*, I, 16, no. 35). See also Delcassé's speech to the Chamber of Deputies in March 1902 (*Journal officiel, Chambre des Députés*, 25 March 1902).

20   For Constans' attitude, see Marschall to Bülow, 2 Feb. 1902, *GP*, no. 5247; Wangenheim (German chargé d'affaires in Constantinople) to Bülow, 28 April 1903, *GP*, no. 5264. Constans ultimately advocated a minority participation (Constans to Delcassé, 24 Oct. 1903, *DDF*, II, 4, no. 37).

21   Thobie (*Intérêts*, p. 549) states that the text of the agreement of 5–6 May is unavailable. Yet a copy is to be found in *DDF*, I, 15, no. 184 (annexe), and it agrees with the British version (FO 78/5102).

22   Note the following dispatches: Constans to Delcassé, 7 Oct. 1899, *DDF*, I, 15, no. 274; Constans to Delcassé, 21 January 1902, AMAE, Turquie, NS 334. On the Paris press, see L. Ragey, *La Question du Chemin de Fer de Bagdad* (Paris, 1936), pp. 30–1. For the uncertainty of the Quai d'Orsay, see 'Note pour la direction politique', 23 May 1899, *DDF*, I, 15, no. 184; 'Note du Département', 8 Feb. 1900, *DDF*, I, 16, no. 71. For Delcassé's attitude, see his annotation of the letter sent to him by Finance Minister Rouvier on 1 Aug. 1903, AMAE, Papiers Delcassé, Vol. 15.

23   On the Syrian railway negotiations, see Marschall to Bülow, 2 Feb. 1902, *GP*, no. 5247; Bompard (ambassador in Constantinople) to Pichon, 15 Feb. 1910, AMAE, Turquie, NS 344.

24   Marschall to Hohenlohe (German Chancellor), 23 Sept. 1899, *GP*, no. 3349.

25   Constans to Delcassé, 30 May 1900, AMAE, Turquie, NS 167; Constans to Delcassé, 28 April 1902, AMAE, Turquie, NS 335.

26   For information on Rouvier's business connections, see R. Poidevin, *Les Relations économiques et financières entre la France et l'Allemagne de 1898 à 1914* (Paris, 1969), pp. 203–7.

27   Turkish lottery bonds, however, were not included. For a detailed account of unification, see Thobie, *Intérêts*, pp. 236–56.

28   Wangenheim to Bülow, 25 April 1903, *GP*, no. 5263; Wangenheim to Bülow, 28 April 1903, *GP*, no. 5264.

29   Delcassé's annotation of Rouvier letter of 1 Aug. 1903, AMAE, Papiers Delcassé, Vol. 15.

30   Rouvier to Delcassé, 20 July 1903, AMAE, Turquie, NS 356.

31   Constans to Delcassé, 24 Oct. 1903, *DDF*, II, 4, no. 37.

32   For example, Andrew, *Théophile Delcassé*, p. 236.

33   Private letter from P. Cambon (ambassador in Constantinople) to Delcassé, 13 Oct. 1898, *DDF*, I, 14, no. 436.

34   The antagonism of the Russian press had been especially marked in late 1901 and early 1902. Yet Delcassé wrote in November 1902 that he was astonished at the 'revival' of Russian hostility to the Baghdad Railway. He thought he had removed the objections of the Russian government in April 1901 (Delcassé to Boutiron, conseiller d'ambassade in St Petersburg, Nov. 1902, AMAE, Papiers Delcassé, Vol. 15).

35   W. I. Shorrock has suggested (*French Imperialism*, pp. 143–6) that Delcassé's dissatisfaction with the agreements accepted by the Beyrouth–Damas–Hauran company in 1900–1 was an important factor in his decision to oppose the quotation of Baghdad Railway bonds. There is no doubt that Delcassé attached much significance to the railway privileges which France possessed, or had once possessed, in northern Syria. But he did not have conclusive evidence of their loss until November 1903 ('Note du Département', 26 Nov. 1903, *DDF*, II, 4, no. 106).

36   Wangenheim to Bülow, 19 May 1903, *GP*, no. 5266.

37   Gwinner to Tschirschky (State Secretary), 10 Oct. 1906, *GP*, no. 8648.

38   On the protectorate, see Shorrock, *French Imperialism*, pp. 33–64.
39   Pichon to Constans, 21 Sept. 1907, AMAE, Turquie, NS 360. See also Bridge, above, pp. 36–7.
40   Delcassé to Constans, 3 Dec. 1903, AMAE, Turquie, NS 356. For still more categorical statements, see Delcassé to Rouvier, 28 July 1904, and Delcassé to Bapst, 1 Sept. 1904, AMAE, Turquie, NS 357.
41   Constans' pro-German inclinations occasionally showed through in his correspondence with the Quai d'Orsay. See Constans to Pichon, 11 Dec. 1906, *DDF*, II, 10, no. 354, and private letter from Pichon to Constans, 15 Dec. 1906, *DDF*, II, 10, no. 361.
42   'Notes du Département' (both dated 26 June 1906), AMAE, Turquie, NS 338.
43   Marschall to Bülow, 10 Dec. 1906, *GP*, no. 7649.
44   On the Debt Council meeting of 10 Dec., see Bertie (British ambassador to Paris) to Grey (Foreign Secretary), 9 Dec. 1906, FO 371/144; Pichon to Constans, 9 Dec. 1906, AMAE, Turquie, NS 388. See also D. C. Blaisdell, *European Financial Control in the Ottoman Empire* (New York, 1929), pp. 167–8, and Kent, below, pp. 176–7 and n. 50.
45   Especially Hardinge note of 16 Dec. 1906, FO 371/144.
46   See P. Cambon to Henri Cambon (his son), 9 July 1907, in P. Cambon, *Correspondance*, 3 vols (Paris, 1940–6), Vol. II, p. 233.
47   On the problems of France's Syrian network: Pean (French consul in Beirut) to Delcassé, 14 Feb. 1905, AMAE, Turquie, NS 358; Shorrock, *French Imperialism*, pp. 147–8.
48   On the Société des Quais: 'Note sur la Société des Quais de Constantinople', 6 Aug. 1901, *DDF* II, 1, no. 349; *Journal officiel, Chambre des Députés*, 5 Nov. 1901; Thobie, *Intérêts*, pp. 384–9.
49   Especially 'Note pour la Ministre', 10 Nov. 1904, AMAE, Turquie, NS 357.
50   Constans to Delcassé, 19 Sept. 1903, AMAE, Turquie, NS 356; Thobie, *Intérêts*, pp. 73–5.
51   Constans to Delcassé, 20 June 1904, AMAE, Turquie, NS 357.
52   See correspondence between Crespi, one of Schneider's Constantinople representatives, and Gemy, the firm's managing director (AMAE, Papiers Constans). This exchange is clarified by a letter which is unsigned, but clearly from Crespi, in AMAE, Turquie, NS 358. It is addressed to 'Schneider et Cie' and dated 16 April 1905.
53   On the diplomatic dispute in Constantinople, see AMAE, Turquie, NS 358.
54   AMAE, Papiers Constans; AMAE, Turquie, Carton 48; Thobie, *Intérêts*, pp. 406–15.
55   Pichon to Constans, 22 April 1908, AMAE, Turquie, Carton 48. According to Hardinge, Permanent Under-Secretary at the British Foreign Office, Constans had 'a very large pecuniary interest' in the Heraclea affair (see K. A. Hamilton, 'An attempt to form an Anglo-French "Industrial Entente" ', *Middle Eastern Studies*, Vol. XI (1975), no. 1, p. 67, n. 23).
56   Pichon to Constans, 1 May 1908, AMAE, Turquie, Carton 48.
57   Pichon to Constans (dispatch), 26 Jan. 1909, AMAE, Papiers Constans.
58   On Constans' unpopularity, see AMAE, Papiers Constans; 'Manifesto of Central Committee of Union and Progress' (March 1909), FO 371/761; *L'Humanité*, 4 April 1909. On the IOB's unpopularity, see Constans to Pichon, 28 Jan. 1909, AMAE, Turquie, NS 362.
59   Dispatch from Pichon to French ambassadors in Vienna and Berlin, 9 April 1909, *DDF*, II, 12, no. 164; Pichon to Constans, 7 April 1909, AMAE, Turquie, NS 362.
60   Caillaux to Pichon, 8 April 1909, AMAE, Turquie, NS 362.
61   Constans to Pichon, 1 June 1909, and J. Cambon (ambassador in Berlin) to Pichon, 29 Aug. 1909, *DDF*, II, 12, nos. 206, 298.
62   See Marian Kent: 'Agent of empire? The National Bank of Turkey and British foreign policy', *Historical Journal*, Vol. XVIII, no. 2 (1975), pp. 367–89. Also, see Ahmad, above, p. 14, and Kent, below, p. 179.
63   Bompard to Pichon, 12 Feb. 1911, *DDF*, II, 13, no. 151; M. Bompard, 'L'entrée en guerre de la Turquie', *La Revue de Paris*, 1 July 1921, pp. 61–85, and 15 July 1921, pp. 261–88.
64   Bompard to Cruppi (Foreign Minister), 5 May 1911, *DDF*, II, 13, no. 282; Note from French embassy in Constantinople, 8 May 1913, *DDF*, III, 6, no. 518; Bompard to Pichon, 31 May 1913, *DDF*, III, 7, no. 5.
65   On the period of hesitation: 'Note du Département', 29 Feb. 1912, *DDF*, III, 2, no. 128; Note by Jean Gout (Sous-Directeur du Levant), 20 May 1912, and 'Note pour le Ministre', 18 Sept. 1912, *DDF*, III, 3, nos 23, 426; Bompard to Poincaré (Foreign Minister), 6 Oct. 1912, *DDF*, III, 4, no. 73. For France's refusal, see *compte rendu* of meeting of 1 July 1913 at Ministry of Foreign Affairs, *DDF*, III, 7, no. 246.

66   Boppe (chargé d'affaires in Constantinople) to Doumergue (Foreign Minister), 9 Feb. 1914, *DDF*, III, 9, no. 249; Boppe–Doumergue, 29 Dec. 1913, AMAE, Turquie, Carton 48 (on German involvement in the coalfields of the Heraclea basin).
67   Bompard to Pichon, 30 Dec. 1910, and Bompard to Cruppi, 2 March 1911, *DDF*, II, 13, nos 109, 168.
68   P. Cambon to Pichon, 17 March 1910, AMAE, Turquie, NS 344.
69   *Bulletin du Comité de l'Asie Française*, Feb. 1911.
70   Bompard to Poincaré, 12 May 1912, *DDF*, III, 3, no. 264; letter from Pichon to Izvolskii (Russian ambassador in Paris), 17 June 1913, and Delcassé (ambassador in St Petersburg) to Pichon, 30 June 1913, *DDF*, III, 7, nos 138, 239. See also Bodger, above, pp. 90–2.
71   Thobie, *Intérêts*, p. 707 (including n. 383).
72   Delcassé to Doumergue, 7 Jan. 1914, *DDF*, III, 9, no. 31.
73   Doumergue to Delcassé, 14 Jan. 1914, *DDF*, III, 9, no. 79.
74   Thobie, *Intérêts*, p. 709; *Bulletin du Comité de l'Asie Française*, Dec. 1912, May and June 1913.
75   On the Comité de Défense see *Bulletin du Comité de l'Asie Française*, June 1913; Shorrock, *French Imperialism*, p. 60.
76   *Compte rendu* of meeting held at Élysée Palace, 6 Nov. 1913, *DDF*, III, 8, no. 445.
77   Bompard to Pichon, 1 April 1913 and 4 April 1913, *DDF*, III, 6, nos 159 and 196; Note from French embassy in Constantinople, 8 May 1913, *DDF*, III, 6, no. 518.
78   P. Cambon to Doumergue, 10 Dec. 1913, *DDF*, III, 8, no. 604.
79   J. Cambon to Doumergue, 28 Jan. 1914, *DDF*, III, 9, no. 177.
80   R. Poincaré, *Au service de la France*, 10 vols (Paris, 1926–33), Vol. IV, pp. 15–17.
81   For details of this agreement, see Thobie, *Intérêts*, pp. 679–82.
82   See U. Trumpener, *Germany and the Ottoman Empire, 1914–1918* (Princeton, NJ, 1968), pp. 19–20; Stanford and E. K. Shaw, *History of the Ottoman Empire and Modern Turkey*, Vol. II (Cambridge/New York, 1977), p. 310.
83   'Note du Département' (by Margerie), 13 July 1914, *DDF*, III, 10, no. 504. See also B. Auffray, *Pierre de Margerie, 1861–1942* (Paris, 1976), p. 265. In his postwar memoirs, Cemal [Djemal Pasha, *Memories of a Turkish Statesman, 1913–1919* (London, 1932), p. 106] said that he had offered France an alliance. But, as Margerie's carefully written report makes clear, Cemal spoke in terms of a reorientation of Ottoman policy and of a *rapprochement* rather than an alliance.
84   A Quai d'Orsay *note du département* of 19 Feb. 1914 suggested that Foreign Ministry officials had a renewed confidence in the Ottoman Empire's capacity for survival (AMAE, Turquie, NS 300). See also Bompard to Doumergue, 21 April 1914, AMAE, Turquie, NS 186.
85   cf. Djemal Pasha, *Memories*, pp. 107–13, and Feroz Ahmad, 'Great Britain's relations with the Young Turks, 1908–1914', *Middle Eastern Studies*, Vol. II, no. 4 (1966), p. 325. See Trumpener, above, p. 120.
86   The French military attaché, Lieut.-Col. Maucorps, pointed to this difficulty in early August 1914 (Maucorps to Messimy, Minister of War, 9 Aug. 1914, AMAE, Grande Guerre, Turquie, 849). See also Bompard to Viviani, 8 and 9 Aug. 1914, AMAE, Grande Guerre, Turquie, 845, and Bompard, 'L'entrée en guerre', pp. 62, 279.
87   Bompard to Delcassé, 30 August 1914, AMAE, Grande Guerre, Turquie, 845; Bompard, 'L'entrée en guerre', pp. 271–2.
88   Delcassé to Bompard, 28 Sept. 1914; Bompard, 'L'entrée en guerre', p. 28.
89   Delcassé to Millerand, Minister of War, 28 April 1915, AMAE, Grande Guerre, Turquie, 850.
90   *L'Asie Française*, Dec. 1914.
91   Delcassé to Millerand, 28 April 1915, AMAE, Grande Guerre, Turquie, 850.
92   P. Cambon to Delcassé, 4 March 1915, AMAE, Grande Guerre, Turquie, 850.
93   Poincaré, *Au service de la France*, Vol. IV, p. 92. Delcassé, in his reply to Sazonov (Russian Foreign Minister), on 7 March, argued that the question of the Straits and Constantinople should not be finally decided until the war was over and until the Allies had agreed on the terms of a peace settlement. (Delcassé to P. Cambon, 10 July 1915, AMAE, Grande Guerre, Turquie, 851.)
94   Poincaré, *Au service de la France*, Vol. IV, p. 94.
95   Delcassé to P. Cambon, 11 March 1915, AMAE, Grande Guerre, Turquie, 851.
96   Note by Berthelot, Director of Political and Commercial Affairs, 9 March 1915, and Delcassé

to P. Cambon, 11 March 1915, AMAE, Grande Guerre, Turquie, 850. It was primarily Delcassé's determination to give detailed shape to the provisional Allied regime which delayed his acceptance of Russia's territorial demands until 12 April 1915.

97 AMAE, Papiers Delcassé, Vol. 25 (copy of an interesting dispatch from Delcassé to the London and Rome embassies, 20 March 1915).

98 Delcassé to Millerand, 28 April 1915, AMAE, Grande Guerre, Turquie, 850.

99 *L'Asie française* April–July issue, 1915.

100 C. M. Andrew and A. S. Kanya-Forstner, 'The French colonial party and French colonial war aims, 1914–1918', *Historical Journal*, Vol. XVII, no. 1 (1974), p. 83.

101 Briand to Georges-Picot, 2 Nov. 1915, AMAE, Grande Guerre, Turquie, 870.

102 Jukka Nevakivi, *Britain, France and the Arab Middle East, 1914–1920* (London, 1969), pp. 36–7; Marian Kent, 'Asiatic Turkey, 1914–1916', in F. H. Hinsley (ed.), *British Foreign Policy under Sir Edward Grey* (Cambridge, 1977), pp. 436–51; Kent, below, pp. 186–7.

103 Andrew and Kanya-Forstner, 'The French colonial party and French colonial war aims', p. 101.

104 On French fortunes in Cilicia and Syria, Nevakivi, *Britain, France and the Arab Middle East*; J. Pichon, *La Partage du Proche Orient* (Paris, 1938), p. 232; H. M. Sachar, *The Emergence of the Middle East, 1914–1924* (New York, 1969), pp. 427–9.

105 On the financial settlement with Turkey, see J. Thobie, *Phares Ottomans et emprunts Turcs, 1904–1961* (Paris, 1972).

106 On French enterprises: AMAE, Levant, Turquie, 297 (Lausanne Conference); 427 (La Société d'Héraclée); 446 (La Société des Quais de Constantinople); 489 (Black Sea Railways); also R. de Gontault-Biron and L. Le Reverend, *D'Angora à Lausanne* (Paris, 1924).

107 *L'Humanité*, 28 April 1909.

108 P. Cambon to Xavier Charmes, 8 Feb. 1909 in Cambon, *Correspondance*, Vol. II, p. 275.

7 Great Britain and the End of the Ottoman Empire 1900–23

Marian Kent, Deakin University

Britain's interests in the Ottoman Empire in the final decades of its existence were concentrated primarily in Mesopotamia and the Persian Gulf. Concerned to maintain British supremacy in an area considered vital to the defence of India and to communications with the eastern Empire in general, Britain could uphold this interest by upholding two others of long standing: her commercial and her political dominance in the region. Foreign commercial interests were not debarred from the area, although any attempt to use them to usurp Britain's political dominance through the local political influence that followed in the train of an established commercial position or, alternatively, by a direct naval and military presence was not to be tolerated. Lord Lansdowne so warned Britain's fellow Great Powers, and particularly, at that time, Russia, in his speech of May 1903 in the House of Lords.[1] The Foreign Secretary's warning was underlined by the Viceroy of India, Lord Curzon, when, six months later, in resounding tones, he reminded the sheikhs of the south Persian Gulf coast of their trucial, dependent relations with Britain:

> We were here before any other Power in modern times had shown its face in these waters. We found strife, and we have created order. It was our commerce as well as your security that was threatened and called for protection. At every port along these coasts the subjects of the King of England still reside and trade. The great Empire of India, which is our duty to defend, lies almost at your gates. We saved you from extinction at the hands of your neighbours. We opened these seas to the ships of all nations, and enabled their flags to fly in peace. We have not seized or held your territory. We have not destroyed your independence but have preserved it. We are not now going to throw away this century of costly and triumphant enterprise. The peace of these waters must still be maintained; your independence will continue to be upheld; and the influence of the British Government must remain supreme.[2]

If the flag had originally followed the trade, the truth now was that the flag was underpinned by the trade, and any harm to the underpinning would bring down the superstructure. In January 1909, when Germany had succeeded Russia as Britain's *bête noire* in the Persian Gulf, the Committee of Imperial

Defence sub-committee reported that 'British claims to political predominance in the Gulf are based mainly upon the fact of our commercial interests
having hitherto been predominant, and should our trade, as a result of a
German forward policy, be impaired, our political influence would propor-
tionately diminish'.[3] Curzon expressed the wider implications of such a
diminution of political influence when he declared to the House of Lords in
March 1911 that 'the Gulf is part of the maritime frontier of India . . . It is a
foundation principle of British policy that we cannot allow the growth of any
rival or predominant political interest in the waters of the Gulf, not because it
would affect our local prestige alone, but because it would have influence that
would extend for many thousands of miles beyond.'[4]

Political and strategic considerations, after all, fitted Britain's Ottoman
Empire interests into the broader framework of British foreign policy. Britain
depended for its greatness on its naval superiority, its commercial strength and
its far-flung strategic positions including, especially, that jewel in the imperial
crown, India, and this strength was reflected in Britain's standing among the
European Great Powers. In the years up to 1914, British leaders were basically
concerned not to let Britain's strength be diminished but to preserve the *status
quo* and hence the peace of Europe against what was seen as the increasing
German threat.[5] Such European preoccupations were mirrored in Britain's
Ottoman Empire concerns. If the key to containing German restlessness in
Europe was intended to be the *entente* with France and, later, that with Russia,
Britain's policy towards the Ottoman Empire in the prewar years had similar
aims. British policy there sought to contain Germany within reasonable limits
and to uphold the solidarity of the *ententes* by not encroaching on French and
Russian spheres of interest; at the same time, none the less, it sought to contain
Russia's traditional southward pressure. More generally, Britain was concerned to prevent any major disintegration of the Ottoman Empire which
would stimulate territorial greed and promote war among the Powers, not least
upsetting her own position of strength in the geographical jigsaw of established
Great Power spheres of influence.

The mechanism for conducting Britain's foreign policy towards the
Ottoman Empire in the years up to the First World War was primarily the
Foreign Office and Diplomatic service, including the consular service.
Where commercial matters were concerned the Board of Trade was also
consulted, drawing on its specialised agency, the Commercial Intelligence
Committee. The government of India, too, was involved. Within its sphere of
administration lay relations with the Persian Gulf sheikhs as well as the
consular establishment in Persia and the Persian Gulf, including a share of the
Baghdad consulate.[6] The Expeditionary Force 'D' that was to conduct the
Mesopotamian campaign in the war was, until 1916, directed by India. The
India Office in London was, further, consulted in virtually all policy decisions
concerning the Ottoman Empire, while Curzon's successor as Viceroy, Lord
Hardinge of Penshurst, filled this post between two phases of being Under-

Secretary of State at the Foreign Office and most powerful adviser to Sir Edward Grey as Foreign Secretary.

Of the four Foreign Secretaries involved in conducting Britain's policy towards the Ottoman Empire in the last two decades of its existence each left a distinctive mark on that policy for those who followed. Lansdowne, Foreign Secretary until 1905, as has been seen, laid down the 'hands off' policy on the Persian Gulf.[7] His successor, Grey, was in office from 1905 until December 1916, the longest spell of all four men. Opposed to the obtaining of more territory for the British Empire, Grey's lasting mark on Britain's Turkish policy was to permit the wartime plans for massively partitioning the Ottoman Empire into what a former consul in Basra was slyly to call 'spheres of affection'.[8] Lord Balfour, who followed him in office until October 1919, handed on the legacy of the Balfour Declaration and the subsequent British control of Palestine.[9] Curzon, the greatest imperialist of them all, was primarily involved during his Foreign Secretaryship in the renegotiation of the Turkish peace settlement at Lausanne, where the Turks regained virtually all of their lost European and Anatolian territory and Curzon returned home congratulating himself on his achievement.[10]

Ambassadors in Constantinople before the First World War were recognised by their Foreign Office chiefs as being required to promote British interests in a difficult diplomatic setting of two regimes which, with only a brief lapse in 1908–9, were pro-German and anti-British. Sir Nicholas O'Conor, who occupied the position from July 1898 until his death in 1908, was regarded as the most successful incumbent in this period, being able and forceful in pressing British interests even if he did not achieve many of his aims.[11] His successor over the next five years, Sir Gerard Lowther, less flexible and less perceptive, was regarded as 'a great disappointment' who had promoted an unfortunate 'anti-Turkish atmosphere' in the embassy with consequent harm to Britain's previously improved position.[12] Lowther had arrived just at the time of the Young Turk revolution when the British had 'the ball at our feet to the great chagrin of our German friends who pivoted their policy on the Sultan and his Camarilla',[13] but he lost his chance and, in October 1913, his job. His replacement, Sir Louis Mallet, a former private secretary to Grey who, at the time of his appointment, had been Assistant Under-Secretary heading the Eastern Department at the Foreign Office, was more closely in tune with his chief. He was a very great contrast to his predecessor and, according to his Acting Chief Dragoman, Andrew Ryan, was intent on conciliating the Young Turk leaders by friendliness and charm.[14] Even charm had its limitations, however, and Mallet was unable to prevent the Turks from going to war against Britain in 1914.

Assisting the ambassador were a number of very able people, plucked, by and large, from the playing-fields of Eton and Oxford and sent to bat on a sticky wicket in Constantinople. Among such junior diplomatic staff of the prewar years were Maurice de Bunsen, Percy Loraine, Alexander Cadogan,

George Clerk, George Kidston, Lancelot Oliphant, Harold Nicolson, George Young, Mark Sykes and George Lloyd. Almost all of these were to attain considerable distinction in their subsequent careers. Of those receiving some prominence in this account, George Lloyd (later, as Lord Lloyd of Dolobran, High Commissioner in Egypt and then Colonial Secretary) was in 1908 to draw up a key report for British commercial policy in Mesopotamia and, during the war, among other activities, worked for the Arab Bureau.[15] De Bunsen (between 1906 and 1914, as Sir Maurice de Bunsen, Ambassador to Madrid and Vienna) was to chair the committee set up in 1915 to inquire into British desiderata in Asiatic Turkey.[16] In 1916, Mark Sykes (then Lieutenant-Colonel Sir Mark Sykes, MP, and adviser to the War Office on Arab matters) was co-author of the Sykes–Picot Agreement.[17] Subsequently, as an ardent Zionist, he was attached to the Foreign Office delegation to the Paris Peace Conference, until his death in February 1919. Harold Nicolson (who resigned his diplomatic career in 1927 at the rank of Counsellor to enter politics and who is best known for his prolific writings on history and diplomacy) was a member of the British delegations to the Paris Peace Conference and to the Lausanne Conference of 1922–3.[18]

Two positions at the Constantinople embassy during this period warrant particular interest – that of Commercial Attaché and that of Dragoman. The Commercial Attaché was to assist in the commercial business of the embassy – a task which involved everything from writing annual and special reports, advising and assisting consuls, merchants, manufacturers and shippers, keeping a watch on tariff movements and helping to settle monetary claims to 'attending to' British mining and industrial concessions and enterprises.[19] During this whole period, from 1897 to 1914, the position of Commercial Attaché was filled by one man, Ernest Weakley. The duties of a Commercial Attaché were so wide that in some matters in particular Weakley played an important part in the presentation to his chief, and through him to the Foreign Office, of information and advice on which policy decisions were made. One such matter was the prolonged negotiations with the Turkish government over obtaining for British interests an oil concession in Mesopotamia.[20] For all his efforts, however, apart from a CMG in 1908, he received little recognition. After the war he was regarded as an expert on the Mesopotamian oil negotiations and became Foreign Office liaison officer with the newly formed Petroleum Executive, but he was not sent with the Foreign Office delegation to the Paris Peace Conference where these negotiations were so important.

The other position of special interest in the Constantinople embassy in the first two decades of this century was that of Dragoman. Filling the position of Oriental Secretary as much as that of interpreter the Dragoman could attain the diplomatic rank of First Secretary[21] and was a well-informed and essential adviser to the Ambassador.[22] Indeed, one incumbent, Andrew Ryan, described the role as being 'in some sense the *alter ego* of the Ambassador in relation to the Turks' or, as his predecessor, Gerald Fitzmaurice, put it, 'a dragoman is merged in his chief'.[23] Under Mallet, in particular, this was essential, in the absence of able senior diplomatic staff to assist him.[24]

Before the war the position of Chief Dragoman was filled by Adam Block (from 1894 to 1903), Harry Lamb (1903 to 1907) and Gerald Fitzmaurice (1908 to 1920). Andrew Ryan was often acting for Fitzmaurice, and at the end of 1920 received the substantive appointment, at the rank, indeed, of Counsellor. Fitzmaurice's grasp of Turkish affairs was so acute, however, that despite considerable illness and absence he long retained his post. His letter of 12 April 1908, for instance, following the death of O'Conor, not only drew attention, in acerbic terms, to the fatal contradictions in Britain's Turkish policy but also set out what he felt ought to be the personality requirements for whoever was to be Britain's next ambassador there.[25] Ryan's main contributions, apart from assisting Mallet when Fitzmaurice was away just before the outbreak of war, came at the Lausanne Conference, when he assisted Sir Horace Rumbold, the High Commissioner and chief British negotiator after Curzon's departure.[26]

The most unusual of the four men was Adam Block. Although Block left consular life in 1903, he kept up contact with the embassy and with the Foreign Office. As Delegate of the British bondholders on the Council of the Ottoman Public Debt Administration as well as alternate President of the Council and President of the British Chamber of Commerce in Constantinople he was ideally placed to be well informed on the position and needs of British commercial interests in the Ottoman Empire.[27] His position on the Debt Council as an Ottoman public servant did not appear to inhibit him unduly from giving information and advice to the Foreign Office, as the Foreign Office documentation of the period constantly shows.[28] One paper in particular which the Foreign Office regarded as highly important was his 1906 memorandum on 'Franco-German economic penetration in the Ottoman Empire', in which he urged that Britain should take steps to buttress her eroded position.[29] He sought to carry out his own advice in 1908–9 when he was instrumental in getting set up in Turkey the British National Bank of Turkey, of which he was one of the directors.[30] During the war he held a number of prominent posts to do with trade, becoming finally Controller of the Finance Section of the Minstry of Blockade (the Ministry where Harry Lamb and Andrew Ryan also served), and, along with Ryan, was a member of the British delegation to the Lausanne Conference.[31] Thereafter he resumed his business life.

The consular service, of which the dragomanate was part, was none the less the Cinderella among Britain's overseas services, where the social status was lower and the rewards for faithful service less exalted. Andrew Ryan's sarcastic description of his fellows in the service as being 'very distinctly of lesser breed, men profane to the mysteries of diplomacy and apt to be infected with a disease known in the language of Olympus as *Morbus consularis* or *l'esprit capitulaire*', undoubtedly reflected the general view of the consular service held by its Foreign and Diplomatic brethren.[32] Ryan achieved a rare transition, albeit through the back door, from the consular to the diplomatic service, and finished his working life with two legations (to his bitter chagrin, neither an important one), in Jeddah and Durazzo. Only two other Middle East consuls made similar progress. One was Sir Reader Bullard, also of the Levant Service, who, from being Acting Consul in Basra in 1914, went on to become Military Governor of Baghdad in 1920 and, between 1936 and 1946, Minister in Jeddah and in Tehran. The other was Sir Percy Cox, who, in the service of the government of India, during his years in the Persian Gulf and Mesopotamia carved out a unique name for himself. From being Consul and Political Agent in Muscat between 1899 and 1904 he became Consul-General in Bushire and from 1909 until the war was 'Political Resident' in the Persian Gulf, filling during those years an almost ambassadorial role with the Gulf sheikhs. During the war he was Chief Political Officer with the Indian Expeditionary Force 'D', after the war was Acting Minister in Tehran, and between 1920 and 1923 was High Commissioner in Mesopotamia.[33]

The work of the consular service was clearly important for the promotion of British commercial interests in the Ottoman Empire. On the one hand, there was the day-to-day administration of matters affecting British subjects and British-protected persons (largely on the authority of Britain's capitulatory rights) and of matters of commerce, particularly the movements of ships in ports. On the other hand, the consul had the most important duty of reporting annually (complete with statistics) on the trade of his region, as well as of sending from time to time any special reports on matters of commercial and general interest, reports which, after editing, were made available to the British commercial community. The balance between the commercial, political and judicial functions of a consulate varied depending on the type of area in which it was located.[34]

British trade and commerce in the Ottoman Empire were also helped directly by the Board of Trade, through its Commercial Intelligence Branch and the weekly *Board of Trade Journal*. Both made available to traders considerable information obtained from consular and special reports, the Constantinople Chamber of Commerce and other sources, on trading opportunities in the Ottoman Empire and elsewhere.[35] If some of the 'intelligence' thus made available included such hopeful but misleading information as the report in late 1908 'that rigorous measures have been taken to eradicate the inveterate habit on the part of Turkish customs officers of receiving bakshish',[36] it could also include the sensible advice from George Lloyd's 1908 'Report on the conditions and prospects of British trade in Mesopotamia'.[37]

Commerce, therefore, however much it was considered below the rarefied notice of some, was nevertheless the basis of Britain's position in Mesopotamia and the Persian Gulf, and represented the 'underpinning' of Britain's foreign policy in the Ottoman Empire. In some ways it even became the 'language' of Britain's diplomacy in the region, where strategic ends were upheld through protection of commercial interests. The prime example of this was the long negotiations over the Baghdad Railway. The political negotiations over the railway have been exhaustively covered in other works;[38] this account will approach the question from a different angle – of the broader, 'commercial' methods used to attain the basic strategic and political ends of British policy.

Basic to all such interests, however, was the state of Britain's relations with the Turkish government of the time.[39] The one British Foreign Secretary whose tenure of office, from 1905 to 1916, spanned both the sultan's and the Young Turk regime, Sir Edward Grey, found his country's relations with either regime unsatisfactory for most of his time in office. This was not only the fault of the Turks. Although Grey was to write later of Sultan 'Abdul Hamid and his detestable camarilla',[40] the policy Grey's ambassadors were obliged to pursue in the early years of the century was not likely to endear their government to the sultan. As Gerald Fitzmaurice, that most experienced of British Dragomans, put it in April 1908:

> During the last few years our policy, if I may so call it, in Turkey has been, and for some time to come will be, to attempt the impossible task of furthering our commercial interests while pursuing a course (in Macedonia, Armenia, Turco-Persian Boundary etc.) which the Sultan interprets as pre-eminently hostile in aim and tendency. These two lines are diametrically opposed and consequently incompatible with one another. In a highly centralised theocracy like the Sultanate and Caliphate combined, with its pre-economic conceptions, every big trade etc. concession is regarded as an Imperial favour to be bestowed on the seemingly friendly, a category in which, needless to say, we are not included . . . any British Ambassador here must necessarily find himself in the equivocal, if not impossible position of having to goad the Sultan with the pinpricks of reform proposals while being expected to score in the commercial line successes which are dependent on the Sultan's goodwill.[41]

It was not surprising, therefore, that the less moralistic approach towards the Turks followed by Germany scored more success with the sultan.[42]

The Young Turk revolution temporarily reversed this situation. On the proclamation of the 1876 Constitution on 23 July 1908 the British government immediately offered its official congratulations, and Grey instructed his Ambassador in Constantinople, Sir Gerard Lowther, to demonstrate Britain's sympathy and encouragement with the new regime.[43] Neither man was without misgivings, however, which grew as the new regime increasingly came to resemble a military despotism. Further, the British government's sympathy and encouragement towards the new regime did not lead it to modify its attitude on a number of questions of practical importance to the new regime. This appeared to the regime – now somewhat changed in membership since the early and pro-British days of the revolution – as disappointing obstructionism and interference in its affairs.[44] Britain, not surprisingly, lost as a result its briefly favoured position. By the time of the First World War, Germany had reoccupied that place, not least through its close connection with the Turkish army, some of whose officers were influential members of the Young Turk regime. The secret Turkish–German military alliance of 1914 marked the culmination of this reversal.[45]

In financial terms Britain's stake in the Ottoman Empire was relatively small among the Powers. In 1914 her share of the Ottoman Public Debt was only 15 per cent and her share of investment in private enterprise was 14 per cent – in both cases well behind Germany and France.[46] Of the very many Turkish loans since the turn of the century only two – the Constantinople municipal loan of 1909 with the National Bank of Turkey, and the naval construction loan of 1913 with the National Bank and Armstrong Vickers – were obtained by British institutions, and both were comparatively small.[47] Indeed, although the Foreign Office wished to see more British investment in the Ottoman Empire, Grey was not prepared to urge British financiers to make Turkish loans which they did not think 'financially sound or desirable in the interests of . . . their banks or to Turkey'.[48] More, he was constantly concerned in the prewar years to try to supplement the political *entente* with France by a financial *entente* with her in the Ottoman Empire, even though this meant bowing to established French financial interests. A major example of this was the Foreign Office's active restraint of the National Bank of Turkey in 1910 from making the loan sought by the Turks that was eventually taken up by German and Austrian interests.[49] British investment in the Ottoman Empire in the prewar years included, apart from the National Bank of Turkey and the sizeable contracts held by Armstrong Vickers for shipbuilding, docks construction, shipyards and arsenal improvements, the Smyrna–Aidin Railway, the Euphrates and Tigris Steam Navigation Company, the Constantinople Telephone Company,[50] and a number of other shipping, transport, mining, engineering, cloth-milling, insurance and import–export enterprises.[51] Some of these activities posed rather greater concern for the British government than did the others, for they were operating in Mesopotamia and the Persian Gulf, Britain's particular areas of concern in the Ottoman Empire.

Britain's commercial 'stake' in this part of the Ottoman Empire in 1906 was a British and Indian share of 79 per cent of the total trade into and out of the Persian Gulf, although the purely British share of this was only 28 per cent.[52] That this 28 per cent represented just over £2¼ million shows clearly that this was not a trade of vital national economic importance. Yet the fact that the major part of the trade of Baghdad and Basra, valued at £2½ million in 1903, was in the hands of British and Indian merchants was used as a stick with which to belabour the Turkish and German governments throughout the period over the Baghdad Railway's threat to Britain's interests in Mesopotamia and the Gulf. The German share of the Gulf import–export trade, after all, had risen already to 4 per cent in 1906 from some 2 per cent ten years before, while the British share had declined from 34 per cent. This trend continued to 1914. By then the British share of Turkey's imports had fallen by a further one-third, while the German share had risen a further threefold.[53]

Shipping in the Persian Gulf, on the other hand, showed a much stronger British position in 1906. The British and Indian share of 85 per cent of the total Gulf shipping had been maintained over the previous ten years, although, somewhat alarmingly for the British government, the German share had increased over that period from less than 1 per cent to 10 per cent, while the Germans also offered reduced freight rates and more reliable sailing dates.[54] As the main goods making up both Britain and India's Gulf trade were Manchester cotton goods, in 1906 worth some £1 million, clearly among the dominant interests that concerned the British government in Mesopotamian and Gulf economic life were the shipping lines and the Manchester cotton trade.[55]

Two further major interests can be added to these. The main inland communications route from the Gulf to central Mesopotamia was from Basra to Baghdad. As George Lloyd pointed out, 'He who controls communications controls trade,' and on this route and on the Karun River the British Lynch firm, the Euphrates and Tigris Steam Navigation Company, had dominated the carrying trade since the mid-nineteenth century, including the mail concession.[56] The other major interest to the British government, though not in this region, was the last remaining British railway in the Ottoman Empire. All the others, which together had given Britain a monopoly of railway development in Anatolia, had been sold to French or German interests.[57] This was the Smyrna–Aidin Railway, only 380 miles long but passing through relatively populous and fertile districts.[58]

For the British government the basic trouble with British trade and commerce in Mesopotamia and the Gulf was complacency in the face of German competition. 'British trade is standing on one leg in the Baghdad market,' complained George Lloyd, in his disgust at the unwillingness of British merchants to diversify and so beat German competition.[59] More, British trade had no British banking facilities to serve it in Mesopotamia, only the Imperial Ottoman Bank, now in effect a French institution. The only genuinely British bank in the region was the Imperial Bank of Persia, which had been forced out of Baghdad and Basra by the Ottoman Bank, and each represented the other in its respective bailiwick.[60] The main Persian Gulf branch of the bank was in Bushire, where its policy was reported to be unnecessarily unadventurous, its rates excessive and its occasional lack of hard currency crippling to local business.[61] Grey himself wrote that when he became Foreign Secretary in 1905 he was

> distressed to find . . how completely we had been ousted from commercial enterprises in Turkey and how apparently hopeless it was to get any footing there . . .
>
> Since then [to August 1908] I have been very disappointed to find what a very poor set of financiers had got commercial enterprises into their hands. It was, I suppose, inevitable under the old regime, for its methods were such that it did not attract the best class of financier . . .[62]

Hence Grey's encouragement of the establishment of the National Bank of Turkey a few years later and his encouragement to Sir Henry Babington Smith, then Secretary to HM Post Office, to become the bank's President.[63]

The British government's main efforts to try to understand the nature of the German threat to the British position in the Ottoman Empire and the action required to counter it crystallised in the period between 1905 and 1909. It was undoubtedly stimulated by the inauguration in 1904, 'with much pomp and ceremony',[64] of the first section of the Baghdad Railway to be added on to the existing Anatolian Railway system. Apart from George Lloyd's fact-finding mission and report, between 1907 and 1909 a number of detailed memoranda and reports were drawn up by the concerned government departments. The Foreign Office,[65] the Board of Trade,[66] the Admiralty[67] and the Committee of Imperial Defence[68] all examined the German threat to Britain's interests in the Persian Gulf and Mesopotamia. Their conclusion, summed up by the Committee of Imperial Defence, was that commercial dominance was the key to political dominance, and this was Germany's method. It was, however, a tactic that could only be fought by a like tactic; any direct political action was bound to be counter-productive.[69] As the Foreign Office had put it:

> . . . the whole history of the Persian Gulf . . . has shown that commercial prosperity inevitably leads to political hegemony, and in these circumstances it is a matter for grave consideration whether, on political grounds, exceptional measures should not be taken to facilitate British enterprise in the Persian Gulf and to neutralise the efforts being made to undermine our existing position . . .[70]

A precedent had, in fact, already been created. As a result of interdepartmental deliberations in October 1907 between the Foreign Office, the India Office and the Admiralty, a secret agreement was made that month with the Sheikh of Koweit.[71] By this agreement Britain was able to secure to herself control over any of the sheikh's land suitable for use as a terminus for the Baghdad Railway.

The British government's commercial strategy from 1907 to the outbreak of war in 1914 was three-pronged. Its first tactic was that of constant diplomatic complaint to the German and Turkish governments about the threat posed by the Baghdad Railway to Britain's long-established commercial interests. These were described, repeatedly, as the valuable Baghdad–Basra trade, the shipping trade entering Basra, the mail trade from India, the carrying trade on the Mesopotamian rivers and the Indian pilgrim traffic to religious shrines.[72] By contrast, 'German commerce, supported by the great local organisation of the railway and its powerful officials . . . would almost inevitably compete with weighted dice'.[73] The Foreign Office never tired of pointing out that basing the railway upon Turkish government kilometric guarantees meant 'that it is in the interest of the Turkish Exchequer . . . that no other railway concessions should be granted in the adjoining regions'.[74] Britain's refusal in 1909–10 to agree to the Turkish request for a further 4 per cent increase in Turkish customs dues unless Britain obtained a satisfactory participation in the line was on the ground that the additional customs revenue would be 'used, whether directly or by liberating other revenues, to facilitate the prolongation of a railway which must, as at present controlled, have a prejudicial effect on established trade interests in Mesopotamia'.[75] As 65 per cent of this trade was British, then British trade would also carry the main burden of the increased customs charge.[76] This argument was undoubtedly merely a lever – a word used by Grey himself – however firmly pursued, to obtain a satisfactory accommodation over the Baghdad Railway. So also was Grey's demand for a 'protective' concession for an alternative railway line down the Tigris valley.[77] As he told the Turkish Ambassador formally in April 1910, the Baghdad Railway without British participation 'would seriously modify, and was indeed intended to modify, the economic position of this country in regard to the trade of Mesopotamia; would affect the political situation in the Persian Gulf to the detriment of British interests; and assuredly would have important influence in regard to the Indian Empire'.[78]

The convention which was finally initialled between Britain and Turkey on 12 August 1913 certainly secured Britain's commercial and political interests very satisfactorily.[79] More, in view of Britain's weakened bargaining position in mid-1912, when it was discovered that the Shatt-el-Arab could be made suitably navigable upstream to Basra for Basra to be the railway terminal and not Koweit, the terms of the convention may be regarded as a considerable *coup* for the British negotiators.[80] Chief credit was due to Alwyn Parker, that junior, background figure in the Foreign Office who handled the details of the long and extremely complex railway and associated negotiations.

In the meantime the British government had two other tactics to follow in its commercial strategy against German competition. The first of these was to try to persuade British merchants and shippers to improve their methods themselves and be more competitive. As with the merchants who had already disappointed George Lloyd, the 1908–9 government reports also concluded that the remedy for most of the deficiencies in British shipping practice to the Gulf lay with the shippers themselves. Like the merchants, however, when faced with concrete suggestions from the Board of Trade, they mostly turned them down. The Board pressed the 'Combine' of three British shipping lines plying the Gulf trade hard, but unsuccessfully, to turn down a profit-sharing proposition made by the German Hamburg–America Line in 1908.[81] The shippers also refused to lower their freight rates without a government subsidy; it was, after all, firmly believed that the Germans were receiving such assistance from their government in one form or another.[82] None the less, this was one option which was not made available to the British shipping companies to the Gulf in the years up to the war.[83] By 1913–14 the British and Indian share of the total Gulf trade (as always, excluding the local Gulf trade) was still 83 per cent, but German competition had made considerable progress in specific

areas.[84] In particular, as Lord Inchcape of the P. & O. Line told the government, the British shipowners had not been able to compete successfully with
the German line ('owing to the German subsidies') and had been obliged to
come to terms with them over freight rates.[85]

George Lloyd's report had also urged direct government intervention in
support of 'the expansion of British trade and interests in a part of the world so
closely connected with the vitality of our Indian Empire'.[86] As he pointed out,
'Trade and politics are closely allied in all countries: in Turkey they are
inseparable'.[87] But direct commercial intervention, although this was the third
tactic in the government's commercial strategy, was the hardest weapon for a
laissez-faire government to use.[88] Apart from the determined negotiations over
the Baghdad Railway, and the securing in 1908 of a British adviser to reorganise the Turkish customs administration – which was in large part a political
move[89] – there was little the Foreign Office could do. It had already, in 1907,
gone so far as to ask the Board of Trade to interview various directors and
managers of Indian and Eastern banks in an effort to persuade them to open a
branch in Baghdad, but none would do so without a subsidy.[90] The National
Bank of Turkey did establish itself in Constantinople in 1909 with warm
Foreign Office encouragement, though this did not solve the Baghdad problem and, anyway, it was intended to offset French influence rather than
German. But this encouragement did not last, and both bank and Foreign
Office became increasingly disenchanted with each other.[91] The Foreign
Office did make great diplomatic efforts to help British interests obtain an oil
concession over most of Mesopotamia, but this was justified on strategic and
not commercial grounds, it involved in the end including German interests,
and the actual concession had still not been obtained by the time the war broke
out.[92] The Foreign Office did press the Porte in June 1909 to allow the Lynch
firm to regain its old monopoly on the Tigris and Euphrates. But so strong was
local protest at the news of this scheme, which appeared to presage a resumption of the company's former, crushing monopolistic freight rates, that the
Turkish Cabinet resigned, at least partly on this issue, the Foreign Office
declined to press the Turks further and the scheme was dropped.[93] British
support of the Lynch firm subsequently was a direct reflection of the government's concern about German competition rather than a belief in the virtues of
the firm, about which they had actually few illusions. To this concern can be
attributed the Foreign Office's (though not the India Office's) decision in May
1914 to revive the old subsidy to the firm and pay it £2,000 a year for two
years.[94] This heresy was saved by the bell.

British interest in the Ottoman Empire other than Mesopotamia and the
Persian Gulf in the years before the First World War was chiefly concerned
with the play of international politics in the western part of the Empire. This
was not an area of primary concern to the British government except in terms
of its relations with the ruling regime in Constantinople or in terms of the
approaches to the Suez Canal and the East. The government could, therefore,

by and large, play a mediatory role in international crises in the Balkans while trying at the same time to preserve the balance of influence among the Great Powers and the continued existence of the Ottoman Empire, with or without all its Balkan dominions. This applied to Britain's attitude to the Bosnian annexation crisis of 1908,[95] the Tripoli War of 1911,[96] the Balkan Wars of 1912–13[97] and even to the major diplomatic conflict between the Powers in the region before the First World War – the Liman von Sanders affair.[98] That quarrel was, after all, a Russo-German one and, anyway, Britain could hardly protest at a German general being appointed to reorganise the Turkish army when a British admiral was busy reorganising the Turkish navy. Over the longstanding Macedonian reform question Britain played only second fiddle to Austria and Russia, and no direct British interests were concerned, although Macedonia's endemic strife posed a constant threat to the stability of the Ottoman Empire.[99] Under pressure from public opinion and especially from the Balkan Committee, a group of political, religious and academic humanitarians,[100] both Landsdowne and Grey were, however, obliged to press Macedonian reform on the sultan, realising well that this was harming Britain's own interests, with efforts that were largely ineffectual.[101]

The most basic British interest directly threatened by the Balkan conflicts was Britain's seaborne position. As far as the Straits themselves were concerned, British policy since the mid-nineteenth century had been to maintain the *status quo* unless it were altered equally for all the Powers.[102] This policy was reaffirmed in October 1908 and maintained throughout the following years up to the First World War. Britain herself had no strategic interest in her navy being able to pass into the Black Sea, although she had commercial shipping through the Straits that was from time to time, between 1911 and 1914, threatened by the series of Balkan crises. Such a threat in early 1912, when Turkey closed the Straits, led to British pressure on the Turks to reopen them, even if only temporarily, to allow bottled-up ships and men and perishable produce to pass through.[103] At no time did Britain dispute Turkey's right to take such measures as she considered necessary for her defence, so long as those measures did not affect the rights of neutrals.[104]

It was Britain's dominant position in the eastern Mediterranean itself that was of most direct concern to her during the Balkan crises. As the Foreign Office stated formally in a memorandum of May 1912, 'It would be difficult to overrate the importance of the part which the sea-power outwardly and visibly exercised by Great Britain in those waters [the eastern Mediterranean] has played in creating the position which she holds at Constantinople . . .'.[105] In the prolonged crisis over the Italian occupation of the Aegean Islands, Britain's Mediterranean dominance seemed to be under threat.[106] Temporary occupations of the Islands by other Powers for specific, short-term objectives were one thing. But, as the Admiralty pointed out to the Foreign Office in June 1912, 'A cardinal factor of . . . [British policy] has naturally been that no strong Naval Power should be in effective permanent occupation of any

territory or harbour East of Malta, if such harbour be capable of transformation into a fortified Naval base . . .'.[107] The Italian occupation, therefore,
'would imperil our position in Egypt, would cause us to lose our control over
our Black Sea and Levant trade at its source, and would in war expose our route
to the East via the Suez Canal to the operations of Italy and her allies . . .'.
There were thus the best of reasons for Britain's earnest mediatory attempts,
however unsuccessful, over this issue.[108]

The First World War was to change very dramatically Britain's relations with
the Ottoman Empire, for now there was no need for either country to exercise
the restraints that had previously marked their relations. The Turks unilaterally abrogated the Capitulations, seized British commercial interests, mined
the Straits and subsequently inflicted humiliating defeat on British attempts to
breach the Dardanelles defences.[109] British forces embarked on a military
campaign in Mesopotamia, as well as later in Palestine, in support of which
their officers were informed that, despite the good qualities of the Ottoman
people they were nevertheless 'cruel to subject races, backward, jealous and
slow-witted', and 'abjectly submissive in the face of Government orders' as a
result of 'want of moral courage'.[110] Such people clearly deserved to lose their
subject races – a fate which was arranged by the middle of the war.[111]

A denial of Turkey's right to the territorial integrity of its Empire represented, indeed, a major change from Britain's prewar policy. As was seen in the
practice of British policy in the Balkans in the years before the war, and as was
repeated frequently by Grey to the other Powers, to the British public and to
the Turks themselves, Britain's policy had been undoubtedly to preserve the
Ottoman Empire intact, so far as was possible, at least from external threats,
for this was in Britain's own interests.[112] But by mid-September 1914 Grey felt,
like Churchill (then First Lord of the Admiralty), that Turkey was 'behaving so
disgracefully' in her actions towards British subjects and British interests while
still a neutral that she 'should be punished'.[113]

Just how such 'punishment' was to be accomplished was to become increasingly clear during the first year of the war with Turkey. Even before Britain's
formal declaration of war against Turkey on 5 November, the Cabinet, as early
as 20 October, presaged the abandoning of the formula of upholding, so far
as was possible, the territorial integrity of the Ottoman Empire. This was
repeated by Grey in the Cabinet meeting of 2 November, having already been
telegraphed by him to St Petersburg for the Russian government.[114] At the
same time Britain sought to shore up her influence in the Persian Gulf and
Arabia by having the government of India issue to the Gulf and Arabian
sheikhs assurances of British support against the Turks, or indeed any foreign
power. The action was to speed up the separation of those areas from Turkish
suzerainty and to provide a foundation for later British promises to the Arabs.
This foundation was strengthened by the landing on 6 November of the
Expeditionary Force 'D' at the head of the Persian Gulf, initially made with

limited and largely political objectives, and by the capture and occupation of Basra only three weeks later.[115] Britain thus controlled the head of the Persian Gulf and the key outlet for Mesopotamia. Further advance up the rivers was largely a combination of replying to Turkish counter-action and continued momentum from success, coupled with the need to impress Muslim opinion following the disastrous Dardanelles campaign, until the setback at Kut-el-Amara in late 1915 halted any further advance for a year.

The Dardanelles failure not only affected British military policy towards Turkey but also triggered off even greater changes in the attitudes of the Allies towards holding Turkish territory after the war. The British government had formally recognised on 14 November 1914 Russia's priority of interest in the future of the Straits and Constantinople.[116] Grey, too, like all his War Council colleagues (until the attack failed), had supported the Dardanelles attack of February 1915, expecting that its success would bring the collapse of Turkey, new Italian and Balkan allies for the British side and moral strength to Russia, already seen by him as an uncertain ally. But Russian mistrust of Britain's motives over the attack brought a firm request on 4 March to annex Constantinople and the Straits in return for guaranteeing British and French interests.[117] Somewhat reluctantly the Cabinet accepted this demand, in the event of the war being won.[118] A few months earlier, when the future of Basra was being discussed, Grey had forbidden the Viceroy to annex it as this would be 'contrary to the principle that occupation of conquered territory by allies is provisional pending final settlement at close of war'.[119] Basra had represented a rich plum to India, whose troops it was, after all, who had shaken the tree. Not only would it 'absolutely consolidate our position in the Gulf', argued the Viceroy, it would also, among other benefits, 'scotch the Baghdad Railway'.[120] Now that Russia had made firm annexationist demands Foreign Office scruples could relax.

The next sixteen months, until July 1916, saw considerable British efforts to define its own territorial requirements in the Ottoman Empire, while at the same time taking account of French and Arab claims. The complex investigations and negotiations of the de Bunsen Committee on Asiatic Turkey, the Hussein–McMahon correspondence and the Sykes–Picot Agreement are now well known.[121] Out of these negotiations, plus the efforts during 1915 and 1916 to win Italian and Balkan allies to the war effort against Turkey,[122] emerged two clear principles for British wartime policy in the Ottoman Empire. First, Britain was committed after the war to obtaining control for herself over the provinces of Baghdad and Basra and to upholding the claims of her Russian, French and Italian allies to other parts of the Ottoman Empire. Secondly, Britain was committed to supporting Arab independence from Turkey so long as the Arabs, under Sherif Hussein of Mecca, revolted effectively against the Turks, thereby helping both themselves and the British war effort. Britain's prewar policy regarding the territorial integrity of the Ottoman Empire was thus totally reversed in less than two years of war. None the less, the area over which she chose to exercise control was still the area long held to be vital to British strategic interests in the East: Mesopotamia, with its command of the Persian Gulf.

By the start of the final year of the war one further area, Palestine, became added to British desiderata. Under the Sykes–Picot Agreement, Palestine, because of its multi-religious character, had been destined to come under international control after the war. But the exigencies of war in the following year were to change that destiny. By the Balfour Declaration of November 1917, Britain sought to ensure a reliable Jewish presence in an area now to be under British control. There were a variety of reasons, all strong at the time, for such a decision,[123] but the most pressing was the strategic. Palestine was, as Curzon put it, 'the military gate to Egypt and the Suez Canal', which must not be allowed to pass back into the hands of Turkey, especially a Turkey dominated by Germany.[124] The impracticability of an international regime for Palestine was increasingly borne in on the British as the Palestine campaign progressed.[125] Hence the decision to avoid more than token Allied participation in occupied Palestine by holding it purely on a military basis; at the conference at San Remo in April 1920 sole British control was ensured.[126]

By the end of the war Britain's feelings towards the Sykes–Picot Agreement had already undergone considerable revision. Not only had Britain's policy regarding the internationalisation of Palestine changed, but also Russia had withdrawn from the secret agreements and made a separate peace. The disillusionment of the Arab leadership on learning, as it happened almost simultaneously, of the Balfour Declaration and the details of the Sykes–Picot Agreement necessitated some sweetening of the pill.[127] Consequently, in the course of 1918 a series of pronouncements interpreting British and French policy towards Arab lands were made.[128] Of the Anglo-French Declaration of November that year it has been said, not unjustly, that 'it did not contradict the Sykes–Picot Agreement: it only concealed its most crucial details'[129] – those, in fact, of Anglo-French tutelage. It was not surprising that such definition of Allied objectives in the Arab lands in idyllic terms of Wilsonian self-determination seriously harmed Allied–Arab relations in the postwar years when the illusion was not sustained.

In yet a further respect – the award of Mosul to France – Britain saw the Sykes–Picot Agreement as deficient, and this raises the broader question of Britain's economic interest in the wartime Ottoman Empire. For almost all of the war in Turkey, thinking in Whitehall was dominated by considerations of strategy and not of economic gain. Defence of the oil installations in Persia and Abadan was for the politicians in Whitehall, no less (at least initially) than for their counterparts in the government of India, merely an unfortunate necessity and not a primary aim.[130] Whitehall was well aware of the oil and other economic advantages of the Mosul province when it accepted the arguments of Sir Mark Sykes, who negotiated the agreement with Picot, that British control over Baghdad and Basra provinces alone were the best terms that could be obtained from the French and in any case secured Britain's essential interests in the region.[131] The obtaining or allocating of new concessions of any sort in Ottoman territory, as the Foreign Office recognised right up to the Peace Conference, was not a viable policy consideration prior to a peace settlement.[132] On the other hand, it was well understood that once the war was won German interests would be excluded from any Turkish territories coming under British control.[133] It was only in the last year of the war, when the question of War Aims had seriously to be considered, that the prime economic asset of Mesopotamia – its likely rich oil supplies – notably affected the conduct of the Turkish war. Even then it really only underlay political authorisation for the hasty occupation of Mosul at the time of the armistice.[134]

That there was any consistency at all in the making of Britain's wartime policy towards the Ottoman Empire is to be wondered at in view of the diverse and conflicting authorities in charge of its different aspects and phases. During these years, certainly, the influence of the Foreign Office waned in the councils of Whitehall. At first this was because Grey had little confidence in his ability to comment on military matters and, concerning Turkish matters, lost his grip on the political negotiations.[135] But even under Balfour from December 1916 onwards the Foreign Office never regained its former control over diplomacy. Dominant personalities of Churchill and Kitchener at the Admiralty and War Office, plus advisers such as Sir Mark Sykes, attached to the Directorate of Military Intelligence, filled the gap of political advice and even negotiation.[136] In any case, in March 1916 the War Cabinet set up a committee of combined Foreign Office and India Office membership, at first known as the Mesopotamian Advisory Committee, then as the Middle East Committee and finally as the Eastern Committee, concerned with the future administration of the Middle East. It was not, however, particularly effective, and Sir Robert Cecil, Assistant Under-Secretary in the Foreign Office, sarcastically described its function to Balfour as 'mainly . . . to enable George Curzon and Mark Sykes to explain to each other how little they know about the subject'.[137] Further, in January and July 1916, in an atmosphere of mounting public criticism at the mishandling of the Dardanelles and Mesopotamian campaigns, the War Office took over from India the direction and administration of Mesopotamian military operations.[138]

One particular organisation was set up at this time which did have a key influence on Britain's wartime Arab policy. In February 1916 a special Foreign Office institution, the Arab Bureau, was set up in Cairo under the existing Soudan Intelligence Department[139] in an attempt to co-ordinate the gathering of political intelligence in Arab lands and its dissemination to a bewildering number of competing authorities in the region and in London and India. It was also intended to co-ordinate local, pro-British and pro-Entente propaganda. Although its information was channelled to the Foreign Office via the High Commissioner in Cairo, Sir Henry McMahon, it was nevertheless dominated by military men of high repute and forceful personality from the Cairo and

Soudan establishment. The Foreign Office, while increasingly uneasy and sceptical about the Arab revolt and promises to support postwar Arab independence which the Arab Bureau was sponsoring, felt unable effectively to question the Bureau's expertise on Arab matters.[140] The verdict of A. T. Wilson, who had been Acting Civil Commissioner in Mesopotamia from the fall of Baghdad in March 1917 until October 1920, was not entirely unfair when he later wrote: 'The Arab Bureau in Cairo died unregretted in 1920, having helped to induce His Majesty's Government to adopt a policy which brought disaster to the people of Syria, disillusionment to the Arabs of Palestine and ruin to the Hijaz.'[141]

After the war Britain's policy towards the defeated Ottoman Empire was based on the same fundamental precept as before the war: to ensure Britain's strategic communications with her Empire in the East. But achieving basic policy aims was no more directly possible now than in the prewar years. If this now meant taking on responsibility, expense and bother for two mandates, Iraq and Palestine (and, as it turned out, a third – Transjordan – created in 1921),[142] in addition, of course, to control of Cyprus, Egypt and Aden, then that was what had to be done. It was, none the less, a time of financial stringency for the government when, as Churchill pointed out with more truth in the theory than in the practice, 'everything else that happens in the Middle East is secondary to the reduction in expense'.[143] If, therefore, an economic boon could be received in the form of Iraq oil, to help meet the mandate administration costs and provide secure and strategically accessible fuel for the navy, then the basic policy was considered doubly justifiable. Moreover, a peace settlement had yet to be reached with the Turkish government, and this took further the wartime reversal of Britain's policy concerning Turkish territorial integrity. There was now little concern to uphold even what remained of Turkey's territorial integrity after the Arab territories were removed. What was more, Britain now supported Turkey's most bitter rival in the region, Greece, to fulfil her territorial appetite at the expense of the European and Anatolian rump of Turkey. Britain's imperial commitments in the Middle East had grown at the very time the new currents of nationalism and self-determination were to make difficult the maintenance of orderly imperial rule in the new mandated territories. This current was also to bring, in the remaining Turkish territory, a nationalist revolution that would confront the British lion and confound many of its postwar intentions. And if such problems delayed the making of a durable peace settlement with Turkey until mid-1923 that delay was also partly due to the quarrels and mistrust among the Allies themselves.

The making of Britain's policy towards the Middle East in these years was complicated further by the number of its designers and their often contradictory principles. Curzon, Acting Foreign Secretary from January 1919 and Foreign Secretary proper from October that year, was constantly frustrated in his attempts to direct Britain's foreign policy. Primarily he came up against the intervention of the Prime Minister, Lloyd George, but he was also by-passed to a considerable extent during the Paris Peace Conference by the Foreign Office delegation to the Peace Conference. The delegation was headed by Balfour (the formal Foreign Secretary until he gave up the post in October 1919) and assisted by Mallet and such able juniors as Harold Nicolson and was, in effect, a policy-making arm of the government. Even if the decisions of this delegation required formal Foreign Office sanction, by the time this was sought Curzon and his colleagues in London were likely to find themselves already committed. And where there were clear differences of opinion between the two groups, over such questions as whether or not the spoils should be divided before or after the mandates were formally awarded, this was to cause much dissension among the policy-makers.[144]

Also dominant in Britain's postwar policy-making was Winston Churchill. Both as Minister for War until the end of 1920 and then as Colonial Secretary, under whose aegis a Middle East Department[145] was set up especially to co-ordinate policy and control the running of the new mandated territories, Churchill was largely responsible during the immediate postwar years for Britain's policy towards those territories. The Turkish peace settlement, nevertheless, remained Lloyd George's dominating interest, in a policy that remained diametrically opposed to that of both Churchill and Curzon until the former, at least, swung passionately to his side in the Chanak crisis that was to bring down the whole British coalition government. Of the former policy-makers only Curzon thereafter remained in power in the new government, and he it was who primarily conducted the British side of the Turkish peace negotiations that finally reached a settlement in the Treaty of Lausanne in July 1923.

In reaching agreement at San Remo on 24 April 1920 that France would obtain the mandate for Syria and Britain mandates over Mesopotamia and Palestine (the latter specifically upholding the Balfour Declaration),[146] British negotiators had completed one phase of their long and acrimonious postwar negotiations with their French counterparts.[147] Britain's priorities in Mesopotamia and Palestine had undergone considerable modification since the early years of the war. Strategic and economic desiderata now influenced equally the thinking in Whitehall, with a sense of imperial responsibility, arising largely from the legacy of wartime British civil administration of the conquered areas and the need for pacification of their disaffected Arab tribes coming an uneasy third. The desire to strengthen imperial communications through 'a chain of contiguous areas under British influence' was explained by the General Staff in late 1919:

> It is hoped that in the future this chain will be strengthened by a line of rail and air communications from west to east, as it is considered that this will strengthen our position in India which, as our greatest possession in the east, may be likened to a most valuable appendage at the end of the chain.[148]

The economic aims in Britain's postwar negotiations with France over the Middle East concerned the desire to secure Britain's future oil supplies. Britain's negotiators were determined to gain for their country *de jure* sanction for their *de facto* military occupation of Mosul as an integral part of the new Iraq state. In return for giving up her 'right' under the Sykes–Picot Agreement to Mosul, France was to obtain participation in the oil company to work the oil concession for the area, once the concession was formally granted by the British-controlled Iraq state.[149] The oil was guaranteed pipeline transit, accompanied by a railway, through French-controlled Syria and a secure debouche to the Mediterranean at the British-controlled port of Haifa. Economics and strategy thus interlocked, as an interdepartmental meeting in Whitehall had concluded earlier in the year:

> British interests . . . cannot be adequately safeguarded on the left flank of India unless the entire frontier of the territory under British control is pushed northward considerably beyond anything contemplated in the Sykes–Picot Agreement in order to afford adequate cover for the pipeline and lateral railway communication from Baghdad to the Mediterranean coast to connect with Egypt . . .[150]

The two years between the award of the mandates at San Remo, their incorporation into the Turkish peace terms signed (under protest) at Sèvres on 10 August 1920, and the League of Nations approval on 22 July 1922 of the terms of the mandates[151] saw Britain getting on with the job of running the mandated territories and defining the superstructure of policy towards them.[152] Churchill, specifically charged with this task, might privately consider that ' "Mandates", "mandatories" and things like that' were 'obsolescent rigmarole' and that 'It is quite possible that in a year or two there will be no mandates and no League of Nations',[153] and his Assistant Secretary of State, Sir John Shuckburgh, admit that 'a certain air of unreality surrounds the whole subject',[154] but these were territories won by right of conquest[155] and neither Turkish regime, sultan's or nationalists', was prepared to challenge their loss.

The Turks did, however, dispute the Allied postwar adjustments of other parts of the former Ottoman Empire. Such parts included those areas in Europe and Anatolia designed to be detached or placed under foreign, especially Greek, influence, and Mosul. Many among Britain's policy-makers recognised the inequity and dangers inherent in the award of Smyrna and Thrace to Greece and the permitted Greek invasion of Smyrna in May 1919.[156] Churchill and the General Staff decried the Greek terms as what Admiral de Robeck, the Allied High Commissioner in Constantinople, called 'a canker for years to come, the constant irritant that will perpetuate bloodshed in Asia Minor probably for generations'.[157] Churchill and the General Staff under its Chief, Sir Henry Wilson, believed Britain's Turkish policy to be likely to throw the

Turks into the arms of the Bolsheviks, with serious repercussions for British policy throughout the whole Middle East and India.[158] Even Curzon, who believed, like President Wilson and Lord Balfour, that the Turks should be expelled from Europe including Constantinople, was appalled at the decision to allow the Greeks to establish a zone in Asia Minor.[159] But Lloyd George, with his aggressively pro-Greek sentiments, dominated British policy over the Turkish peace. He was convinced, like Venizelos, the Greek Prime Minister, that the Turks could not stand up militarily or morally to the Greeks, who, he believed, were 'the coming power in the Mediterranean', and such was his personal standing among his government colleagues that dissenting views had little influence on his desired decisions.[160] The decision not to deprive the Turks of Constantinople had been taken in January 1920, following much argument to the contrary;[161] and the nominally international, but initially actually British, occupation of the city two months later was essentially an *ad hoc* measure taken primarily to pressure the Turkish government to accept the Allied peace terms.[162] It had, not surprisingly, the further effect of strengthening Kemal's Nationalist movement. Britain's remaining in Constantinople was upheld by Cabinet on the grounds 'that having regard to the very strong and even dramatic line of policy taken in regard to the Treaty of Peace with Turkey, to retire from Constantinople before a bandit like Mustapha Kemal would deal a shattering blow to our prestige in the East'.[163]

The period up to the Chanak crisis of September 1922 saw a continuation of this pattern of policy-making. It was notable, chiefly, for constant attempts by Curzon to uphold the need for Turkish ratification of the Treaty of Sèvres, with the Allies making concessions on small points only. At the same time Curzon endeavoured to uphold the united Allied front, well disintegrated now with the defection of France through the Franklin–Bouillon agreement with the Nationalists and the difficulty of his acrimonious, personal negotiations with the new French premier, Poincaré.[164] The Allies had agreed in the meantime to cease either financial assistance[165] or the supply of war materials to Greece, and by mid-1922 it was clear to British policy-makers that France and Italy were secretly supplying the Turkish Nationalists.[166] Lloyd George, on the other hand, maintained his encouragement of the Greek military advance.[167]

With the collapse of the Greek army in September 1922 and the Turkish Nationalist advance into Smyrna and the 'neutral zone' around the Straits, Britain's policy-makers were forced to modify their demands on Turkey.[168] Not only were France and Italy refusing to fight the Turks, most of the Dominions refused also, and British honour and military mastery in the Middle East were under grave threat. Churchill had immediately joined Lloyd George and the 'militants' once British prestige was at stake, and the bellicose statement which he issued to the press on 16 September,[169] in Curzon's absence and against his views, typified the stance of himself and the premier that Britain would fight (it was hoped, not alone) rather than give in. As the

War Office explained to the General Officer Commanding the Allied Forces of Occupation, General Sir Charles Harington:

> The foundation of all our policy is the Gallipoli Peninsula and the freedom of the Straits. For this it is of the highest importance that Chanak should be held effectively. Quite apart from its military importance it has now become a point of immense moral significance to the prestige of the Empire . . . A blow at Chanak is a blow at Britain alone, whereas Ismid and Constantinople are matters of international consequence affecting all the Allies . . .[170]

In a slightly different version, the United State government was informed that Britain's 'sole aim is to place beyond all jeopardy the future freedom of the Straits, which is a world interest just as much as one affecting the British Empire'.[171]

Britain very nearly went to war over the Chanak crisis. That this was averted was due as much to Curzon's continued protracted and difficult negotiations with Poincaré as it was to the tempered judgement of the men on the spot, Harington and Sir Horace Rumbold, the High Commissioner. Curzon's efforts to prop up the united Allied front[172] produced a joint Allied Note of 25 September to the Turks proposing a conference at Mudania,[173] and succeeded in holding the French to it[174] (the Italians did whatever the French did). Harington and Rumbold continued negotiations with Kemal, delaying passing on the British ultimatum of 30 September, and eventually brought the Turks to the conference table at Mudania; this resulted in the Convention of 11 October.[175] Sir Maurice Hankey, Secretary to the Cabinet, wrote in his diary of these tense days that all the talk in Cabinet was of war. Lloyd George, Churchill and others, he recorded, 'dreaded' Kemal's accepting the conference since that implied compromise terms for Britain, bringing back the Turk to Europe and losing credit with both sides.[176]

This, however, was the price of peace. The final peace treaty with Turkey was signed at Lausanne on 24 July 1923 and was ratified by the Assembly in Angora the following month, the sultan having quietly left Turkey on a British ship before the conference commenced.[177] Churchill called the Treaty of Lausanne 'a surprising contrast to the Treaty of Sèvres',[178] but for many of Britain's policy-makers there was little surprise in it, however much contrast. Britain attained its now greatly reduced essential policy points, although at the price of many concessions. Turkey had to observe the freedom and demilitarisation of the Straits, but there was now no international supervisory commission or zone.[179] Further, she recovered all the territory previously awarded to the Greeks, up to the River Maritza, while Armenia was not detached from Turkey. These terms, ironically, were almost precisely those advocated by the British General Staff, supported by the Admiralty, early in 1919.[180] Britain had also to acquiesce in the abandonment of the Capitulations and of any attempt to supervise Turkish finances.

Curzon had compared 'Sisyphus and his stone . . . [as] tame performers compared with my daily task' of negotiating with the Turks and coping with the lack of support of his allies.[181] Consequently, he counted it a triumph for British policy that he was at least able to ensure that the problem of Mosul was excluded from the peace negotiations. It was left, first, to separate Anglo-Turkish negotiations and, failing them, to the League of Nations to settle. This problem, none the less, haunted the Lausanne negotiations, for its oil implications were only too obvious.[182] Yet, despite the aims of Britain at San Remo and after, it was not until 1925 that the League awarded Mosul to Iraq and nearly a decade after that before oil was to start flowing through the pipeline.

If Harold Nicolson could later describe Britain's Turkish peace policy before Lausanne as 'trying to tie up a kicking hen in tissue paper',[183] he none the less rationalised that policy at the time in terms more acceptable to his seniors in the government:

> The idea which prompted our support of Greece was no emotional impulse but the natural expression of our historical policy: – the protection of India and the Suez Canal. For a century we had supported Turkey as the first line of defence in the Eastern Mediterranean. Turkey had proved a broken reed and we fell back on the second line, the line from Salamis to Smyrna . . . The Treaty of Sèvres was thus an immense asset had it succeeded.[184]

The Treaty of Sèvres did not succeed, and its failure brought the end of Ottoman rule in Turkey. Britain's contribution towards that end was, in the short term, very clear indeed. Not only did she help her allies, France and Italy, press the hated treaty on the defeated and shaky Ottoman regime, but she also supported the invasion of Anatolia by Turkey's traditional enemy, the Greeks. This, together with other moves of the time, such as the occupation of Constantinople, helped consolidate Nationalist feeling and organisation. The recognition implicit in the Allies negotiating and signing an international treaty with the Turkish Nationalists (while helping, albeit with some embarrassment, Turkey's hereditary ruler to flee the country) transformed a revolutionary regime into a national government. More directly, in the immediate postwar years Britain had helped herself and her allies to slices of the former Ottoman Empire so that, in fact, after 1920, apart from the later Mosul award, all that remained for the Great Powers to squabble over was the European and Anatolian rump: the Empire had disappeared if the Ottomans as yet remained.

In the long term it is harder to ascertain Britain's responsibility for the fall of an empire that was widely seen as imminent for a very long time. Indeed, in the decades before 1914 as in the preceding century, Britain's clear policy was to maintain the independence of Turkey and the territorial integrity of at least the central and Asiatic portions of its Empire. This did not inhibit Britain from using that Empire for her own purposes and so in effect undermining Turkish authority in many ways. None the less, as an individual Great Power involved in getting what she could out of the Ottoman Empire and using it as a pawn in the play of Great Power politics, Britain was no more responsible than any of the other Great Powers for weakening Ottoman authority, and rather less responsible than some. As the rise of the Young Turks showed, nationalist forces were likely to have arisen anyway, given the weak state of the sultan's regime, and sooner or later could have overthrown it. It so happened that in a war in which Britain, just as much as Turkey, was fighting for its survival Britain won and, in exacting the traditional compensation of a victor as well as rewards for her allies, helped destroy the Ottoman Empire.

Notes: Chapter 7

Abbreviations

Adm.   Admiralty records, Public Record Office, London
BD   *British Documents on the Origins of the War, 1898–1914*, ed. G. P. Gooch and
                 H. W. V. Temperley, 11 vols (London: 1926–38)
Cab.   Cabinet Office records, Public Record Office, London
Cmd   Command Papers
CO   Colonial Office records, Public Record Office, London
Confid. Print   Confidential Print, Foreign Office records, Public Record Office, London
DBFP   *Documents on British Foreign Policy 1919–1939*, first series (London: 1947–72)
FO   Foreign Office records, Public Record Office, London
PD, H of C   *Parliamentary Debates, House of Commons*
PD, H of L   *Parliamentary Debates, House of Lords*

1   *PD, H of L*, 4th ser. Vol. CXXI (1903), col. 1348. See also B. C. Busch, *Britain and the Persian Gulf 1894–1914* (Berkeley, Calif., 1967), pp. 255–7.
2   Foreign Office 'Memorandum respecting British interests in the Persian Gulf', 12 Feb. 1908, FO 881/9161; and included as app. 2 to FO Confid. Print no. 9953* and to Cab 16/10; Curzon's speech is also quoted in Earl of Ronaldshay, *The Life of Lord Curzon*, 3 vols (London, 1928), Vol. II, p. 316. See also Lord Newton, *Lord Lansdowne: A Biography* (London, 1929), p. 243.
3   'Report of the Sub-Committee of the Committee of Imperial Defence on the Baghdad Railway, Southern Persia, and the Persian Gulf', 26 Jan. 1909, Cab. 16/10.
4   *PD, H of L*, 5th ser., Vol. VII (1911), cols 587–8. Also see draft Foreign Office dispatch to Sir Louis Mallet, FO 371/2125, no. 33655. The draft was drawn up and initialled by Alwyn Parker, Assistant Clerk in the FO, on whom see below, p. 182.
5   See, for instance, Zara Steiner, 'The Foreign Office under Sir Edward Grey, 1905–1914', in F. H. Hinsley (ed.), *British Foreign Policy under Sir Edward Grey* (Cambridge, 1977), pp. 48–9.
6   D. C. M. Platt, *The Cinderella Service. British Consuls since 1825* (London/New York, 1971), pp. 131–2.
7   Lansdowne's policy towards the Gulf had already been anticipated by Curzon, both in his book, *Persia and the Persian Question* (London, 1892), and in his dispatch no. 615 to the Secretary of State for India (Lord George Hamilton), 21 Sept. 1899, *BD*, Vol. IV, no. 319, pp. 356–63. On the Foreign Secretaryship of Lansdowne, see also Zara Steiner, *The Foreign Office and Foreign Policy, 1898–1914* (Cambridge, 1969), ch. 2.
8   Sir Reader Bullard, *The Camels Must Go* (London, 1961), p. 61.
9   See below, p. 187.
10 See below, pp. 193–4.
11 See, for instance, private correspondence between Grey and O'Conor, 17 and 25 Dec. 1907, *BD*, Vol. V, nos 174 and 276, pp. 219–21.
12 Private letter from Lord Hardinge (Viceroy of India) to Sir Thomas Sanderson (now retired, previously Permanent Under-Secretary at the Foreign Office until 1906), 22 May 1913, Cambridge University Library, Hardinge MSS, 93/II/26.

13   Private letter from G. H. Fitzmaurice (Chief Dragoman at the Constantinople embassy) to William Tyrrell (Grey's Private Secretary and confidant), 25 Aug. 1908, *BD*, Vol. V, no. 210 Ed. Add., pp. 268–9.

14   Andrew Ryan, *The Last of the Dragomans* (London, 1951), p. 84.

15   See below, pp. 177, 180–3.

16   Marian Kent, *Oil and Empire: British Policy and Mesopotamian Oil, 1900–1920* (London/New York, 1976), pp. 121–2; and the same author's 'Asiatic Turkey, 1914–1916', in Hinsley, *British Foreign Policy*, pp. 443–4.

17   Kent, *Oil and Empire*, pp. 122–4; 'Asiatic Turkey', pp. 447–451; and see below, pp. 187, 191.

18   See below, pp. 189–93. Nicolson wrote perceptive first-hand accounts of both of these conferences in his two books, *Peacemaking 1919* (London, 1933) and *Curzon: The Last Phase, 1919–1925* (New York, 1934).

19   'Memorandum' containing instructions to a commercial attaché on taking up appointment, 1909 FO Confid. Print, no. 9421.

20   See, for instance, his views reflected in the correspondence in FO 371/1486, nos 53729, 55372 and 55479; FO 371/1760, nos 4977 and 4984; and FO 195/2449, file 18.

21   Ryan, *Last of the Dragomans*, pp. 152–3.

22   See, for instance, the sections in the Annual Report for Turkey for 1906 which Lamb and Fitzmaurice were acknowledged to have written, *BD*, Vol. V, pp. 7–20, 24–9.

23   Ryan, *Last of the Dragomans*, p. 124; private letter from Fitzmaurice to Tyrrell, 25 Aug. 1908, *BD*, Vol. V, no. 210, p. 268.

24   See, for instance, the comment in Sir Edwin Pears, *Forty Years in Constantinople* (London, 1916), pp. 344–7.

25   Private letter from Fitzmaurice to Tyrrell, 12 Apr. 1908, *BD*, Vol. V, no. 196, pp. 147–8. Although this was a 'private' letter to Grey's Private Secretary, he knew that it would be shown to the Foreign Secretary. See also below, p. 178.

26   Ryan, *Last of the Dragomans*, pp. 174–98. On Rumbold he was later to write that the High Commissioner exemplified 'solid qualities as opposed to brilliancy. It could be said of him that he saw little farther than the end of his nose, but saw exactly what was at the end of it' (ibid., p. 152).

27   According to E. G. Mears (*Modern Turkey* (New York, 1924), p. 350), the Constantinople Chamber of Commerce had a published membership of approximately 600 and was an active body with important affiliations not only in Constantinople but also extending through the Balkan states, south Russia, the Transcaucasus and the Levant. As the *Board of Trade Journal* shows, much of its Turkish information was received via the Constantinople Chamber of Commerce. See below, p. 177. On Block, see also below, n. 50, and in Fulton, above, pp. 153–4.

28   See, for instance, his letter to Hardinge, 21 June 1908, on the proposed Turkish customs increase and other matters, FO 371/762, no. 23941. Sir Edwin Pears's view on Block's actions is loyal but misleading; Pears, *Forty Years*, p. 346.

29   Enclosed in dispatch no. 452 Confidential, from Lowther to Grey, 3 July 1906, *BD*, Vol. V, no. 147, pp. 174–84.

30   Marian Kent, 'Agent of empire? The National Bank of Turkey and British foreign policy', *Historical Journal*, Vol. XVIII, no. 2 (1975), pp. 370–1.

31   Ryan, *Last of the Dragomans*, pp. 117–18.

32   ibid., p. 48; also see pp. 251–2. For similar sentiments from a fellow retired Levant Service consul, see Laurence Grafftey-Smith, *Bright Levant* (London, 1970), p. 13. Both are also quoted in Platt, *Cinderella Service*, p. 2.

33   For a biography of Cox, see Philip Graves, *The Life of Sir Percy Cox* (London, 1941).

34   'Duties of His Majesty's Consular Officers', Foreign Office Memorandum, 17 March 1913, Confid. Print no. 10344; Platt, *Cinderella Service*, ch. 4; and the autobiographical accounts already noted. See also Fulton, above, pp. 142–3.

35   The Commercial Intelligence Branch, set up in 1897, was a centre for the collection, organisation and dissemination of commercial information on such matters as trade statistics, tariffs and customs regulations, lists of firms abroad engaged in particular lines of business in different localities, contracts abroad open to tender, sources of supply and prices, regulations for commercial travellers, and so forth. It also provided a sample-room at its offices in Basinghall in the City and a confidential information service for a registered British clientele. Sir H. Llewellyn Smith, *The Board of Trade* (London, 1928), pp. 70–80; also descriptions in

successive issues of the *Board of Trade Journal*. Platt gives a detailed discussion on the whole question of commercial diplomacy in his *Finance, Trade and Politics in British Foreign Policy* (Oxford, 1968), pp. 102–40, 371–97. See also n. 27 above.

36 *Board of Trade Journal*, Oct.–Dec. 1908, p. 283. See also Ahmad, above, p. 23.

37 *Board of Trade Journal*, Oct.–Dec. 1908, p. 71. Some of this advice is discussed below, pp. 180–1, 182–3.

38 Notably the classic account by Maybelle K. Chapman, *Great Britain and the Baghdad Railway 1888–1914*, Smith College Studies in History, Vol. XXXI (Northampton, Mass., 1948). For some more recent writings on the subject, see Richard M. Francis, 'The British withdrawal from the Baghdad Railway project in April 1903', *Historical Journal*, Vol. XVI, no. 3 (1973), pp. 168–78; Marian Kent, 'Constantinople and Asiatic Turkey, 1905–1914', in Hinsley, *British Foreign Policy*, pp. 150–4. See also above, Trumpener, pp. 117, 122, and Fulton, passim.

39 For more detail on the following section of the chapter, see Kent, 'Asiatic Turkey', pp. 148–50.

40 Viscount Grey of Fallodon, *Twenty-Five Years, 1892–1916*, 2 vols (London/New York, 1925), Vol. I, p. 174.

41 Private letter from Fitzmaurice to Sir William Tyrrell (Grey's Private Secretary), 12 April 1908, *BD*, Vol. V, no. 196, pp. 247–8.

42 See, for instance, *Twenty-Five Years*, Vol. I, pp. 133, 172–4, 211–12, 257–60.

43 Annual Report for Turkey for 1908, *BD*, Vol. V, p. 251; private letters from Grey to Lowther, 21 July and 23 Aug. 1908, ibid., Vol. V, no. 204, pp. 263–4, and no. 208, pp. 266–7.

44 Dispatch no. 521 Confidential, from Lowther to Grey, 30 July 1910, *BD*, Vol. IX, pt 1, no. 161, pp. 180–3. Britain had appeared as interfering in Mesopotamia and the Persian Gulf; obstructive over Crete, Egypt, frontier relations with Persia, Turkey's desire to purchase a British warship and over seeming to be the leader among the Powers in imposing unwelcome conditions on Turkey in return for allowing an increase in Turkish customs duties; and, finally, she appeared unreasonable in the criticism increasingly voiced by British public opinion over the unconstitutional and restrictive acts of the new Turkish regime.

45 See Trumpener, above, p. 124.

46 Z. Y. Hershlag, *Introduction to the Modern Economic History of the Middle East*, 2nd rev. edn (Leiden, 1980), p. 67; he bases his figures on Mears, *Modern Turkey*, p. 357. Note that before the turn of the century Britain was in second place. The figures in Charles Issawi, *The Economic History of the Middle East, 1800–1914* (Chicago, Ill./London, 1966), are a little different (p. 94), using a Turkish source.

47 Kent, 'Agent of empire?', pp. 381, 388; and see below, pp. 180, 183. See also Issawi, *Economic History*, pp. 104–6. He omits to list the Constantinople Municipal Loan.

48 Minute by Grey, n.d., but 14 Sept. 1909 or later, on FO 371/762, no. 33649. See also Kent, 'Agent of empire?' p. 374.

49 ibid., pp. 374–81. See also above, Ahmad, p. 14, Bridge, p. 40, and Fulton, p. 157.

50 See below, pp. 180, 183–4. Sir Adam Block was Vice-Chairman of the Constantinople Telephone Company and a director of the Imperial Ottoman Docks, Arsenals and Naval Construction Company. On German obstruction at the Porte against this concession, see correspondence from Mallet to Grey, 6 and 25 Nov., 3 Dec. 1913, FO Confid. Print 1913, 10485, nos 54, 82 and 92.

51 W. W. Gottlieb, *Studies in Secret Diplomacy during the First World War* (London, 1957), p. 19.

52 'Memorandum on the position of British Trade in the Persian Gulf', Board of Trade, 1908 (n.d.) FO Confid. Print no. 9953*; also included as app. 8 to Cab. 16/10 of Jan. 1909, see especially pp. 245–6. The total value of Persian Gulf seaborne trade (but including trade with south Persian ports) was £8,205,000. Of this the combined British and Indian share was £6,467,000.

53 ibid; also *BD*, Vol. VI, no. 250, pp. 355–6, no. 352, pp. 468–72, and enclosure to no. 414, pp. 550–3. See also Hershlag, *Introduction*, p. 80, who cites Mears, *Modern Turkey*, p. 349.

54 Board of Trade Memorandum, 1908; also 'Trade and shipping in the Persian Gulf', memorandum by the Director of Naval Intelligence, 1908 (n.d.), included as app. 7 to FO Confid. Print no. 9953*; also in Cab. 16/10. Of the five British shipping lines which plied the Gulf trade three worked together as a 'Combine' or 'Shipping Conference' in organising their sailings. These were the Anglo-Algerian Shipping Co. (run by Messrs Strick & Co. Ltd), the

Bucknall Lines and the West Hartlepool Steam Navigation Co. A fourth company, the British Indian Steam Navigation Co., had the mail concession from Bombay (where it was brought by the P. & O. Co.); the fifth company was Messrs Andrew Weir & Co.

55　Board of Trade Memorandum, 1908.

56　ibid., also, 'Report upon the conditions and prospects of British trade in Mesopotamia', submitted by George Lloyd, Special Commissioner, to the Board of Trade Advisory Committee on Commercial Intelligence, 1908, FO Confid. Print 9324A, pp. 64–5. See also Hanna Batatu, *The Old Social Classes and the Revolutionary Movements of Iraq* (Princeton, NJ, 1978), pp. 238–9, 242. See also below, pp. 183–4.

57　The Mersina–Adana, the Smyrna–Cassaba and the Smyrna–Aidin lines had all been British built, financed and managed, and the Haidar Pasha–Ismidt line had for some years been leased to British subjects. Since 1857 a Euphrates Valley Railway Co. had held a concession for a railway from Alexandretta to Basra, but the scheme was, by the turn of the century, moribund. An interesting commentary on these matters is in the draft FO dispatch for Mallet (n. 4 above). See also Fulton, above, passim.

58　Kent, 'Constantinople and Asiatic Turkey', p. 155; see also Bosworth, above, p. 66.

59　George Lloyd's 'Report', p. 4.

60　On the Imperial Ottoman Bank, see 'The Imperial Ottoman Bank', Treasury Memorandum, 23 Dec. 1918, FO Confid. Print no. 11054; D. C. Blaisdell, *European Financial Control in the Ottoman Empire* (New York, 1929), passim; Kent, 'Agent of empire?'; Fulton, above, pp. 141–2, 145–6.

61　George Lloyd's 'Report', p. 5; Board of Trade Memorandum, 1908.

62　Private letter from Grey to Lowther, 23 Aug. 1908, *BD*, Vol. V, no. 208, p. 267.

63　Kent, 'Agent of empire?', pp. 370–2.

64　'The development of railway interests in Turkey, and the negotiations concerning the Bagdad Railway', FO Memorandum, n.d., FO Confid. Print no. 10890, p. 11. Although unsigned, the identical phraseology in parts of this memorandum, with the article on 'The Baghdad Railway negotiations', published in *The Quarterly Review*, Vol. 228 (Oct. 1917), anonymously but known to be by Alwyn Parker, shows identical authorship; some of the phraseology is also identical with the draft FO dispatch to Mallet, n. 4 above.

65　FO Memorandum, 12 Feb. 1908, FO 881/9161.

66　Board of Trade Memorandum, 1908; and 'British and German shipping in the Persian Gulf', further Board of Trade Memorandum, 23 Dec. 1908, signed A. Wilson Fox.

67　Director of Naval Intelligence memorandum, 'Trade and shipping in the Persian Gulf'.

68　'Report of the Sub-Committee of the Committee of Imperial Defence on the Baghdad Railway', FO Memorandum, n.d., FO Confid. Print no. 10890, p. 11. Although unsigned,

69　ibid., p. vii, and see pp. 172–3, above.

70　FO 'Memorandum respecting British interests in the Persian Gulf', p. 58.

71　ibid., p. 11, and Committee of Imperial Defence Sub-Committee Report, p. x; see also Kent, 'Constantinople and Asiatic Turkey', p. 152, and Busch, *Britain and the Persian Gulf*, ch. 10.

72　These disabilities were spelled out to Britain's Entente partners, France and Russia, and to Turkey and Germany. See, for instance, *BD*, Vol. VI, nos 250, 292, 352 and enclosure to 414. No. 352 was an important policy statement by Grey, the draft of which was prepared from May 1909 onwards with Board of Trade concurrence; Lowther, however, when asked for his views on the draft, wrote a detailed reply, among other things stating that he felt the Foreign Office was much too pessimistic about the likely damage to British trade – a reply considered by Hardinge and Grey as 'not helpful' and generally missing the point; correspondence of 27 May and 19 June 1909, FO 371/762, no. 20209. As the result of further correspondence reaching the Foreign Office the dispatch sent to Lowther officially was on quite different lines and the material in the draft was saved for later use; *BD*, Vol. VI, pp. 371–5.

73　FO confidential 'Memorandum' enclosed in dispatch no. 312 Secret, from Grey to Sir E. Goschen (Ambassador in Berlin), 23 Nov. 1910, ibid., enclosure to no. 414, p. 551. See also Trumpener, above, pp. 114–16, 118–19.

74　*BD*, Vol. VI, enclosure to no. 414, p. 551, and also in dispatch no. 107 Secret from Grey to Lowther, 20 April 1910; no. 352, pp. 468–72.

75　Repeatedly stated by Grey to Lowther and to the Turkish Ambassador (Tewfik Pasha), ibid., nos 292, 324, 340, 350, 352, 377, 388. See also memo by Grey to Tewfik Pasha, 23 Sept. 1909 and dispatch no. 840 from Lowther to Grey, 11 Oct. 1909, FO Confid. Print no. 9566, nos 118 and 208.

76 Letter from Grey to Goschen, 5 May 1910, *BD*, Vol. VI, no. 361, pp. 478–9; reproduced in Grey, *Twenty-Five Years*, Vol. I, p. 245. As Grey also wrote privately to Lowther on 14 July 1909, 'I am much more anxious to secure our interests against being damaged by the construction of the Baghdad Railway than to secure special advantages for ourselves, and I do not quite see how we are to guard against the construction of the Baghdad Railway without our participation unless we take advantage of such opportunities as the increase of the customs dues may give us for making conditions' (*BD*, Vol. VI, p. 374).

77 Telegram no. 61 from Grey to Lowther, 4 April 1910, *BD*, Vol. VI, no. 340, pp. 446–7, and memorandum from Grey to Tewfik Pasha, 30 April 1910, ibid., Vol. VI, no. 357, p. 474. Grey himself uses the expression 'lever' in his minute of early January 1911, ibid., Vol. X, pt 2, p. 16. The customs increase was by now also a lever to obtain recognition of the *status quo* of Koweit, as it was always also a lever for having lifted the restrictions on the borrowing powers of Egypt. See also minute by Eyre Crowe (then Senior Clerk, but in 1912 to become Assistant Under-Secretary at the Foreign Office), 27 March 1911, initialled by Grey, and again using the term 'lever'.

78 Reported in dispatch no. 96 Secret from Grey to Lowther, 18 April 1910, ibid., Vol. VI, no. 350, pp. 466–7, which Lowther was asked to read to both the Grand Vezir and the Minister for Foreign Affairs; see also his dispatch no. 107 Secret, 20 April 1910, ibid., Vol. VI, no. 352, pp. 468–72. For Lowther's reading of the dispatch, see no. 359, pp. 475–7, and for the official response to it of the Turkish Minister for Foreign Affairs, see no. 378, pp. 493–4.

79 Kent, 'Constantinople and Asiatic Turkey', pp. 153–4.

80 'The prospects of British trade in Mesopotamia and the Persian Gulf', report by R. E. Holland and J. H. Wilson, Joint Trade Commissioners (Delhi, 1917), FO Confid. Print no. 10988, p. 95.

81 Board of Trade Memorandum, 1908, and A. Wilson Fox memorandum; see also Busch, *Britain and the Persian Gulf*, pp. 373–4. On the Combine, see n. 54 above.

82 Board of Trade Memorandum, 1908, sect. 4, and Committee of Imperial Defence Sub-Committee report, p. viii. Holland and Wilson's 1917 report noted, moreover, in app. XXIII on the 'Result of a preliminary examination of Messrs Wönckhaus' office records seized in the Gulf', that the company 'was evidently in receipt of support from the German Government and took an important part in the Baghdad Railway enterprise', although 'All important records and books . . . seem to have been successfully destroyed' (p. 153). This is in contrast to the verbal account reported in Eugene Staley's 'Business and politics in the Persian Gulf: the story of the Wönckhaus firm', *Political Science Quarterly*, Vol. XLVIII, no. 3 (1933), pp. 367–85. In the same 1917 report, app. II deals with 'The operations of the Hamburg–America Steamship Company in the Persian Gulf', pp. 75–82.

83 Holland and Wilson's 1917 report, p. 78, refers to government of India dispatch no. 62, 23 May 1912; and pp. 79–80 to the fact that Sir Percy Cox recommended subsidies, April–July 1913, but the government of India accepted the opinion of the Board of Trade and did not advocate them.

84 ibid., pp. 79–81, and Statistical Tables, pp. 146–7. The Germans had captured almost all the sugar trade to the Gulf; by 1913 the shipping line operated into London, while the British lines had been forced to abandon loading from Hamburg and Antwerp. On competition in Arabistan, see n. 94 below.

85 Letter from Lord Inchcape, 13 Dec. 1913, ibid., pp. 80–1.

86 George Lloyd's report, p. 68.

87 ibid., p. 31.

88 The difficulties of such active government intervention are well brought out in Platt, *Finance, Trade and Politics*, pp. 114, 117–18, 123–4. He describes in particular the reluctance of larger firms, with their own information networks, to countenance such government intervention, which was most likely to assist small firms.

89 Kent, 'Constantinople and Asiatic Turkey', p. 163.

90 Board of Trade memo, pp. 250–1.

91 Kent, 'Agent of empire?', pp. 377–89.

92 Kent, *Oil and Empire*, chs 3–6, which corrects the account given in Fritz Fischer's *Krieg der Illusionen: Die deutsche Politik von 1911 bis 1914* (Düsseldorf, 1969), trans. as *War of Illusions* (New York, 1973).

93 Batatu, *Old Social Classes*, pp. 237, 275–6; also Holland and Wilson's 1917 report, app. VII, 'Navigation on the Tigris and Euphrates', p. 94.

94   ibid., pp. 81, 133. It was German competition in the form of an openly expressed German intention to drive the firm off the Karun River that led the Foreign Office in 1912 to approach Lord Inchcape to 'stiffen' the firm by reorganising it. By May 1914, German exports from Bushire and Arabistan virtually equalled British. Arabistan was an area of particular sensitivity to the British government because of its proximity to the oilfields and to Mesopotamia. On the British rejection of repeated Turkish offers of alliance, however, see Ahmad, above, pp. 13–14.

95   See D. W. Sweet, 'The Bosnian Crisis', in Hinsley, *British Foreign Policy*, pp. 178–92, and F. R. Bridge, *Great Britain and Austria-Hungary 1906–14: A Diplomatic History* (London, 1972), pp. 111–38; also Grey, *Twenty-Five Years*, Vol. I, pp. 168–86. See also Bridge, above, pp. 37–9.

96   See C. J. Lowe, 'Grey and the Tripoli War, 1911–1912', in Hinsley, *British Foreign Policy*, pp. 315–23. See also Bosworth, above, pp. 60–3.

97   See R. J. Crampton, 'The Balkans, 1909–1914', in Hinsley, *British Foreign Policy*, pp. 256–70; see also speech by Grey in the House of Commons, 12 Aug. 1913, included in Paul Knaplund, *Speeches on Foreign Affairs 1904–1914 by Sir Edward Grey* (London, 1931), pp. 208–24, and *Twenty-Five Years*, Vol. I, ch. 14. See also Bodger, above, pp. 93–4.

98   On Britain's part in this diplomatic flurry, see Kent, 'Constantinople and Asiatic Turkey', pp. 159–62. See also above, Bodger, pp. 94–5, and Trumpener, p. 120.

99   See Bridge, *Great Britain and Austria-Hungary*, pp. 5–10 and passim, also his 'Relations with Austria-Hungary and the Balkan States, 1905–1908', in Hinsley, *British Foreign Policy*, pp. 166–74; also Grey's speeches in the House of Commons on 1 Aug. 1907 and in Berwick-on-Tweed, 19 Dec. 1907, in Knaplund, *Speeches*, pp. 36, 42. See also above, Fulton, pp. 150–1, 153–4.

100   For detail on the Balkan Committee, see T. P. Conwell-Evans, *Foreign Policy from a Back Bench 1904–1918* (London, 1932).

101   Lansdowne's biographer described the scheme of Macedonian reform as 'little better than a gigantic sham' and wrote that 'it was the local jest in Salonica that whenever an effective reform was proposed the only doubt was whether it would be the Russian or the Austrian Agent who would be the first to oppose it' (Newton, *Lord Lansdowne*, pp. 302–3); cf. Bridge, above, pp. 34, 36–7.

102   Kent, 'Constantinople and Asiatic Turkey', pp. 156–9. Compare this British interest with Russia's: Bodger, above, pp. 77–80, 82–4, 100–1.

103   Telegram no. 260 from Grey to Lowther, 30 April 1912, and reply, telegram no. 402, 1 May 1912, *BD*, Vol. IX, pt. 1, nos 390 and 402, pp. 390–1.

104   Dispatch no. 77 and telegram no. 130 from Grey to Sir Fairfax Cartwright (Ambassador in Vienna), 22 and 25 Nov. 1912, ibid., Vol. IX, pt 1, nos 317 and 320, pp. 328, 330.

105   'Memorandum on the effect of a British evacuation of the Mediterranean on questions of foreign policy', FO, 8 May 1912, *BD*, Vol. X, pt 2, no. 386, p. 588.

106   See Crampton, 'The Balkans, 1909–1914': R. J. Bosworth, 'Britain and Italy's acquisition of the Dodecanese 1912–1915', *Historical Journal*, Vol. XIII, no. 4 (1970), pp. 683–705, and his *Italy, the Least of the Great Powers: Italian Foreign Policy before the First World War* (Cambridge, 1979), ch. ix, and also above, p. 66.

107   'Italian occupation of Aegean Islands and its effect on naval policy', Admiralty memorandum by Rear-Admiral E. C. T. Troubridge (Chief of War Staff, Admiralty), 29 June 1912, *BD*, Vol. IX, pt 1, no. 430, pp. 413–15. See also accompanying minute (n.d.) by Nicolson.

108   See Crampton, 'The Balkans, 1909–1914', pp. 266–9.

109   For the build-up to the war with Turkey, see Ulrich Trumpener, 'Liman von Sanders and the German–Ottoman alliance', *Journal of Contemporary History*, Vol. I, no. 4 (1966), pp. 179–92; Kent, 'Asiatic Turkey', pp. 436–8; and Trumpener, above, pp. 124–5.

110   Office of the Chief Political Officer I[ndian] E[xpeditionary] F[orce] 'D' [Sir Percy Cox], *A Sketch of the Political History of Persia, Iraq and Arabia, with Special Reference to the Present Campaign* (Calcutta, 1917) (For Official Use Only), p. 40.

111   For British wartime policy in the region, see B. C. Busch, *Britain, India and the Arabs, 1914–1921* (Berkeley, Calif., 1971), chs 1–5; also Kent, 'Asiatic Turkey', pp. 436–51, and *Oil and Empire*, ch. 7; and below, pp. 186–7, 188.

112   See above, pp. 183–4, and also Kent, 'Constantinople and Asiatic Turkey', pp. 154–6. But note also Grey's frank advice to the Turks to cede Edirne (Adrianople) to the Bulgarians in the First Balkan War; Ahmad, above, pp. 14–15.

113 Note by Grey (n.d.) on letter from Churchill to Grey, 16 Sept. 1914, Grey MSS, FO 800/87. This is ascribed to Kitchener in Martin Gilbert, *Winston S. Churchill*, Vol. III, *1914–1916* (London, 1971), p. 211. See also Cd 7628, Misc. no. 13 (1914), Correspondence Respecting Events Leading to the Rupture of Relations with Turkey. Sir Reader Bullard, then Acting Consul in Basra, gives his own account in *The Camels Must Go*, pp. 84–9.

114 Bodleian Library, Oxford, Asquith MSS, Cabinet Letters to the King, 1913–14, Vol. 7, meeting of 3 Nov. 1914; also Gilbert, *Churchill*, Vol. III, p. 217, and J. A. Spender and C. Asquith, *Life of Herbert Henry Asquith, Lord Oxford and Asquith* (London, 1932), Vol. II, p. 129.

115 For details of the decision to dispatch the force, see Brig.-Gen. F. J. Moberly, *Official History of the Great War: The Campaign in Mesopotamia 1914–1918*, 4 vols (London, 1923–7), Vol. I, pp. 89–106. The landing was particularly intended to assure the local Arab populations of British support against the Turks and to encourage Britain's Moslem subjects in India.

116 Winston Churchill, *The World Crisis*, 5 vols (London, 1923–32), Vol. II, pp. 197–8.

117 War Council discussions, 19 and 24 Feb. and 3 March 1915, Cab. 2/1 and 2, and memoranda by Hankey and Kitchener, 17 Feb., 4 March and 28 May 1915, Balfour MSS, Vol. 49703, fol. 167; Cab. 24/1, G. 10. and Asquith MSS, Vol. 129, fol. 89. See also Lowe, 'Italy and the Balkans', in Hinsley, *British Foreign Policy*, pp. 412–14, and his 'The failure of British diplomacy in the Balkans, 1914–1916', in *Canadian Journal of History*, Vol. IV, no. 1 (1969), pp. 77–80; Grey, *Twenty-Five Years*, Vol. II, pp. 180–3; J. T. Shotwell and F. Deak, *Turkey at the Straits* (New York, 1940), pp. 98–102; Paul Guinn, *British Strategy and Politics 1914–1918* (Oxford, 1965), p. 56. See also above, Bodger, pp. 96–9, and Fulton, pp. 162–3.

118 Bodleian Library, Oxford, Asquith MSS, Cabinet Letters to the King, 1915–1916, Vol. 8, meetings of 9 and 10 March 1915. See also Lowe, 'Italy and the Balkans', p. 418.

119 Telegram from Secretary of State for India to Viceroy, Secret, 16 Dec. 1914, Asquith MSS, Vol. 125, fol. 23, 'Précis of correspondence regarding the Mesopotamian expedition – its genesis and development', II, mentioned but not quoted in Moberly, *Official History*, Vol. I, p. 140. Grey's minute (n.d.) on which this telegram was based was on telegram from Viceroy to Crewe, 5 Dec. 1914, FO 371/2144.

120 Private letters from Hardinge to Sir Valentine Chirol (Foreign Editor of *The Times*), 2 Dec. 1914, and to Sir Arthur Nicolson (Permanent Under-Secretary of the Foreign Office), 4 Feb. 1915, Hardinge MSS, 93/II/263 and Public Record Office, London, 290, and Nicolson MSS 1915 I. See also Busch, *Britain, India and the Arabs*, pp. 15–23.

121 See, for instance, Kent, 'Asiatic Turkey', pp. 442–51; Isaiah Friedman, 'The Hussein–McMahon correspondence and the question of Palestine', *Journal of Contemporary History*, Vol. V, no. 2 (1970), and the comments by Toynbee and Friedman's reply, ibid, Vol. V, no. 4 (1970); Elie Kedourie, *In the Anglo-Arab Labyrinth* (Cambridge, 1976).

122 See, especially, C. J. Lowe, 'Britain and Italian intervention 1914–1915', *Historical Journal*, Vol. XII, no. 3 (1969), pp. 533–48; also his 'The failure of British diplomacy', and his 'Italy and the Balkans, 1914–1915'. The Treaty of London is to be found in Cmd 671, Misc. no. 7, Agreement between France, Russia, Great Britain and Italy, signed at London April 26 1915. Some of the difficulties of adjusting Italian ambitions to Anglo-French intentions are shown in minutes of meeting of War Cabinet, 2 Aug. 1917, Cab. 23/13, p. 61. See also Bosworth, above, pp. 69–71.

123 For a summary of these reasons, see Isaiah Friedman, *The Question of Palestine, 1914–1918* (London, 1973), pp. 286–91. On German interests in the region, see Trumpener, above, pp. 119–20.

124 'German and Turkish territories captured in the war', memorandum by Curzon, 5 Dec. 1917, Cab. 24/4, G.182; quoted in Friedman, *Question of Palestine*, p. 165. Already in April 1917 similar views had been noted by Leopold Amery and General Smuts, both newly appointed to Curzon's Sub-Committee on Territorial Desiderata on the Terms of Peace, while on 10 Aug. 1917 such arguments formed the basis of the War Cabinet's instructions to General Allenby, Commander-in-Chief of the Egyptian Expeditionary Force, to launch an all-out offensive against Turkey; ibid., pp. 172–4, 186.

125 ibid., pp. 168–9.

126 ibid., pp. 285–6. See also Jukka Nevakivi, *Britain, France, and the Arab Middle East, 1914–1920* (London, 1969), pp. 51–8, 94, 100–1.

127 ibid., pp. 59–84; Zeine N. Zeine, *The Struggle for Arab Independence*, 2nd edn (New York, 1977), pp. 22–3, 46–7, 186–8.

128 See Nevakivi, *Britain, France, and the Arab Middle East*, app. B, and Cmd 5964, Misc. no. 4 (1939), Statements made on behalf of His Majesty's Government in regard to the Future Status of certain parts of the Ottoman Empire. Some precedent had been set in the declarations made by the British government on the capture of Baghdad in March 1917 and of Jerusalem in Dec. 1917, see Nevakivi, *Britain, France, and the Arab Middle East*, p. 60.

129 ibid., p. 82.

130 Kent, *Oil and Empire*, pp. 118–19.

131 ibid., pp. 122–3. In any case, reciprocal assurances concerning concessions, rights and privileges of each Power in the other's sphere were reserved in the Grey–Cambon letters of 15 May 1916, as Sir Arthur Hirtzel (Secretary, Political and Secret Department, India Office) put it, to provide 'material for bargaining' (ibid., p. 124). Hirtzel's letter, sent on behalf of the Secretary of State for India, Sir Austen Chamberlain, mentioned with equal weight oil and religious interests.

132 Take, for instance, the Foreign Office's attitude over oil concessions, even if its arguments did, in the end, have to compromise with the need for a postwar accommodation with France; ibid., pp. 128–9, 145.

133 ibid., pp. 113, 129.

134 Minutes of War Cabinet meetings, 3, 21, 24, 25, 26, 31 Oct. 1918, Cab. 42/14, Mins 482A, 489A, 490A, 491A, 491B, 494A; also Moberly, *Official History*, Vol. IV, pp. 320–1, 324–8; Kent, *Oil and Empire*, pp. 125–7; V. H. Rothwell, 'Mesopotamia in British war aims, 1914–1918', *Historical Journal*, Vol. XIII, no. 2 (1970), pp. 286–94.

135 Keith Robbins, *Sir Edward Grey* (London, 1971), pp. 301–4; Kent, 'Asiatic Turkey', pp. 445–51; Zara Steiner, 'The Foreign Office and the war', in Hinsley, *British Foreign Policy*, pp. 516–31.

136 Sykes was also intended as the first Director of the Arab Bureau (see below), but India objected that it had 'no confidence' in him; see private letter from Hardinge to Nicolson, 18 Feb. 1916, Nicolson MSS 1916 I; also cited in Busch, *Britain, India and the Arabs*, p. 102.

137 Private letter from Cecil to Balfour, 8 Jan. 1918, British Museum, Balfour MSS, Vol. 49738. See also Busch, *Britain, India and the Arabs*, pp. 141, 207–8. On the successor to this committee, the Middle East Department, see below, pp. 188–9.

138 See Cab. 24/2, G.51 and 52, and Moberly, *Official History*, Vol. II, pp. 287 and app. XVIII.

139 'Establishment of an Arab Bureau in Cairo', proceedings and report on an inter-departmental conference, chaired by Brig.-Gen. G. M. W. Macdonogh (Director of Military Intelligence), 7 Jan. 1916; Cab 4/6 no. 1. See also FO Confid. Print 10812*, pp. 44–5, and report on the history of the *Arab Bulletin* (the publication of the Bureau) by D. G. Hogarth, who had been the first Director of the Bureau, in issue no. 100, 20 Aug. 1918, FO 882/27. See also, Busch, *Britain, India and the Arabs*, pp. 98–109, 202, 205.

140 Kent, 'Asiatic Turkey', and Elie Kedourie, 'Cairo and Khartoum on the Arab Question 1915–18', *Historical Journal*, Vol. VII, no. 2 (1964), pp. 280–97.

141 John Marlowe, *Late Victorian: The Life of Sir Arnold Talbot Wilson* (London, 1967), p. 249.

142 On the reasons for setting up Transjordan as a separate state, see Martin Gilbert, *Winston S. Churchill*, Vol. IV, *1917–1922* (London, 1975), pp. 538, 553–4, 559–62; A. S. Klieman, *Foundations of British Policy: The Cairo Conference of 1921* (Baltimore, Md, 1970), pp. 115–19, 230–5; Viscount Samuel, *Memoirs* (London, 1945), pp. 160–1; also 'Report on the Middle East Conference Held in Cairo and Jerusalem, March 12 to 30, 1921' FO Confid. Print no. 11683*, pp. 7–8, and documentation in CO 732/1, 2.

143 Minute from Churchill to Sir Archibald Sinclair, his Private Secretary, 12 Nov. 1921, Gilbert, *Churchill*, Vol. IV, p. 638.

144 Kent, *Oil and Empire*, pp. 141–5. See also Nicolson, *Curzon*, pp. 71–5, 110, and his *Peacemaking*, p. 314.

145 See especially Gilbert, *Churchill*, Vol. IV, ch. 29; also the very informative Report of the Inter-Departmental Committee on the Middle East, 31 Jan. 1921, CO 732/3 no. 8389.

146 The San Remo Agreement is to be found in Cmd 675, Misc. no. 11 (1920), Memorandum of Agreement between M. Philippe Berthelot, Directeur des Affaires Étrangères, and Professor Sir John Cadman, Director in Charge of His Majesty's Petroleum Department. See also Cmd 1785. League of Nations. Mandate for Palestine . . . December 1922, p. 2.

147 See especially Nevakivi, *Britain, France, and the Arab Middle East*, passim; Kent, *Oil and Empire*, ch. 8 and app. IV; and *DBFP*, Vol. IV, chs 2 and 4, Vol. VII, ch. 1.

148 'Memorandum by the General Staff on Mesopotamia', circulated to the Cabinet by the

Secretary for War (Churchill) on 12 Nov. 1919, Cab. 24/93, CP 120 Secret, app. I; despite the political objections of the Foreign Office to such a scheme its military significance was upheld at an interdepartmental meeting held at the War Office on 29 Oct. 1919, FO 371/4231, no. 148291.

149   See discussion between Lloyd George and Berthelot at the Allied Conference held at 10 Downing Street on 17 Feb. 1920, *DBFP*, Vol. VII, no. 12, pp. 103–7; and Kent, *Oil and Empire*, pp. 151–5.

150   Memorandum by Hardinge, 26 Feb. 1919, of an interdepartmental meeting on 'The future of the Baghdad Railway', FO 608/231, no. 2633. Ironically, it was Hardinge who, in 1915, as Viceroy of India, had written of his intense dislike of Britain's financial involvement in Persian oil and the imperial commitments that went with it; private letter from Hardinge to Chirol, 21 April 1915, Hardinge MSS, 93/II/325, and repeated more formally in a private letter to Nicolson, 26 April 1915, ibid., 93/II/327.

151   The Treaty of Sèvres is to be found in Cmd 964, Treaty Series no. 11 (1920), Treaty of Peace with Turkey. Signed at Sèvres, August 10 1920. See also Cmd 1195, Misc. no. 4 (1921), Franco-British Convention of December 23 1920, on Certain Points connected with the Mandates for Syria and the Lebanon, Palestine and Mesopotamia; and Cmd 1500, Mandates. Final Drafts of the Mandates for Mesopotamia and Palestine . . . August 1921. And see dispatch no. 3435 from Curzon to Hardinge, 29 Dec. 1921, FO Confid. Print no. 11942, no. 316, p. 429.

152   See, for instance, Gilbert, *Churchill*, Vol. IV, passim, and *Companion Volumes* 2 and 3; Klieman, *Foundations*; Busch, *Britain, India and the Arabs*, chs 7–9; Cmd 1700, Palestine. Correspondence with the Palestine Arab Delegation and the Zionist Organisation, June 1922.

153   Letter from Churchill to Sir Archibald Sinclair, 9 July 1921, Gilbert, *Churchill*, Vol. IV, p. 798.

154   Minute for Churchill by Shuckburgh, 28 July 1921, CO 732/2, no. 37194.

155   Churchill's response to the Arab deputation, 28 March 1921, Gilbert, *Churchill*, Vol. IV, p. 565. Curzon expressed the same view to the French Ambassador the following year; dispatch no. 990 from Curzon to Hardinge, 6 April, 1921, CO 732/1, no. 17713. See also Hubert Young, *The Independent Arab* (London, 1933), p. 277.

156   Michael Llewellyn Smith, *Ionian Vision: Greece in Asia Minor 1919–1922* (London, 1973), pp. 74–9; *DBFP*, Vol. VII, no. 20, pp. 186–8, no. 26, pp. 238–9, and no. 29, pp. 229–34, on giving the Greeks Smyrna (though under nominal Turkish suzerainty); B. C. Busch, *Mudros to Lausanne: Britain's Frontier in West Asia, 1918–1923* (New York, 1976), pp. 86–98 and ch. 4. See also Cmd 963, Treaty Series no. 12, 1920, Tripartite Agreement between the British Empire, France and Italy respecting Anatolia. Signed at Sèvres, August 10 1920, *DBFP*, Vol. VIII, nos 13 and 19, pp. 132–6, 141–3, 210–14, and relevant correspondence in Adm. 116/3240.

157   Letter from Adm. Sir John de Robeck to Curzon, 9 March 1920, *DBFP*, Vol. XIII, no. 17, p. 18, also no. 32, p. 48, and no. 513, p. 765. On Churchill and the General Staff's views see 'Turkey', Cab. memorandum of 7 June 1920, Cab. 24/107, quoted in Gilbert, *Churchill*, Vol. IV, pp. 485–6; 'General Staff memorandum on the situation in Turkey' (secret), 15 March 1920, Cab. 24/101, CP 966 and *DBFP*, Vol. XIII, no. 23, p. 38; 'General Staff memorandum on the Turkish Peace Treaty' (secret), 1 April 1920, ibid., no. 40, pp. 54–7, and Churchill's Cab. memorandum, 'Greek territorial claims in Turkey', Dec. 1920, Cab. 24./116, CP 2275, app. D., pp. 7–8. See also Churchill, *The World Crisis*, Vol. V, *The Aftermath*, p. 388, and Smith, *Ionian Vision*, pp. 122–3.

158   See Gilbert, *Churchill*, Vol. IV, pp. 477–8, 485, and *Companion Volume 2*, pp. 991–2, 1114–16, 1122–3, 1245–50, 1260–1; C. E. Callwell, *Field Marshal Sir Henry Wilson: His Life and Diaries*, 2 vols (London, 1927), Vol. II, p. 244. Churchill, *The Aftermath*, p. 419.

159   Ronaldshay, *Curzon*, Vol. III, pp. 262–3, 266, 270–1; Nicolson, *Curzon*, pp. 106–7; on Wilson's views see 'Notes of a meeting held at President Wilson's house . . . June 25', *DBFP*, Vol. IV, no. 426, p. 644; on Balfour's views see 'The future of Constantinople. (Note by Sir Maurice Hankey)' (secret), 6 Jan. 1920, Cab. 24/95, CP 390; on Clemenceau's views see 'Notes of a conversation at 10 Downing St . . . on Thursday, December 11, 1919 . . .', *DBFP*, Vol. II, no. 55, pp. 727–33.

160   Apart from the documentation above, which bears out this conclusion, see also the remarks of his contemporaries. e.g. in Churchill, *The Aftermath*, pp. 414–17; cf., too, the mutually mistrustful views about each other of the Prime Minister and his Chief of the Imperial General

Staff, Sir Henry Wilson, in Callwell, *Wilson*, Vol. II, p. 243, and Lord Ridell's *Intimate Diary of the Peace Conference and After, 1918–1923* (London, 1933), p. 208.

161 'Memorandum by Earl Curzon on the future of Constantinople', *DBFP*, Vol. IV, no. 646, pp. 992–1000; see also Stephen Roskill, *Hankey: Man of Secrets*, 3 vols (London, 1970–4), Vol. II, pp. 142–3, and Nicolson, *Curzon*, pp. 112–15.

162 Allied Conferences held at 10 Downing Street, 5, 8 and 10 March 1920, *DBFP*, Vol. VII, no. 38, pp. 300–6, no. 50, pp. 411–23, no. 55, pp. 450–7; also nos 36 and 37, pp. 291–9. See also Smith, *Ionian Vision*, p. 120, and Busch, *Mudros to Lausanne*, pp. 201–8.

163 Minutes of Cabinet meeting, 17 June 1920, Cab. 23/22; quoted in Gilbert, *Churchill*, Vol. IV, p. 487.

164 The Agreement is printed as Cmd 1556, Turkey No. 2 (1921). Dispatch from His Majesty's Ambassador at Paris, enclosing the Franco-Turkish Agreement signed at Angora on October 20, 1921, and included in *DBFP*, Vol. XVII, no. 502, pp. 564–9; on the correspondence between Britain and France over the agreement, see Cmd 1570, Turkey No. 1 (1922). Correspondence between His Majesty's Government and the French Government respecting The Angora Agreement of October 20, 1921; and correspondence in *DBFP*, Vol. XVII, nos 432, 434 and 436, pp. 461–9; CO 732/2, nos 55227 and 55726. On Curzon and Poincaré's discussions, *see DBFP*, Vol. XVII, nos 496 (enclosures) and 627, pp. 536–56 and 813–17. See also Nicolson, *Curzon*, pp. 260–4, 273–4.

165 Telegrams nos 218, 319 and 320 between Curzon and Earl Granville (since 21 Aug. 1917 'H.M. Minister to the King of the Hellenes', Athens), 2–3 Dec. 1920, *DBFP*, Vol. XII, nos 457, 460 and 461, pp. 533–5. See also Smith, *Ionian Vision*, pp. 166–8, and Churchill, *The Aftermath*, p. 412.

166 See documentation in *DBFP*, Vol. XVII, nos 112, 130, 517, 684, 729, 738 and 746, pp. 130, 150–2, 595–8, 883–4, 920, 930–1, 937–8; CO 732/2, no. 63244; Ronaldshay, *Curzon*, Vol. III, p. 283. One of the Foreign Office's worries was that the arms would be used against Britain in Iraq.

167 Smith, *Ionian Vision*, pp. 192–7, and Roskill, *Hankey*, Vol. II, pp. 223–4, on the advance in March; Hankey also recorded his own 'grave misgivings' about its outcome, and noted that Lloyd George looked 'very tired and ill'. See also FO 371/6466, no. E2960, and FO 371/7853, no. E415. On Lloyd George's speech in the House of Commons, 4 Aug. 1922, see *PD, H of C*, 5th ser., Vol. 157, cols 1997–2006, especially, 2004; *DBFP*, Vol. XVII, no. 727, pp. 918–19; Nicolson, *Curzon*, p. 270, and Smith, *Ionian Vision*, pp. 282–3.

168 On the Chanak crisis and especially Britain's Cabinet discussions and her relations with the Dominions, see Gilbert, *Churchill*, Vol. IV, pp. 820–62, and *Companion Volume* 3, Sept.–Nov. 1922. Britain's diplomatic efforts over the crisis are documented in *DBFP*, Vol. XVIII, ch. 1. See also Roskill, *Hankey*, Vol. II, pp. 283–95, and his *Naval Policy between the Wars*, 2 vols (London, 1968–76), Vol. I, pp. 199–200.

169 Reproduced in Churchill, *The Aftermath*, pp. 452–4. See also unnumbered telegram, Private and Secret, from Curzon to Rumbold, 16 Sept. 1922, *DBFP*, Vol. XVIII, no. 32, pp. 29–30.

170 Telegram no. 312, Urgent, Most Secret, from Crowe to Hardinge (now Ambassador in Paris), 21 Sept. 1922, ibid., no. 43, pp. 62–3. Since 1920 Crowe had been Permanent Under-Secretary at the Foreign Office.

171 Telegram no. 290, Secret, from Curzon to Sir Auckland Geddes (Ambassador in Washington), 26 Sept. 1922, ibid., no. 60, p. 102. For the American reply, see ibid., n. 3.

172 Notes of conferences held at the Quai d'Orsay, 20, 22 and 23 Sept., and unnumbered telegram from Hardinge to Crowe, 23 Sept., ibid., nos 41, 42, 48, 51 and 52, pp. 38–50, 50–61, 66–85, 88–96, 96–7. Curzon was formally congratulated by the Cabinet on his 'firmness and self-restraint' in his 'painful interview with Monsieur Poincaré', ibid., no. 49, pp. 85–6.

173 See ibid., nos 51 and 52, pp. 93 n. 8, 96–7.

174 Notes of conferences at the Quai d'Orsay, 6 and 7 Oct., ibid., nos 106–8, pp. 155–76; telegram no. 369 from Crowe to Hardinge, and telephone message from Curzon to Prime Minister, 7 Oct. 1922, ibid., nos 109–10, pp. 176–7; Cmd 1641, Misc. no. 3 (1922). Pronouncement by Three Allied Ministers for Foreign Affairs respecting the Near Eastern Situation. Paris, March 27, 1922.

175 Ultimatum (War Office telegram no. 91255) included in telegram no. 332 from Curzon to Hardinge, 30 Sept. 1922, *DBFP*, Vol. XVIII, no. 78, pp. 117–18; see also Gilbert, *Churchill*, Vol. IV, pp. 841–2, and for Harington's reply of 1 Oct., pp. 849–50. In Cabinet, Curzon urged

cancellation of the ultimatum but was opposed by Chamberlain (then Lord Privy Seal), Lord Lee (First Lord of the Admiralty), Lord Birkenhead (Lord Chancellor) and Churchill; Gilbert, *Churchill*, Vol. IV, pp. 844–5. On the Convention see telegram no. 554, Most Urgent, from Rumbold to Curzon, 11 Oct. 1922, *DBFP*, Vol. XVIII, no. 119, pp. 186–7, and Gilbert, pp. 860–1. On congratulations to Harington see *DBFP*, Vol. XVIII, no. 119 nn. 3 and 4, p. 187.

176 Roskill, *Hankey*, Vol. II, pp. 289–90. The 'militants' (Hankey's apposite term) also included Sir Robert Horne (Chancellor of the Exchequer) and Frederick Guest (Secretary of State for Air).

177 On the negotiations and the Treaty see *DBFP*, Vol. XVIII, chs 2–4; Cmd 1814, Turkey No. 1 (1923). Lausanne Conference on Near Eastern Affairs 1922–1923. Records of Proceedings and Draft Terms of Peace; Cmd 1929, Treaty Series No. 16 (1923), Treaty of Peace with Turkey and other instruments signed at Lausanne on July 24 1923 . . .; Cmd 1946, Treaty Series No. 17 (1923), Notes exchanged between the British and French Delegates at Lausanne regarding Certain Concessions in Territories detached from Turkey. Signed at Lausanne, July 24 1923. See also Roskill, *Naval Policy*, Vol. I, pp. 200–1, and Ryan, *Last of the Dragomans*, pp. 169–70.

178 Churchill, *The Aftermath*, p. 465.

179 See also 'Memorandum by Mr H. G. Nicolson respecting the freedom of the Straits', FO, 15 Nov. 1922, *DBFP*, Vol. XVIII, app. I, pp. 974–83. Of the Straits agreement Churchill wrote: 'The control of the fateful Straits reverted to the Turk under the thinnest of disguises', *The Aftermath*, p. 465, but cf. with Editor's note, *DBFP*, Vol. XVIII, p. vii.

180 Cabinet Memorandum by Churchill, Dec. 1920, 'Greek territorial claims in Turkey', and General Staff memorandum, 'General Staff desiderata regarding territorial adjustments', 19 Feb. 1920, Cab. 24/116, CP 2275, app. D and annexure, pp. 7–8.

181 Telegram no. 198, from Curzon to Crowe, 12 Jan. 1923, FO 839/17, no. 1032.

182 See, e.g., documentation in FO 371/9085–9.

183 Nicolson, *Peacemaking*, p. 340.

184 'Memorandum by Mr Nicolson on future policy towards King Constantine', 20 Dec. 1920, *DBFP*, Vol. XII, no. 488, p. 55. The memorandum also included summaries of French and Italian policy.

Bibliography

Because of the fullness of the annotation for the individual chapters the following bibliography is compressed and, for its secondary sources, selective. Most of the works cited are in English, but some works not in English that have been of particular use in the chapters or are of particular intrinsic merit for the subject have also been included. It should also be recalled, as pointed out in the notes to Chapter 4, that Western students of Russian foreign policy in the decades preceding the October Revolution have not yet been given access to Soviet archives and are therefore dependent on selective material published in the Soviet Union between the wars, on the works of ex-Tsarist officials and scholars in emigration, and on material published in the diplomatic document collections of the other Powers.

Primary Sources

Manuscripts
(a) *Austrian*
       Haus-, Hof-, und Staatsarchiv, Vienna
       Administrative Regisratur
       Politisches Archiv
       Nachlass Aehrenthal
       Nachlass Berchtold
       Nachlass Mensdorff

(b) *British*
       Public Record Office, London
       Admiralty records:
       Secretary's Department   Adm. 116

       Cabinet records:
       Committee of Imperial Defence
              Memoranda, Misc.   Cab. 4
       Committee of Imperial Defence
              Ad Hoc Sub-Committees of Inquiry   Cab. 16
       Cabinet Minutes   Cab. 23
       Cabinet Memoranda   Cab. 24

       Colonial Office records:
       Original correspondence, Middle East, 1921–   CO 732

       Foreign Office records:
       Embassy and Consular, 1906–, Turkey   FO 195
       Political   FO 371
       Peace Conference of 1919–20   FO 608
       Private collections: including
              Grey papers
              Nicolson papers   FO 800
       Eastern Conference, Lausanne, 1922–3   FO 839
       Confidential Print, Numerical Series   FO 881
       Arab Bureau Papers   FO 882

Bodleian Library, Oxford
Asquith papers

British Museum, London
Balfour papers

Cambridge University Library, Cambridge
Hardinge papers

(c) *French*
Archives du Ministère des Affaires Étrangères, Paris
Grand Guerre, Turquie
Levant, Turquie
Turquie
Papiers Constans
Papiers Delcassé

Archives de la Préfecture de Police, Paris

Bibliothèque Nationale, Paris
Papiers Étienne

(d) *German*
(including collections in the United States of America)

Auswärtiges Amt, Bonn
Microfilmed files of the German Foreign Office, 1867–1920
Nachlass Miquel, Hans von
Nachlass Weitz, Paul

Bundesarchiv, Koblenz
Nachlass Bülow, Bernhard von

Bundesarchiv-Militärarchiv, Freiburg
Nachlass N40, Mittelberger, Hilmar Ritter von
Nachlass N227, Morgen, Curt von
Nachlass N80, Mudra, Bruno von

Hoover Library, Stanford University
The Papers of Dr Heinrich Kanner of Vienna

Yale University Library
Ernst Jäckh papers

(e) *Italian*
Archivio Centrale della Stato, Rome

Archivio storico, Ministero degli Affari Esteri, Rome
Archivio riservato di gabinetto
Archivio di gabinetto
Archivio politica

Printed Documentary Collections
Adamov, E. A. (ed.), *Evropeiskie derzhavy i Turtsiia vo vremia mirovoi voiny: Konstantinopol' i prolivy. Po sekretnym dokumentam byvshego Ministerstva inostrannykh del*, 2 vols (Moscow, 1925–6).
Adamov, E. A. (ed.), *Razdel aziatskoi Turtsii po sekretnym dokumentam Biblioteki Ministerstva inostrannykh del* (Moscow, 1924).
Anderson, M. S., *The Great Powers and the Near East, 1774–1923* (London, 1970).
British Documents on the Origins of the War, 1898–1914, ed. G. P. Gooch and H. W. V. Temperley, 11 vols (London, 1926–38).
I documenti diplomatici italiani, 4th series, Vol. XII and 5th series, Vol. I, ed. A. Torre (Rome, 1954–64).
Documents diplomatiques français, 1871–1914 (Paris, 1929–55).
Documents on British Foreign Policy 1919–1939, Series I (London, 1947–72), Vols II and IV, ed. E. L. Woodward and R. Butler; Vols. VII, XII and XIII, ed. R. Butler and J. P. T. Bury; Vols XVII and XVIII, ed. W. N. Medlicott, D. Dakin and M. E. Lambert.
Die Grosse Politik der Europäischen Kabinette, 1871–1914, ed. Johannes Lepsius, A. Mendelssohn-Bartholdy and Friedrich Thimme, 40 vols (Berlin, 1922–7).
Ebel, Gerhard (ed.), *Botschafter Paul Graf von Hatzfeldt: Nachgelassene Papiere*, 2 vols (Boppard, 1976).
Eliav, Mordechai (ed.), *Die Juden Palästinas in der deutschen Politik: Dokumente aus dem Archiv des deutschen Konsulats in Jerusalem 1842–1914*, 2 vols (Tel Aviv, 1973).
Hurewitz, J. C., *Diplomacy in the Near and Middle East*, 2 vols (Princeton, NJ, 1956).
Mezhdunarodnye otnosheniia v epokhu imperializma. Dokumenty iz arkhivov tsarskogo i vremennogo pravitel'stv 1878–1917, Series II, Vols 18–20; Series III, Vols 1–6 (Moscow, 1931–). Translated into German as: Hoetzsh, O. (ed.), *Die internationalen Beziehungen im Zeitalter des Imperialismus* (Berlin, 1931–).
Vietsch, Eberhard von (ed.), *Gegen die Unvernunft: Der Briefwechsel zwischen Paul Graf Wolff Metternich und Wilhelm Solf 1915–1918* (Bremen, 1964).

Official Journals

Board of Trade Journal
Command Papers, House of Commons: Cd 7628; Cmd 671, 675, 963, 964, 1195, 1500, 1556, 1570, 1641, 1700, 1785, 1814, 1929, 1946, 5964
Journal officiel, Chambre des Députés, Paris
Krasnyi arkhiv, Tsentral'nyi arkhiv: RSFSR, Moscow, Vols VI, 1924; XVIII, 1926; XLVI–XLVIII, 1931; LVIII, LXI, 1933; and LXIX, LXX, 1935
Parliamentary Debates, House of Commons
Parliamentary Debates, House of Lords

Secondary Sources

Books and Theses

Ahmad, Feroz, *The Young Turks: The Committee of Union and Progress in Turkish Politics, 1908–1914* (Oxford, 1969).
Albertini, Luigi, *The Origins of the War of 1914*, 3 vols (London, 1952–7).
Albrecht-Carrié, R., *Italy at the Paris Peace Conference* (Hamden, Conn., 1966).
Allen, W. E. D., and Muratoff, P., *Caucasian Battlefields: A History of Wars on the Turco-Caucasian Border, 1828–1921* (Cambridge, 1953).

Anderson, M. S., *The Eastern Question, 1774–1923* (London, 1966).

Andrew, C., *Théophile Delcassé and the Making of the Entente Cordiale* (London, 1968).

Askew, William C., *Europe and Italy's Acquisition of Libya, 1911–12*, (Durham, NC, 1942).

Atatürk, Kemal, *A Speech Delivered by Mustafa Kemal Atatürk 1927* new edn (Istanbul, 1963).

Auffray, B., *Pierre de Margerie, 1861–1942* (Paris, 1976).

Balfour, Michael, *The Kaiser and His Times* (New York, 1972).

Barker, A. J., *The Bastard War: The Mesopotamian Campaign of 1914–1918* (New York, 1967).

Batatu, Hanna, *The Old Social Classes and the Revolutionary Movements of Iraq* (Princeton, NJ, 1978).

Bayur, Yusuf Hikmet, *Türk inkilâbi tarihi*, 3 vols in 10 parts (Ankara, 1940–67).

Berkes, Niyazi, *The Development of Secularism in Turkey* (Montreal, 1964).

Bernstorff, Johann Graf, *Erinnerungen und Briefe* (Zurich, 1936).

Bestuzhev, I. B., *Bor'ba v Rossii po voprosam vneshnei politiki, 1908–1910* (Moscow, 1961).

Bihl, Wolfdieter, *Die Kaukasus-Politik der Mittelmächte*, Part I, *Ihre Basis in der Orient-Politik und ihre Aktionen 1914–1917* (Vienna, 1975).

Biliotti, A., *La Banque Imperiale Ottomane* (Paris, 1909).

Blaisdell, D. C., *European Financial Control in the Ottoman Empire* (New York, 1929).

Bosworth, Richard J. B., *Italy, the Least of the Great Powers: Italian Foreign Policy before the First World War* (Cambridge, 1979).

Braude, B., and Lewis, B. (eds), *Christians and Jews in the Ottoman Empire*, 2 vols (New York, 1982).

Bridge, F. R., *From Sadowa to Sarajevo* (London, 1972).

Bridge, F. R., *Great Britain and Austria-Hungary 1906–1914: A Diplomatic History* (London, 1972).

Bullard, Sir Reader, *The Camels Must Go* (London, 1961).

Busch, B. C., *Britain and the Persian Gulf 1894–1914* (Berkeley, Calif., 1967).

Busch, B. C., *Britain, India and the Arabs, 1914–1921* (Berkeley, Calif., 1971).

Busch, B. C., *Mudros to Lausanne: Britain's Frontier in West Asia, 1918–1923* (New York, 1976).

Callwell, C. E., *Field-Marshal Sir Henry Wilson: His Life and Diaries*, 2 vols (London, 1927).

Cambon, P., *Correspondance*, 3 vols (Paris, 1940–6).

Cecil, Lamar, *The German Diplomatic Service, 1871–1914* (Princeton, NJ, 1976).

Chapman, Maybelle K., *Great Britain and the Baghdad Railway 1888–1914*, Smith College Studies in History, Vol. XXXI (Northampton, Mass., 1948).

Churchill, Winston S., *The World Crisis*, 5 vols (London, 1923–31).

Ciasca, R., *Storia coloniale dell'Italia contemporanea* (Milan, 1938).

Conwell-Evans, T. P., *Foreign Policy from a Back Bench 1904–1918* (London, 1932).

Craig, Gordon, A., *From Bismarck to Adenauer: Aspects of German Statecraft*, rev. edn (New York, 1965).

Crampton, R. J., *The Hollow Détente: Austro-German Relations in the Balkans 1911–1914* (London, 1980).

Dakin, D., *The Greek Struggle in Macedonia, 1897–1913* (Thessaloniki, 1966).

Dallin, A., *et al.* (eds), *Russian Diplomacy in Eastern Europe, 1914–1917* (New York, 1963).

Davison, Roderic, 'Turkish diplomacy from Mudros to Lausanne', in G. Craig and F. Gilbert (eds), *The Diplomats 1919–1939*, Vol. I (Princeton, NJ, 1953).

Decleva, E., *Da Adua a Sarajevo: la politica estera italiana e la Francia, 1896–1914* (Bari, 1971).

Del Boca, A., *Gli italiani in Africa orientale: dall'unità alla marcia su Roma* (Bari, 1976).

Demirhan, Gen. Pertev, *General-Feldmarschall Colmar Freiherr von der Goltz . . . Aus meinen persönlichen Erinnerungen* (Göttingen, 1960).

Djemal Pasha, Ahmed, *Memories of a Turkish Statesman, 1913–1919* (London, 1922).

Ducruet, Jean, *Les Capitaux européens au Proche-Orient* (Paris, 1964).

Earle, E. M., *Turkey, the Great Powers and the Baghdad Railway: A Study in Imperialism* (New York, 1924).

Emin, Ahmed, *Turkey in the World War* (New Haven, Conn./Oxford, 1930).

Feis, Herbert, *Europe the World's Banker 1870–1914* (New Haven, Conn., 1930).

Findley, Carter V., *Bureaucratic Reform in the Ottoman Empire: The Sublime Porte 1789–1922* (Princeton, NJ, 1980).

Fischer, Fritz, *Griff nach der Weltmacht: Die Kriegszielpolitik des kaiserlichen Deutschland 1914–18* (Düsseldorf, 1961); trans. as *Germany's Aims in the First World War* (New York, 1967).

Fischer, Fritz, *Krieg der Illusionen: Die deutsche Politik von 1911 bis 1914* (Düsseldorf, 1969); trans. as *War of Illusions* (New York, 1973).

Fleury, Antoine, *La Pénétration allemande au Moyen-Orient 1919–1939* (Leiden, 1977).

Florinksy, M., *Russia: A History and an Interpretation*, 2 vols (New York, 1947).

Friedman, Isaiah, *Germany, Turkey, and Zionism 1897–1918* (Oxford, 1977).

Friedman, Isaiah, *The Question of Palestine, 1914–1918* (London, 1973).

Geiss, Imanuel, *German Foreign Policy 1871–1914* (London, 1976).

Geyer, D., *Der Russische Imperialismus* (Göttingen, 1977).

Giessler, Klaus-Volker, *Die Institution des Marineattachés im Kaiserreich* (Boppard, 1976).

Gilbert, Martin, *Winston S. Churchill*, Vol. III, *1914–1916*, Vol. IV, *1917–1922*, and *Companion Volumes* to Vol. IV, nos 2 and 3 (London, 1971–5).

Gontault-Biron, R. de, and Le Reverend, L., *D'Angora à Lausanne* (Paris, 1924).

Gothaischer Genealogischer Hofkalender nebst Diplomatisch-statisticschem Jahrbuch (Gotha, 1871–1919).

Gottlieb, W. W., *Studies in Secret Diplomacy during the First World War* (London, 1957).

Grafftey-Smith, Laurence, *Bright Levant* (London, 1970).

Grey of Fallodon, Viscount, *Twenty-Five Years, 1892–1916*, 2 vols (London/New York, 1925).

Gurko-Kriazhin, V. A., *Blizhnii Vostok i derzhavy* (Moscow, 1925).

Hallgarten, George W. F., *Imperialismus vor 1914*, 2nd edn, 2 vols (Munich, 1963).

Haslip, Joan, *The Sultan: The Life of Abdul Hamid II* (London, 1958).

Helmreich, E. C., *The Diplomacy of the Balkan Wars* (Cambridge, Mass., 1938).

Helmreich, Paul, *From Paris to Sèvres: The Partition of the Ottoman Empire at the Peace Conference of 1919–20* (Columbus, Ohio, 1974).

Hershlag, Z. Y., *Introduction to the Modern Economic History of the Middle East*, 2nd rev. edn (Leiden, 1980).

Hinsley, F. H. (ed.), *British Foreign Policy under Sir Edward Grey* (Cambridge, 1977).

Hohorst, Gerd, *et al* (eds), *Sozialgeschichtliches Arbeitsbuch: Materialien zur Statistik des Kaiserreichs 1870–1914* (Munich, 1975).

Hopwood, D., *The Russian Presence in Syria and Palestine, 1843–1914* (Oxford, 1969).

Hovanissian, R., *Armenia on the Road to Independence* (Berkeley, Calif., 1967).

Howard, Harry N., *The Partition of Turkey: A Diplomatic History 1919–1923* (Norman, Okla., 1931; new edn, New York, 1966).

Hunczak, T. (ed.), *Russian Imperialism from Ivan the Great to the Revolution* (Rutgers, NJ, 1974).

Issawi, Charles (ed.), *The Economic History of the Middle East, 1800–1914* (Chicago, Ill./London, 1966).

Issawi, Charles (ed.), *The Economic History of Turkey, 1800–1914* (Chicago, Ill./London, 1980).

Jany, Curt, *Die Königlich Preussische Armee und das Deutsche Reichsheer 1807–1914* (Berlin, 1933).
Jelavich, Barbara, *The Ottoman Empire, the Great Powers and the Straits Question, 1870–1887* (Bloomington, Ind., 1973).
Kalmykov, A. D., *Memoirs of a Russian Diplomat* (New Haven, Conn., 1971).
Katkov, G., and Futrell, M., 'Russian foreign policy, 1880–1914', in G. Katkov *et al.*, *Russia Enters the Twentieth Century* (London, 1971), pp. 9–33.
Kedourie, Elie, *In the Anglo-Arab Labyrinth* (Cambridge, 1976).
Kent, Marian, *Oil and Empire: British Policy and Mesopotamian Oil, 1900–1920* (London/New York, 1976).
Kinross, Lord, *Atatürk* (London, 1964).
Klein, F., 'Probleme des Bündnisses zwischen Oesterreich-Ungarn und Deutschland am Vorabend des ersten Weltkrieges', in F. Klein (ed.), *Oesterreich-Ungarn in der Weltpolitik* (Berlin, 1965), pp. 155–62.
Knaplund, Paul, *Speeches on Foreign Affairs 1904–1914 by Sir Edward Grey* (London, 1931).
Kühlmann, Richard von, *Erinnerungen* (Heidelberg, 1948).
Kurat, A. N., *Türkiye ve Rusya: XVIII yüzyil sonundan Kurtulus Savaşina kadar Türk-Russilişkileri (1789–1919)* (Ankara, 1970).
Langer, W. L., *The Diplomacy of Imperialism, 1890–1902* (New York, 1968).
Laue, T. H. von, *Sergei Witte and the Industrialization of Russia* (New York, 1963).
Lauren, P. G., *Diplomats and Bureaucrats* (Stanford, Calif., 1976).
Lederer, I. J. (ed.), *Russian Foreign Policy: Essays in Historical Perspective* (New Haven, Conn., 1962).
Lewis, Bernard, *The Emergence of Modern Turkey*, 2nd edn (London, 1968).
Liman von Sanders, Otto, *Fünf Jahre Türkei* (Berlin, 1920).
Lindow, Erich, *Freiherr Marschall von Bieberstein als Botschafter in Konstantinopel, 1897–1912* (Danzig, 1934).
Löding, Dörte, *Deutschlands und Oesterreich-Ungarns Balkanpolitik von 1912 bis 1914 unter besonderer Berücksichtigung ihrer Wirtschaftsinteressen* (Hamburg, 1969).
Lorey, Hermann, *Der Krieg in den türkischen Gewässern*, 2 vols, *Der Krieg zur See 1914–1918* (Berlin, 1928–38).
Lowe, C. J., and Marzari, F., *Italian Foreign Policy, 1820–1940* (London, 1975).
Macartney, M. H. H., and Cremona, P., *Italy's Foreign and Colonial Policy 1914–1937* (London, 1938).
Malgeri, F., *La guerra libica (1911–1912)* (Rome, 1970).
Maltese, P., *La terra promessa: la guerra italo-turca e la conquista della Libia, 1911–1912* (Milan, 1968).
Mantegazza, V., *Italiani in Oriente: Eraclea* (Rome, 1922).
Mantegazza, V., *Il Mediterraneo e il suo equilibrio* (Milan, 1914).
Mantegazza, V., *La Turchia liberale e le questioni balcaniche* (Milan, 1908).
Mears, E. G. (ed.), *Modern Turkey* (New York, 1924).
Meyer, Henry Cord, *Mitteleuropa in German Thought and Action 1815–1945* (The Hague, 1955).
Miège, J.-L., *L'Imperialisme colonial italien de 1870 à nos jours* (Paris, 1968).
Miller, Margaret, *The Economic Development of Russia, 1905–1914* (London, 1926).
Moberly, Brig.-Gen. F. J., *Official History of the Great War: The Campaign in Mesopotamia 1914–1918*, 4 vols (London, 1923–7).
Mogk, Walter, *Paul Rohrbach und das 'Grössere Deutschland'* (Munich, 1972).
Möhring, Rubina, 'Die Beziehungen zwischen Oesterreich-Ungarn und dem osmanischen Reich 1908–1912', PhD dissertation, Vienna University, 1978.
Mühlmann, Carl, *Das deutsch-türkische Waffenbundnis im Weltkrieg* (Leipzig, 1940).
Mühlmann, Carl, *Oberste Heeresleitung und Balkan im Weltkrieg 1914–1918* (Berlin, 1942).

Mulligan, R. J. J., 'Great Britain, Russia and the Turkish Straits, 1908–1923', MA thesis, University of London, 1953.

Musulin, A. von, *Erinnerungen eines österreichisch-ungarischen Diplomaten* (Munich, 1924).

Nebioglu, Osman, *Die Auswirkungen der Kapitulationen auf die türkische Wirtschaft* (Jena, 1941).

Nevakivi, Jukka, *Britain, France, and the Arab Middle East, 1914–1920* (London, 1969).

Nicolson, Harold, *Curzon: The Last Phase, 1919–1925* (New York, 1934).

Nicolson, Harold, *Peacemaking 1919* (London, 1933).

Novichev, A. I., *Ocherki ekonomiki Turtsii do mirovoi voiny* (Moscow, 1937).

Okyar, Osman, and Inalcik, Halil (eds), *Social and Economic History of Turkey (1271–1922)* (Ankara, 1980).

Pears, Sir Edwin, *Forty Years in Constantinople* (London, 1916).

Pichon, J., *La Partage du Proche Orient* (Paris, 1938).

Platt, D. C. M., *The Cinderella Service: British Consuls since 1825* (London/New York, 1971).

Platt, D. C. M., *Finance, Trade and Politics in British Foreign Policy* (Oxford, 1968).

Poidevin, Raymond, *Les Relations économiques et financières entre la France et l'Allemagne de 1898 à 1914* (Paris, 1969).

Poincaré, R., *Au Service de la France*, 10 vols (Paris, 1926–33).

Pomiankowski, Joseph, *Der Zusammenbruch des ottomanischen Reiches* (Vienna, 1928).

Portal, R., 'The industrialization of Russia', in H. J. Habakkuk and M. M. Postan (eds), *The Cambridge Economic History of Europe*, Vol. VI, part 2 (Cambridge, 1965), pp. 801–72.

Raab, Alfons, *Die Politik Deutschlands im Nahen Orient von 1878 bis 1908* (Vienna, 1936).

Raabe, Ingrid, *Beiträge zur Geschichte der diplomatischen Beziehungen zwischen Frankreich und Oesterreich-Ungarn 1908–12* (Vienna, 1971).

Raffalovich, A., *Russia: Its Trade and Commerce* (London, 1918).

Ragey, L., *La Question du Chemin de Fer de Bagdad* (Paris, 1936).

Ramsaur, Ernest E., *The Young Turks: Prelude to the Revolution of 1908* (Princeton, NJ, 1957).

Rathmann, Lothar, *Berlin–Bagdad: Die imperialistische Nahostpolitik des kaiserlichen Deutschlands* (Berlin, 1962).

Reichsarchiv et al., *Der Weltkrieg 1914 bis 1918: Die militärischen Operationen zu Lande*, 14 vols (Berlin, 1925–44).

Rich, Norman, *Friedrich von Holstein: Politics and Diplomacy in the Era of Bismarck and Wilhelm II*, 2 vols (Cambridge, 1965).

Ridell, Lord, *Intimate Diary of the Peace Conference and After, 1918–1923* (London, 1933).

Ritter, Gerhard, *Staatskunst und Kriegshandwerk: Das Problem des 'Militarismus' in Deutschland*, 4 vols (Munich, 1954–68).

Robbins, Keith, *Sir Edward Grey* (London, 1971).

Röhl, John, *Germany without Bismarck: The Crisis of Government in the Second Reich, 1890–1900* (Berkeley and Los Angeles, Calif., 1967).

Romano, S., *Guiseppe Volpi: industria e finanza tra Giolitti e Mussolini* (Milan, 1979).

Ronaldshay, Earl of, *Life of Lord Curzon*, 3 vols (London, 1928).

Rosen, Friedrich, *Aus einem diplomatischen Wanderleben*, 2 vols (Berlin, 1931).

Rosen, Baron R., *Forty Years of Diplomacy*, 2 vols (London, 1922).

Roskill, Stephen, *Hankey, Man of Secrets*, 3 vols (London, 1970–4).

Roskill, Stephen, *Naval Policy between the Wars*, 2 vols (London, 1968–76).

Rossos, A., *Russia and the Balkans, 1909–1914* (Ann Arbor, Mich., 1971).

Ryan, Andrew, *The Last of the Dragomans* (London, 1951).

Sachar, H. M., *The Emergence of the Middle East, 1914–1924* (New York, 1969).
Sarkissian, A. O., 'Concert diplomacy and the Armenians, 1890–1897', in A. O. Sarkissian (ed.), *Studies in Diplomatic History and Historiography in Honour of G. P. Gooch* (London, 1962), pp. 48–75.
Sazonov, S. D., *Fateful Years, 1909–1916: Reminiscences* (London/New York, 1928).
Schmidt-Richberg, Wiegand, *et al.*, *Vor der Entlassung Bismarcks bis zum Ende des Ersten Weltkrieges*, Handbuch zur deutschen Militärgeschichte, Vol. V (Frankfurt, 1968).
Schmitt, B. E., *The Annexation of Bosnia, 1908–1909* (Cambridge, 1937).
Schulte, Bernd F., *Vor dem Kriegsausbruch 1914: Deutschland, die Türkei und der Balkan* (Düsseldorf, 1980).
Schuman, F. L., *War and Diplomacy in the French Republic* (Chicago, Ill., 1931).
Shatsillo, F. F., *Russkii imperializm i razvitie flota* (Moscow, 1968).
Shaw, Stanford, and Shaw, E. K., *History of the Ottoman Empire and Modern Turkey*, Vol. II (Cambridge/New York, 1977).
Shorrock, W. I., *French Imperialism in the Middle East: The Failure of Policy in Syria and Lebanon, 1900–1914* (Madison, Wis., 1976).
Shotwell, J. T., and Deak, F., *Turkey at the Straits* (New York, 1940).
Silberstein, Gerard E., *The Troubled Alliance: German–Austrian Relations 1914–1917* (Lexington, Ky, 1970).
Silin, A. S., *Ekspansiya Germanii na Blizhnem Vostoke v kontse XIX veka* (Moscow, 1971).
Silin, A. S., *Ekspansiya germanskogo imperializma na Blizhnem Vostoke nakanunye pervoi mirovoi voiny, 1908–1914* (Moscow, 1976).
Smith, C. J., *The Russian Struggle for Power, 1914–1917: A Study of Russian Policy during the First World War* (New York, 1956).
Smith, Elaine D., *Turkey: Origins of the Kemalist Movement (1919–1922)* (Washington, DC, 1959).
Smith, Sir H. Llewellyn, *The Board of Trade* (London, 1928).
Smith, Michael Llewellyn, *Ionian Vision: Greece in Asia Minor 1919–22* (London, 1973).
Stavrou, T. G., *Russian Interests in Palestine, 1882–1914* (Thessaloniki, 1963).
Stavrou, T. G. (ed.), *Russia under the Last Tsar* (Minneapolis, Minn., 1969).
Steiner, Zara, *The Foreign Office and Foreign Policy, 1898–1914* (Cambridge, 1969).
Stieve, F., *Izvolsky and the World War* (London, 1926).
Sullivan, Charles D., 'Stamboul crossings: German diplomacy in Turkey, 1908–1914', PhD thesis, Vanderbilt University, Nashville, Tenn., 1977.
Thaden, E. C., *Russia and the Balkan Alliance of 1912* (University Park, Pa, 1965).
Thayer, J. A., *Italy and the Great War: Politics and Culture* (Madison, Wis., 1964).
Theodoli, A., *A cavallo di due secoli* (Rome, 1950).
Thobie, J., *Intérêts et impérialisme français dans l'Empire Ottoman, 1895–1914* (Paris, 1977).
Thobie, J., *Phares Ottomans et emprunts Turcs, 1904–1961* (Paris, 1972).
Trumpener, U., *Germany and the Ottoman Empire, 1914–1918* (Princeton, NJ, 1968).
Turkish National Commission for UNESCO, *Ataturk* (Anharn, 1963).
Wallach, Jehuda L., *Anatomie einer Militärhilfe: Die preussisch-deutschen Militärmissionen in der Türkei, 1835–1919* (Düsseldorf, 1976).
Weber, Frank G., *Eagles on the Crescent: Germany, Austria, and the Diplomacy of the Turkish Alliance, 1914–1918* (Ithaca, NY/London, 1970).
Webster, R. A., *L'imperialismo industriale italiano 1908–1915* (Turin, 1974).
Williams, Beryl J., 'The revolution of 1905 and Russian foreign policy', in C. Abramsky and Beryl J. Williams (eds), *Essays in Honour of E. H. Carr* (London, 1974), pp. 101–25.
Williamson, John G., *Karl Helfferich, 1872–1924: Economist, Financier, Politician* (Princeton, NJ, 1971).

Wolf, J. B., *The Diplomatic History of the Baghdad Railroad* (Columbia, Miss., 1936).
Yerasimos, Stefanos, *Türk-Sovyet İlişkileri* (Istanbul, 1979).
Zoli, C., *La guerra turco-bulgara* (Milan, 1913).

Articles

Ahmad, Feroz, 'Great Britain's relations with the Young Turks 1908–1914', *Middle Eastern Studies*, Vol. II, no. 4 (1966), pp. 302–29.
Albrecht-Carrié, R., 'Italian foreign policy, 1914–1922', *Journal of Modern History*, Vol. XX, no. 4 (1948), pp. 326–39.
Andrew, C., and Kanya-Forstner, A. S., 'The French "colonial party": its composition, aims and influence, 1885–1914', *Historical Journal*, Vol. XIV, no. 1 (1971), pp. 79–106.
Anonymous (Alwyn Parker), 'The Bagdad Railway negotiations', *Quarterly Review*, Vol. CCXXVIII (1917), pp. 487–528.
Bosworth, R. J., 'Britain and Italy's acquisition of the Dodecanese 1912–1915', *Historical Journal*, Vol. XIII, no. 4 (1970), pp. 683–705.
Bridge, F. R., *'Tarde venientibus ossa:* Austro-Hungarian colonial aspirations in Asia Minor, 1913–14', *Middle Eastern Studies*, Vol. VI (1970), pp. 319–30.
Carlgren, W. M., 'Informationsstycken från Abdul Hamids senare regeringsår', *Historisk Tidskrift*, n.s., Vol. XV (1952), pp. 1–35.
Carmel, Alex, 'The political significance of German settlement in Palestine, 1868–1918', *Jahrbuch des Instituts für Deutsche Geschichte*, Beiheft 1 (1975), pp. 45–71.
Charykov, N. V., 'Sazonov', *Contemporary Review*, Vol. CXXXIII, no. 3 (1928), pp. 284–8.
Cole, S. M., 'Secret diplomacy and the Cyrenaican settlement of 1917', *Journal of Italian History*, Vol. II, no. 2 (1979), pp. 258–80.
Cunsolo, R. S., 'Libya, Italian nationalism, and the revolt against Giolitti', *Journal of Modern History*, Vol. XXXVII, no. 2 (1965), pp. 186–207.
Davison, R. H., 'The Armenian crisis, 1912–1914', *American Historical Review*, Vol. LIII, no. 3 (1948), pp. 481–505.
Dyer, Gwynne, 'The Turkish armistice of 1918', *Middle Eastern Studies*, Vol. VIII (1972), pp. 143 ff., 313 ff.
Dyer, Gwynne, 'Turkish "falsifiers" and Armenian "deceivers": historiography and the Armenian massacres', *Middle Eastern Studies*, Vol. XII (1976), pp. 99–107.
Flanigam, M. L., 'German eastward expansion, fact and fiction: a study in German–Ottoman trade relations 1890–1914', *Journal of Central European Affairs*, Vol. XIV, no. 4 (1955), pp. 321–33.
Folco, A., and Biagini, M., 'La rivoluzione die Giovani Turchi nel carteggio degli addetli militari italiani', *Rassegna Storica del Risorgimento*, Vol. LXI (1974).
Franchetti, L., 'L'Italia e L'Asia Minore', *Nuova antologia*, no. 1087, 1 May 1917, pp. 109–13.
Francis, Richard M., 'The British withdrawal from the Baghdad Railway project in April 1903', *Historical Journal*, Vol. XVI, no. 3 (1973), pp. 168–78.
Friedman, Isaiah, 'The Hussein–McMahon correspondence and the question of Palestine', *Journal of Contemporary History*, Vol. V, no. 2 (1970), pp. 83–122.
Grishina, M., 'Chernomorskie prolivy vo vneshnei politiki Rossii, 1904–1907', *Istoricheskie zapiski*, Vol. XCIX (Moscow, 1977), pp. 145–8.
Grunwald, Kurt, *'Pénétration pacifique* – the financial vehicles of Germany's "Drang nach dem Osten"', *Jahrbuch des Instituts für Deutsche Geschichte*, Beiheft 1 (1975), pp. 85–103.
Guillen, P., 'La politique de Delcassé et les relations Franco-Allemandes', *Revue d'Allemagne*, Vol. IV, no. 3 (1972), pp. 455–64.

Hamilton, K. A., 'An attempt to form an Anglo-French "Industrial Entente" ', *Middle Eastern Studies*, Vol. XI, no. 1 (1975), pp. 47–73.

Heslop, Derwent G., 'The Bagdad Railway', *The Engineer*, November–December 1920, pp. 469–80, 523–7, 551–4, 601–3.

Hoffmann, Walter, 'Deutsche Banken in der Türkei', *Weltwirtschaftliches Archiv*, Vol. VI (1915), pp. 410–21.

Honig, N., 'Schiffahrt und Schiffahrtspolitik der Türkei', *Weltwirtschaftliches Archiv*, Vol. VII (1916), pp. 79–92.

Jäschke, Gotthard, 'Die christliche Mission in der Türkei', *Saeculum*, Vol. VII (1956), pp. 68–78.

Kahan, A., 'Government policies and the industrialization of Russia', *Journal of Economic History*, Vol. XXVII, no. 4 (1967), pp. 460–77.

Kedourie, Elie, 'Cairo and Khartoum on the Arab Question 1915–18', *Historical Journal*, Vol. VII, no. 2 (1964), pp. 280–97.

Kent, Marian, 'Agent of empire? The National Bank of Turkey and British foreign policy', *Historical Journal*, Vol. XVIII, no. 2 (1975), pp. 367–89.

Kerner, R. J., 'The mission of Liman von Sanders', *Slavonic Review*, Vol. VI, no. 16 (1927), pp. 12–27; no. 17 (1927), pp. 344–63; no. 18 (1928), pp. 543–60; Vol. VII, no. 19 (1928), pp. 90–112.

Kerner, R. J., 'Russia and the Straits Question, 1915–1917', *Slavonic and East European Review*, Vol. VIII, no. 24 (1930), pp. 589–600.

Kerner, R. J., 'Russia, the Straits and Constantinople, 1914–1915', *Journal of Modern History*, Vol. I, no. 3 (1929), pp. 400–15.

Köymen, Oya, 'The advent and consequences of free trade in the Ottoman Empire', *Etudes Balkaniques*, Vol. II (1971).

Langer, W. L., 'Russia, the Straits Question and the origins of the Balkan League, 1908–1912', *Political Science Quarterly*, Vol. XLIII, no. 3 (1928), pp. 321–63.

Lowe, C. J., 'Britain and Italian intervention 1914–1915', *Historical Journal*, Vol. XII, no. 3 (1969), pp. 533–48.

Lowe, C. J., 'The failure of British diplomacy in the Balkans, 1914–1916', *Canadian Journal of History*, Vol. IV, no. 1 (1969), pp. 73–100.

McLean, D., 'British finance and foreign policy in Turkey: the Smyrna–Aidin railway settlement 1913–1914', *Historical Journal*, Vol. XIX, no. 2 (1976), pp. 521–30.

Mandelstam, A. A., 'La politique russe d'accès à la Méditerranée au XXe siècle', *Academie de Droit International. Receuil des cours*, Vol. I (Paris, 1934), pp. 597–802.

Manuel, F. E., 'The Palestine question in Italian diplomacy, 1917–1920', *Journal of Modern History*, Vol. XXVII, no. 3 (1955), pp. 263–80.

Mejcher, Helmut, 'Die Bagdadbahn als Instrument deutschen wirtschaftlichen Einflusses im Osmanischen Reich', *Geschichte und Gesellschaft*, Vol. I, no. 4 (1975), pp. 447–81.

Melka, R. L., 'Max Freiherr von Oppenheim: sixty years of scholarship and political intrigue in the Middle East', *Middle Eastern Studies*, Vol. IX (1973), pp. 81–93.

Mosely, P., 'Russian policy in 1911–12', *Journal of Modern History*, Vol. XII, no. 1 (1940), pp. 69–86.

Pick, Walter, 'Der deutsche Pionier Heinrich August Meissner-Pascha und seine Eisenbahnbauten im Nahen Osten 1901–1917', *Jahrbuch des Instituts für Deutsche Geschichte*, Vol. IV (1975), pp. 257–300.

Pönicke, Herbert, 'Heinrich August Meissner-Pascha und der Bau der Hedschas-und Bagdadbahn', *Welt als Geschichte*, Vol. XVI (1956), pp. 196–210.

Popov, A., 'Ot Bosfora do Tikhogo Okeana', *Istorik Marksist*, Vol. XXXVII (1954), pp. 3–28.

Renzi, W. A., 'Great Britain, Russia and the Straits, 1914–1915', *Journal of Modern History*, Vol. XLII, no. 1 (1970), pp. 1–20.

Rothwell, V. H., 'Mesopotamia in British war aims 1914–1918', *Historical Journal*, Vol. XIII, no. 2 (1970), pp. 273–94.

Silberstein, Gerard E., 'The Central Powers and the Second Turkish Alliance 1915', *Slavic Review*, Vol. XXIV, no. 1 (1965), pp. 77–89.

Smith, C. J., 'Great Britain and the 1914–1915 Straits Agreement with Russia: the British promise of November, 1914', *American Historical Review*, Vol. LXX, no. 4 (1965), pp. 1015–54.

Sontag, J. P., 'Tsarist debts and Tsarist foreign policy', *Slavic Review*, Vol. XXVII, no. 4 (1968), pp. 529–41.

Staley, Eugene, 'Business and politics in the Persian Gulf: the story of the Wönckhaus firm', *Political Science Quarterly*, Vol. XLVIII, no. 3 (1933), pp. 367–85.

Stanley, W. R., 'Review of Turkish Asiatic railways to 1918: some political–military considerations', *Journal of Transport History*, Vol. VII, no. 3 (1966), pp. 180–204.

Sumner, B. H., 'Tsardom and imperialism in the Far East and Middle East, 1880–1914', *Proceedings of the British Academy*, Vol. XXVII (London, 1941), pp. 25–65.

Thaden, E. C., 'Charykov and Russian foreign policy at Constantinople in 1914', *Journal of Central European Affairs*, Vol. XVI, no. 1 (1956), pp. 23–44.

Toscano, M., 'Le origini diplomatiche dell'art. 9 del patto di Londra relativo agli eventuali compensi all' Italia in Asia Minore', *Storia e Politica*, Vol. IV, no. 3 (1965).

Toynbee, Arnold, 'The McMahon–Hussein correspondence: comments and a reply', with reply by Isaiah Friedman, *Journal of Contemporary History*, Vol. V, no. 4 (1970), pp. 185–201.

Trumpener, Ulrich, 'The escape of the *Goeben* and *Breslau*: a reassessment', *Canadian Journal of History*, Vol. VI (1971), pp. 171–87.

Trumpener, Ulrich, 'German military aid to Turkey in 1914', *Journal of Modern History*, Vol. XXXII, no. 2 (1960), pp. 145–9.

Trumpener, Ulrich, 'German officers in the Ottoman Empire, 1880–1918', *Jahrbuch des Instituts für Deutsche Geschichte*, Beiheft 1 (1975), pp. 30–43.

Trumpener, Ulrich, 'Liman von Sanders and the German–Ottoman alliance', *Journal of Contemporary History*, Vol. I, no. 4 (1966), pp. 179–92.

Trumpener, Ulrich, 'War premeditated? German intelligence operations in July 1914', *Central European History*, Vol. IX (1976), pp. 58–85.

Zechlin, Z., 'Die Turkischen Meerengen – ein Brennpunkt der Weltgeschichte', *Geschichte in Wissenschaft und Uterricht*, Vol. XVII, no. 1 (1966), pp. 1–31.

Zotiades, G., 'Russia and the question of the Straits and Constantinople during the Balkan Wars', *Balkan Studies*, Vol. II, no. 2 (Thessaloniki, 1970), pp. 285–98.

Index

Index

Abdul Aziz (Turkish Sultan, 1861–76) 33
Abdul Hamid II (1842–1918) (Turkish Sultan, 1876–1909) 2, 7, 11–12, 20, 25, 26, 33, 57, 151, 166, 174; attitude towards Great Powers 11–12, 77, 122, 174, 177, 178; financial pressure on, from France 154, 156; British attitude towards 174, 180; attitude towards Ottoman Public Debt Administration 24; attitude towards army 11, 12; and Macedonian reform question 36, 153; visit to, by Kaiser Wilhelm II, 1898 112; replaced by brother, Mehmed, 1909 123; and financing of Baghdad Railway 148
Adalia 52, 65, 66, 67–8, 69, 72
Admiralty, British 181, 184–5, 193
Adrianople (Edirne) 15, 43, 124
Adriatic see also Dodecanese 69–70
Aehrenthal, Alois Lexa, Count von (1854–1912) (Austro-Hungarian Ambassador at St. Petersburg, 1899–1906; Minister for Foreign Affairs, 1906–Feb. 1912) 33–41, 61
Africa see also Libya 1, 70, 111, 144
Agadir Crisis, 1911 60
Ahmed Izzet Pasha, General (1864–1937) (Turkish War Minister 1913–14; army group commander, 1917; Grand Vezir, Oct. 1918) 116, 124, 130, 136 n.36
Ahmed Nesimi Bey (Sayman) (d. 1958) (Prominent member of CUP and deputy, becoming, during the war, Minister for Agriculture, then Foreign Minister, Feb. 1917–Oct. 1918) 8
Ahmed Riza Bey (1859–1950) (Prominent Young Turk, deputy for Istanbul 1908, 1912, and President of the Chamber) 13
Ahmed Rüstem Bey de Bilinski 9, 27 n.18
Albania, interest of Austro-Hungarian Empire in 4, 20, 33, 35, 38, 40–2, 44, 57, 64, 70–1; rising against Turks, Spring 1911 40–1, 56, and in July 1912 42; Turkish attempts to conciliate, mid-1912 42; Italian designs on 52, 56, 61, 64–5, 74 n.65; Greek ambitions for (called 'northern Epirus'): 64; Italian-Austrian competition over 64–5
Alexandretta 144, 147, 150, 161
Alexandria 53, 54
Alekseev, General Mikhail Vasil'evich (1857–1918) (Russian Chief of the Army Staff, Aug. 1915–Mar. 1917) 109 n.160
Ali Pasha, Mehmed (1815–1871) (Tanzimat Grand Vezir or Foreign Minister for most of the years between 1846 and 1871) 6, 10
Allies (Britain, France, Russia and Italy) see also individual countries, and for pre-war

years see Entente, Triple, Russian Empire and Italy 17, 19, 125, 130; Dardanelles campaign 98–9; changes in attitude of Allies towards holding Turkish territory after the war 186–7; determination to avoid post-war German domination of Turkey 187, 188; and the Turkish peace settlement 190–4
Anatolia see also Armenia, Black Sea Agreement 19, 20, 26; Russian interests in 4, 20, 22, 23; Austro-Hungarian plans for colony in south 44–5; Italian designs on 52; Russia and 84–5, 86, 99; Pan-German League and 120
Anatolian Railway Company 146, 147, 181
Andrew Weir & Co. (British shipping company) 197–8 n.54
Anglo-Algerian Shipping Co. 182, 197–8 n.54
Anglo-French Declaration, Nov. 1918 187, 202 n.128
Angora (Ankara) government see also Nationalist regime, formed, 23 Apr. 1920 9; Treaty with Bolshevik regime, 2 Dec. 1920 19; Treaty with France (Angora Agreement) 20 Oct. 1921 19, 164, 192; Treaty of Lausanne, 24 July 1923, ratified Aug. 1923 193; Republic established 19
Angora (Ankara) Treaty (Franklin-Bouillon Agreement), 20 Oct. 1921 19, 164, 192
Arabia 1, 70
Arab Bureau 175, 188, 202 n.136
Arab provinces of Ottoman Empire 23, 40, 45, 60, 164, Arab revolt 163, 186; Arab disillusionment with Allies 187; pacification of disaffected tribes needed post-war 190
Armenia and Armenians see also Transcaucasia, Cilicia, Anatolia 19, 46, 100, 178, 193; Armenian communities in Ottoman Empire 20; persecution of Armenians 34–5, 45, 46, 128, 133, 143; crisis of 1896 77; reform scheme for 44; threat from Russia in 45, 101; Russia and 85, 86, 90, 96, 97, 99, 101
Armstrong Vickers Company, 179, 197 n.50
Artin Dadian Pasha (Under-Secretary, Turkish Foreign Ministry, under Abdul Hamid II) 7
Atatürk, Mustafa Kemal Pasha, see Mustafa Kemal Pasha
Austria-Hungary and the Ottoman Empire see also Macedonia, Ottoman Empire, Great Powers, First World War, Young Turks, Nationalist Movement, basic interests in 4, 31, 35, 43; common borders, problems of Balkan nationalism and military weakness 1, 20, 31, 43, 45, 48–9, 77; policy towards, always includes Balkan consideration 32, 42,